A TEST OF

Faith and
COURAGE

Patton's Raiders in WWII

Memories of
a combat infantryman
in World War II in the
65th Infantry Division of
General Patton's 3rd Army

Oscar B. Ladner

Liberty & Freedom Productions
GULFPORT, MISSISSIPPI

Although the author and publisher have made every effort to ensure the accuracy and completeness of information contained in this book, we assume no responsibility for errors, inaccuracies, omissions, or any inconsistency herein. Any slights of people, places, or organizations are unintentional.

First printing 2002

ISBN 0-9711286-7-7

LCCN 2001133004

ATTENTION CORPORATIONS, UNIVERSITIES, COLLEGES, AND PROFESSIONAL ORGANIZATIONS: Quantity discounts are available on bulk purchases of this book for educational, gift purposes, or as premiums for increasing magazine subscriptions or renewals. Special books or book excerpts can also be created to fit specific needs. For information, please contact Liberty & Freedom Productions, 176 Allan Drive, Gulfport, MS 39507-1503; ph 228-896-7244.

TABLE OF CONTENTS

DEDICATION

I dedicate this book to my beloved parents, Oscar Lawrence Ladner and Irene Baker Ladner, through whose love, care, and teachings I learned so much. I learned such things as courage, determination, responsibility, and faith in my Almighty God and our Savior Jesus Christ, whose teachings and inspirations gave me much courage in the many times of peril in my life.

My dear mother lived to be over one hundred years of age. It was her prayers, as well as my father's, for my safety in that war, that I credit to bringing me through the many dangers I encountered.

INTRODUCTION

It has been said he who has no history, has no future. Our great Heritage in America, which is our birthright, our traditions and legacies that have been bequeathed to us from the past, gives us our individuality, and makes us the proud citizens that we are. If we do not have a Religion, a History, a Heritage, and a meaningful government; of, for, and by the people, that we believe in, we are then a worthless and insignificant people.

Without a History we will have no Heritage, and cannot learn from the past, and we will make the same mistakes again, and again, and no progress in human endeavors for the betterment of mankind will ever be accomplished.

So, we must learn the history of WWII so the mistakes and blunders made then will never occur again. We must look back at WWII to be able to identify those great qualities in Americans that made them accomplish such greatness as they then did, and try to perpetuate them the best that we can. We must learn from mistakes, as well as from achievements, so as to then make this world a better place for all mankind to live in, in peace, freedom, harmony, and prosperity.

For the citizens of this great country to remain free, we must all have something that we believe in immensely, and a cause that we are willing to die for. Without such, we are a meaningless and empty people that are easily destroyed by the forces of evil.

There have always been two forces at work opposing each other in this world: one of good and one of evil. It has always been inherent upon the good people to put down and defeat the evil forces. This is a fact that we must always face, and be vigilant to successfully deal with.

To protect and preserve our History, our Heritage, and our Religious faiths and freedoms, it takes brave men, men of strong heart, to endure the hardships of the trials and tribulations of war. These must be men with a legacy, a birthright to live up to, a Heritage and tradition to follow in the footsteps of, that has been bequeathed to us by our forbearers who have fought for what is right, who have won over evil and passed the rewards on down to us.

It is necessary to know the true worth of our Heritage and legacy that have been passed on to us, to protect and defend it.

We must have great faith in our birthright, to muster the courage it takes to defend our great American Heritage, our constitutional government, and our inheritance of these great values, that have been handed down from our forbearers who struggled so hard to create them, and pass them on to us to protect and preserve for posterity.

WWII was a time of great peril for all freedom-loving people everywhere. Our Constitution that guarantees us the inalienable right to life, liberty, and the pursuit of happiness, as well as freedom of our religious faiths, all was in great peril of being eradicated.

Had we Allies not won that war, all of us would have lost those things that were so precious to us. We would not now have our History and Heritage to be proud of, no Religion to give us the moral strength of character to inspire us, to carry us through times of great difficulties and tribulations. We would have been reduced to dumb downed zombies and slave laborers.

A monument at Mauthausen Concentration Camp Memorial Museum, in Linz, Austria, where over 100,000 political enemies of Adolph Hitler died, bears the inscription, "May the living learn from the fate of the dead."

My purpose in writing this book about my war time experiences was driven by the need for the citizens of America to come together as one great nation again, as one nation indivisible and under God. This is the only way that our people can be secure to live in peace, happiness, and prosperity.

What I observed and experienced in Europe in WWII I hope and pray will never happen here, to the people of America, or in fact, to any other people of the world. We can make this possible by studying and being thankful for our History, our Heritage, and believing in our God Almighty, and His powers over all things.

It is inevitable that henceforth, down through history, American citizens will be called upon to again, and again, put down the forces of evil in this world, both from without, and from within this great Country.

To be able to succeed in preserving our History, our Heritage, and our freedom, we must remain prepared to defend against the forces of evil, and to overcome them, through faith in Almighty God, and all that is good, and with the courage to win over the forces of evil.

The author, Oscar B. Ladner

CHAPTER 1

America at War

> *"Let every nation know, whether it wishes us well, or ill, that we shall pay any price, bear any burden, meet any hardship, support any friend, oppose any foe to assure the survival of, and the success of liberty."*
>
> —DANIEL WEBSTER (1752–1852)

In 1944 the war in the Pacific and in Europe was raging like a forest fire. Most Americans were behind the war effort. Many wives and mothers were working in defense factories, while their sons, fathers and husbands were off fighting the war. Others were supporting the war effort by keeping the home fires burning, as well as donating all of their aluminum pots and pans to make airplanes. Patriotism was at an all-time high. Our freedom was at stake if we lost the war. All of my friends were off to war, fighting in the Pacific or in Europe. Friends, neighbors, cousins, classmates, almost everyone I knew was in some way contributing to the war effort.

I thought I would be accepted by the draft board when I turned eighteen, but they found a small lump in my groin that I knew was there, though I thought it was insignificant. I was turned down by the induction center at Camp Shelby, Mississippi. It was a great shock and disappointment to me. My parents were pleased somewhat, that I would

1

not be going to war. They needed me badly to help work the big family farm. We had several hundred head of cattle, even more sheep, as well as six or eight saddle horses used in herding the livestock. I trained my own horse and had my own saddle. Running the farm was a big job. I was an integral part of keeping the farm going and without me, my parents, my younger brother, and two younger sisters would have a great deal more work to do.

I had finished high school and had entered college at Pearl River Junior College at Poplarville, Mississippi, which was also where I had attended the last two years of high school, and then I had over one and a half years of college; as a result, I had three and a half years of ROTC. I didn't know exactly what I wanted to become in life at that time, but I did know that I wanted to do something for the betterment of mankind. I wanted to go into the Army and do my part in liberating the oppressed people of Europe, as well as to do my part, and put out all of my effort to save the world from Communism and Fascism, as well as to preserve Christianity and freedom of religion for all people. At that period in the history of this country, people seriously valued their liberty and freedom, and everyone I knew was patriotic, loyal to the Constitution and the American flag.

The good people of America had met the threat of war and were dealing with it in a heroic manner. When our security became threatened, people willingly went off to fight the war. I felt that everyone should meet his or her responsibility to help win the war. I also was fully aware that no amount of money would be sufficient to pay someone to fight a war. The courage, dedication, sacrifices, and hardships that it takes to fight a war had to come from the belief in the greatness of America and the yearning to defend it.

It was apparent that most all of the servicemen were fighting not because they had been drafted, but because they were patriotic American citizens who were willing to fight to protect and defend the American way of life. I would not like to go into combat with soldiers who were there fighting just because they got drafted. Who would go to war for a private's pay alone? History reveals that without loyalty and patriotism, a nation will never survive.

I read every book I could find regarding the war, as well as every news magazine, about what was happening on the battlefields of Europe, as well as in the theaters of combat in North Africa, Sicily, Italy, and the South Pacific. I saw every James Cagney movie that he made about the French Resistance and Underground. These heroic French people were fighting the occupation of their country by the Nazis, risking their lives daily to fight their enemy. I read every word and studied every picture in Life magazine. I wrote letters to the editors of Look magazine, as well as PIC magazine, both of which were published. They simply stated that it was everyone's duty to fight for their country in order bring about peace in the world, and that we should work hard to protect and preserve liberty and freedom, and to make this the war to end all wars.

During the war years everyone listened to Glenn Miller and his band, as well as other great bandleaders, like Benny Goodman, who played music written by Cole Porter, such as "Begin the Beguine," "Night and Day," "This Thing Called Love," and "I've Got You Under My Skin." Duke Ellington played "Mood Indigo" and "Solitude." Ella Fitzgerald sang her own inimitable style of soothing, melodious jazz. All of this music was part of the era of WWII.

My father was of French descent, going back to the early 1700s. He volunteered to serve in the Navy, and fought in WWI as a crew member on the destroyer S.S. San Diego. He made fourteen trips across the Atlantic, escorting troop and supply ships to France, through German submarine-infested waters. On my father's birthday, July 19, 1918, a German torpedo hit his ship the S.S. San Diego seventy-five miles off New York City, and the destroyer quickly sank. Official reports said that the ship had hit a mine; however, there were no mines in such deep waters. American leaders did not want the citizens to believe that a German submarine had come that close to our shores. My father told me that the sailor in the crow's nest of the San Diego told him that he saw the torpedo coming toward the ship and that he called down to the bridge and reported it. My father survived in the cold water for over four hours. He had no clothes on, in that he was taking a shower when the torpedo hit the destroyer. He told me that the explosion was so great that the ship sank very quickly. After they had spent four hours in the water, hanging onto a raft, a passing freighter rescued them and carried them to New York City. When he walked down the gangplank, he had no clothes on, and two Red Cross women placed blankets on him to warm him and to cover his nudity. I admired him very much for his efforts in that Great War. I wanted to do the same for my country, in this war, WWII.

My father had also voluntarily joined the Navy to fight for his country in WWI. He was of pioneer stock, and descended from early French settlers who settled on the Mississippi Gulf Coast. Christian Ladner and two brothers were the first to settle what is now Pass Christian, Mississippi. Christian opened a trading post, constructed of logs. He sold and traded goods to the early settlers, as well as to the Biloxi and Choctaw Indians.

My great grandfather, Jeremiah Ladner had served in the Confederate Army in the Civil War in Steed's Cavalry. His father, Carlos Ladner, at age 18, volunteered as a citizen soldier to fight the British in the Battle of New Orleans in 1814. He served in the 18th Regiment of the Mississippi Militia as a member of Captain Joseph Vallio's company under the leadership of Andrew Jackson. They defeated the British who were under the command of General Sir Edward M. Pakenham, who had defeated Napoleon in the Battle of Waterloo.

My ancestors greatly valued the freedom they enjoyed in this new country and they were willing to fight and die to preserve that freedom. I knew that I had a tradition and a heritage to uphold, and that I must not shirk my responsibility and duty to my country in these perilous times.

I spoke with my parents as well as my grandmother about having surgery to correct the small hernia in my side, so the military would accept me. I had also talked with my grandmother, with whom I was very close, and told her of my desires and plans, and I wanted to have the surgery and then volunteer for the combat infantry. She agreed that I should have it done and told me that since I was so determined and dedicated, she would pay for my surgery.

My grandmother was the aunt of then U.S. Senator Theodore G. Bilbo, my second cousin, who had served two terms as governor of Mississippi and was at that time serving his third term in the U.S. Senate. I worked for him at times during the summer after sheepshearing was over. I paid close attention to the many sayings that he coined, like, "Agree with me if you can, disagree with me if you must, but please don't ignore me." I poured his bourbon for him and he always instructed me to "put just enough ice in it to cool it, but not enough to dilute it."

My grandmother, Louesa Bilbo Ladner, in fact my grandparents on both sides, came from rugged pioneer stock. She was a person who always spoke her mind. She told me many stories about when her father was off fighting for the Confederacy. Her mother and her two young children, who were my grandmother Louesa and her twin sister Louisa, were home alone. Their closest neighbors were miles away. They would learn that the Jay Hawkers were in the area. They were a group of marauding raiders who robbed, raped, murdered, and pillaged throughout the South during that war, when the men folks were away fighting.

She related to me that when they learned that the thieves were in the area they would take quilts and sleep in the jam of the rail fence near the house. When the raiders pillaged and plundered their home, they would watch as they were robbed of their meager valuables and livestock. She was a noble, rugged, and patriotic lady who strongly believed in fighting for what was right, fair, and honest, as well as for the preservation of the Constitution and the safeguarding of liberty and freedom. My grandmother's uncle, Poplar Jim Smith, an early settler that the town of Poplarville, Mississippi was named after, was killed during the Civil War by the Copeland Gang, another group of marauding thieves who raided his home and killed him while robbing him. He was on his knees begging them not to kill him when they shot him in the head. The thieves found only fifteen cents on him. There was no effective law enforcement during that period of time, and soon thereafter a group of citizens formed a posse, captured all of the Copeland Gang, gave them a quick trial, and hanged all of them at a public hanging.

My parents reluctantly agreed on my surgery and that upon recovery, I would join the Army. The surgery was uneventful. My doctor told me that in three months I would be fully recovered and could then enter the military.

I was aware that it would place an added burden on my family, a younger brother, two small sisters, and my mother and father for me to go into the Army, but I heeded the call. I felt duty bound to do so. They assured me that they would be behind me all the way and they would do all of the chores at home, but that they would miss me very much, as well as pray for our victory in the war and for my safe return.

I went to the draft board, right after my doctor released me and told them I wanted to volunteer for the infantry. They must have thought I was nuts. I had these three and one half years of ROTC training in infantry tactics, which I enjoyed. I loved geography and map reading. I could field-strip a Browning automatic rifle blindfolded in a matter of seconds. I had studied and read everything I could about military strategy, combat infantry tactics, weapons and many other aspects of the infantry, as well as keeping up with the progress of the war in both the European and Pacific theaters. Joining the infantry was something that I felt I was to some extent, prepared to do. I wanted to do it, and I did it. I was placed in the next shipment of draftees sent to Camp Shelby, Mississippi, for induction.

Before I left my mother gave me a small Bible to carry in my shirt pocket and she made me promise that I would not just carry it through combat, but that I would read it often for an inspiration of God's word. I was lectured on taking care of myself and doing at all times, those things that were right, fair, and honest, as well as sensible and well thought out. She told me to say my prayers each and every day, to have faith in my Almighty God, to let everyone know that they could have great trust and confidence in me, and that I would do my job well. She instructed me in my prayers to ask God to give me the faith, strength, courage, and ability to do what was right, and that having faith in God would carry me through all the perilous times that I would be likely to encounter. She instructed me to have great faith and trust in my leaders, to pray for them that they also be given the strength, courage, and ability to carry out their duties.

My mother told me, "Your father and I have always taught you children to do the right thing, always. We have taught you to never walk by a situation that needs to be taken care of, and not do anything about it. If you see something that is needed to be done, do it. Don't wait for someone to tell you to do it, don't wait for someone else to do it, you do it, and do it well. Never be a shirker, always meet all of your obligations and responsibilities to yourself and to others as well."

She told me to always be brave and courageous, and to be determined, sincere, and dedicated in all that I did. She taught all of us to always be polite and respectful, and to show kindness, consideration, humility, and understanding to others. She had always told me that without humility, no one could ever achieve greatness. She taught me that some people thought that a person with these characteristics was a weak person and that I should never let that deter me, but instead let such people know how mistaken they were, by doing the right thing. She told me that she would pray for me all the time, asking that God keep me safe and return me home, safe and sound.

It was difficult leaving my family, especially my mother to whom I was very close. I had the full support of my family. My father was a hero in my mind, and I wanted to be able to do everything that he had done for his country. I had the full support of my family.

My local junior college band played martial music as the train pulled into the station early that morning. I had played trumpet in this band. My group of inductees arrived at Camp Shelby and were housed in new wooden barracks equipped only with cots, pillows, and mattresses. We were issued sheets, a pillowcase, and a blanket. We went through the physical examination. One doctor examined my groin for a hernia and when he found a recent surgical scar, told me that he couldn't understand why I had the surgery just so that I would be accepted into the Army.

After a few days of processing there, we were placed on a passenger train to an undisclosed destination for infantry basic training. No one knew where we were going. The train ride was nice and we had Pullman coaches. The train included a vacant boxcar with doors at each end, where a kitchen was set up to feed us. Using our mess kits for the first time, we walked through the kitchen where we got our food.

We arrived at Camp Blanding, Florida, where immediately the discipline and training commenced, that day, full force. After further processing we were assigned to a company to receive combat infantry training. The organization was three squads of twelve men each to a platoon, and three platoons to the company. Our company commander was Captain Arthur Teague from Texas.

The barracks were crude wooden construction, windows that were just screened holes cut in the wall with wooden shutters on the outside that had to be propped open with a board. Two coal-burning stoves provided heat. The large latrine was down the way with rows and rows of lavatories, urinals, commodes, and showers.

One day during training, one of the men kept calling his rifle his "gun." The captain ordered him to stand just inside the latrine door with his penis in his left hand and his rifle in his right, and each time someone entered, he had to shake his penis and say, "This is my gun." Then he would salute with his rifle and say, "This is my rifle." This put a stop to trainees using the wrong terminology. Without such humor and a little lightheartedness, we would have had a difficult time adjusting to the strict army life.

We were trained in the use of and identification of many kinds of gasses, as well as gas masks, grenades, booby traps, camouflage, cover and concealment, bangalore torpedoes, bazookas, rifle grenades, explosives, flamethrowers, both 40mm and 81mm mortars, machine guns, both .30 and .50 caliber, the Browning Automatic Rifle, even first aid, and of course the M-1 rifle and bayonet. This is far from an exhaustive number of things that we were taught. The training usually commenced at 5:00 A.M. and ended anywhere from 6:00 A.M. and sometimes lasting all night.

Each day we worked harder in our training and kept at it for longer hours. Our training was so strenuous that even the sergeants, who were our training cadre, could not hold up to it. We marched many miles to rifle, machine gun, mortar and other ranges, usually six miles there and six miles back, carrying a mortar, machine gun or whatever we were working on that day. We fired mortars, rifle grenades, flamethrowers, and bazookas at old tanks and other vehicles. We had night training where we would crawl through bushes, woods, and tangled barbed wire, with real machine guns firing over our heads.

We also had extensive bayonet training on a special course, using burlap-padded dummies, and we would attack the dummies, usually getting skinned knuckles as we parried, slashed, smashed, and stabbed it. If we missed with the bayonet, we slashed and smashed, using butt strokes with the butt of the rifle. We learned to use that rifle to kill the enemy in hand-to-hand combat. We were taught how to aggressively attack enemy soldiers with the bayonet fixed on our rifle by stabbing him, and if we missed, to come up with a smash to the head with the butt of the rifle, then a downward slash, followed by an upward butt stroke. We were shown many movies and training films that depicted the real thing, from which we learned an awful lot about killing the enemy. We practiced doing all these things and many more, studying such things as enemy tactics, map reading, village fighting, reconnoitering, hand-to-hand combat, camouflage, and most of all, military discipline, as well as an awful lot of physical conditioning. We often started the day by doing calisthenics and running obstacle courses. I already was in great physical condition from the hard work on the farm. I was 19 years old, five-feet, ten-inches tall, weighed 180 pounds, was solid as a rock, and had lots of energy.

About half of our company was from New York, Massachusetts, Ohio, Indiana, Virginia, Pennsylvania, Kentucky, and other northeastern states. The other half was from the Deep South and the West. We formed up into two teams, the Yanks and the Rebs, and competed as to who was the best group in swimming, foot racing, target shooting, and many other things. We, the Rebs, always won.

One of the Yanks asked why we Rebs always won. I told him that in my civilian life I rode my saddle horse herding cows and sheep, farmed and sheared sheep by the hundreds during the summer. Also, my father would put a lot full of his bull yearlings together, and I would bulldog them for him to mark their ears, castrate, and brand them with a hot branding iron. In order to do this, I had to run up to each of the bull yearlings that weighed about two or three hundred pounds, catch him in his slippery, slobbery nose with one hand and by the ear with the other, and give his head a big twist, throw him down, and then lie on the ground holding the young bull's head against my chest while my brother grabbed his hind feet and pulled them while my father marked, branded, and castrated him. I explained that this farm life was a rugged and strenuous life and that in order to do this, one had to be pretty fit and have a lot of guts. I related how I went deer and turkey hunting and always brought home the game for us to eat. We would get up at 3:00 A.M. to go sheep hunting, to drive several hundreds of them in at a time, to shear, mark, and brand.

I further explained that 95 percent of the people in America at that time lived in rural areas of America, and only 5 percent lived in urban areas, which accounted for some of the difference, there being fewer urban areas in the South. Those figures are reversed today. Most of the men from the North lived in urban areas. He had never experienced anything like farm life, but he now understood.

One of the many things that I knew I was going to miss was my mother's home cooking. No one could cook better than my mother. During the summer months when fruits and vegetables were growing, dinner, the big meal, was at noon sharp, in our big dining room, and anyone helping with the livestock was there to eat with us. Supper was a lighter meal in the evening because we went to bed early.

She would prepare a meal like no one else could. There would be country fried mutton; beef steak; fried chicken; brown onion gravy over rice; creamed sweet corn baked in a large black iron skillet, seasoned with our own hickory smoked bacon; fresh fried okra cut that morning, breaded with cornmeal, and deep fried; vine ripened tomatoes picked that morning; fresh carrots pulled that morning, seasoned with bourbon; and her own homemade butter; hot cornbread made from our own corn, and just recently ground, that was so good that it tasted like cake; and the best cobbler that one could imagine, either blackberry, peach, pear, or huckleberry, with thick sweet cream on top—and the berries were always picked that morning. No French gourmet restaurant could prepare a meal as good as my mother. I knew that I was going to miss her and her cooking more than anything else.

My captain was a short, strong, gutsy man full of energy, and who seemed never to get tired. He was a very dedicated soldier, and one of the finest and fairest men that I had ever known. He made us tough and rugged, as well. He inspired and motivated us all. When we marched somewhere, say, to a rifle or machine gun range—some of them were six or seven miles away—he would march at the head of the column. He often made me his guidon bearer. The guidon is a small flag on a pole with our company initial on it, so that if anyone wanted to find us, it wouldn't be hard to do. So my daily job was to march at the head of the column of threes, made up of three, thirty-six man platoons, with him on the left side and me on the right, carrying the guidon.

Each night after returning from a rifle or machine gun range we would have to clean our weapons before we could lie down and get some rest, no matter how tired we were. If nothing was scheduled for any of the weapons ranges that day, then you could bet that right after breakfast we would be doing physical training, running obstacle courses, and doing other strenuous exercises. Everyone gained weight and got into great physical condition. I don't know how this training could have been more rigorous than it was; but though I was already conditioned, I got tougher. I maintained my weight of 180 pounds as I have all my life, except while at the front in Europe, during which time I lost twenty pounds. I really felt that I was in great physical condition when I finished basic training.

Upon nearing completion of this intensive training, we had a thirty-five-mile forced march with full field pack consisting of a mess kit, tent pole and pegs, tent half, blanket, and a change of clothes. In addition to that, we carried a gas mask, rifle, bayonet, steel helmet, cartridge belt, canteen, entrenching tool, all of which weigh seventy-five pounds or more. We learned that this was the most comprehensive and rigorous training ever given to American fighting men at this large training camp.

We would march and then take a break, then march some more and take another break, continuing until we arrived in a wooded area, thirty-five miles from our barracks. Then we had to pitch a pup tent in the pouring rain. Each man carried one half of a tent, one pole, and half the wooden pegs to pin the tent down to the ground with, and a blanket, while his buddy carried the other half of the tent and his blanket.

It was pouring rain when we arrived at the wooded area about midnight, and we had to pitch these two-man pup tents in the dark. My buddy and I dug a trench around this tent with our field shovel, to drain the water away, then we took the dirt from the ditch and put it around the edge of the canvas tent to keep the water out, but it didn't help much. With nothing but sand in Florida, the rain ran right off the tent and then flowed right inside. After a while we felt a stream of water running through the tent; but we were so tired, it really didn't matter, we just let it run and tried to sleep. So we slept in that wet pup tent on a soaking wet blanket, in our wet clothes. I was so exhausted at the end of that 35-mile march, carrying 75 pounds on my back, plus a rifle, gas mask, and steel helmet, that every muscle in my body ached.

After doing quite a few combat-like exercises of taking hills and fighting imaginary enemy soldiers for two weeks in the woods, we finally marched the thirty-five miles back to camp. One man I saw substitute several rolls of toilet paper in his pack, in place of the seventy-five pounds of equipment, to make his pack a lot lighter. Anyone who fell out of this march or otherwise goofed up, such as this man did, for any reason, had to do it over again, if he were caught. He would have also gotten about a week working in the mess hall peeling potatoes and washing greasy pots and pans. God forbid.

It was there in these sandy woods that we all learned the importance of the buddy system. If an enemy sees only one soldier, his chances of surviving are very slim. So, now we had to obey all the rules of combat, and that meant that if you got out of your tent to go to use the slit trench, you had to wake up your buddy to go with you; otherwise, if you were caught by yourself you did 50 pushups, right then and there, no matter how tired you were, or how hard the rain was coming down.

While on bivouac, I and several others who had been recommended by the captain to go to Officers Candidate School, were called to meet with a committee of field officers, all ranked above captain, who were clustered in a group of trees, seated in chairs. Their job there was to interview those recommended by the captain for Officers Candidate School, OCS.

I reported to them, saluted with my rifle, and I was asked, "What will your duties be in combat?"

My reply was, "To kill as many enemy as I can, take their territory, destroy their equipment, and to keep on fighting like hell to win the war as quickly as possible, sir."

The next question by a colonel was, "Why do you want to go to Officers Candidate School, soldier?"

My reply was, "Sir, I do not want to go to Officers Candidate School."

"Would you tell us why?"

"Sir, I had a hernia that caused the draft board to turn me down, which delayed me considerably in getting here. I had surgery to correct it, just so that I could go into the army as a combat infantryman and do my part to hurry up and finish this war, then return home and go to college. Sir, I am running late now. The war in Europe will soon be over, and I need to get over there as quick as I can to do my part."

The colonel replied, "Thank you soldier, you have given us some very interesting answers. Your answer to our question as to what your job in combat will be, was very good. You job as a combat infantryman is to kill as many enemy soldiers, destroy their equipment, and take and hold as much of their territory as you can. That is the only way that a war can be won. That is the job of a combat infantryman. That is what we are here to train you to do. Good luck, and God speed. You are dismissed."

I thanked him and saluted with my rifle, did an about face, and returned to my bivouac area.

CHAPTER 2

On My Way To Europe

"I have nothing to offer but blood, toil, tears and sweat."

—WINSTON CHURCHILL (1874–1965)

Upon completion of basic training I had a few days at home and then caught the train to Fort Meade, Maryland. We stayed there several days. I think that they were trying to fatten us up for combat, in that it was the best food I ever ate in the military. There were no chow lines to stand in and wait, the food was served family style in bowls, and you could just sit there and eat all you wanted. I received my orders there and was assigned to the 65th Infantry Division, which was currently somewhere in France. I now had my orders and was on my way.

After about three days of processing there, we were on the train again to Camp Shanks, NY, just outside New York City. This was the coldest place I had thus far been. The snow was deep and the temporary barracks were hard to heat. After about three days there, one night we got on trucks and were taken to the docks in New York City where we boarded the HMS Queen Elizabeth. I had never seen such a huge ship in my life. It was awesome. We went up a steep gangplank with full combat gear, plus our duffel bag, which contained our clothing and personal items—like extra clothing such as socks, underwear, overcoat, stationery, etc. We were assigned to a room that at one time had been a luxurious stateroom on this giant luxury liner. Everything had been removed from it and about four steel bunks, each three or four bunks high, had been placed in there. Each bunk was just a steel frame with a piece of canvas laced around the edge with a rope to hold it. There was no mattress, just canvas to sleep on, with one blanket, which we brought in our duffle bags. There was little room for all our equipment. Nothing had ever been so cramped, so we crawled over each other's equipment.

While every soldier there was a stranger, in some respect we all were real friends. We talked as if we had known each other all our lives. We worked and cooperated with each other so much that it made one proud to be a part of such a great endeavor. No one would ever believe so many men could be placed in such cramped quarters for so long, and there not be any conflicts, yet there was none of that. Everyone was kind, helpful, and considerate of each other, more like brothers, which in a sense we were.

Before daylight, we sailed out of New York Harbor, past the Statue of Liberty, and on out to sea. We were surprised that soon the weather was like it had been in Florida, sunny and balmy. We had gone south to avoid the Nazi submarines in the North Atlantic. Several days later, however, we were in the North Atlantic with heavy seas, some fifty feet high. This huge ship was like a cork in a bathtub bucking the waves. As the ship rode the crest of the big waves its propellers came out of the water, and you could hear and feel their loud vibration.

There were so many troops on this ship that each of us was given a button to wear. I had heard that there were many thousands of men on board, over fifteen thousand troops, plus crew. So the men in the bow section wore a red button, those in the middle section wore a white button, we in the stern, wore a blue button, and no one could go into the other sections. This was to keep the ship balanced.

We got two meals a day. Breakfast was always two boiled eggs, two pieces of bread, some strawberry jam, and coffee. Someone asked a cook in the chow line why we always got strawberry jam, and he replied that it was because it looks just as good coming up as it does going down, in case you get seasick. I never got seasick, but there were some who were not so lucky. Each morning we would go to the top deck for lifeboat drill and to enjoy the fresh air and the salt spray from the huge waves. I enjoyed feeling the salty mist in my face.

Early one morning, on the seventh day at sea, someone awoke, removed the blackout curtain, looked out the porthole, and saw a small ship, a British destroyer called a Corvette, running right along beside us. In fact we saw several of them on each side of the Queen. I knew then that we were getting near our destination, which heretofore had been a secret. The weather was very cold. Then we learned from others that these Corvettes were all around us, protecting HMS Queen Elizabeth from German submarines, and that they had been with us the entire night.

About mid-afternoon we pulled into a large harbor and dropped anchor. I learned that this was Glasgow, Scotland, or a safe harbor very near there. Immediately, huge barges, each towed by a tugboat, came along each side of the ship to carry us ashore. Big doors, that I did not know were there in the side of the ship, opened up and we were the first ones to leave the ship, supposedly, because we were the last getting on to debark. The barge was quickly filled to capacity and we were told that those of us who were the first to unload were all combat infantrymen who were assigned to front-line action where they needed us badly.

We boarded a long passenger train and headed for South Hampton, England. Then, almost immediately we were on our way to the South of England to board a ship to cross the English Channel.

I recall going through New Castle, England, and could see the iron smelting mills glowing red-hot, with huge plumes of smoke billowing from the large furnaces. I recalled reading what Shakespeare said, "…It is like taking coals to New Castle." I explained it to some of the men in our compartment on the train, trying to break the silence and boredom and trying to relieve some of the tension. What Shakespeare meant was, if one was traveling with his family in a wagon, with their food, they usually carried a clay bucket of hot coals to start a fire with, to cook their meals. But if you went to New Castle there were lots of iron smelting mills there with many red-hot coals lying around where one could get all they wanted, so why carry coals when you are going to New Castle? Then one man replied, "Well, in that case I am going to throw my duffel bag out this window. After we get in combat we will never see it again until the war is over, and we won't need it then." And he was right. We all then began talking to each other. I could feel the tension, anxiety, and fear that had been built up amongst all of the men in our compartment, and now I had broken it with only a few words. There was now a more relaxed mood and all of us began to talk to each other, which relieved lots of tension.

As we traveled through London we saw some large buildings that were burning and a lot of flames and smoke. We learned that a Nazi buzz bomb V2 ballistic missile had just hit the city and caused a lot of fires. At Southampton we got off the train and walked about three miles, carrying our duffle bags on our shoulders to the docks, where we slept that night in a cold, damp north wind that went right through us. We found some large cargo canvases, and many of us got under them for protection from the wind and cold, but it didn't help much, in that the cold wind was coming up through the cracks between the planks of the huge pier.

The following morning we boarded an old rusty British ship that looked as though it had seen lots of action. We slept in hammocks so close together that it was impossible to get up to go to the latrine without crawling on the floor, underneath the many hammocks to get there. The food they gave us was pitiful, only some oatmeal with no sugar or cream. At dark we set sail with a convoy of other ships about this same size and arrived at daylight in Le Havre, France, where we tied up alongside a sunken ship that was lying on its side. We walked across the hull of this sunken ship to get ashore, then walked twelve miles, all uphill, to a tent city called Camp Lucky Strike. We only spent one night there.

The next morning early, we boarded a French train of boxcars called forty and eights. Where it got its name from was because they would hold forty men, or eight horses. These boxcars were of WWI, 1917 vintage when they had a cavalry with horses that had to be transported along with the troops. We actually had about thirty-five men in each car, with our duffel bags, backpacks, everything we would need in combat, except ammunition and grenades. We traveled all day and all that night. We were packed so tight that it was actually painful. Always someone's equipment was poking you in the ribs, or else some GI was asleep, and he kept kicking you in the face with his combat boots. We were literally sleeping on top of each other.

German planes strafed us that night, I heard the machine guns firing and the bullets hitting something, but no one in our car was hit. That night we would often stop in a rail yard for some reason, and French women would come up to the train trying to sell bottles of wine. I felt sorry for the women standing on the ground, dodging the many streams of urine from the men trying to relieve themselves, while the women were trying to sell their bottles of wine. I bought a bottle of the wine just to be kind; it tasted more like vinegar. It was actually green wine, not very good at all, but what could one expect under the conditions that they had endured through years of Nazi occupation and then trying to survive the fighting through these towns and villages as the Nazis were being driven out of France. One could see the devastation everywhere, especially in the railroad yards.

CHAPTER 3

Arriving at the Front in Saarlautern, Germany

> *"The Third Army moved further, and faster, and engaged more divisions, in less time than any other Army in the history of the United States, possibly in the history of the world."*
>
> —GENERAL GEORGE S. PATTON (1885–1945)

The next morning the train stopped, and we were ordered to debark. We walked many miles to an old French military installation near Metz, France, which has always been called the "Fortress City of Europe." We each picked up our rifle, bandoleers of ammo, and hand grenades that we hooked onto our cartridge belts. We left our duffel bags in a room there. After a speech from General Patton, welcoming us, we were sorted out and went in various directions on trucks. This was one time that we didn't have to ever "hurry up and wait." Not one moment was ever wasted in getting us to the front lines.

A truck pulled up. I and three others were instructed to board that truck, which would take us to our respective units up on the front lines. There were a long line of trucks loading men on them to obviously go to other places on the front. I had been assigned back in the States, to the 65th Infantry Division of the Third Army and I presumed that he would take us there, wherever it was in action. I learned from the truck driver who was to take me and three others to our assigned units, that we were going right up to the front lines, on the Siegfried Line, at Saarlautern, on the Saar River right now. The four of us loaded on this two-and-one-half ton open cab truck and we left right away. This driver drove like a maniac the east, along a dirt road full of shell holes, sometimes he would have to hit some of these holes that were impossible to avoid, and we would bounce at least a foot off the seat.

Along the way we saw thousands of abandoned pieces of German war materiel, tanks, 88mm cannons, trucks, and every conceivable kind of German vehicle and weapon of war, all of which were either demolished or abandoned.

There were abandoned farms, homes, and farm equipment everywhere along the road to the front. Not one French civilian could be seen anywhere, except in one small town that we passed through, where a few of the older men and women had returned to their partially destroyed town. The houses everywhere were most all, totally destroyed. Not one whole window was in any house.

Soon we arrived at a large building at the edge of what was once a big city that was now totally demolished, and abandoned by all citizens, and had been for almost six months. This was the battle zone of the Siegfried Line, a city called Saarlautern, on the Saar River.

This city, Saarlautern, as we knew it then in 1945, was founded by Louis XIV of France, in the seventeenth century, and in 1680 he named it Saarlouis, after himself. It was in that year that King Louis XIV of France made this a fortified city, which it has been ever since. King Louis had a famous French architect, Sebastien le Prestre de Vauban, to plan the City of Saarlouis and its fortifications, as well as the fortifications of Strasbourg and Metz, France. His tomb is in Les Invalids, in Paris where Napoleon is buried.

After Hitler came into power, in 1936, he changed the name to Saarlautern, in that he didn't want a city in Germany that was named after a French king. After WWII ended, it was renamed Saarlouis, which accounts for Saarlautern not being on the present-day maps of Germany.

The truck driver drove right up to the front of this large military-type building that was partly demolished, with debris lying around. Shell holes and bomb craters were everywhere and there was not one window anywhere that had any glass in it. There were larger craters that were bomb craters, made by our B-17s before any American GIs ever arrived.

The four of us soldiers were told by the assistant driver before the truck even stopped, to hurry in getting out when the truck stopped, because they had to leave quickly, because they had to get out of range of those 88mm cannons. We got out of the truck immediately after it stopped. The driver had also told us that he had to leave quickly so that he wouldn't be hit by Kraut artillery. He left driving in just as big of a hurry. I looked around everywhere and there were no signs of life to be seen anywhere, just devastation and desolation everywhere.

After we got out of the truck, we were left just standing there, not knowing where to go or what to do. We looked around to try to see what the situation was like. There was this big partially demolished building with no windows or doors in it; they had all been knocked out, either by artillery or bombs. It was a ghostly looking area, like nothing I had ever seen before. We were afraid to go into this building, not knowing what to expect if we did. We were in a combat zone, if ever there was one. We just stood there and didn't see anyone anywhere. I couldn't see anyone that we could report to. We didn't know whether to go into this desolate-looking building, or just what to do. I asked the soldier with me, "Are we to fight this war here, alone, by ourselves?"

Suddenly, 88mm artillery shells began landing right near us. We hit the ground. I was at a loss to know where we would be the safest, out there lying in the dirt with the shells landing nearby, or inside where it now may be occupied by booby traps or Krauts. We had no way of knowing. About five or six rounds came in and landed on the same side of the building we were on, just a few yards from us. The first burst was not too close, but then they kept getting closer and closer, too close for comfort. The ground shook, my ears almost burst, my head roared. We had hit the ground after the first round and now we were afraid to get up off of the ground. I was fearful of going into this building, in that it may be full of Krauts, or in getting up those steps, where we would more easily be exposed to 88 artillery shrapnel than we would be lying there flat on the ground.

While we were lying there with the shells getting closer and closer to us, a major stuck his head out of a broken window and said, "You guys get your asses in here, now. You are going to get us all killed by those damned 88s if you just stay out there making yourself a target. You are drawing fire—get in here now."

I thought, to myself, "Major, now you tell us, after we have been nearly killed by these 88s. Where have you been?" He was just inside that broken-out window when we arrived and he had to be deaf not to have heard that truck arrive. I thought that under these circumstances someone in that room should have stuck their head out then—to determine if anyone was outside, what that truck was doing there—and he should have been professional enough to have told us to come on in then, before the 88s started coming in, and not after. I didn't want to become a casualty immediately upon arrival, nor did I want to fight under the command of this man.

So, we ran inside as the shells still were coming in. Luckily we got up the steps before the next round came in. Running up those steps scared me in that we were higher than being on the ground. I knew that the shrapnel flies upward in a cone shape when a shell lands and goes off. We were lucky that no shells landed while we were running up the steps. I often wondered why this major who was just inside the broken-out window when we arrived, didn't tell us sooner to come on in, because he was just inside that broken-out window and he had to have heard the truck that brought us there. I thought to myself that he had to be pretty irresponsible by not sticking his head out that window sooner and telling us to come on in.

There was just this major and a couple of sergeants sitting around a table with a bunch of battery-operated, hand-crank GI telephones, a few maps, and the remains of a few consumed rations. Their table was covered with plaster that had been knocked from the ceiling by shrapnel coming in through the windows. It was a filthy-looking place that would never pass any kind of inspection. In the next room was the company, or battalion, aid station with a couple of medics and two GIs with minor injuries that were being patched up. There were also some stretchers and a few medical supplies. No one ever told us what organization this was, and none of us ever asked.

The sergeant told us that the Krauts started shelling about this time, about 4:00 P.M., every afternoon and it continued usually until midnight, and they would fire at any vehicle, even at one or two individuals, and these 88s were deadly accurate.

I had no idea they were targeting us, in that I could not see where there could be any artillery observers anywhere around there, that would be close enough to see us, but I now knew better. I knew that he was out there somewhere near, watching the front of this building. He had to be. I wondered why someone hadn't sought him out and killed him. I didn't like the idea of being shot at with 88mm cannons and bounced around on the ground. I felt that someone should do something about this. I also thought that it was damn sorry of someone not to have told us about them the moment we got off that truck. I couldn't conceive of enemy soldiers being all around us, and so close as this spotter had to be.

Soon two GIs just walked in from somewhere. They had come for two of the men who arrived with us. They left right away. It just left the one other GI—Lenny—and myself. We were not told what to do, or what not to do. We explored this large old former Nazi military building that was strongly built, but was now pretty well shattered. After entering the building, the hall made a right turn; this long hall ran the length of the building and then cornered for the other entrance. There, at the other end, was a large doorway that had also been demolished, which was unguarded and unprotected, where any Kraut patrol could just walk in. There were many rooms like a dormitory, or barracks, in this old abandoned building. All the windows in the entire building were broken out and no longer there, holes were in the roof, and all the doors and windows were all shattered. I could see where shrapnel had come in through the windows and shattered the wall, and ceiling plaster was everywhere on the floor. It was a ghostly sight, dirty, dark, dusty, dank, and desolate, as well as very cold.

It got late in the evening quickly, as well as much colder. Things got awfully quiet. One of the sergeants came out of the room near the door where we came in and told us that tonight we would stay there and to find a place to sleep, that there were some old mattresses in the rooms that we could find to sleep on, and there were some blankets in the office.

While I had the sergeant's ear, I asked him what conditions here were like. He told us that the enemy soldiers were everywhere in the area and to be very careful, not to go outside unless it was totally necessary—especially in the daylight hours—and never to be without a buddy, which was continuously drilled into our minds. Also, they were short of men there, and they had no way to really guard the building from enemy soldiers just walking in, anytime, so be always on guard, and to be extra careful.

He told us that our objective was to take the bridge there across the Saar River, that were protected by big pillbox bunkers that were across the river on the Siegfried Line. There were many bridges across the Saar River, but we were to be concerned with the one nearby. We were to neutralize those bunkers, take the bridge, and cross the Saar River, and then cross the Siegfried Line and those Dragon's Teeth, at such time that this could be accomplished. He related to us that this wasn't going to be an easy job, in that there were so many Kraut soldiers in this area trying to defend the Siegfried Line, that we would just have to kill off as many as we could in order to make any advances to even get up to that river, which was only about two blocks away. The sergeant told me that the entire 65th Division was deployed all along the Saar River, and that the Siegfried Line was just across the river, which was a continuous line of big concrete bunkers protecting the entire area from as far away as Switzerland, all the way north along the French border, to the Belgium border. He also explained that these bunkers kept all of the bridges that crossed the Saar River well covered with weapons fire.

He plainly said, "You men are going to have to kill them as you go; there is no other way. This whole area is supersaturated with Krauts. You have only one choice, either kill the hell out of them, or be killed." We got the message.

I also realized they were happy to have us there with them and would like to keep us there. I hoped he didn't get any ideas about keeping us there, because I didn't think I could stand the boredom. He related that a lieutenant would be here tomorrow and take us to the platoon we were temporarily assigned to. We were to simply make ourselves as comfortable as possible, afford as much protection for the building as we could, and await further orders. I thought, "This is one hell of a big building for just two men to have to protect, especially when there are Kraut artillery spotters nearby, watching everything that takes place here." I wondered, "Who is going to stand guard at this old building when we leave?"

Just outside the entrance we had used, there was a slit trench in the ground that served as a toilet. You had to use this slit trench in a hurry unless you wanted one of those lurking Kraut artillery spotters to call in some 88 artillery fire on you. They had a reputation of firing the 88s at only one soldier, just as they would fire a rifle at you, as we soon learned. So, to use the slit trench toilet, you had to literally take your life into your own hands. After you went outside and the Krauts spotted you, it took at most about a minute or two for the 88 shells to start hitting all around you.

I didn't venture outside that night except to quickly use the slit trench. When I did go outside, I noticed a light almost like a full moon; however I could see that it was coming from large antiaircraft-type searchlights, far to the rear, shining low to the ground overhead, where we were. These lights illuminated the particles in the atmosphere, and they reflected the light, illuminating the area in a flood of ghostly light. It provided a dim light all night, making it possible to see someone else maybe fifty yards away. At least you could see where you were going, which was better than total darkness. But you couldn't see anyone at any great distance. The men there called it the GI (Government Issue) Moon. Some called it the artificial moon. By whatever name, it made it possible to see a little at night, when otherwise it would be impossible to move around at all, not to mention in daylight, which we were told was suicide.

We explored the building without going outside, peeping out the windows trying to find the Kraut artillery spotters, or any enemy soldiers. We were really trying to determine where the Kraut spotters were located. They were the ones I wanted to find and deal with. There were no men to serve as door guards, other than Lenny and me. An enemy soldier could have just walked into that building, and blown all us all away with just one burp gun. I figured it would be wiser to eliminate the spotters, then we wouldn't have to worry about them shelling the place as much. It sure angered me to know that they were out there firing at me with an 88mm cannon, and me with only my M-1 rifle. I thought this was an unfair advantage, and that they ought to be eliminated. I was beginning to understand what war was all about.

The weather in Saarlautern was cold, hazy, with a heavy atmosphere of smoke, dust, and burnt gunpowder. Even if there were a full moon, you wouldn't be able to see it for the haze. It was very cold at night, a little warmer in the day, if the sun shined.

Across the hall from the "office," Lenny and I found a room where we would stay and hopefully get a little sleep for the night, before the lieutenant came for us to take us up to the cellars the next day. We both were tired because we'd had no sleep riding that freight train from Le Havre to Metz last night. We got two mattresses from another room and put them on the floor rather than on the bed, because being on the bed would put us too close to the blown-out windowsill, where we could more likely be hit by shrapnel because the height of the bed was the same height as the windowsill. To be safer, we put the mattresses on the floor. As it got late, we quickly learned that the blankets were not enough to keep us warm.

The night became tiresome, it got much colder, we couldn't sleep. It had been a long day. Only three days before, we had left Southampton, England, and yesterday we had left Le Havre, France, on that train. Just this afternoon we had left Metz, France, on a truck and here we were, right up on Hitler's Siegfried Line, his West Wall as it was often called. We were totally confused as to what we were to do and how we were to do it. But first, we needed some warmth, which we hadn't had for a while. It had gotten so cold it was impossible to go to sleep.

There was a small potbellied stove in the room where we planned to sleep. We fixed the stovepipe, poked it out the broken window, and propped it up so that the draft of the stove would draw and the smoke would go outside. Lenny found a bucket of burned coal called coke. He said that it wouldn't make any smoke like wood or coal and that it would glow red-hot all night once we got it burning. He commenced to make a fire with some wood splinters from pieces of the shattered building, and piled the coke on top. Soon it was smoking like a train. We needed a little warmth badly.

Just as a little heat began to come out of the stove, artillery shells started landing on that side of the building, just outside our smoking window. Shells were landing right outside of our window. Shrapnel was coming through the window and knocking the plaster off of the walls and ceiling, down onto us. This was on the opposite side of this same building where they had just shelled us, in the late afternoon when we arrived. I told Lenny that it looked like those Kraut artillery spotters were determined to get us.

The shells were also hitting on top of the building. Glass and plaster were falling everywhere and the whole building was shaking. We quickly decided that it was the smoke that was attracting the attention of their artillery spotters. I knew now that those spotters had to be very close to where we were, in order for them to see the smoke. There was not a great deal of smoke coming out of the stovepipe that would make it so visible to anyone, unless they were close by. This disturbed me greatly. I thought that something should be done about these Kraut artillery spotters that were lurking out there. It was hard for me to conceive that we were in such close quarters with these Kraut soldiers who were trying so hard to kill us.

We tried in vain to put the fire out to stop the smoke, but the more we tried, the more the smoke came out and the heavier the artillery fire got. I emptied the coke out of the bucket, crawled on the floor out into the hall to avoid the shrapnel, ran outside and got a bucket of dirt from a shell hole on the other side of the building, wet it with water from my canteen, and covered the fire with the mud. Quickly the smoke diminished, and soon the artillery shells stopped. We found another way to try to keep warm. We found two more dirty, dusty mattresses, dragged them into the room by crawling along the floor to avoid the shrapnel, and we each slept on one and covered with the other. We got very little sleep that night and I wondered if every night would be something like this. I was so cold that the only thing that I could think of was being back home in my cozy bed where it was warm, quiet, and peaceful. I thought that this would not be the way to think here, in this situation, and that I should devote all of my time trying to first stay alive and survive. I was determined that I would take all of the misery and discomfort that I was confronted with and I began to think of other men in combat in Europe and what they have had to endure. I would not allow me to feel sorry for myself.

The next morning I went into the office across the hall, near the main door, and asked the sergeant for some rations.

He remarked, "Man, those Krauts were sure pissed off at something last night; they really gave us a hell of a shelling."

I didn't say anything in response to that. I now really knew what "cover and concealment" meant: "Keep yourself completely hidden and concealed, and don't make any smoke, or else become a casualty."

About that time, a lieutenant came in and introduced himself as Lt. Anderson. (I have been unable to recall his name, so I will refer to him as Anderson.) He told us that we were being temporarily assigned, in that the platoon that the captain had assigned me to, the 2nd Platoon, was in the process of crossing the old bridge at the opportune time, and occupying cellars beyond it, and at the foot of one of those big concrete and steel bunkers. No one could get into or out of where they were going without having to cross that old bridge, which was a deadly undertaking. He told us that they would be living in cellars, right in front of a big concrete Kraut bunker on the Siegfried Line. He told me that since no one could get to my platoon, they needed as many men as they could get, there in the cellars, to go on patrols, and that I would be temporarily assigned to a platoon here until my platoon could regroup, or was accessible. I never did learn what platoon or squad I was temporarily assigned to. That was the least of my thoughts.

The lieutenant told Lenny and me, "We have only been in action here for a few of days, so don't feel like you are new. I will try to tell you all the do's and don'ts. You will learn the ropes in a little while. We are sleeping in cellars a little ways down the street. We won't go there till after it gets dark—it is safer that way. I'll take you there tonight, and you can help these men out until we can regroup; they are kind of short-handed. Grab yourself a blanket before we leave, because it is cold at night, and you will need it—or maybe take two."

I knew that the nights were cold, like last night. The lieutenant helpfully tried to brief us as much as he could, which would help us stay alive. I was glad he was trying to tell us how things were. I prodded him for more answers about the situation that we would be facing.

He continued describing the situation to us. "The Krauts are everywhere around here. You can hardly ever see one, but they always see us. We have to take cover and stay out of sight all the time. They know this area very well and have every inch of it covered by artillery observers, snipers, reconnaissance and ambush patrols. They start firing those 88s every afternoon and continue firing them until about midnight. We will leave here after it gets dark and go to the cellars we are holed up in, and soon we want to start clearing the Krauts out of here and eliminating some resistance. If we only clear a block of this old demolished city every day, we will be doing great. The problem is that they always keep infiltrating right back in, no matter how many of them we eliminate. Our objective is that bridge up there, which crosses the Saar, which is right near the foot of some big concrete bunkers. We have to get up there and take it. I will take you where your new platoon is, up the street a ways, after it gets dark, about 8:00 o'clock."

I asked the lieutenant, "Well, sir, how are we to get to the river and across it and the Siegfried Line, with so many Krauts around in this area?"

"That is going to take a while. We will just have to kill them as we go. That is the only way. This Siegfried Line is heavily fortified and well defended. There are lots of Kraut soldiers in this area that came in when they were squeezed out of Normandy, before any American troops arrived here. They all seem to be still here. The only way that we can make any advances is to kill them off as we go, and this is not that easy to do. They are ahead of us, behind us, and on each side of us, and you never know where they are. The only way to win is to fight like hell and kill all of them you can, but don't ever let them get a bead on you."

I thanked him and we waited, looking over the old partially demolished building, without going outside and giving a Nazi observer the pleasure of seeing us again, anymore than we had to.

That morning after talking with the lieutenant, we just wandered around in this once large and elaborate military headquarters building of the Nazi regime, bored to death. We found a large black granite bust of Adolph Hitler. There was a slit trench just outside the door of this building near where we first came in. This was a narrow slit trench that our troops dug in the ground and used as a toilet, where you just squat down across it to do your thing. Lenny and I carried this very heavy black granite bust of Hitler out into the yard and placed it down in the slit trench. We then stood inside, near a window where we could see this trench, and soon a sergeant came out to use the toilet. We wanted to know how he would react to Hitler's bust being there. We heard him say, "Piss on Hitler, piss on Hitler!" as he suited his action to the words. There is nothing better than a little humor, during times like these, to lift morale. I later told the captain that this should merit a write-up in the *Stars and Stripes* but he was so busy, that while he found it humorous, he didn't have time for any of our foolishness.

I thought it very strange that there could be Kraut spotters in buildings somewhere nearby, in and around this building, and no one is trying to seek them out and kill them, and that they were allowed to just sit out there somewhere in a building right nearby and call in artillery fire on us anytime that they see some smoke, or see someone outside. I thought that they ought to be hunted down, which shouldn't be too difficult, and dealt with accordingly. Both the sergeant and the lieutenant had told us that the only way that we could ever make any advances is to "just kill them off as we go." They also told us that they didn't have enough men there to hunt them down and eliminate them, and for the time being, there was nothing that we could do about the spotters but to stay out of their sights.

Lenny said to me, as we sat on the floor out in the big hallway, bored to death, "Remember what the sergeant said, 'Just kill them off as you go, or be killed'?"

I replied, "Don't you remember what the lieutenant said?"

He said, "The only way to win, is to fight like hell, and kill all of them that you can."

That afternoon we were bored to no end, just standing around in that old building. I told Lenny that we were going to go look for those spotters, that is, if he would cover me and do a good job. He agreed, and assured me that he would do just that. We had a long talk, rehearsing what we intended to do and how we were going to do it, because this was something new for me, but not too different from deer or turkey hunting back home. I told him that I saw nothing wrong with us trying to do this. I explained that it was better than just sitting here like ducks in a pond, waiting for the Krauts to kill us with those 88s. I told him that we didn't have any orders not to kill a few Krauts, and that is what we were trained to do, what we came over here to do, and that we should either do it, or else go visit Paris, meet some pretty girls, drink some fine wine and have a good time. No one had instructed us not to hunt down these spotters, and it was something that badly needed to be done. So we began planning our strategy. We two privates planned this operation like some general would do it. After all, that is what we were trained to do, and what we were sent over here to do. I felt this was something that needed to be done, and that we should go do it. I didn't want anyone to think that we were shirking our responsibilities. I was also now as angry as one could be. I felt we should fight back, not just sit here and wait till someone told us what to do and when to do it.

I knew that I had to come to grips with fear, as well as with having to kill another person. I had thought about it quite a bit. I had reservations about just killing an enemy soldier that was not a threat to me, like, just because he was there. This would be more difficult for me to do than if an enemy was firing at me, or directing 88s at me. This seemed to be the time to straighten things out in my mind. If I was to engage in mortal combat with enemy soldiers, I felt that now was the time to settle it in my mind that I would and could kill an enemy soldier. It was not that I yearned to do it; it was that I was angry now, and I wanted to stop those observers from firing those 88s at us, trying to kill us, as well as other American soldiers here. It was obvious to all of us there that this was a situation that needed to be taken care of. I also wanted to prove to myself that I could do what I was trained and sent over here to do. We both were very scared, but we both tried hard not to show it, because we could now see that we had an awful lot of killing to do if we ever wanted to extricate our selves out of this place. We were in a situation where there was no other way out and no turning back, as I saw it. It was, a do-or-die situation. We agreed that it was time to conquer that fear, and then go on about this business of "killing them before they kill us."

So I told Lenny, "Let's do it."

Lenny replied, "Yes, let's go do it."

We had a mutual understanding of how we were to do this job. We both felt pretty cocky, somewhat infallible, and determined to get this war over with. We had to be very cautious though. I instructed him that

I would go ahead and look for the Kraut spotters, and he would stay behind me and look for anyone trying to draw a bead on either of us. I told him to not keep an eye on me, but to watch all around, all the time, in every direction, high and low, and in a 360° direction, for anyone that would spot us, or try to fire on us, or who might be lurking in one of these old demolished buildings.

I cautioned him that because he looks in one spot and don't see anyone, then he has got to keep looking again and again at those same locations, because the enemy wasn't going to just sit there somewhere; he was going to keep moving, and hiding, peeping out, and trying to stay out of our sight, or he would be trying to draw a bead on us. That meant that we would both have to keep a constant lookout for Krauts. We also agreed that we would find our next place of cover, make sure that there were no enemy soldiers observing us, then move to the next cover, one at a time, each covering for the other, and as quickly and quietly as we could. He agreed and convinced me that he would do a good job and keep a good lookout while I would be out front, trying to spot the spotters. We agreed that each of our lives depended upon how alert and observant the other was.

We crept out the back door of the big building, and alongside another building to a spot where we had good visibility over a pretty wide area. We had already determined that the spotters had to be to the north side of the big building to have spotted us when we arrived, and also to have spotted the smoke coming out of our window last night on the other side of the building. There were no likely places to the south for an observer to hide, where there were just a few one-story buildings and then the river.

We took our time and moved slowly and then only after making sure that no one was observing us. We stayed ten or fifteen feet apart and never out in the open. We would hide behind some structure or debris, locate our next position, wait awhile, look in every direction, and then move one at a time as fast and as quietly as we could to that location, always being very quiet. Sit very still, just as if we were hunting deer or turkey, and look, listen, and closely observe every upstairs opening in all of the old partially demolished buildings. It was like a ghost town, quiet, scary, and very eerie, like something you could never imagine. There were no birds chirping, nothing moving anywhere. It was as quiet as a tomb.

We were two or three hundred yards from our CP (command post) building when I spotted a bay window in the alcove of the top of a three-story building that was further to the north, about a hundred yards. One of those glassless windows would give a person a broad view of both sides of the long building we were staying in, and in fact, a broad view of the entire area where we were staying. Also, it was the highest point of any building around there. Common sense told me that this would be an ideal place for a spotter. This was a spot I would have chosen if I were a spotter.

I whispered to Lenny as I pointed to this window, "This has to be the spot, it's an ideal location for them."

We just sat, waited, watched, stayed quiet and out of view, just peeping from time to time at this window on the third floor, as well as keeping an eye out all around everywhere else. I was concerned that the spotters might have some guards around the building they were occupying, protecting them. Lenny was taking cover about fifteen feet behind me in some rubble. We moved closer, but very slowly. I positioned myself by a corner of a demolished building where I was not visible to anyone from either side, but where I could peep through an opening and see the alcove windows. We were now no further from this building than two hundred feet or less. This was my favorite shooting range. I couldn't miss at this range. We waited patiently. It was not long before we saw a shadow, like a person moving around, back away from one of the windows. I got excited, and my heart began to pound. I gritted my teeth and got a good grip on my rifle.

Then I saw a Kraut helmet appear near one edge of the window. I got even more excited. He peeped around, looked in all directions, then backed away, and I could see him faintly as he moved away from the window and then around to the other side, and he peeped out. Then he dropped lower as if he was stooping or sitting down, looking out over the windowsill. Apparently he was now confident that there was no one out there who could spot him. Then his elbows were up on the windowsill and he was holding a pair of field glasses, looking through them toward the front side of our building. He was two hundred yards or more from our building and was looking right toward the entrance everyone used. Now, this was about 4 P.M., about when the shelling started yesterday afternoon. He obviously was looking right at the entrance of our building. I was now more determined than ever to eliminate this enemy that was right now trying to see if there was any of us that he could eliminate with his 88s.

Lenny watched quietly, tensely, but patiently waiting to see what I intended to do. I glanced at him and saw a faint smile on his face. He understood that his job was to cover me. I was on one knee; I slowly raised my rifle, braced it against the brick wall, and took aim at the Kraut, right in the center of his head just below the field glasses. I squeezed off one round. I saw his head snap back from the impact of the bullet. I knew that we dared not move right now. I also wondered if I was doing the right thing. I had to finish the job; it was too late to stop now. I knew there had to be at least two of the Kraut spotters. I didn't want to get Lenny killed or wounded, or myself either. I knew that we couldn't leave even one of them alive who could then shoot us as we tried to get back to our building. We both just froze as we waited to see what would happen next.

I then saw another Kraut looking out the lower corner of the window. He was looking in every direction. I quickly drew a bead on him right between his eyes, just below his helmet. I fired and he fell back.

Lenny said, "Let's get the hell out of here."

We left as quickly and quietly as we possibly could, staying out of the view from this window as much as we could. We ran into the back door of our building. We casually walked up to the room being used as an office with our rifles slung over our shoulders as though nothing had happened. The major and a sergeant were standing out in the hall. One of them asked if we had heard any rifle fire. We told him that we did, that it came from over that way—pointing to where the two dead Krauts were.

The major said, "I can't figure out what that was all about. We don't have anyone in that area."

I tried to change the subject, not knowing what he might think about what we did if we told him. I certainly didn't trust his judgment after he failed to stick his head out that window yesterday evening when we arrived, to see who we were and tell us then to come on in. Instead, he'd waited until we were almost shelled to death to then tell us to come on in. He certainly didn't bother to tell us to come in the building until he thought that the shells were going to "get us all killed."

I said to him, "Sir, this back door is wide open. Any number of Krauts can just walk right in here anytime they want to, sir."

His tart reply was, "I know that! We need some door guards if we plan to stay here any longer, but we just don't have any men to spare for that. You men will be leaving as soon as it gets dark."

Lenny and I both were out of breath and shaking like a leaf, but they didn't seem to notice it. This was not something we were accustomed to doing every day. No 88 shells landed anywhere around the old building that afternoon or evening before we left with the lieutenant at about 8 P.M. I later learned that no shells landed there that night either. I felt very proud of myself, and I also felt that I had conquered my fear of combat and killing, or as much so as one could expect to. I had always felt that fear could be conquered by facing the fearful situation head-on, becoming involved in what your were afraid of and accomplishing something.

I now felt much better and I believed that I could deal with just about any situation without being overcome with fear. My father had always taught me to always "catch the bull by the horns." I had now done that, and I felt some pride and satisfaction in having been able to destroy two of the enemy. I was as much afraid as any of the other men, and I never saw a soldier that didn't appear to be afraid in combat. I reasoned that I should put fear behind me as much as possible and just do my job as I was trained to do and as I intended to do as a patriotic American soldier. I had asked for combat, I got it, and here I was up to my ears in it. There was no possible way to now avoid it, so the only alternative was to call upon all of your resources and fight like hell, like we were supposed to. It never occurred to me to let fear deter me in fighting to kill as many of the enemy as I could and help win this war.

Before we departed to the cellar that night I picked up two blankets. It was already freezing cold. I also grabbed three K rations and put them inside my field jacket. With my cartridge belt around my field jacket, I had lots of room for such things as rations. I also filled my canteen from a five-gallon Jerry can of water. I knew now that there were not many people on the front lines that would do one's thinking for them, and a man in combat had to do his own thinking and not wait for anyone else to tell him what to do. I also believed that I should never just wait around for someone to tell me what to do. It wasn't my nature to do that anyway. I was anxious to see what the cellars were like, and also what tomorrow would be like, as well.

There was certainly no spit and polish here. There was no sign at the entrance of any cellar saying that this is the Headquarters of Company G or the 1st Platoon, as there would be back in the States. All the military formalities and protocol had no place here on the front. No officer or noncommissioned officer displayed their rank, because the Krauts had rather shoot one of them than a private like me. There was also no saluting for the same reason. It was now only a matter of fighting and killing the enemy, taking our objectives, and trying to survive. Learning the ropes came quick. There are some things you just don't need to be told about survival, it just comes naturally.

This situation here was extremely serious, and I now knew that fighting here had to be a full-time job, with undivided and dedicated attention given to it. Training and discipline with a heap of guts, are the three primary ingredients that make a good fighting man.

I could see now that it takes a lot of guts, a lot of thought, common sense, and determination, to apply all that we had been taught in basic training, as well as all of my experiences of life, in order to fight and do it all well. But more than anything else, it took Faith in Jesus Christ and God Almighty, as well as faith in our leaders, before one could acquire the courage to face the enemy, as one should. Here and from now on, would be a test of faith and courage. From what I could see, this is war in its purest sense. A hostile war, a mean and dirty war, but we would fight it clean and honorable, and never become so evil as to commit atrocities against the human race as our enemy was doing. Christian values, loyalty to our fellow soldiers and our commanders, all played a great part in our ability to fight a war, to win.

I prayed to my Almighty God in Heaven and promised Him that if He would keep me safe and sound and return me home all in one piece, that I would continue to fight tyranny and oppression as long as there was a breath left in my body.

CHAPTER 4

The Cellars of Saarlautern

> *"Listen, Brad [Gen. Omar Bradley], don't spoil my show. The Third Army has sweated and bled to bring this thing to a head. Without the 10ᵗʰ Armored we won't be able to exploit the breakthrough at Saarlautern."*
>
> —GENERAL GEORGE S. PATTON (1885–1945)

Our entire 65ᵗʰ Infantry Division had moved into the region of the Saar River Valley on the French-German border, only a few days prior to my arrival there. The 95ᵗʰ Infantry Division had previously taken and occupied this entire area in mid-September of 1944.

The Battle of the Bulge commenced, which was a large counterattack by German Wehrmacht, SS, and Panzer tank units to try to stop our troops to the north from entering Germany, through the lowlands of Belgium and the Netherlands, north of where the Siegfried Line ended, at the Belgium border. When this happened, General Patton ordered the 95ᵗʰ Division occupying this area to pull out from its positions along the Siegfried Line and move immediately to the north, to Bastogne, to aid the 101ˢᵗ Airborne Division the Krauts had pinned down there. Our troops were fiercely fighting and suffering many casualties, as well as freezing to death in the frigid cold. The fighting in that area was taking place in the bitter cold of the coldest winter in forty-three years.

The 26th Infantry Division replaced the 95th Division that had previously taken and occupied the territory along the Saar River, the Siegfried Line, and the surrounding area and held it for quite some time before General Patton withdrew it. The 65th Division arrived, replaced the 26th Division, and was assigned the area of the Siegfried Line, which encompassed the Saar River from Saarbrucken in the south to as far north as Bitburg and Trier.

Now the 65th was committed into action here and had to retake much of the territory that was given up by the 26th Division when it moved northward. We also occupied many of the cellars that had been occupied by the men of the 95th and 26th Divisions. The German soldiers driven out of Normandy in the north central part of France, had assembled in the Saar region to help defend the Siegfried Line, hence, the invasion of Germany proper.

The men of the 26th Division had crept out a few at a time during nighttime, and then our men of the 65th Division had infiltrated the defenses and occupied the positions in cellars that the men of the 26th had occupied—and the men of the 95th had occupied before them. Many of our men were killed doing this. Also, Hitler had given the order for his soldiers to hold the Siegfried Line at all costs, which accounted for the presence of so many Nazi troops being here, and a life-or-death battle going on to prevent the invasion of Germany.

Saarlautern, Germany, is on the German-French border, located right on the Saar River. This area is located in the Saar Valley coal, iron, and steel producing area. It was a very old industrial city. Hitler's Siegfried Line with its line of large concrete bunkers and other defenses, also known as the West Wall, was located on a ridge along the east bank of the Saar River. Saarlautern was on the west bank of the Saar. The Siegfried Line was Hitler's main line of defense of the homeland, and it extended from near Switzerland to the south; all the way north to Belgium. Along the Saar River and the West Wall were cities, including Saarlautern—or Saarlouis as it is now called—Saarbrucken, Saarburg, Bitburg, and other cities in that area. This was Hitler's strongest fortification between France and Germany.

In each of these cities, as well as in between them, there were bridges across the river that were protected by a series of big German concrete and steel bunkers that had three machine guns firing out of them, almost continuously. General Patton wanted these bridges badly, and intact, so that his tanks and equipment could get across, so he could spearhead to the Rhine River and then on to Berlin—and be the first to do it. The Germans were holding onto the Siegfried Line as much as they could, so that they could commit their tanks, infantry, and artillery to the north to try to stop Allied advances in that area from advancing around the north end of the Siegfried Line.

The bunkers along the Siegfried Line were extremely large, with walls three feet thick, reinforced with steel that could withstand heavy artillery bombardment. Some had a wide, boxed-off rectangular slit in them, about twelve inches high and four feet wide, with a shelf inside to hold the machine gun tripods. Others had a slit in them that was stepped inward. There were steel hatch-type doors in the rear of the bunkers for the German soldiers to leave and to enter, so that they could place weapons positions outside, alongside the big bunkers at nighttime. Supplies were brought in through the back doors to the bunkers. These rear doors were also used to take machine guns, mortars, and other arms outside the bunkers to strategic and well-camouflaged positions on both sides of the bunkers, to be able to fire down streets and other lanes of fire. All of them were located along a hilltop, or ridge, along the east bank of the Saar River, and strategically spaced to stop any army attempting to invade Germany. Hitler had given orders that the Siegfried Line, especially along the Saar area where the main bridge was, was not to be breached by the Allies under any circumstance. The Siegfried Line was the last, strong, main line of defense of Germany. This area was assigned to General Patton and his men of the Third Army.

We men of the 65th had to retake the entire area that the 95th and the 26th Infantry Divisions had fought so hard to take. It was now filled with German soldiers who had fled out of France as the Third and First Armies advanced, pushing them eastward. Now, the men of the 65th Division were taking it back, cellar by cellar, in a plan to breach the Siegfried Line, to capture and save the bridges, and then cross the Siegfried Line's Dragon's Teeth tank traps further east.

It was the bridges across the Saar River that General Patton desperately wanted to take control over, so as to get his tanks and other support, men, and equipment across, in order to spearhead his drive to Berlin. Every bridge was protected by one of the many big bunkers and their outlying defenses all along the French-German border, all of which had to be neutralized.

Patton worried about how much armored equipment, tanks, and other armored vehicles that he had access to, so that when we did breach the Siegfried Line he would be able to exploit it with his armor spearheading out front, and move rapidly to Berlin.

One of our instructions was to go to our bridge and to protect it with mortar and machine gun fire, to keep the Krauts on the other side from getting to it, to blow it up. But first, our infantry had to fight their way through the mass of rubble that the city had been turned into, as well as the mass of Wehrmacht soldiers that now held and controlled the area, in order to get into a position to do that.

When I arrived at G Company, which was only a couple of days after the division had moved into position along the Saar River, all of the four platoons were spread out, in their sector, up and down the Saar, in the Saarlautern area.

My orders assigned me to the 2nd Platoon, Second Squad, Company G, 260th Infantry Regiment. However, the 2nd Platoon was already committed to an area that they had to take, which was across the old Roman bridge across the Saar in an isolated area to the northeast of where we were, with no way for anyone to get in to them, or for any of them to get out of there without quickly and surely being killed. There was no communication with the 2nd Platoon, not even telephone communications, so I was temporarily assigned to a squad of a platoon that was fighting in the rubble of this old demolished city. This, I learned, meant that they wanted me temporarily until our company could later be regrouped. This was certainly all right with me, so long as I was fighting the Nazis somewhere, and it didn't matter in what outfit. That was what I came over here to do.

The entire Saar River area was crawling with German soldiers. They were everywhere. There were no whole buildings standing anywhere, that I was able to determine. The dust, smoke, and fumes from exploding shells, as well as the stench of dead bodies, rotting potatoes, and other waste and debris of a no man's land in a long dead and decaying city, hung heavily over the old city, making breathing difficult and very unpleasant. Rubble was everywhere, even out into the center of the streets. The air was so thick that you felt that it could be cut with a knife. Without the floodlights, fighting in this area at night would have been impossible. All of the fighting would then have to be done in the daylight. This would have been suicide, in that the Germans had the advantage of knowing the area, as well as it being on their own turf. They had well-defined lanes of fire, hidden observation posts, accurate maps, and weapons that were just as accurate, which were well-suited to this kind of situation. It would have been hand-to-hand fighting in broad daylight without the light from the GI moon at night.

In the daylight one could see rather clearly for a great distance, making anyone an easy target to any enemy soldier hiding in the mass of rubble. Seldom did any of our men go outside in daylight. I quickly learned that to do so would be putting your life at great risk. The Germans were in such a position that they had their lanes of fire that their machine guns fired down, and snipers positioned in strategic locations, where they could fire on us day or night. It was much easier for the Krauts to kill our men in the daylight than at night.

So the fighting had to be done mostly at night, so they couldn't see us very well for any distance. That was when the Krauts came out of their bunkers on the hill across the river and placed their machine guns alongside the bunkers and behind rock boulders, and fired down streets and other lanes of fire. The enemy soldiers also came out of their cellars that were all around us at night, to do their night patrolling. They came out en masse to fire on American GIs who were doing the same thing, like combat and reconnaissance patrols going after rations and water, laying new communication wire, and communicating with other GIs located in nearby cellars. Telephone communication wires were strung, and hanging everywhere like cobwebs. Radio communications were out of the question, because the Krauts would monitor every word that was transmitted. They would also locate your position with direction finders, and shell you. If a wire was broken by shellfire or cut by the enemy, it required laying a new wire, and this was an almost nightly job.

We soon learned that the German soldiers who held the city were living not only in their bunkers up on the hills, but also in cellars throughout the city. Often they occupied cellars only a short block away from our positions. They were beside us, as well as oftentimes behind us, and always in front of us. They had well-established positions. They also had observers everywhere watching closely, our every movement. Their observers not only reported our positions, movements, and strength to their 88 artillery batteries, but also to their mortar crews. This made it necessary for us to not let the Krauts know what cellar we were in, by us going in and out without being seen, as much as possible. At times their 88s would fire only at one man. On occasions they fired at a particular intersection, then the next intersection a block away, and so on.

We had to become entrenched sometime, somewhere. But, moving around in the daylight was terribly dangerous because we could be seen for a long distance by the enemy machine gunners, snipers, and artillery observers who hid in parts of the devastated buildings that they used as observation posts. Their bunkers were on high ground across the river, which made it easy for them to observe our activities in the city. When we moved to a different cellar, we had to find an entrance in the daytime before it got too dark to do so, in spite of the artillery and machine guns. This meant that we had to run and take cover quickly.

It seemed that all of these enemy soldiers who had been squeezed out of France and into the Saar Valley Region had all remained. The retreating Krauts were ordered to hold that area, and to hold the Siegfried Line, especially along the Saar. One man described the enemy soldiers in the Saar Valley as being "as thick as fleas on a dog." They had to be forced from cellar after cellar in the Saarlautern area by us killing as many of them as we could, in our attempt to get up to the bridge that crossed the Saar River and the Siegfried Line, where we were to cross. We could not cross the bridge and the Siegfried Line until we had eliminated these Nazi forces in this city, so that these bunkers could then somehow be neutralized in order to cross the bridge, and then go between the neutralized bunkers. This was a mighty fortress that we had to fight through.

The Kraut soldiers hiding in the city would go behind the bunkers for supplies at night. German artillery positions were hidden behind the Siegfried Line bunkers, as well as in the hills in the entire area around us. We learned that the Krauts had confiscated farmers' horses to pull their 88mm cannons around through roads and trails to new locations, to fire barrages upon us, then move to another location before they were zeroed in on and wiped out by our artillery. Wheels on the 88s could be lowered or raised for this purpose. Artillery observers and snipers were everywhere, in partially standing buildings, hidden in places that gave them a clear view of any movements that we made. This was very frightening, as well as deadly, street fighting.

CHAPTER 5

Killing, Saarlautern Style

"The only thing we have to fear is fear itself."

—FRANKLIN D. ROOSEVELT (1882–1945)

Lenny and I left the command post with Lieutenant Anderson on our way to our squad, in the cellar of a demolished building. We crept along in the light of the GI moon, keeping as close to the old demolished buildings as possible, arrived at a shattered building, and entered it through a demolished wall. The door guard greeted us like we greeted Sunday company that was visiting us back down on the farm. Down the steps were about eight or ten men, lying and sitting on the floor amongst piles of potatoes and junk, just waiting for whatever was to happen next. I sat down in the dark cellar, leaned back against a wall, and just said hello to all the men there, not knowing their mood or what to say to them.

Fear in everyone was running high. Very few people talked. Everyone was very tense. This kind of street fighting was totally new and different from anything that we had ever heard of. What we had been taught about street and village fighting was that we were on the offensive, and had no cellars, GI moons, artillery observers, 88s, nor snipers, or machine gunners with well-defined lanes of fire that you dared not even try to cross. All of this kind of fighting was totally new and different to us. This was the real thing. We first had to learn how to stay alive.

We were just now beginning to move into these cellars and fight, killing enemy soldiers in order to take more territory and reduce their numbers. That seemed to be the order of the day, to see how many enemy soldiers you could kill today. As we were told in basic training, we were being trained to kill enemy soldiers, that is the only way you can take enemy territory and win a war. Killing is an infantryman's job, duty, and responsibility. It was instilled in us that we were the men on the front, the ones who are trained to fight and kill, up there on the front, hand-to-hand, in no man's land. There was no other way out. The killing had already begun here, and there was a lot more of it to be done.

Since I was new to the men of this squad, I wasn't asked to go on patrol that night. I wrapped up in my two blankets and got a little sleep. I really felt more safe here, more so than back at that big old building with no door guards, and as well as almost constant shelling all night. When the patrol returned that night I was awake to greet them, and all of the men returned safely, which was great for my morale.

It was very cold and it seemed that I was never warm. I, as well as everyone else, always slept fully dressed, including combat boots and steel helmet. Under the helmet was a fiberglass liner that looked like an ordinary helmet. The liner had webbing in it that acted like a cushion. Under the liner I wore my wool knit cap that could be pulled down over my ears when it was extremely cold. I never removed my helmet because it was comfortable when you had no pillow, so I just slept with it on. Our uniforms were certainly inadequate for the cold and rugged wear. I wore long johns, a wool shirt, and wool dress pants that had always been used only for dress wear, like at parades. I also had a wool sweater that was quite warm, and then on top of all that, my field jacket, the finest and most practical garment that the quartermaster had thus far issued.

I always slept with my rifle butt between my legs and the barrel beside my cheek, as almost everyone else did. Not once was I ever separated from my rifle. It becomes a part of you. I had learned in basic training that you never even lay your rifle down, for even one second. You always keep it in your hands and ready to use. It becomes an integral part of your own body. Occasionally, I would remove my shoes, massage my feet, and air out my shoes and socks. Never was I able to sleep warm or comfortable. Finally we brought some more wool blankets back from the CP. A shave and a bath were totally out of the question. We used the water that we brought back very frugally, and for drinking only. We ate mostly ten-in-one and C rations, which were much better than K rations because they came in a large wax-coated box with more of a choice of food, and more of it, the best being the sausage in oil, and the spaghetti and meatballs.

Never had I ever even dreamed of such devastation of any city. The streets were filled with rubble overflowing from the destruction of the buildings on both sides of the street. Before any American units ever arrived here, it was first bombed by our B-17 bombers, and later constantly shelled by heavy artillery. I never saw even one single building that was not completely destroyed, or left half-standing at best. The cellars were the safest place to be. I took a look at a map of the city. It was once a fine old city with distinctive buildings. I saw the location of the river, the bridge, the hills beyond, where that so-called formidable barrier was located. According to those who knew, the bunkers had rooms underneath the pillboxes; some said that they led to the other pillboxes and gun emplacements. They housed an aid station, ammo and weapons dumps, food supplies, command centers, and quarters for the troops. I also learned that here in the Saarlautern area, was the strongest part of the entire Siegfried Line. It was a mighty stronghold, to say the least. It was said to be Adolph Hitler's pride and joy. Hitler had said that it was impregnable.

We would have to face these weapons firing at us from the huge pillboxes. They also had many weapons of all descriptions located on the ground, and camouflaged at a lower level than the bunkers, and on each side of them. They also had their machine gun nests located and hidden at a lower level, where they could fire grazing fire along any thoroughfare that was frequently used by American GI foot soldiers. Not to mention the very mobile 88mm artillery pieces that were hidden in the hills behind the Siegfried Line, as well as up in the hills on the west side of the river. We were essentially walking right into Hitler's strongest stronghold. I was anxious to see what the situation was up close, near the river, and to get a good look at the Siegfried Line weapons emplacements, as well as that extremely important bridge across the Saar. It was to happen sooner than I expected. Now we had to adapt to living in the cellars of demolished buildings and fighting in this rubble and debris, until we could make that happen.

We occupied this and other cellars of demolished buildings along what was once a street, but which is now piled high with rubble. We moved closer to the river. Before we occupied a new cellar, we had to make certain that the squads on our left and right flanks were also occupying one next to us, and that no squad got too far away from the other ones. It was not easy to enter a dark cellar, not knowing what was down in there. So the way that we did it was, you yelled into it that you were going to toss in some grenades, by yelling, "Fire in the hole," then, wait a moment to see if you get an answer, then you would throw in two hand grenades to make sure that you eliminate any resistance in there. So, before entering this one cellar, I did just that, then I crawled down into it, and in the dim light coming through a small window that was partially covered with rubble outside I could see what was in there. I could see junk, rubble, a pile of rotting potatoes, crates, boxes, furniture, and about anything you could imagine.

This cellar was our new home until we took other demolished buildings farther down the street and moved in there. We occupied it and placed a guard near the entrance. We were out of view of the enemy—so we thought—and we posted guards in strategic positions in the area, as well as a man at the entrance of the cellar, which was inside the demolished building where one would normally enter a cellar from the inside of the building. Some cellar entrances were hard to find in the rubble, but there was always a guard there at the entrance, which was sometimes hidden inside the building, obscured by rubble. When the shells started coming in, it appeared rather homey, safe, and protective. It reminded me of a safe haven in a hurricane; as some say, "Any old port in a storm."

Lieutenant Anderson told us to pass on to all of the others everything that he was telling us about this area. He related how the Germans have the entire city mapped so well and they know it better than you know the palm of your hand. In learning where we are holed up, they know that we have to go back for rations, ammo, and water, so they will be placing mines, mostly their Schu mines, in our paths. These mines are about the size of a brick, hard to distinguish, and they will blow your leg off. Everyone has to watch for them, everywhere, all the time.

Their observers and scouts keep tabs on where we are, how many of us there are, what kinds of support weapons we have. They will locate our routes back for supplies and then mine and booby trap that area, or have snipers to cover it, or do both. We had to find out the same thing about them, which was not easy. We had to try to be invisible as much as possible, like very little, if any kind of movement in daylight. Don't expose yourselves to their view and don't do anything to attract their attention. I learned that if we ever wanted to get out of this devastated city, we would have to outsmart the Krauts and beat them at their own game.

As the lieutenant said, "We have got to take this city, at all costs, a foot at the time, whatever it takes to rout them out and take this city over. We will live in these cellars and come out only to advance and occupy another cellar further to the east, to get supplies, go on patrols, and maintain communications with the command post, and with each of the squads in this platoon. We will eat, sleep, and fight in this mess of rubble, and clear one cellar at a time, until we arrive at that river on the east end of town. Then we will be faced with the so-called formidable Siegfried line, that we will have to cross some way, sometime. We will always have one man posted outside the cellar where a squad will be housed. We use the buddy system all of the time. No one is to go any-where or to do anything alone without his buddy being with him, and that is an order. All patrols will consist of a minimum of six men. Are there any questions?" the lieutenant asked in a firm tone. There were none.

We knew that we were not to go outside during daylight, because, naturally, this was a busy part of town, and their observers could see us and fire at us with everything that they had—which mostly was their 88mm artillery pieces, machine guns, mortars, snipers, and screaming meemies, as we called them, in the absence of a more technical name that we could not pronounce. They could also see where we were going in and out of, locate our cellar, and shell us, or toss in concussion gre-nades. This was a dangerous place to be.

Lieutenant Anderson gave us further instructions: "We will send out a reconnaissance patrol from this squad just as soon as it gets dark. We won't go very far, just cover enough of the area to make sure we won't be attacked during the night. Our mission will be to seek out where the enemy is, how many of them there are, what kind of weapons they have, where they are quartered, or where their grouping is located, and destroy them, as many as we can, with whatever it takes. This will be very limited at first, in that we won't go very far, just far enough in the immediate area to make sure that we are not about to be overrun by these Krauts, and that they are not sleeping in the next cellar to us, or if they are about to move in on us.

"Now, I don't want anyone starting a war within a war that you can't win, like shooting at a lone German on patrol, and then getting yourself killed by the others in his patrol. If it places you at risk, hide, let them go on their way. But if you have the advantage, take it. Be invisible, and low-profile as possible, but if you have the backup and the advantage and the weapons capable of wiping out one or more, without great risk to yourself, do it. Always be sure that you have backup and adequate support before starting a fight with the enemy."

The lieutenant continued to lecture to us, making sure that we didn't go anywhere without our buddy being with us. He constantly emphasized that this had been proven—as we all now knew—as the best method of protecting yourself and in fact, surviving. He emphasized, "Each man protects the other at all times. Going anywhere alone is asking for it. But come back alive and in one piece. We will need you again. We need all the help we can get. That means, protect your buddy and he will protect you."

The lieutenant continued his instructions to us, and told us that by midnight he wanted all men on patrol to be back in their cellars. "We will have volunteers for all patrols, two men to go back to the supply dump to pick up rations, water and ammo, two others to string telephone wire from this platoon to the CP. Don't be surprised if at night they find our telephone wires and tap a line into them, or cut them. Also, their mortar and artillery fire often cuts the wires, which puts us out of communication with any of our units. We will be moving out early tomorrow night and advance further into the city, as far as we dare to go at one time, even if we can only clear it a block at the time, but we will take it. We will kill the enemy, drive them from their bunkers and totally defeat them, and take this city in its entirety by eliminating all of the enemy that are here."

The lieutenant continued; "We can expect enemy artillery, mortar fire, 88 artillery fire, machine gun fire, as well as those screaming meemies—and don't forget, close range small arms fire. Tonight and every night you are going to hear some strange-sounding noises from their screaming meemies and burp guns. The screaming meemies are rocket-propelled shells that are fired randomly from a rack of them. In addition to their demoralizing sound, they use them to lay down a blanket of fire in one area, like when they spot a patrol; they use them to try to knock out that patrol, or their location. They have a whistle on their fins that make them give off that demoralizing screaming sound."

The lieutenant continued telling us those many things that we needed to know in order to stay alive. "Their machine guns fire fifteen hundred rounds per minute, and ours fire about one-third that fast. In some of their machine guns, near the end of the barrel, they have three slots cut into the barrel, each a different width with a sleeve over these slots, and the sleeve can be rotated, covering one, two, or all three, or all of the slots. And as they rotate this sleeve, it sounds like a different gun at a different place; in other words, one burp gun will sound like a whole group of burp guns firing at you. It has a confusing and demoralizing effect on our soldiers until you learn to detect that sound and realize that it is only one gun firing.

"Don't forget that these Krauts like to use a garrote to strangle you with, a piano wire with handles on it, to toss around your neck. With their knee in your back, they ease you down to the ground as you are choked to death. They kill you quietly, quickly, and bloodlessly, as you may be walking by where they are lurking in any of these demolished buildings here. Look for them everywhere, because they are everywhere, and for God sake, don't let them slip up on you to garrote you or take you prisoner, and don't underestimate their abilities as soldiers to do such things. What they are accustomed to doing is hiding behind a wall or something, and as a patrol goes by, he steps out and garrotes the last man in the patrol. Just keep a sharp eye out as you move through this rubble to wherever you have to go, especially if you are the last man in a patrol. You must keep a good lookout ahead, behind, and on both sides of you at all times if you want to stay alive."

He continued to reiterate many things that we already well knew, but this being such serious business, no one minded hearing it over and over again. I appreciated him telling us this. This officer was determined to really take care of his men. As for myself, I appreciated being well informed about what conditions were like here.

"Remember that before you enter any cellar or room for the first time, that you cannot see into, throw in several grenades to clean the place out. Be careful that you do not throw them in on any of our own troops that may be in there. There is to be no one in these places unless there is a door guard at the entrance protecting and warning the men inside, who are resting and sleeping, of an attack on our position. You can expect the enemy to be hiding behind a wall, in an alleyway, anywhere they can hide and attack you. They have been trained to kill for a long time now, and they are good at it. They know how to do it real well, but don't give them the opportunity. Do it to them before they do it to you. One patrol returned, and the man who brought up the rear was missing. It was later determined that he had been garroted by a Kraut who obviously was hiding, and stepped out and garroted the man in the rear, without any of the others being aware of it. Any questions?" the lieutenant asked.

No one said a word. It was as quiet as a mouse in the cellar of this old demolished building.

After dark, I with five other volunteers—including a Sergeant who I will refer to as Carson, who led the patrol—left the cellar, keeping a distance from each other of about twelve or fifteen feet apart. We walked to the east, this time along the walls as close as we could get to a wall of demolished buildings, stopping occasionally to get our bearings so as to not forget where our cellar was, but more so, to look, listen, smell, and wait, in order to see if there were any Kraut soldiers out there anywhere. We well knew there were. We took our time, each crouched beside some sort of a knocked-down structure, and then one of us at a time moved forward to another location, where we took cover. We were good at this.

After we had gotten about four blocks away, moving very slowly, Sergeant Carson signaled that he saw a Kraut patrol coming from our left, at this intersection. They also used about six men for a patrol. It takes that many in order to lay down enough firepower to accomplish anything. Sergeant Carson signaled with his arm for us to take cover in the rubble. We took cover behind debris and walls and waited. The Kraut patrol crossed the street that we were on, all six of them about ten feet apart. We could hear their footsteps with their hobnail boots, only about thirty feet from Sergeant Carson who was at the front. As they walked slowly in front of us and to our right, the moment that Carson signaled to us—we were all watching him for a signal—we all opened fire on them, wiping all six of them out completely, in just a matter of a few seconds. I think that each of us got one of them. There were six of them and six of us. One apiece. We had been trained to fire at the one that represents the corresponding position in the patrol, so that there are no wasted shots; every shot counts and the job is done quicker.

Immediately after we quit firing on them, we returned to our cellar. We didn't want to press our luck. Everyone was breathing hard when we got back, and no one would talk about it. It took quite some time for everyone to get over the excitement and back to normal, if that can be done. Not every day do any of us knock out a Kraut patrol completely, as we did to this one. We were gradually, every day, diminishing their numbers. We were also gaining a lot of confidence in our ability as fighting men, and everyone was becoming more courageous.

It was after this patrol that I told Lieutenant Anderson about Lenny and me hunting down and eliminating the two Kraut artillery spotters in that third-story alcove window back by the CP. He didn't seem to like the idea, claiming that it was too risky and dangerous, it being in daylight where we could have gotten ambushed by guards they may have had guarding their observation post. He agreed with me that it was something that should have been done, and it probably saved lives, but they replaced them with other observers the next day. He didn't get on my case, but strongly cautioned me about taking too much of a chance, and in daylight, and without more support, too.

"Just be awfully careful," he cautioned me.

CHAPTER 6

Serious Fighting in Saarlautern

> *"The quickest way to get to heaven is to advance across open ground swept by effective enemy fire."*
>
> —GENERAL GEORGE S. PATTON (1885–1945)

There was now heavy fighting, serious fighting, everywhere, no skirmishes or mere sniping. We were shot at by German soldiers who were there in numbers to stop us any way that they could, and were determined to kill as many of us as they could. I told my buddies my thoughts on how to stay alive, and how to get them before they got us. You didn't have to have three stars on your shoulders to know this. It was simple: you just go out looking for them—like deer hunting—and kill them, all of them that you can. Have your buddy cover you, wait until they show up, then take them out.

I figured that my good judgment was worth something. My idea was to move slowly, never get in a hurry, stay out of sight of the enemy, observe everything, don't stand, walk, or even be seen out in the open anymore than possible. Then locate your next position, which affords you cover from more than one direction, and when you are sure that you are not being observed, run for it while your buddy covers you. Then you turn around and cover for him. Take your time, don't get in a hurry, take cover, hide, stay there, and make sure it is a good vantage point. Choose a location where you get some protection from a wall, an inside corner, or something like that, where you won't have a blind side. Protect the other men, as many as you can, and they will be protecting you. When you plan to move to a new position, tell or signal to the other men what you are going to do, so that they will cover you as you expose yourself running to your next location. Do that for each other. I didn't want to see any man wounded or killed, and I tried to do my part to prevent this from happening, as much as possible, without seeming to give orders or telling them how to fight a war. I considered it all to be just teamwork, helping to win the war. I listened carefully to every word that anyone said to me.

For everyone's safety, I wanted to make sure that none of us were killed or wounded. Removing a wounded man from a main line of defense position was very dangerous for everyone doing it. I, for one, didn't want to have to carry one end of a stretcher under these conditions, nor did I want to be carried out on a stretcher, or otherwise.

I learned from the lieutenant that a lieutenant in another of our companies was leading a patrol just south of us one night, and he stepped on a Schu mine, and it blew his leg off. He was quickly carried to the rear by the men on the patrol with him, and he had a minimum loss of blood due to the quick and thoughtful, as well as bravery of his men that got him away from that area and to where he could receive medical help, quickly, which saved his life.

We worked like a highly skilled precision team, and were getting better by the moment. I came to the conclusion that when we routed the Germans out of their cellar hiding places, the only place for them to run was down the streets. So I just waited, kept hiding myself, in a strategic location, barely visible, and waited for my targets to appear, after they were routed out by others in the squad. That is the way that I hunted deer and turkey back home on the farm. I quickly learned that the best way to do this job was to take it very slow and easy, get into a good vantage point where you could see in all four directions, such as a street intersection, and just quietly wait until the enemy wanted to go somewhere, and then bring him, or them down.

It was somewhat frightening to know that last night we were sleeping in a cellar with enemy soldiers all around us, even though we had a guard near the entrance to warn us if any Krauts came near our holdout position.

We only would be able to clear out an area of about two or three blocks at a time, meaning that at the end of each day we had to occasionally find a different cellar to sleep in for that night, if we wanted to hold our position. Anywhere out of the cold with just some protection from the elements, was a blessing. It didn't matter to me which cellar we were in, they were all bad. We also had to stay in contact with the men on each side of us, making sure that one squad didn't get too far out ahead of the men on their flanks, and we coordinated everything with them.

Each day we were moving more to the east, closer to that River Saar, shooting and killing the enemy as we went, clearing them out. We would just let them lie where they were shot; this applied to our dead soldiers as well. It was virtually impossible for anyone to even attempt to remove the dead bodies of our own men, so there were many dead soldiers everywhere in that city—most of them were German.

On one occasion, one of our men on patrol saw a dead enemy soldier lying in the GI moonlight. Always it seemed to me, that a dead soldier's skin would seem to glow at night under the light of the GI moon. So this soldier sees a wristwatch on the dead German's wrist and attempted to remove it, when suddenly an explosion killed the American soldier. It was reported that the dead German had been booby-trapped with a German potato masher grenade placed under his arm. The string that triggers it was attached to the watch, and when the American pulled on the watch, he set off the grenade that killed him.

A potato masher grenade is about the size of a can of tomatoes. It has a wooden handle about ten inches long. At the end of the handle is a metal cap, like on a medicine bottle, which you unscrew and discard, and underneath the cap is a ring with a string tied to it. You put the ring on your finger, lob, or throw the grenade by the handle. The string being pulled activates it, and five seconds later it explodes. It is mostly concussion, in that it has only a thin layer of metal that the explosive is contained in. It is not a fragmentation grenade. It makes a very loud noise. In an enclosed building, or cellar it makes a loud explosion with lots of concussion that can cause considerable physical damage.

Each day we suffered more and more casualties. More replacements were sent in, new men, scared as hell, and as one replacement told me, "I never dreamed that it would be like this. This is just pure hell." He soon got over it and accepted the fact that he was there to kill and destroy the enemy and win the battle and eventually the war at all costs, no matter what it takes to do it—there was no other alternative—and then he was just like all of the rest of us.

Most of our casualties were fatalities, some were men who had lost a leg from a Schu mine and survived, or in one case a man lost his leg from tripping on one, fell, and landed on another one that killed him. We had more medics now as our casualty rate rose. The medics were all great guys, lots of guts, passionately determined to save their patients and get them to an aid station quickly. The medics carried plenty of large bandages, morphine syringes, and bottles of glucose drip solution. An aid station had been set up at company CP to receive casualties and care for them until an ambulance could come for them, under cover of darkness, and carry them to the field hospital near Metz, France. One couldn't help but think, who is going to be next, when, and how will it be? I tried not to think about it.

I had gotten to know one of the men of this squad who I found to be a very fine person, intelligent, courageous, very kind and considerate, as well as a person that I could relate to well. One night, back at the CP, Mark and I were talking to another soldier and his buddy, who was from West Virginia. We were casually discussing the situation there, and making lighthearted conversation with a little humor. So I said something to the West Virginia GI, trying to get him to talk to us, something that he had not done. I only asked him what he thought of the situation here, to get him to join in the conversation. I just thought that he was apprehensive or shy. Suddenly he pointed his rifle at my chest, unlocked the safety, and said, "I don't want to talk to you or anyone else, so if you open your mouth again, I will kill you."

We all just stood there in a state of shock. I had only made a kind and friendly remark to him. The first thing in my mind was that this guy was a mental case, which he was—or we were led to believe by him that he was. Finally he put his rifle down, sat down, and never said another word. His buddy with him told me that he had never heard him speak hardly one word, and that he acted real strange all the time.

I reported this to the lieutenant and told him that this man was nuts, dangerous, and that he never went on a patrol or for rations and was just deadweight for the others to have to support. I also told him that if this man did this again to me, or to any of the other men, he would be a dead soldier. I also told him that now I knew that he was either crazy, or mean as hell trying to play crazy. He was removed to the rear that day. I later heard that they put him to work in the rear, filling up five-gallon gas cans with gasoline and loading them on trucks all day long. This was my first, but not my last experience with mental cases, nuts, psychos, cowards and the like. There were only two other such people that I ever encountered.

All of the other men that I ever knew, except maybe one person, were the greatest people that you would ever want to know, and people who would die for you, who you could trust with your life, and who would not try to take it. For one of your own men to do something like this, is more frightening than facing the enemy because you wouldn't expect one of your own fellow soldiers that your life depended upon, and his depended upon yours, to be so treacherous, contemptible, and dangerous. I would hate to have to kill one of our own soldiers, especially a mental case who wasn't responsible for his actions.

That same night while we were at the CP, a jeep arrived with Captain Teague in it. He came in and a few minutes later an 88 shell hit just outside. When I looked out the window, all I could see was a big ball of black smoke and a pile of twisted metal that had been Captain Teague's jeep.

I told him what my captain in basic training at Camp Blanding, Florida—who was also named Teague—had told us one day: "I have a brother over there in Europe, and he is a company commander, and he told me not to send any half-assed trained soldiers over there to his outfit, that he wanted well-trained, well-disciplined men with some guts."

He chuckled at that and had a big grin on his face, in spite of the fact that he had just lost his jeep to a Kraut 88. I thought that I should go back to that third floor bay window and take care of the spotters in there. I don't know how it happened so often, but it seemed that every time that I turned around, there was Captain Teague. He seemed to be everywhere the action was. He was not my company commander, but he was really on the ball, getting things done. In fact, I encountered

Captain Teague more often than I did my own company commander, Captain Graham, who was one great commander, as well as one fine and fair-minded man who really knew how to get the job done. He was always up front where the action was. Both of these great men stand out in my mind.

It was a long siege taking and holding onto this devastated city. Fighting was everywhere. No one was safe at any time. We had progressed further east to the edge of the city, by the river, facing the formidable Siegfried Line, eliminating the enemy as we went. If only they would stay eliminated. Now we became entrenched more than ever. This made it further to go from our cellars to the company CP. We would stay in these cellars until we were able to somehow and at some time cross the bridge and the Siegfried Line. No one knew just how we were going to do that. The Krauts were awfully persistent and determined. They were still everywhere.

We arrived at this most forward cellar location near the river, and at the west side of what we called the old bridge. There was a big bunker across the bridge that protected it. Our artillery in the rear commenced a continuous bombardment of that bunker as well as the area on each side of, and behind it. We knew that the Krauts in that bunker couldn't take it much longer. The shells would explode right on top and appear to just bounce off without even making a dent in that bunker, but it caused a hell of a concussion to those inside, I am certain. This strategy of bombarding all of these bunkers with our artillery seemed to send a message to the Krauts manning them that we were coming, and were going to drive them out of there. The concussion from our artillery shells pounding this bunker all day, every day, certainly made it very unpleasant for those inside. Our artillery pounded away, not only at this bunker, but all around it, making it impossible for them to emplace machine guns, mortars, screaming meemies, and other weapons on the outside of the bunker.

One of our squads, about eight men living in the cellar of a bombed-out building suffered severe concussions when a concussion grenade that was thrown in through a cellar window one night. These grenades were seldom fatal, but always caused enough concussion that one suffered brain damage, loss of hearing, dizziness, headaches, and other related ailments, especially if one explodes in a confined area like a cellar. They cause one's nose, eyes, and ears to bleed, severe headaches, unconsciousness, loss of memory, hearing loss, drowsiness, and all sorts of symptoms. No one was killed, but all of these guys had to be removed from the front line and taken to a hospital. That is what the Nazis wanted; they preferred to cause injury rather than death, so as to involve the time of other soldiers to care for them. So, we had to be more cautious and constantly on guard.

We captured some of their grenades. The concussion ones were small, thin-shelled, round, the size of an orange, with a fuse on top, and a handle that operated like our own fragmentation grenades. The potato masher grenades also produced a hell of a lot of concussion, and they could be lobbed, or thrown a very long distance by a person who could throw a ball well. Neither had much fragmentation, having only a thin metal shell like a tin can.

Living in the squalor of these cellars was miserable to say the least. We oftentimes defecated and urinated into the wax-coated boxes that the ten-in-one rations came in, and then, under cover of darkness, take it out of the cellar and throw it as far away as possible, all the time exposing yourself to any enemy that may be around—and they always were. If you went out of the cellar at night you had to wake up your buddy to go with you, to afford protection, each to the other. We also used the wax-coated boxes to burn like a candle, to heat rations, and to heat our aluminum canteen cups of Postum, a dried instant coffee substance that came in a small foil envelope in the rations. This was about the neatest trick that the War Department came up with. The ten-in-one rations were much better than the K or C rations. Many guys made jokes about the K rations. One GI remarked that the ham and eggs that came in a small tuna-size can, had a lot of butter or fat in it. It stated on the can that Thrivo Dog Food Co. in Philadelphia, Pa., manufactured it. This one GI goes around asking others if they have any cans of Thrivo Dog Food to spare. The boxes with the ham and eggs in them were labeled as "Breakfast" and the ones with the potted meat in them were labeled "Dinner." They both were tasty and nourishing, considering the circumstances.

Enduring lots of stress and anxiety, many GIs complained about lots of things, most of them were about the conditions that we lived in, as well as the deadly risks that we constantly were exposed to. One was that our uniforms were totally inadequate for combat, which they were. Combat boots were made of leather, with the suede side of the leather on the outside, making it impossible for the leather to repel water. This made it absorb water readily, so if your boots got wet, they stayed wet. The senseless explanation, or the reason for making them this was that the smooth side of the leather would reflect light. This argument was absolutely nonsense. Even if it were shiny new leather when it was new, it wouldn't be shiny after just one day of combat. I assumed that they had never heard of shoe dye. Because of the suede being on the outside, many GIs got trench foot and became casualties from it.

No one could imagine an overcoat with a lapel on it being used in combat. I was thankful that we had left our overcoats in our duffel bags back at Metz, France. When I wore the overcoat in the cold I got colder, in that the wind came in underneath it and funneled right up to the collar where it exited, just like the stove pipe did back at the CP a few nights ago that made all of the smoke the Nazi spotters saw. It acted just like a chimney, carrying all of your body heat right up and out the collar. What I did regret then, and more so later, was that I hadn't brought several pairs of socks that I had left in my duffel bag at Metz. The uniforms of the German soldiers were far superior to our uniforms, much more practicable and functional.

Then try drinking anything hot out of your aluminum canteen cup without blistering your lips, which was a real hassle. The designers apparently weren't aware of the fact that, although aluminum is light-weight, it conducts heat very rapidly. After you heated it, by holding it over a burning part of the wax-coated ration boxes, you had to cool it to drink it. So, when the metal was cool enough to not burn your lips, the liquid was then too tepid to be of any good to you.

All the cellars had potatoes in them; many were rotting and they smelled like hell. The air was putrid. Another contributing factor for the foul air was that many of the men had dysentery. Some said that this was due to bacteria in the digestive tract; others said that it was a symptom of stress and anxiety. I was always glad to have an opportunity to get out of there, to go on a patrol, go back to the company CP for rations and water, lay new telephone wire, or whatever was necessary, to get out, day or night, even though nighttime was the safest time to get out.

Speaking of telephone wire, we constantly laid new wire. The telephones were battery operated, like Grandma's old telephone. They were in a leather carrying case, a hand crank, and a handset. You had to crank it to generate the extra power to make the phone ring at the other end of the line. We would tie off one end of the line to something solid near the portable telephone where it couldn't be pulled loose, then connect the wires to it and run with the reel, that had a handle on it, to the CP and connect that end to their telephone, then test it. Wire in Saarlautern where I was, was hanging from everywhere like cobwebs. It was an unbelievable sight to see so many wires strung everywhere. It was impossible to find a break or cut and repair it, so we laid new wire almost daily, when there was no connection on the phone.

One night my friend Ray and I volunteered to go for water and rations with these backpacks made specifically for carrying a five-gallon can of water or a box of ten-in-one rations. It was a strong, lightweight, fiberglass rack that you wore on your back, and it had several straps on it. One could strap a five-gallon can of water or a case of ten-in-one rations onto it, and carry it rather comfortably, except, if you had to run while you were carrying the Jerry can full of water, it would be uncomfortable, sloshing around and shifting the load. We made it to the CP all right, but Ray wanted to carry the rations, so I carried the can of water, which was much heavier.

On the return to the front line cellars, we came under machine gun fire and hit the ground. The bullets were flying right over our bodies, too close for comfort. When a bullet comes close to you, you know it because it cracks just as if you had fired the rifle, but not quite as loud. We lay on the ground for a while, the machine gun fire continued, and we couldn't move. We were totally pinned down. Suddenly Ray began to cry, telling me that he was hit, and was bleeding to death. He was shaking like a leaf. I asked him where he was hit, and he told me it was in his butt somewhere. I felt his rear end and couldn't find any blood. I did feel some kind of liquid, but I knew immediately that it was not blood, because it was oily and not sticky like blood. So, I smelled it, and it was the oil from the big can of sausages that was in the ten-in-one rations—the can of sausage in oil had taken one of those machine gun bullets. I had a terrible time convincing Ray that he was not hurt or hit at all, but that a bullet had gone through the box of rations and the oil in the can of sausage was leaking out into his crotch. When the firing stopped, we made a mad dash for cover, stayed there for a while, then continued on to our cellar. When all the other guys heard of what happened, everyone had a good laugh. It was the first that I ever heard some of them laugh.

Lieutenant Anderson came to our cellar one evening where we discussed the patrol that night. He was a conscientious officer and worked hard to prevent any casualties. He was a perfectionist, to say the least, probably a Virgo like me. He didn't go on patrols often, but he wanted each one to be a big success, and everyone to return safely. He always gave everyone a lecture, hoping that it would pay off by preventing someone from becoming a casualty. I paid close attention to everything he said. His typical lecture and instructions are as follows:

"Now, I want a patrol leader and five other volunteers to go on patrol here, in about an hour. Don't bunch up, I don't want to see a whole squad wiped out by one of their shells; stay several yards apart, keep moving, keep hidden, keep quiet, and observe closely for the enemy. Make sure your canteen is full of water at all times. The main reason is that if you bleed from a wound, you will need water to drink, and to keep your guts wet if you should get a belly wound, which may save your life. The Krauts have been putting out lots of Schu mines here, where there is lots of rubble; they look about like this brick here, the same size and color. If you just touch the top of it in any manner it will explode, blow your legs off and most likely kill you. I hear that lots of men in the area have lost a leg from one. One man lost his leg to one of them and when he fell, his chest hit another one, and of course it killed him. So watch out for them the best you can. You don't know if that brick there is one of them or not. The moral of the story is not to disturb any bricks anymore than you must, especially when you are walking in a path frequently used, like going after rations, laying wire, or whatever. The Krauts watch what routes and paths we take, and then they come back and lay mines and booby traps.

"Remember though that you are not going out there to see how many German soldiers you can kill or capture tonight; your mission is to observe the enemy's location, his strength, and any other facts that you can find out. I am not saying though, if you find a patrol, like you did the other night, not to take them out. If you locate where they are billeted, or holed up, we will deal with them in broad daylight tomorrow by letting our mortars or artillery take care of them. Take prisoners if you can, though it won't be easy here. But if we could capture some and make them give us information as to their whereabouts and numbers, we would be ahead of the game.

"So, good luck and get your men organized for this patrol. Be prepared to relate where you went, how far away, what direction, and other pertinent details so we can evaluate the results and determine the strength of the enemy, where they are, and any other information you can learn. Remember where you departed from, and don't forget how to get back here, safely. All of these rubble-filled streets look alike, especially at night, until you learn your way around. Passwords will change at midnight. Remember what it is, and don't go on patrol without knowing it. We will use the word 'aluminum' tonight; the Germans can't say that word like we do. You will be challenged when you return. All patrols are to be back before midnight. Remember it is no man's land out there, and right here, as well. Good luck, men, and do a good job." The lieutenant looked exhausted as he finished his lecture.

Lieutenant Anderson was an excellent officer. He never appeared to be tired, hungry, or cold and was always neat in appearance, considering the circumstances. His men always came first, and he would go the extra mile for any of us, anytime. He had remarkable leadership qualities. His greatest quality was his sincere concern for the welfare of all of his men. He was very thorough, as well as very detailed in his job. I was glad to be serving under a man like him.

CHAPTER 7

An Early Morning Reconnaissance

> *"The only thing that I am afraid of is fear."*
> —ARTHUR WELLESLEY, DUKE OF WELLINGTON
> (1759–1852)

Every soldier contributes and does his part, and then some. Anyone who can communicate well and has some guts is a leader, regardless of rank. In combat here, it is not rank that counts, it is the men who know what to do and when to do it, and aren't afraid to do it. That is what counts.

I was in a squad that was supposed to consist of twelve men, more or less, but now there were only seven or eight of us. There was not a spare moment; even though we slept most of the daylight hours, the nights were the busiest time. I wanted to help win this war as soon as possible, go home, live in peace, and let everyone else do the same. I took everything that I was doing very seriously.

I had gotten to know one friend more than anyone else. I only knew him as Mark, a hell of a nice guy from the West Coast who possessed a strong body and mind, a soldier with lots of guts and determination. He was the man that I chose to be my combat buddy, a man I knew I could depend upon, who would not hesitate to fight to the finish and would never let a fellow soldier down. He was always keen and alert.

Sleeping on the floor of a cellar that was cluttered with junk, rubble, and trash, not to mention the stench of rotting potatoes, was not conducive to rest or sleep. I had not gotten much sleep due to the anxiety of not knowing what the next day, and night, was going to be like. I was awake just before the crack of daylight. I told Mark that he and I should go out and get us a few Krauts before it got too light. I knew that no one had ever been out on patrol after midnight or at this early hour. So I wondered what it would be like outside, between midnight and daylight. Would all the Krauts be asleep too, or would they be out there laying mines, tapping into our telephone lines, or whatever, at this early hour? Is this the reason that their 88s quit firing at midnight? Would these late hours be when the Krauts went across the old bridge to their bunkers to get rations and ammo?

I wanted to find out what the Krauts did after we retired to our cellars for the night. I was thinking that from midnight until after dark that following night, it was like a curfew for us, in that all our men were in cellars and off of the streets. For all that any of us knew, the Krauts could be out in the streets cutting telephone lines, planting mines, setting booby traps, and otherwise having a ball. I really wanted to find out. I did not want to be outsmarted by them.

Mark thought I was joking at first. And then after I told him my feelings about it, he agreed and we left the cellar, telling the door guard what we were going to do. We just told him we were going down the street about a block to kill a few Krauts before it got daylight. He thought we were kidding. I then sincerely told him that I had a strong feeling there were Krauts nearby, and that we were most likely about to be attacked. I wanted to take a look around and check the area out to make sure we were not about to be overrun, so that we could go back to sleep, all of which was true.

We went down the street very cautiously and hid behind a shattered corner of a building at an intersection a block from our cellar. I could see down both streets in all four directions. There, I told Mark to cover me, to stay a safe distance from me, to keep under cover, and to keep a good lookout for anyone trying to take a sight on either of us. Also, so that one grenade, bullet, or shell would not kill us both, and to cover me, make sure that a Kraut would not fire on me, and I would do the same for him. He understood and did his job extremely well.

It was early that morning, not even daylight yet, so we waited very patiently in the light of the GI moon. I positioned myself as though I was deer hunting, on one knee, mostly hidden by the rubble, quietly waiting, peeping through the corner of what was once a doorway and a partial wall at this corner. Suddenly I saw two German soldiers who casually came out of the rubble, about a half a block to the east of us. They were coming right to where we were. They were a little more than a block away from the cellar that we occupied. I quickly dropped both of them.

Then in the other direction I saw two more who had to have heard the shots. They ran out of another building in the same block, about a block down the street to the south, running away from where we were, and I dropped both of them as they ran down the street. Just about the time that I shot the last two, I heard Mark fire from over my right shoulder. He shot a Kraut who was in a second-story window of a shattered building just across the street, who was taking aim at me. Mark saved my life by being alert and very observant.

I told Mark this was a close call and that we had probably done enough for one day. He remarked to me, "Don't you think that five is enough for one day, before it even gets daylight?"

It was getting daylight and dangerous for us to be out here where they could see us more easily. We cautiously went back to our cellar, and when we got through answering all the questions that the others there wanted to know, like what the shooting was all about, we went back to sleep.

CHAPTER 8

A Bad Night on Patrol in Saarlautern

"I did not know the dignity of their birth,
but I do know the glory of their death."

—GENERAL DOUGLAS MCARTHUR (1880–1964)

Our platoon sergeant asked me to go on patrol with him that night, which I did. There were a total of six of us, three two-man buddy teams. There were always six men on a reconnaissance patrol. You always have a buddy with you, and my good friend Mark was with me as my buddy. We headed out, staying ten to fifteen feet apart in a staggered, single-file column, going north from our hangout cellar into an area where we suspected German soldiers to be billeted, to find out how many of them were there, what kind of weapons they had, and everything else that we could.

We walked about a quarter mile along the deserted, debris-filled street, passing some of our own platoon's cellars, with their door guards hiding in the rubble near the entrances, to stop any enemy from approaching their billets. Soon, down the way a piece, nearly a quarter of a mile away, we smelled potatoes cooking. Hunger pains began to hit my stomach. We approached the house that we suspected, because of the smell of potatoes being fried. We crept along close to the row of buildings to try to avoid being seen. Our platoon sergeant could speak good German. As we sneaked up to the house that the smell was coming from, he was challenged by the German door guard of this house that faced the river. The Sergeant answered him in German, but with the incorrect password, naturally. Then the door guard attempted to fire on him, but before he could fire, our sergeant cut him down with his automatic .45 caliber grease gun. Then, men in an upstairs window threw out several hand grenades, which landed nearby, but we were already dispersed and on the ground, and all that we got was some concussion.

We all ran when we could find the right time to get up and sprint away, as the machine gun fire grazed the ground all around us. We had to cross an open vacant block area, which was a shortcut to return to our cellar, and it was littered with old bomb craters and shell holes. As Mark and I, hunched over, running, attempting to cross this area during a break in the machine gun fire, all hell broke loose with mortar, screaming meemies, and artillery fire hitting all around us.

Suddenly a big shell landed nearby and knocked us both down. All that I recall was that one moment I was running, and the next moment I was lying on the ground, waking up with my head roaring. It was a hell of a concussion. It felt as though I had been hit by a freight train. More shells came in, as well as grazing machine gun fire. The Germans shot flares into the air so that they could hopefully see us, and kill us. We were bounced around on the ground like a rubber ball. My helmet had bounced off my head from the concussion of the first shell. The urine was shaken out of my bladder by the concussion, and I was wet from that, which was a common occurrence when a big artillery shell would hit nearby. I had to crawl out a few feet to retrieve my helmet. You never fasten the chin strap of your helmet in combat because the concussion of a shell bursting close by will get under it and break your neck.

I was right beside a large bomb crater partly filled with mud. I rolled over into it. Mark didn't respond to me talking to him, with me trying to get him to move over into this crater for protection from the shellfire, as well as the machine gun grazing fire that we were getting right over the tops of our heads. I crawled out, grabbed him by his ammo belt, and pulled him into the hole with me, and he rolled on top of me. I felt blood on my face and neck. He seemed limp and unconscious. I attempted to examine him to see where he was hurt. I first felt his head; it was awfully bloody. Then I discovered that half of his head was missing, and that I had his blood and brains all over me. I rolled him over on the other side of me in the hole.

He and I both now lay in the mixture of blood and mud in this bomb crater. I just lay there beside him, senseless, half-conscious from the concussion of the shelling and the shock of losing my closest friend and buddy. I felt as though I was lost, in a daze, or somehow dreaming. I had difficulty believing that this sort of thing was occurring. I felt totally lost. I had trouble at first trying to figure out where I was, and what I was doing here.

I asked myself, where am I, and what am I doing here, and how will I ever get back home? It was like a nightmare. I was confused. I wasn't sure that this was really happening. My head was spinning. I didn't know where I was, which direction to go, to return to where we came from. I was very much disoriented, to put it mildly. I didn't know what had happened to the others on patrol with us. I had never felt so alone and abandoned in my life, out there in the middle of no man's land, lying in a bomb crater with my dead buddy, and blood all over me. So I decided to just lie there for a while until the shelling subsided.

I later realized that I had fallen asleep from the effects of the concussion. I had no idea how long I was unconscious, or whatever it was that was wrong with me. I was dizzy, confused, disoriented, depressed, and I felt all alone, late at night, in very cold weather, lying in a bomb crater with blood and mud all over me, with my dead buddy, with shells still landing all around us, but not quite as bad now.

Finally I became stronger and came to my senses a little more, from the shock of all of it.

I spoke to Mark and said to my dead buddy, "Mark, we won't forget you. We will be back for you, soon. Don't worry, my friend, we will make it. I have to leave you now and go get some help. We will be back for you, and I will kill these damned sonsabitchin' thugs that did this to you."

I thought to myself, 'But for the Grace of God here, I also lie dead.'

Then I crawled out of the bomb crater and crawled on my belly for about fifty yards to the corner of what was once a building, hoping that I was going in the right direction and on the right street to return to my squad in the cellar. I realized that it wasn't much of a place to go to, but it was all we had. Things all around looked a lot different and very strange to me.

I slowly and quietly crept along this deserted rubble-strewn street, close to the buildings that were still partially standing, and was able to see by the light of the GI moon's reflected floodlighting.

Suddenly, behind me I heard footsteps, the sound of enemy footsteps, hobnail boots hitting the pavement very slowly. I crept into a small alley between two buildings where there was a broken-down wooden gate, and some firewood was stacked. I crawled into this alley, and I sat there with my rifle ready as a lone German soldier with a potato masher grenade sticking out of each of his boots, slowly walked past me. He was so close to me that I could have reached out and touched him. I knew not to fire at him because I didn't know how many of his buddies were behind him and who might throw one of those potato masher grenades in there on me. I remembered what the lieutenant had told me, so I let him go on his way, reluctantly.

My intentions were to wait awhile until this Kraut, and possibly a patrol that he was most likely a scout for, got out of the way before I resumed trying to find my cellar, in case that there was a patrol with him. I had no idea what time it was. I don't recall going to sleep again. But I must have, because I recall waking up a little more alert, listening, cautiously looking out onto the street to see if it was clear. When I was sure there were not any Krauts around, I then continued moving on down the street, hunting for my cellar, wondering if I would ever find it again. I prayed that this German soldier had gone on his way and was no longer near me. I had no earthly idea how much time had passed since he had passed by me. I walked for quite a while, when suddenly I heard an American soldier say, "Halt! Who goes there?"

I had a hell of a time convincing this GI who I was and that I was not an enemy, and for him not to shoot me. He was a new and inexperienced replacement, I learned later. Then, Lieutenant Anderson's welcome voice rang in my ears, like music from Heaven. I heard the soldier say to him, "Let me shoot him, lieutenant—he is not one of ours. All of our patrols, all came back before midnight. We don't have anyone out there now."

I then assumed that all of the other men returned, and that everyone thought that Mark and I had been killed.

I didn't know the password that had changed at midnight. In fact I didn't even know that it was past midnight. I don't believe that I even could recall the password. But upon recognizing Lieutenant Anderson's voice, I yelled out to him and told him who I was, and he recognized me and told me to come on in. He asked me to relate to him what had taken place. I told him, and he saw the blood all over me, and the bits of Mark's brains on my field jacket and shirt. I was embarrassed by my wet pants, even though he couldn't see them in the darkness, it was as though I had been so scared that I had wet my pants, and I didn't want anyone to think that, so I explained this to the lieutenant. He told me that this is sure to happen when a big shell hits nearby, that the concussion will knock the urine out of you as it bounces you around on the ground.

He told me to go below and get some sleep. I was still wet with the mud and urine, and soaked in Mark's blood and brains, hungry, my stomach hurting and growling like a guard dog. I was so exhausted that I felt like a brainless zombie, totally confused and disoriented. I went below and fell suddenly to sleep on a pile of rotting, stinking potatoes. I later learned that it was 3:00 A.M. when I returned to my cellar that night.

I went to sleep believing that there was an angel looking after me. My sister had written me that my mother would get on her knees every night beside her bed and pray for an hour or more for my safety. She and my father had placed a large map of Europe on the wall, and each time she heard the news that told where the Third Army was and what it was doing, she would mark it on the map. My sister later told me each time that the news came on the radio that both of our parents would sit close to the radio with their ear right up close to the speaker and listen to the war news. Then my mother would mark it on the map on the wall over the radio. I was convinced beyond any doubt that there was a power more powerful than any president, or general, who was looking after and protecting me. I renewed my solemn promise to my Almighty God, that if He would return me home safe and sound and in one piece, I would continue to fight terrorism and oppression so long as I lived.

After days that seemed like weeks of this kind of fighting and killing, day after day, maddening, unrelenting, and endless, the crossing of

Hitler's formidable Siegfried Line at last seemed near. The minds of our troops had become mesmerized. Many were asking themselves, "Who will be next and how will it happen?"

At night in the cellars, one could hear the men saying their prayers. We all were suffering from the stress, tension, anxiety, and fear, as well as exhaustion and undernourishment. Every day we woke up in the stench of rotting potatoes, human waste, and filth, in the cellars of a devastated city that had been under siege for over five months.

Some soldiers were getting that "mile-long stare," which was a look in their eyes that appeared that they were steadily staring at something a mile away, a stare where the pupils were fixed, the eyes looked glassy— maybe my eyes looked that way, but I didn't know it if they did. The stress of wounded and dying men, the constant threat of death kept us vigil, and on edge. I could tell that our reaction was slowed considerably. Hardly anyone talked at all. There was no longer any sense of humor, laughter, or jesting. Everyone was extremely serious. It was impossible to become friends with a fellow soldier because you felt that if you developed a friendship, that it would be devastated by this war, as everything else was, leaving you even more despondent. Nevertheless, there was still a closeness, a camaraderie, loyalty, and trust beyond belief. We all were like blood brothers. However, there were exceptions.

There was one man who never did anything, hardly ever leaving the cellar. He always broke the silence when nothing was happening, by running his sick mouth, saying smart-assed things, bragging, trying to talk tough and brave. He never did anything to prove that he was tough or brave, and generally annoyed everyone, until it came time for someone to go on a reconnaissance or combat patrol, or to go for water, rations, ammo, or to lay wire. Then he would suddenly develop a headache, crawl into a corner, and pretend he was asleep. He would talk so much about how bad he was, and what a fighter he was, until I didn't think I could take much more of him. I considered him a total liability and a hindrance. I will refer to him as Tony from Brooklyn.

Some of the men told me that when they had so much built up fear and anxiety, that when they went on patrol at night to search for enemy hideouts, they would go into a nearby partially demolished building and just sit there for about an hour or two. Then they would swear to each other that they would report having gone on this patrol, and fabricate what they would report they did. They would then return and make a report to the platoon leader. I never did that, and wouldn't even entertain such an idea. I don't think any of them wanted to experience what I had on the night Mark was killed. Each day was another day of pure unrelenting misery and hell. Hopefully we would not be too much longer in this devastated place.

We had a little less opposition now, which came about kind of all of a sudden—not so many enemy soldiers throwing concussion grenades into cellar windows. There were fewer instances of the enemy stringing fine trip wire across our usual paths we used to get to the rear for supplies, with the other end of the wire attached to a fragmentation hand grenade encapsulated in its box, with the pin already pulled allowing the trigger to fire it, when pulled from the box. When you tripped the wire of such a booby trap, it pulled the grenade out of its canister, releasing the handle, and it exploded, killing or injuring the persons in the area, usually more than one person. It was the most simple booby trap that I had ever seen.

We had to find new paths to travel where there were fewer Schu mines and booby traps set for us, and not as many lines of fire from their machine guns. We had more support personnel with us now, like engineers with flamethrowers, and explosives, like bangalore torpedoes that one could put under a roll of barbed wire, or any kind of barricade, and when it exploded it opened up a gap in the wire or wall for us to pass through. However, we did not encounter any barbed wire there. Machine gun and mortar crews came up to help protect that bridge from the Krauts who were trying to blow it up.

I refused to believe things were getting better. It was apparent, though, that we were more versed in the tactics of staying alive in a war like this, and that we were now winning it. We all suddenly developed a sense of accomplishment and success. But it wasn't over yet. We had to neutralize those two big bunkers, as well as all the other small weapons locations all around them, and then cross the bridge. All of us were aware that in crossing the bridge, if there was only one Kraut artillery observer out there that could call in fire on that bridge, it would be deadly to try crossing it.

73

CHAPTER 9

Crossing the Saar River and Siegfried Line

"I had rather die on my feet than to live for eternity on my knees."

—GENERAL GEORGE S. PATTON (1885–1945)

The time was getting close for us to put down all enemy resistance and cross the Saar River and that impenetrable Siegfried Line. We believed it was now or never, a do-or-die situation. We went to where this old, strong concrete bridge crossed the Saar River. Beyond the bridge the road led through the many strategically placed concrete bunkers that made up the Siegfried Line, and then on to the Dragon's Teeth tank traps further over the hills.

This was an old stone and concrete Roman bridge that apparently was constructed several centuries ago. The Krauts had tried many times to blow it up, but it would always remain intact. Also, they kept it loaded with explosives, with detonator wires leading to their side of the bridge. However, we had been so successful in being able to keep the other side of the river at this bridge clear of the enemy, with almost constant mortar and machine gun fire, so that they could not even get close to it to try again to blow it up.

We were not yet able to cross this bridge because the Krauts still had it covered with 88 fire, as well as machine gun, mortars, and other small weapons fire, and anyone trying to cross it, was very visible to their observers, and they would commence firing. Trying to cross this bridge now would be certain death for anyone. But neither could the Krauts cross it, because we also had it covered with mortar and machine gun fire. So, we couldn't safely cross this bridge until we had neutralized all of their weapons that covered that bridge with weapons fire.

We could not yet see the Dragon's Teeth, as GIs called that part of the Siegfried Line. This fortification consisted of many rows of concrete and steel pylons that would stop any tank or other vehicles. They were further beyond the bridge and the big concrete bunkers. The road that crossed this bridge led through the roadway pass that went through the Dragon's Teeth. This passageway through these strong pylons was fortified with heavy steel beams that had to be cleared away before anyone or any vehicle could pass through.

We had been briefed on what to expect beyond the river. No kind of vehicle could crawl over these concrete pylons of the Dragon's Teeth. In the roadway opening between these many rows of teeth were numerous large steel structures of heavy steel railroad rails, or I beams, that were used to block the road through the rows of the Dragon's Teeth's concrete and steel pylons. There were also other barricades of steel bars set in strong concrete frames that would prevent a vehicle from passing through on the roadway. I knew then what all of the explosives were for, that the engineers were bringing up. It had to be used to blow the barricades apart so our tanks and other vehicles could get through the pass. Naturally the engineers could only do this, when it was safe to cross the bridge and go east on the road that went through these rows of pylons.

"I need six of my best men to volunteer for a dangerous mission tonight, who is it going to be?" Lieutenant Anderson asked of our group in the cellar.

"Lieutenant, may I ask what kind of mission that this is going to be, and where we are going, and what we are to do?" I asked him, even though I already surmised what it was all about, but I wanted an understanding of what our objective was, which was that bunker across the river at the newer bridge.

"Tonight, some of our engineers are going to paddle across the river, in an assault boat. They will be carrying flame-throwers, and they are going to go up to this big pillbox from the side and burn the hell out of it with the flamethrowers. I need six men: two men to protect the engineers with the flamethrowers, plus two rearguard men to make sure you are not attacked from the rear and to cover your hind side on your return after your successful mission. Two flank men, eight men total, to accompany them, to clear the way, to put down any machine gunners, riflemen, snipers—or whatever else that is out there—who tries to impede this important mission, and to make sure that you guys get back safely. How many volunteers do I have?" he asked the men of my squad. That was about all that there was in the squad, no more than ten men total.

I am ready to go now, sir. It won't be any more dangerous out there, than it is right where we are now." I looked around and counted heads; there were only nine men in the cellar then. All volunteered but Tony from Brooklyn who complained about a severe headache. As usual, he never volunteered for anything. To be honest, I really didn't want him with me, or anything to do with him.

"I am anxious to get across that so-called impenetrable line and head for Berlin, or wherever General Patton decides we are going," I told my lieutenant.

There were enough volunteers. We prepared for it. Two of our biggest and strongest men had BARs (Browning Automatic Rifles) that would be on each side of the operation, protecting the flanks. By nightfall we commenced our preparation. The engineers put the olive-drab aluminum boat near the river, with paddles in it. At the proper time we put them in the water and paddled across with the two BAR men left on the bank, to protect us while we crossed. We paddled like hell. When on the other side, my buddy Ken and I accompanied two engineers with their flamethrowers. We crawled unobserved up to about thirty feet from the large pillbox, just to the side, enough so that the gunners inside couldn't see us. We could see the three machine guns protruding out of the slit, and they fired almost continuously—not at us, they never saw us, we were too far to the side. Our artillery had already shelled, all out, and around the sides, and behind the bunker, so as to eliminate any weapons there, which they did, effectively, as usual.

The engineers advanced to within about thirty feet, and fired their flamethrowers simultaneously at the concrete pillbox gun emplacement—I am sure, charring everything in it. What fireworks—the whole area lit up like daylight. But come to think of it, I hadn't seen much daylight in a long time. As soon as they had expended their fuel, we ran back to the waiting boat and paddled like hell back across the river.

I could hardly believe that this could have occurred without almost all of us being killed or wounded. But the mission was not over yet, just as we got out of the boat and ran, all hell broke loose. The Nazis fired flares into the air to try to see us. Mortar and artillery fire was very heavy, burp guns burping, and screaming meemies screaming at us as they came in and landed all around us; but we suffered no casualties, thank God.

Our observers, who saw the entire operation, including the captain, seemed more excited than children watching fireworks on the Fourth of July. We had accomplished what was thought to be impossible. There were also some top brass who watched the whole operation. However, in about one hour or two, the Germans had replaced the burned gunners and the burned-out machine guns with others—a new crew—and they were firing out from that hole again in that concrete and steel bunker, as usual, with three machine guns. Our artillery, the greatest and the most accurate in the world, I am sure, began a continuous, around-the-clock bombardment of the bunker, as well as the other side of it, and all around the outside of the bunker by our 155mm cannons. In effect, surrounding those locked in that fortress, with no egress and ingress that we were aware of, on the backside. Our heavy artillery fired 155mm shells, which plummeted that bunker with high-explosive shells all day, day after day, which also put an end to all of the lower-level machine gun emplacements, and now we had less to worry about when coming out of our rat holes. The only fire was from the bunker only, and there was none from any surrounding area outside of it.

We stepped up our patrols during the next day, more than ever. We went to many places in that dead city, including large partially standing buildings, like a bank building, for instance, to search out the area. We went into it, and there were still hanging large beautiful, but damaged, window drapes, on the partially standing wall. So, one man who had dysentery had to defecate, and he used the drapes to clean himself with. So then the bazooka man decided that he wanted to blow the bank's safe open. He did, from across the street, firing through a window, and hit the big safe door with the first shot. It flew open, but it was empty. The Hitler regime money was no good anyway. We learned that we were going to be issued invasion money, German marks, soon.

CHAPTER 10

The 259th Regiment Attacks the Siegfried Line at Saarbrucken

"…all of us must have a desperate desire to close with the enemy, and destroy him."

—GENERAL GEORGE S. PATTON (1885–1945)

We learned from Lieutenant Anderson that some of the men in the 259th Regiment of our division also located on the Saar River, at a bunker there that protected a bridge, had crossed the Saar at Saarbrucken to the south of us, had gotten across the river in assault boats, and had come up behind the big bunker and found a door open, had gone inside, and they, all twelve of them, were captured after they had gone into the back doors of the pillbox bunker. The Germans had come upon them from the outside, probably knew that they were coming, locked them inside, and captured all twelve of them. This tactic had been considered not the safest thing to try doing. Their mistake was going into that pillbox without leaving some men outside as a rear guard, to prevent the Germans from coming up and catching them all inside the bunker. The German soldiers were very clever and shrewd.

After this incident, another attempt to take that bunker was undertaken. Another patrol crossed the river, came up behind the bunker, but the Krauts didn't know that they were coming this time. They blew the big steel doors open with a bazooka and captured twelve Nazi soldiers inside, and brought them back across the river as POWs. This was a great and historical accomplishment, especially for our 65th Division. Taking prisoners along the Siegfried Line had almost been impossible to do. This was the break that the generals were looking for. It was now very possible to cross the Siegfried Line—but in what strength and at what cost?

I learned that it was the bridges across the Saar that General Patton wanted to take more than anything else. This was his sector, and if he got control of the bridges that crossed the Saar, and if they were still intact, then he could get his tanks across the Siegfried Line. He would then spearhead his drive to the Rhine and then on to Berlin.

The 261ST Regiment Crosses the Siegfried Line at Merzig and Bitburg, Germany

We learned that the 261st Regiment of our division, against heavy resistance and with many casualties, had crossed the Siegfried Line to the north at a town called Merzig, Germany, and after getting across, they were moving at an angle to the southeast into Germany. We also learned that the 259th Regiment had now crossed the Siegfried Line to the south of us at Saarbrucken and they were moving in a northeasterly direction. Both regiments were making a triangle that was encircling the area where we were fighting a diehard bunch of radical, extremist holdouts there in the Saarlautern area, leaving a pocket of fierce fighting there, where we, the 260th Regiment, were still fighting it out, trying to neutralize those bunkers and get across the two bridges there.

This was the strongest and most fortified part of the entire Siegfried Line. It contained most all of the diehard soldiers of the Third Reich that Hitler was depending upon to save the Siegfried Line and stop the Allied push into Germany. They continued to fight, knowing of course that our other two regiments were encircling them. It was now obvious that the resistance in our sector was weakened and most likely the holdouts there would flee to where their own main line of defense now was, further to the east.

We all knew that it was about time for us to move out of this demolished city. We were about to wrap up this operation and were now ready for some open country. Everyone was in better spirits thinking that soon we would be abandoning our rat-hole cellars—however, a rat wouldn't even stay in there. We vigorously and aggressively intensified our patrols and attacks, killing as many enemy as we could find, making it difficult for them to coexist there with us.

I told my lieutenant, "It is time that we were mopping up these Kraut fanatics here. We've been playing their game for too long now, it's time for a showdown. We have got to eliminate all of them, as well as destroy all their bunkers, so we can get out of here and get a bath, some hot water, clean clothes, brush our teeth, get some real food for a change, new clothes, and some rest from this kind of fighting. We are all tired, sick, mentally and physically, and we need some rest and relaxation very bad."

I wanted to hear him reply that we would soon destroy all the Kraut defenses here and be leaving this area. I was just hoping he could do something to expedite matters, but I knew he was doing all that he could.

He wholeheartedly agreed and said, "This has to be a real test of stamina and courage for all of us." I knew there was nothing that he could do about it, but I got my gripe off my chest for a while. I always believed that the leaders needed to know what the gripes and needs of their men were, and how they felt about any situation. I just felt that he should know we were nearing complete mental and physical exhaustion.

I would lie in the cellar trying to rest, and often think about where we were and what we were doing here. I thought of back home and what my family was doing. I knew this was war, a big war, and the whole world was riding on the outcome of it. I knew this war would be forever recorded in the history books, but I was anxious to see it over and peace restored everywhere.

Each day I felt I needed to do more to help win this war quicker, and I wanted to do more. It dwelled on my mind what we were fighting for. I well knew that it was our American way of life that we were fighting for. Not only that, the price we were paying was for all the great values we Americans possessed, and most of us took them for granted, unlike people in the rest of the world, who wished they had what we had, things like liberty and freedom.

We were fighting to make the world safe for democracy. If we believed in all these things, then what we were enduring would be well worth it. It was those intangible things that we looked forward to enjoying, when this terrible catastrophe ended. No amount of money could purchase things like life, liberty, and the pursuit of happiness. They had to be fought for or they would be lost forever.

Never once did I forget about those that I had seen make the supreme sacrifice. Nor did I ever forget about other American soldiers there, near us, who had no cellars to sleep in but only an open foxhole in the snow. I thought about those American prisoners who were shot in cold blood at Malmedy, Belgium, especially my good friend and high school classmate, Jack Richardson, whose father was the Baptist Minister in my hometown of Poplarville, Mississippi.

Jack Richardson would come out to my house and hunt deer with me. He was one of the finest young men that I ever knew, as well as a great deer hunter, and he enjoyed doing it immensely. He was mowed down by Kraut machine gun fire, in cold blood, after he was captured. He was standing in knee-deep snow in a field at a crossroads near Malmedy, Belgium, along with more than eighty other American GIs when they were slaughtered there by orders from an SS lieutenant. Those brave men gave all that they had for their country, and I was determined to never forget them, nor ever to forget my buddy Mark, and the ultimate price they all had paid.

CHAPTER 11

Crossing of the Siegfried Line

"Never in the field of human conflict have so many owed so much to so few."

—SIR WINSTON CHURCHILL (1874–1965)

I knew that it wouldn't be long before we finalized this operation. Lieutenant Anderson told everyone in the platoon, and they listened: "I will tell you this, two TDs [Tank Destroyers that have a 105mm Howitzer mounted on them] are back there coming forward right now to fire point-blank right into this pillbox, to silence it. They will do bore sightings on the openings of the pillbox, and fire right into it from up close. When they finish their bombardment, we will then cross the river over the bridge, or in the assault boats. We will blow open the back doors of the bunker after the TDs finish firing into it." I told the lieutenant that I would gladly guard the bazooka man who would blow open the bunker's back doors.

The TDs came forward and did a bore sighting on the opening where the three machine guns were firing from. The TD fired close-up, directly into the opening of the pillbox, causing an inferno inside, which eliminated the contents of that pillbox temporarily, but in no way totally destroyed it. We took cover and observed the whole battle. The operation was a complete success. Our artillery and mortars bombarded that entire area around this huge, thick concrete pillbox, completely neutralizing that big bunker, as well as everything in and around it. We all then crossed the bridge over the Saar River, and came in behind the bunker to give it the coup de grâce by blowing open the big steel back doors and going inside it.

After the bazooka man had blown open the back doors to the bunker, we found nothing but charred bodies inside it, a ghastly sight that would sicken anyone.

The old concrete bridge that had definitely been mined by the Germans and reportedly now ready to blow at any time, had been protected, was now safe and under the control of our engineers. We had neutralized one of the big bunkers and established a bridgehead beyond the Saar River to prevent the Germans from coming up to it and attempting to demolish it. The bridge was old, built very strong out of stone and concrete, which seemed to be almost indestructible. Now it was ours. They wanted to blow it, but they couldn't get up there to it—we wouldn't let them.

The credit should go to the artillery and the tankers who used the 105 Howitzer self-propelled cannon, for doing such a great job of saturating the bunker and the other side of the Saar with heavy artillery fire, which caused the remaining Krauts to flee to the east to find safety from our artillery.

We kept guard over this bridge until daybreak, when we moved out east, crossing through Hitler's impenetrable West Wall.

CHAPTER 12

Crossing the Dragon's Teeth

*"Let us have faith that right makes might;
and in that faith let us, to the end, dare to
do our duty as we understand it."*

—ABRAHAM LINCOLN (1809–1865)

Just before daylight on this same morning, on our last day in Saarlautern, we got orders to move out. No one had gotten any sleep and we all were like walking zombies. The bridge was clear, there was no enemy resistance that we could see or hear. The big bunkers were now neutralized and quiet. We assumed that they had abandoned their heavily fortified, impenetrable Siegfried Line fortresses and fled into Germany proper. The old city of Saarlautern was now deserted of both our and the Nazi troops, leaving only the dead bodies of both sides that lay everywhere. We assembled and walked across the bridge and down the road to the east, toward the Dragon's Teeth. There was a complete absence of enemy opposition. No Krauts were to be seen anywhere, nor did we hear any enemy fire. We nevertheless kept up our guard.

We walked down this road until we arrived at the Dragon's Teeth, that is, through the pass in the opening where the road passed through these many rows of concrete and steel pylons. Our engineers had already arrived there immediately before we arrived, and had cut or blown the steel barriers apart so our foot soldiers and vehicles could pass through the roadway opening in the apparently never-ending multiple rows of concrete and steel pylons.

I shall never forget that hazy early morning as we crossed this barrier of many rows of concrete and steel pylons. It was an awesome sight. It was a great relief to know that those deadly menacing concrete bunkers on the Siegfried Line were now neutralized and were some distance behind us.

As we walked through the passageway through these many rows of concrete pylons, I looked to my right and to my left, and saw those seemingly endless rows of pylons that faded into the gray gloom of gun smoke and dust-laden smog of the early morning atmosphere, as we walked through that narrow roadway pass in the Dragon's Teeth of the Siegfried Line and entered Germany proper. These rows of pylons permanently implanted in the earth, appeared as ugly scars on God's beautiful planet. It was a very exciting experience to say the least, to know that we had breached Hitler's impenetrable West Wall. This was one great event that words will never be able to adequately describe, as well as one that will be forever indelibly imprinted in my memory.

Soon, as we walked in staggered formation down this road to the east, we heard heavy tanks rumbling us from our rear. Then came tanks, and more tanks, large tanks, medium tanks, light tanks, tank destroyers with Howitzers on them, more tanks than I had ever seen in one operation anywhere in my combat experience. This seemingly endless line of heavy armor lined up behind us in a convoy was an awesome sight to behold. Any enemy seeing this much power coming at them would surrender for sure, I thought.

Then came the trucks, the big two-and-one-half-ton open cab vehicles that carried many soldiers and supplies. We loaded onto them and left at a high rate of speed toward the east. We knew this was one of the most decisive and historical moments of the entire war. Where all of these vehicles came from was some great astonishment. We all were thrilled to no end to know that the many people in the rear were doing a fantastic job, and that we were not all alone up on the front, as it had oftentimes seemed.

We couldn't wait for a hot bath, a shave, and some clean clothes, not to mention hot food. Then behind our trucks came more infantry riding two-and-one-half-ton trucks. They were riding tanks, half-tracks, trucks, jeeps, and all kinds of vehicles. Tears came into my eyes, thinking of the price that so many loyal and patriotic Americans had paid to accomplish this feat of crossing the Siegfried Line. It was a momentous occasion, to say the least, an experience that I shall remember always with tears in my eyes.

It was not long before we arrived at a small town, though I never actually knew the name of it. Our trucks stopped there by the rail station, at an old schoolhouse where my unit was assembling. There was no damage to any buildings in this village. As I recall, it was Neunkirchen, or some other small town near there. Many of its citizens had left; only a few remained.

It was here that I met for the first time the other men of my squad and platoon, who had survived the battle of Saarlautern and the Siegfried Line. Many were not so lucky and had not survived. My platoon, 2nd Platoon of Company G, had been in an isolated location between the old bridge across the Saar and a large bunker of the Siegfried Line, located across the river from where I was. We had now regrouped here.

I met for the first time my platoon sergeant, Technical Sergeant Lars Agneberg, who I liked immediately. He was tall, lanky, reserved, and very knowledgeable. I wanted to get to know as many of the men of my squad and platoon as I could. They were dirty, unshaved, exhausted, and the most starved bunch of critters that I had ever seen. Well, so was I; we all were in that condition. It was with this great group of brave and fearless fighting men that I would now be fighting with the rest of the way across Europe, till the end of the war or until death do us part.

One soldier stood out in my mind. He was the BAR man of my squad, named Al Sperl, who was what one would call a great guy. He was a soldier that all of the others could count on to be there and finish the job. No one talked about the terrible experiences that we all had recently endured. I quickly had learned that one never looks back. We got to know each other fairly well, and respected each and every other one greatly.

It was Al Sperl who told me—not then, but 54 years later at a reunion at my home in Gulfport, Mississippi—about his terrible experiences along the Siegfried Line and the Saar River. He recounted what it was like at the foot of that big bad bunker that was manned by Hitler's elite soldiers whose job it was to stop us at all cost.

Things were a little different for each individual, each squad, and every platoon, company, and regiment, in that there were different conditions, locations, objectives, and terrain that made each person's job different than any other. Nevertheless, without cellars in the destroyed houses of Saarlautern, the fight would have been much bloodier. Without the artificial moon, things would have been substantially different.

It was heartbreaking after the end of the war to read where some rear echelon fake hero wrote that we were only in a holding position there at Saarlautern. I wished he had been there, he would have found that statement to be totally false.

CHAPTER 13

Al Sperl Relates his Squad's Action in Saarlautern

> *"Destiny is not a matter of chance, it is a matter of choice; it is not a thing to be waited for, it is a thing to be achieved."*
>
> —WILLIAM JENNINGS BRYAN (1860–1925)

The following is what Al Sperl told me about the action that he participated in around Saarlautern, Germany, in March 1945. Anxious to learn as much about the history of my new outfit, I prodded Sperl to relate to me as much as he could about my division and particularly my company, platoon, and squad prior to my rendezvousing with them. I will quote Sperl as accurately as I can as follows:

"The 65th Infantry Division, consisting of about sixteen thousand men, arrived at Le Havre, France, about mid-January 1945. They were at Camp Lucky Strike there for a few days until the division could get reorganized and move into action. Where they would be assigned to fight was unknown to anyone in the platoon.

"After about a week, all of our equipment, such as trucks, weapons, ammunition, and other supplies had been unloaded off the ships and were in place. We loaded onto French freight trains, known as forty and eights, and moved toward the front. The front constantly moved, so we did not know where we would be fighting until we arrived there. We first stopped in Metz, France, to reorganize and disperse to our assigned sectors of the front lines, which were along the Siegfried Line, which was right beside the Saar River on the French-German border in and around the area of Saarlautern.

"We left Metz, France, riding two-and-one-half-ton trucks, and arrived at an area west of the city of Saarlautern, Germany, just inside the German border on the Saar River. We unloaded from our trucks about six or seven miles from that city and walked to a predetermined location, just a few blocks from the Saar River. We came under German artillery fire before we even got near the river. The Germans seemed to be everywhere and also knew where we were at all times. Their 88mm artillery fire came at us, seemingly from every direction, from behind us, from our right and left flanks, as well as from the front, or east, toward the Siegfried Line.

"When we left our trucks we carried with us our personal items that could be carried in our pockets or backpacks. We carried a lightweight backpack, which one could strap onto his back and carry items, such as boxes of K rations, ammunition, and other supplies that could be placed in or strapped onto this backpack. We did not know exactly what our objectives were, but we headed east toward the Saar and the Siegfried Line. We did not know that we were being assigned to occupy and fight in one of the most deadly and dangerous areas of combat in the entire European Theater, at that time.

"Our platoon sergeant, Technical Sergeant Lars Agneberg was a courageous man with great leadership abilities. All of us had complete faith in him, and every man in his platoon would die for him. He was admired and respected by every man in the outfit. I would follow him to hell and back. His ability as a leader was unquestionable. He put out a tireless effort that was beyond what would be expected of any soldier.

"We knew from previous reports that we were part of the Third Army under the command of General Patton, also that we were now a part of and were in the XXth Corps, which was a part of the Third Army, and which was commanded by Major General Walton H. 'Bull Dog' Walker. We also knew that the Third Army had squeezed the German army into a large pocket that was in the north central part of France, in Normandy, and mostly around Metz, France. Also, that the disorganized remnants of the German Army that had been caught in this large pocket were being pushed toward the German border along the Saar River Valley. The Siegfried Line was located in this area, and it was Hitler's strong line of defense on the French border. It was a heavy fortified line of defenses consisting of large, strong concrete and steel bunkers with wide rectangular openings in their thick wall, where more than one machine gun would fire out of, at an approaching enemy. It was the main line of defense of the German Fatherland.

"Enemy soldiers were all around us, including behind us. After leaving the trucks and walking about six or eight miles, we arrived at an area by the Saar River. We entered a residential area of buildings that were almost all demolished, wooden frame buildings. This was the part of the city of Saarlautern that we were assigned to occupy and presumably move out from, and cross the Saar River, and then to cross this impregnable Siegfried Line, whenever and however that could be accomplished.

"We spread out, took cover from enemy artillery, snipers, and just plain Wehrmacht soldiers that fired upon us. It seemed that the entire area was flooded with German soldiers. A little after dark we arrived at some houses, which were only one or two short blocks from the Saar River, and right in front of a long concrete bridge that crossed it.

"When we got to our objective, it was late at night and Sergeant Agneberg directed each squad leader to occupy a cellar near the other three of the four squads, most all of which were in the same block. This area was a ghostly sight. It was 'No Man's Land' in the truest sense of the word. Before we entered any cellar to occupy it, we threw in several hand grenades to make sure that there were no enemy in there, before we entered it, in the dark. We were just feeling our way around trying to find a safe place to protect us from artillery and machine gun fire, as well as a place where we could get a little rest and be out of the elements. It was quite frightening going into the cellar of a partially demolished building late at night, with no lights of any kind, not knowing what was in there and just feeling our way around, trying to find a place to sit or lie down and get some rest.

"We had about ten soldiers in each squad that occupied each cellar. We had no idea then that other American infantry had occupied this area previously. The division that had been here had been withdrawn days before we arrived. We found letters and other items that had been left in these cellars by American soldiers from another division that had previously occupied this area. It was quite a surprise and a shock to then learn that we were not the first GIs to be in this area. It became a mystery as to why they had pulled back, letting the Krauts take the area back, then making it necessary for us to retake that entire area. So, what it amounted to was, as we learned from rumors, that this area had previously been taken and occupied by the 95th Infantry Division in September 1944. They had been pulled back and moved to Bastogne, in the Ardennes Forest, during the Battle of the Bulge, to help defend against the German Panzer counterattack there. The 95th had been replaced later by the 26th Division, who had recently been pulled out and moved north.

"We found a cellar for the ten men in my squad. The other squads occupied cellars of demolished houses, all in the same block as where we were. We slept in them that night and continuously for four or five days. We did not go on any patrols, ate the rations that we brought with us, conserved our ammo, and awaited our next move toward what was known as the impregnable Siegfried Line, which everyone knew that we were to, somehow, someday, cross it. When and how we were to breach the Siegfried Line was the big question in everyone's mind. There in our first 'dug in' location, we did not receive any 88mm artillery fire, for some unknown reason. However, we received around-the-clock machine gun fire. We stayed in our cellars all day, only to come out at night to do only short patrols in the immediate area to make sure that we were not about to be attacked by the Krauts. We had a guard at the entrance of each cellar all the time. Each one of us alternated in pulling guard duty. No one was to venture outside the cellars after midnight, or during daylight, in any situation. To do so meant instant death from the Kraut machine guns.

"The isolation, the sound of artillery and machine gun fire, as well as the entire combat situation that existed here was frightening. We got little or no sleep or rest. We had to be on alert all the time. I slept with my arms wrapped around my rifle, as most everyone else did. We knew that when you hear a shell come in, you are safe from it. It's the one that you never hear that kills you. We never knew where the enemy soldiers were. The fact that we had no communications with any higher command was also frightening. We did not have any radio communications with our command due to the fact that the Krauts would intercept what was said. We did not have any telephone communications because of the situation we were in, and it was too far to where our command was located in the rear. We also had to live with the fear of being wounded, knowing that we would not receive hardly any kind of treatment, other than just some first aid. There was no possible way that any of us could be medically evacuated. It was really a do-or-die situation there.

"My mother had given me a St. Christopher medal that I wore around my neck. I prayed silently many times each day. I had been brought up in a strict Catholic home, and believed strongly in Jesus Christ and my God Almighty. I had faith that my God would carry me through this ordeal. This faith that I had in my God gave me much strength and courage that was essential to make it through each day. All of my buddies believed the same as I did about faith in God. I could hear many of them saying prayers at night as we slept in these cellars, on piles of potatoes. It was also my belief that I was fighting for a very worthy cause. My parents had immigrated to America from Germany early in life, and America was now their country that they were totally loyal to.

"I knew that I was fighting not only for the protection of America, but also for those in Germany who had suffered as a result of Germany being overrun by a group of nothing more than terrorist thugs, who in the final analysis were destroying Germany, as well as the rest of Europe. I was devout in my faith. I never lacked the courage to do my job in fighting and killing the enemy. I sincerely believed that I was continuously risking my life for a very worthy cause, one that would, hopefully, save the world from another world war, and make the world safe for democracy and freedom-loving people everywhere.

"There were several rows of houses between the street that our four cellars were on and the river. Each night we would get an awful lot of machine gun fire, and for this reason we had to stay in the cellars most all of the time day and night. Machine guns fired down almost every street, most all of the time. In the daytime we were subject to sniper fire, never knowing when a sniper would pick one of us off, if we left the cellar. Our platoon, consisting of four squads of about ten men each, was the only unit that I was aware of that was fighting in this area, and at this particular bridge and bunker across the river.

"We later realized that this was just a holding position before having to cross that bridge across the Saar River. We correctly surmised that the real fighting and patrols were to happen over across the river, if we could make it across that bridge.

"We anxiously waited—bored, tired, and very uncomfortable, having to live in these dark cellars day after day and night after night. The cellars were dark, damp, musty, smelly, and frightening.

"In making short patrols at night we found that there, just ahead of us, about two blocks to the east, was the Saar River. We observed that long stone concrete bridge that crossed it and we knew that we would have to cross this bridge when the time came.

"After being in these cellars for about five days, Sergeant Lars, as we called him, told us one night, 'It is now time for our platoon to move out, and to cross that bridge and occupy cellars beyond the Saar and between the river and that bunker up on the hill, which is about several short blocks east of the bridge.' Our platoon was the only platoon that I knew of that was in this entire area that had crossed the river. I did not know of any other American soldiers in that immediate vicinity, or anywhere on the east side of that river. If any were there, they stayed in their cellars.

"We did not know of any enemy machine gun fire that was covering the bridge, which was coming from the bunker up on the hill, or from any machine gun positions out beside the bunker. The bridge never appeared to be under machine gun fire in that just east of the bridge was this large hotel, three floors tall, very wide, and it stood right in the center of the street that crossed over this bridge. Anyone crossing this bridge would then have to go around the hotel, either on the north, or the south side. There was a railroad track that ran alongside the river and on the east side of the hotel. It ran north and south and right up alongside the east entrance of the hotel, and that was the reason for the name of the hotel. Its name was the Bahnhoffs-Hotel [*Bahnhoffs* meaning, in German, a rail station].

"The bunker on the hill was located right at the end of that same street that crossed the river, but for the fact that the hotel had been built

94

there, for some curious reason, right in the center of the street that ran from the bridge to the big bunker on the hill. Had the hotel not been located there, the machine guns in the bunker would have had a direct line of fire right over the bridge. That would have made it impossible for anyone to try to cross the bridge. We observed that after one crossed the bridge you would have to go around one side or the other of the hotel to get around it, to get on the street that led up the hill, from the front of the hotel toward the bunker. This street, we called it the 'main' street, and it only led from the east side of the hotel to the bottom of the hill where the bunker was located, which was about a three or four block distance. So, this was the 'lay of the land' that we would have to cope with when the time came to cross the bridge.

"We knew the enemy observers saw us all the time and knew where we were. They also knew that we knew they were occupying that hotel. What we had to worry about was machine gun fire that may come from almost every direction and down every street, grazing fire, making it deadly to try to go across any street. It was not only machine gun fire that worried us, but all of the other weapons that they used, like the 88s, mortars, screaming meemies, and other artillery.

"The Krauts would come out of their big bunker at night with machine guns, and set them up in positions beside the bunker, in the bushes, and behind large rocks, all along the ridge that the bunker was on. These machine guns would have a lane of fire down almost every street that ran perpendicular to the ridge, except, of course, the main street. If the Krauts had fired down that street, they would have hit the hotel. They had their men in that hotel, was the reason that I concluded that they didn't fire down that street toward it.

"From the west side of the river we could come out of the cellar at night and see machine guns firing out of the big bunker at night, and directly in our direction hitting our partially demolished houses. We were located off to one side of the hotel, and it did not obstruct our view of the machine guns firing out of the bunker. Had we been further to the right, the hotel would have obstructed the view of the bunker. I found a picture postcard in the cellar that we were in, that was of the hotel right in front of us, and between the big bunker and us, and I later mailed it home. The hotel appeared to be pretty much intact and suffered little or no damage, for some mysterious reason.

"I could never understand why the German government ever allowed the hotel to be built right crosswise of the street that ran from and across the bridge, up the hill to the foot of the bunker, where it ended. It certainly defeated the purpose of that huge bunker and its ability to fire across the bridge, but that was to our advantage. The bunker was built in 1932. This was written in concrete on its side. I surmised that the hotel was probably built prior to that.

"We did not know when we were expected to cross this bridge that was about two hundred feet long. We could see that it was covered by heavy mortar and artillery fire. Machine gun fire covered it at times from machine guns firing from positions outside of the bunker, and on each side of it. We knew well enough that we were going to have to cross it, but we didn't want to think about it until the time came. What we did know was that it would be a hell of an ordeal. When we were to make a strategic advance, it was always kept a secret from most all of us, except from those that had to know. The reason being that if anyone having such information would be captured and tortured, the information may be learned by the enemy and cost the lives of many of our soldiers.

"As time passed, there on the west side of the Saar, we became anxious and very nervous. We could not become accustomed to the almost continuous, around-the-clock, nerve-racking machine gun fire. One evening late, Sergeant Lars came to our cellar and told us that we would be moving out of these cellars and not coming back. We would be crossing the bridge that night, all four squads of the entire 2nd Platoon would be crossing the river and moving into cellars across the river, and between it and the east edge of the town where the bunker was located up on the hill. He further explained that we would then be right at the foot of the hill that the bunker was located on. He told us that the 1st Squad would cross first; the 2nd would then cross next, and then the 3rd, and then the 4th. Everyone prepared to leave, we gathered our meager personal items that we could carry in our pockets and backpacks, as well as ammo and our weapon.

"Sergeant Lars gave instructions that each squad was to stay together, cross over together, and to be ready to advance across that bridge at the exact moment that he gave the order. There was to be no dragging around. This had to be done quickly, quietly, efficiently, and orderly, without any foul-ups. This is a good description of how Sergeant Lars did things.

"We all moved up to within the first block of the bridge behind some buildings, waiting our time to cross. Each squad leader was at the head of his squad.

"The 1st Squad moved up to the edge of the bridge, but behind a row of houses that were right by the river, and Sergeant Lars told all of us, 'Keep spaced out, about twenty feet apart, and run across the bridge when I tell you to. Stay together as a group, but keep spread out. We can expect some 88 fire in making this crossing.'

"Then he said to the squad leader of the 1st Squad, 'You men follow me.' Lars ran across the bridge with the men of the 1st Squad following him, as he had directed them to.

"Lars positioned himself to the right, or at the southeast side of the bridge, so he could see and give orders to the others waiting on the other side to cross. He told the 1st Squad to stay against the walls of the first row of houses across the river, which was between the river and close to the big hotel.

"He then yelled at the leader of my 2nd Squad to come on across. We all ran across, all spaced out about twenty feet apart, and all got across without an incident. We took cover alongside the buildings near where the 1st Squad was waiting.

"He then told the leader of the 3rd Squad to come on across. The squad leader was in an embarrassing situation in that one of his men acted as though he was not ready, kept adjusting his equipment, just fiddling around, just standing there, holding up the whole squad. He just stayed there, holding up all of the others. The squad leader could not commit his men to cross until all of them were ready. So they waited. Lars shouted at the squad leader to stay back. He then ordered the 4th Squad come on across.

"The 4th Squad then ran across uneventfully, still there was no shelling, which was a great surprise to everyone. It now came time for the last, the 3rd Squad, to come across. As the number two man got almost across, about twenty feet from the east end of the bridge, an 88mm artillery shell landed right beside him, and I saw this man fly through the air and into the river on the south side of the bridge. The other men kept coming across. The shelling continued at a rapid rate of fire, with shells landing all around, on each end of the bridge, on the bridge, and in the water, on each side of the bridge.

"As the last man of the 3rd Squad came onto the bridge and was about one quarter of the way across it, a shell hit right beside him on the bridge, and I saw him fly through the air, and into the water on the north side of the bridge.

"The shelling continued for a long time after all of the squads had crossed. We could only conclude that either the Kraut observer, probably in that hotel, was not observing closely and didn't see our men crossing until sometime later, when the last Squad was coming across, or that the 88mm cannon was not in position to fire until then.

"The entire platoon remained against the wall of the buildings right beside the river, on the south side of the road over the river, until the artillery fire had subsided. In a short while, Lars told all of us to follow him. We followed in a staggered formation. We came upon one house about two blocks east of the hotel. Lars told the squad leader to take his squad into the cellar of that house, and so on, until three squads had been shown what cellars to go into.

"Finally he took the 2nd Squad, my squad, to the last house up the hill, and it was on the right, or south side of the main road that led from the hotel up the hill to the big bunker. This main street was only a few blocks long, and it only ran from the hotel up to the base of the bunker where it ended.

"Lars had told all of us, when we first got to Saarlautern, to not go into any cellar or building without first throwing in a couple of hand grenades. So, after we arrived at the 'last house,' as it became known, we threw into the cellar some grenades. This house, like all of the others in that area, was not totally demolished, as they were in other sections of the city. There was a stove in it, a roof, but the windows were all blown out. We settled in and awaited further orders from Lars.

"Lars seemed like the busiest man I had ever seen, getting the men of all four squads situated in cellars where he would remember where they were. He seemed to be everywhere at the same time, always with his .45 caliber grease gun that he was very partial to, slung on his shoulder and ready for action. We posted our door guard at the entrance, and the remainder of us went to sleep.

"We were dreadfully tired and still shaking from the river crossing. We lived in this cellar about ten days. No one dared to leave it during daylight. Snipers, machine gunners, and observers were everywhere.

"The following morning, very early, we were awakened by heavy artillery fire. It was our 155mm artillery, we soon learned, in the rear, firing on that bunker just ahead of us and no more than about 150 yards up the hill from our house. We could look out and see our artillery shells hitting the bunker, and it appeared that the shells just bounced off it. The impact of the all-day shelling hardly left a mark on that huge bunker. The shelling of this bunker would stop at dark every night. The concussion hurt my ears so bad that I could not hear very well, and still can't. We could not find anything like cotton to put in our ears to ease the pain of the concussion.

"The following night Lars came to our cellar and ordered several of us to follow him. We crossed the main, east-west road that ran from the base of the bunker to the big hotel. After we crossed that street, darting across as quickly as we could, we continued north along a path parallel to the river and to the base of the hill the bunker was on. This path led to the north, alongside a single row of houses to our right, or on the east side. This row was the last row of houses beneath and closest to the bunker, and was aligned with our house across the main street. On the west side of this path, toward the river, was an open area about two hundred feet wide. It also ran north and south, parallel to the river, for about two or three city blocks. It was a rectangular piece of vacant land. It was once a city park, or a playground, and most recently it was a field where corn had been grown, and prior to that it was probably a park for the kids to play in. Now it was covered with about a hundred bodies of both American and German soldiers. It was heavily mined with anti-personnel mines and Schu mines. No one could go across or walk into this area without being killed. Across this field, or park, to the west, toward the river, was also a long row of houses that ran north and south. This row was just east of the big hotel. These houses were occupied by Krauts, which were just two blocks from where we were staying.

"I thought long and hard about this minefield that everyone feared and that no one would dare to even make one step out of our well-worn path. Why there were so many dead soldiers, both American and German, in that small three-block area, we were at a loss to understand how this could have occurred. They were there when we arrived. None of the dead GIs were any men in our division. They had been there for some time.

"My friends and I discovered that the German soldiers fleeing from the Normandy pocket fled by the thousands into this area. Many of them, in their rapid, disorganized withdrawal, crossed that bridge across the Saar, went around the hotel, between the rows of houses, and attempted to run across this dirt surfaced area where the Germans had planted mines, and they were caught in their own minefield. There was no way the German command could have informed them that this area was mined.

"Then, when the 95th Division took this city in September 1944 they occupied many of the cellars and buildings here. The 95th was moved north during the Battle of the Bulge to help the 101st Airborne Division, and the 26th Division moved into this area. The 65th Division had now replaced the 26th Division. These men of the 95th had also fallen into this minefield trap, the same as the German soldiers had done. I feel certain that these Americans soldiers of the 95th Division, who were the first to take this area, were killed there after they came across the bridge, some going on one side of the hotel, as we did, and others going on the north side, then through the row of houses to the east of the hotel, and attempted to cross that open area in a hurry.

"When a land mine goes off in a situation like that, one does not know if it was a mortar or an artillery shell coming in, that made the explosion, so the men keep coming. This is the only conclusion that we could draw from there being so many dead soldiers in this small area.

"Lars led us along a path right beside this minefield, cautioning each of us not to step even one inch out of that path, as we went further north to a supply dump that was located underneath an underpass, that ran under a railroad track that ran alongside the river. Close by the supply dump was the cellar of an old house, where about six men from E Company were billeted. They controlled the supply dump where we got our rations, ammunition, and a few other items of necessity.

"I got to know one of the six men who guarded the supplies. He was Tom Stroud, one of the kindest and most likable soldiers that I ever met. He always had a kind and encouraging word, not only for me but also for everyone. He attended to his job there of protecting and issuing the supplies in a very helpful way. He was always glad to see any of the men in my squad when we came for supplies. He told me that he was a Mennonite, who were also called Pennsylvania Dutch, as well as Amish, and he lived in Pennsylvania, like me. He was a conscientious objector because of his religious faith, but was drafted and fulfilled his responsibility to defend his country.

"I never learned how the supplies got to this location. My friend Ladner and I learned later that these supplies had been brought in first by the 95th, and then the 26th Division. They had apparently been brought in across this old Roman bridge. It was a real mystery how and when these supplies actually got there.

"The 95th Division had been pulled out by General Patton and sent to fight north of where we now were, during the battle of the Bulge. The German soldiers had not bothered the supplies during the time between their pullout, and the time the area was retaken by the 26th Division, and then by our 65th. None of us were able to determine how long of a lapse of time this was. The Krauts probably thought they were booby-trapped.

"Each night, going for rations and ammo in the dim light of the GI moon, we could see enemy soldiers patrolling the area just across the park, or minefield and in front of that row of houses that were just to the east of the hotel.

"The light from the GI moon was a diffused light that gave us just enough light to be able to see approximately two hundred feet, or a little more, but at that distance the figure of a person was very faint, almost like what you would expect a ghost to look like. It was enough light for us to see across the minefield, or the 'graveyard' as some called it, and to see the German soldiers walking or standing on that street in front of that row of houses.

"As we walked from our cellar to the supply dump to get supplies we had to stay right on this narrow path that was right beside the minefield open area. It was mined right up to the edge of this path. In the moonlight, we could see the dead American and German soldiers. The flesh was rotting off of their faces. Many of these bodies were lying just within inches of the edge of this path. Lars constantly cautioned us about even getting inches off of this well-worn path.

"Without this GI moon, we would have been totally annihilated, since we could not go out in the open during daylight, nor would we have been able to go out any at night, in that we would not have been able to see anyone or anything. The constant hazy overcast of dust and fumes from explosives would even keep a real full moon from being seen, but it helped to diffuse the light of the large antiaircraft spotlights, which gave us lots of reflected light in the area.

"We well knew that the German soldiers were staying in that hotel day and night, and that they used it to observe from. They got from there to their bunkers at night by following a route alongside that row of houses just east of the hotel, to the north behind our supply dump, and then to the east up into the hills where their bunkers were located. We saw these German soldiers every night, and they saw us as well. There was nothing to prevent them from going into the hotel because they couldn't be seen by us, due to the row of houses on the hotel's east side.

"Another reason to believe that they were staying in the hotel was that the machine guns in the bunker never fired right down that main street in front of the bunker, and toward that hotel. We felt fairly safe crossing that main road to go get supplies, for that reason, but when we had to, we crossed it quickly.

"One night we went on a six-man patrol in and around the area of the supply dump. We had to do some reconnaissance at night to determine if there were any Krauts assembling in that area and ready to attack us. I was wearing a backpack so that I could bring some supplies back after we returned from the patrol. However, I had my Browning Automatic Rifle and a big ammo bag on my shoulder that I had filled with ammo at the dump, so I did not bring any supplies on my backpack, but nevertheless, I was still wearing the fiberglass backpack. The ammo that I brought back was so heavy that I was not able to carry any rations on the backpack. It would be too heavy.

"That night, returning from the patrol, when we got close to the main road and near our cellar, one of the German soldiers across the minefield threw a potato masher grenade at us. The explosion killed the man behind me, and part of the grenade hit me in the low back and knocked me down on my face. When I fell, luckily I hit the ground in a firing position, and my BAR was aimed right at the Krauts who threw the grenade. I immediately looked across this cornfield, and could see about five German soldiers there, just standing there looking in my direction, so I opened up on them, and fired an entire magazine of twenty rounds, mowing all of them down. I could see them falling as I fired, and also I could see the tracers that I fired, going right into them.

"When I was hit, all the men with me in the patrol ran toward our cellar. They didn't know what had happened or what to expect. I didn't know how bad I was wounded, but I was able to crawl back to our cellar. A GI infantryman who had been trained as a medic carried medical first aid equipment, cleaned the wound, and put sulfa bandages on it for about a week. The fiberglass backpack took the worst of the impact of the grenade, otherwise the injury would have been fatal, or would have severed my spine. I was not able to do any more patrols for about four days.

"Our BAR man for our squad had gotten killed, and I took his rifle, and I became the BAR man. I had been carrying that weapon for only several days when I was hit. I had received special training stateside in the BAR, at Camp Shelby, Mississippi, and had wanted to use that weapon ever since. When I first got the BAR, I took the bipod off of the end of the barrel, in that it got in the way and was just something to rest the end of the barrel on. I liked firing it so much that I had mastered firing it from my hip and fired it often from that position all across Germany. I could even fire it from my hip as I was walking either forward or backward.

"I thanked my God in Heaven that I had not been more seriously wounded. Had I or anyone else been severely wounded, it would have been impossible to be evacuated to the rear, because no one in their right mind would try to go back across that bridge that we had come across. In the situation that we were in there, it was every man was on his own. Of course, each of us looked after the others the best we could. We all knew that if any of us were seriously wounded that we could not be evacuated, and that we would just have to stay there, and die there. There was no help that could be forthcoming.

"We did not have to bring water because there were artesian wells in lots of places in that area, in and around the houses. These wells flowed artesian water out the spigot of a pump all of the time. We had one man, Billy Gilliam, who was a very daring and courageous soldier and a good friend of mine, but he had difficulty in believing that he could get hit, wounded, or hurt in any way. He violated every order to stay in the cellars during daylight. One day he took a bucket from the cellar and went down the street in the day time, of course, and was at a pump catching a bucket of water to carry back to the cellar with him, when suddenly a machine gun up on the hill fired at the bucket and riddled it with holes, without even one bullet hitting him. He ran back the short distance to the cellar carrying this bucket with numerous holes in it, with water pouring out through them.

"Billy never went out of the cellar again during daylight, until the day we went over the top. It was apparent to us that the Krauts did not intend to kill him, but to just have some fun and scare him. They could have easily killed him if they had wanted to.

"No smoking was allowed anywhere. The enemy could smell the smoke and possibly see the light from it at nighttime. We never wanted to attract them to us in any manner.

"Patrols began at 9:00 P.M. every night. For whatever reason the Germans had, we didn't get a lot of 88 fire in our area. We did get continuous machine gun fire down almost every street that ran from the hills west toward the river. One night some of our men built a fire in the stove in the house to heat some water for instant coffee. Just as soon as the smoke started coming out of the chimney, the machine guns in the bunker started firing at the top of the chimney, and each time knocked off a few more bricks that fell on the roof. We took it as a warning if the smoke continued we may be hit by artillery fire.

"Soon after we arrived there, and not knowing what strategy the higher command had in mind for us, we just didn't think about what we were expected to do to get ourselves out of the pocket that we found ourselves in. We had no known way out other than over the hill the bunker was on. There was another big bunker just south of this one that covered the other bridge across the Saar.

"We observed and studied the Nazis' strategy, habits, and methods. We detected that they would come out the back doors of the big bunker at night and bring machine guns out, and set them up beside the bunker in the bushes and behind large rocks, fire them at us and others back across the river. We also learned that they used teams of horses to pull their 88mm artillery pieces along back roads behind and beside the bunker, and fire at us from these various locations. They would fire them for a while then quit and move them to a new location. This was so that our artillery could not zero in on them; they moved before we could do that. These 88s had wheels on the base that could be lowered when they wanted to move them, so they pulled them with horses, which didn't make much noise, to different positions on the hills. As soon as they thought that we could have zeroed in on them with artillery, they would move to another position and fire from there.

"Soon after we arrived at this forward position east of the river, our big 155mm cannons set up somewhere behind us, almost continuously fired their big shells at this bunker, as well as all around it. The 155mm cannon is a very heavy artillery piece that fires a shell that is about 6.25 inches, or 155 millimeters in diameter, with a hard steel case filled with high explosives, and is detonated by a fuse in the nose of it. They are mounted either on a gun carriage towed by a heavy vehicle, or some are mounted on a tank-like vehicle with tracks making it highly mobile like a tank. The firing of these 155mm cannons started the day after the night that we crossed the river, and they would fire at this bunker every day, all day, but would stop at night. I assume that it was because with the light of the GI moon at night we had to go on patrols and get rations and it would not be safe for us. It kept us awake all day and we patrolled at night, so we seldom slept.

"When the 155s hit the bunker they would bounce off, however they created one huge explosion with tremendous concussion and noise. It shook the old house and our cellar, tremendously. In fact, the noise was so great that I got severe headaches and lost most of my hearing. Our cellar was located only about one hundred and fifty yards from the bunker up the hill. We had no cotton or anything else to put in our ears to ease the pain of the noise. We knew that the Krauts in the bunker were also suffering from concussion, however many times at night we could hear them singing, or playing a radio or record player, just as though nothing had happened. We often heard what appeared to be a radio that they had placed in the opening of the big bunker, playing the German song, 'Lilli Marlene.' This was a very popular song written by a Hans Leip, a German poet, during WWI. A German, Norbert Schultze put it to music."

Marlene Dietrich was a very popular American singer with a sensual, sexy, and soothing voice. She had immigrated to America from Germany prior to WWII. She sang Lilli Marlene in WWII for American infantrymen under the name of "The Girl Under the Lantern." She sang it to American soldiers in North Africa, Sicily, Italy, Alaska, Greenland, Iceland, and England. It was sung by Miss Dietrich to servicemen in American military hospitals, and her recordings were broadcast over loudspeakers on American Army trucks, to German soldiers on the front lines in France, Belgium, and Germany during fighting there, to make them sentimental and homesick. Adolph Hitler had tried hard to get Miss Dietrich to renounce her American citizenship and return to Germany, but without success.

Lilli Marlene was well liked by both American and German servicemen. It became a classic and its historical words are as follows:

Vor der Kaserme vor dem grossen Tor
Stand eine Laterne, und stebt noch davor,
So wolln wir uns da wiedersehn
Bei der Laterne wolln wir stehn,
Wie einst Lili Marleen, wie einst Lili Marleen.

Unsre beide Schatten sahn wie einer aus.
Dass wir so lieb uns hatten, das sah man gleich daraus
Un alle Leute solln es sehn,
Wenn wir bei der Laterne stehn,
Wie einst Lili Marleen, Wie einst Lili Marleen.

Schon rief der Posten: Sie blasen Zapfenstreich
Es kann drei Tage kosten! Kam'rad, ish komm ja gleich.
Da Sagten wir auf Wiedersehn.
Wie gerne wollt ich mit dir gehn,
Mit dir Lili Marlene, mit dir Lili Marleen.

Deine Schritte kennt sie, deinen zieren Gang

106

Alle Abend brennt sie, mich vergass sie lanp
Und sollte mir ein Leids geschehn,
Wer wird bei der Laterne stehn,
Mit dir Lili Marleen, mit dir Lili Marleen?

Aus dem stillen Raume, aus der Erde Grund
Hebt mich wie im Traume dein verliebter Mund.
Wenn sich die spaeten Nebel drehn;
Werd' ich bei der Laterne stehn
Wie einst Lili Marleen, Wie einst Lili Marleen.

The English version of Lilli Marlene is as follows:

Underneath the lantern, by the barrack gate,
Darling I remember the way you used to wait;
'Twas there that you whispered tenderly,
That you lov'd me, you'd always be,
My Lilli of the lamplight,
My own Lilli Marlene.

Time would come for roll call time for us to part
Darling I'd caress you and press you to my heart.
And there 'neath that far off lantern light
I'd hold you tight, we'd kiss goodnight,
My Lilli of the lamplight,
My own Lilli Marlene.

Orders came for sailing somewhere over there,
All confined to barracks was more than I could bear,
I knew you were waiting in the street,
I heard your feet, but could not meet,
My Lillie of the lamplight,
My own Lilli Marlene.

Resting in a billet just behind the line
Even tho' we're parted your lips were close to mine,
You wait where that lantern softly gleams

Your sweet face seems to haunt my dreams,
My Lillie of the lamplight,
My own Lilli Marlene.

2nd Platoon—Over the Top of the Siegfried Line

Al Sperl continues his description of being in Saarlautern;

"After about ten days of the shelling and living in these cellars, Lars told us that we were going over the top early the next morning to cross over this formidable Siegfried Line. Early that morning just after daylight we could not hear any machine guns or 88s firing, nor could we hear any of our 155mm artillery firing on the bunker either.

"All was quiet on the western front, the Siegfried Line, for the first time in a long time. We gathered up our few depleted and worn-out belongings that evening, got a little rest that night, and at the break of day we all moved out. I was awake and up, looking the area over to try to see how we would fare going over the Siegfried Line. I saw two of our engineers who had to have lots of courage, who came up to our position, almost in front of the bunker, and fired two flamethrowers into the bunker opening. We saw smoke coming out a small stack in the top. They yelled down to us to come on up. We then ran up the hill to the bunker and around behind it.

"There, behind this giant bunker we saw three doors leading into it; they were all open. There was one door on each side of the backside of the bunker. The other one was in the center, up at a higher level. There was a dirt road that led to the upper door, from somewhere in the rear. It was where vehicles could deliver ammo and supplies right up to the back entrance. From that top door, or hatch, there were steps leading down on each side to each of the two side doors. The doors, or steel hatches, were all open, apparently left open by the fleeing Nazi soldiers who had obviously left that night. The Krauts had left, apparently because they couldn't stand the bombardment of our 155s pounding on them all day, every day. This was their last chance to retreat along with their other troops before we captured them in this pocket. I am sure that they got a real concussion from all of our artillery.

"The artillerymen are to be commended for the great job that they did there and elsewhere. They are always on the ball, as well as being extremely accurate. They were so accurate that all of their shells landed on the bunker. Some landed beside and behind it, purposely, to knock out any surrounding weapons positions. We all lived in constant fear throughout that entire ordeal in that house so close to the bunker they were shelling, hoping that none of the shells would fall short and hit our house. None did. I also had great faith in all of our men of the 65th. Infantry Division.

"Inside the large room of the bunker where the firing came from, there was a concrete shelf inside of the big slit that was about six feet wide and about fifteen inches high—where three machine guns could fire out of it—which afforded a wide dispersing fire. We looked out of the opening from which as many as three machine guns fired at us, all at one time, and which had caused the loss of so many of our men. We had a view of the entire area where we had lived and fought in while there. We could see everything, the minefields where all of the dead bodies lay, the house where the cellar was that we stayed in with part of the chimney shot off, the underpass where we went for supplies, the hotel, the far end of the bridge beyond it, and we had a good view of the Saar River. It was an exciting thing to do, but terrifying to be there looking at where we had been and had come so close to being killed. Now we were finally victorious in crossing that impregnable Siegfried Line. Yes, we did it. It was a triumphant feeling.

"After going into the other rooms of the bunker, we found nothing but burned papers and documents, bunks, a small kitchen and dining area, storage rooms, showers, toilets, and other areas necessary for those living there. They could come and go through the top entrance to the roadway that led to a road outside. They could also go out of the bunker through the two side doors in the back, at the lower level. We saw the trails that the 88s were brought in on, pulled by teams of horses, leading to different positions to fire at us from.

"It was a shock and a relief to go inside this monstrous killing facility. After we finished looking it over, all of us in the 2nd Platoon that had been living at the foot of that bunker, left and walked east toward the Dragon's Teeth, the many rows of large concrete and steel pylon tank traps that made up part of the Siegfried Line. Our engineers had now cleared the steel structures from the roadway leading through the

Dragon's Teeth of the Siegfried Line. Upon arriving at the roadway that went through the Dragon's Teeth, and crossing it, we walked through the passageway.

"As we got to this pass, we met other men from our company that had been fighting in the area of Saarlautern who had come across the other bridge, and who were walking through this narrow passageway, who had come there on another road. Behind us came many tanks and other armored vehicles.

"After we had walked along this road that went through the Dragon's Teeth, we got on trucks that came from the rear to meet us and pick us up. It was here that we again met up with the men of our other platoons that had been fighting near where we were, one of whom was Ladner, who became my close friend and combat buddy.

"We traveled to a nearby town, Neunkirchen, Germany, where we regrouped and all had a hot shower at a coal mine. We then stayed there for regrouping and a few days rest before commencing our spearhead on tanks across Germany. Any conditions were better than those cellars in Saarlautern. Here the air was clean and smelled fresh.

"All of us felt as though we had done the impossible—one of the great accomplishments of this war. We had utmost faith in all of our leaders, both military and political. This faith gave all of us the strength and courage we needed to do our jobs. We had renewed faith in our God Almighty, without whom we could not have ever accomplished what we had. Faith in Him also gave us an unbelievable amount of strength and courage. I became convinced that no man could endure what we had endured, and accomplish what we had accomplished without the faith that we had in our God, and in our leaders, and in our fellow soldiers, with the belief that what we were doing was the right thing. It was this great faith that gave us the courage that took us through this terrible ordeal, as well as all of the other ordeals that were to follow.

"We were dirty and needed a bath. We were exhausted, almost totally, from nerves, lack of proper nourishment, loss of sleep, and overexhaustion. However, when we walked over that hill where the bunker was we felt like heroes who had conquered an enemy, which we had. Nothing else mattered, we had accomplished what was said to be impossible."

CHAPTER 14

Into Germany

*"Older men declare war. But it is youth
that must fight and die. And it is youth
that must inherit the tribulation, and the
triumphs that are the aftermath of war."*

—HERBERT HOOVER (1874–1964)

We arrived riding trucks, in a small town in the hilly coal mining country of the Saar River basin, and as I learned when we arrived, this was a small quiet town off the beaten path that so far had escaped the ravages of war. It was Neunkirchen, the location where a part of the 65th Division had stopped to regroup. Only a few civilians remained in this town and one was the town crier. An old man at midnight would ring his bell out in the street and say something, I surmised, like, "Midnight and all is well." He also conveyed messages or news to the remaining citizens there. He is what early Americans would have called the town crier. I found a place to sleep, but it too was on the floor, in a schoolhouse, but I did have a sleeping bag that Technical Sergeant Lars Agneberg passed out to all of us. Some of the men refused to sleep in the sleeping bags for the reason they would not be able to fire their rifle quick enough in the event that they needed to.

Someone learned that there was a coal mine near town with lots of hot water and showers. That afternoon we got in trucks that took us there to get a hot bath—the only place in the entire country probably that had lots of hot water. We went into this large shower room, a circular room with chains all around the wall that were hooked onto a hook, with a number. You lowered the hook and placed your clothes on it, and then hoisted them up in the air to keep them from getting wet while we showered. I didn't use it for anything but my combat boots, rifle, cartridge belt, hand grenades, my field jacket, and my steel helmet, which held my personal items. I threw my nasty clothes on the floor and turned a shower onto them, stomped them with my feet to wash them. I must have showered and laundered my clothes for a half hour. I washed my pants, shirt, underwear, and socks on the floor by stomping on them to wash them, as the hot water poured onto them. No one had any soap. My clothes were so dirty and bloody, no one would believe it. They should have been thrown away, but we still had no supplies, hot food, or any other amenities like we had looked forward to. I went into the boiler room and placed my wet clothes on the boiler pipes to dry, then returned and showered more while they dried. We had no towels, so I recalled from stories in my Latin class that the Greek and Roman soldiers used a small scythe to scrape the water off their bodies after a bath. So, I figured that my bayonet would accomplish the same thing, which it did. Finally my clothes were dry enough to wear and I returned to our peaceful little village, on the next truck.

That night the kitchen crew arrived and prepared a hasty meal, heavy, not very digestible, but no one complained; at least it was hot and different from K, C, and ten-in-one rations. The mess sergeant and his crew had apparently been on vacation for a while, not having to prepare food for us back there on the Saar. They really took a lot of kidding and ridicule as well, about not having anyone to cook for while we were up there in those cellars eating canned rations. Many men kidded them by asking how their vacation on the Riviera or Paris had been.

Sergeant Lars, always concerned about his men, saw that every man got a sleeping bag. They had just arrived on a truck. They were rather warm, better than nothing. I fell asleep on the floor of the old schoolhouse. About midnight a sergeant woke me up to pull two hours' guard duty at the railroad station just a short distance away. It was lonely there but it was a relief to stand guard duty without worrying about shells and bullets exploding around you.

I awoke the following morning with a high fever. I spoke to the medic who took my temperature and it was very high. He sent me by jeep to the Battalion Aid Station just a short distance away, where I was examined by another medic who told me that I had a bad infection of my sinuses and that he was sending me to the hospital. I tried to argue with him but it didn't do any good. He told me that because of the fever, if I had some contagious infection I could possibly spread it to all of the other men. He had me get into an ambulance to be transported to a hospital. I had to turn in my rifle and ammo, which was in my cartridge belt, and my hand grenades before they would put me in an ambulance to be taken to a field hospital. On the way there it had begun to rain, a slow drizzle as occurs often in Europe. We had to go over country dirt roads that were muddy and slippery. The ambulance plowed through the mud almost getting stuck several times. At one point we stopped. I got a look outside and saw armed German soldiers carrying submachine guns. They were talking to the driver. I, as well as the others in the ambulance, were now very apprehensive. I recalled the Malmedy incident where my closest friend was murdered by the Nazi SS troops in Belgium.

Then the rear door of the ambulance was opened by one of the Nazis. Two of them searched inside the ambulance for weapons then closed the door and waved us on. Upon arrival at the tent hospital there were several large tents with a big red cross painted on the top. The weather was very cold and damp. The hospital was set up in the corner of a field near a large forest; further to the east was the Rhine River.

I wondered what a field hospital that looked this crude was like. Inside there were a couple of coal-burning heaters that really warmed that big tent well. I was placed on a series of blankets on a folding cot. The cot was made up of one blanket that was half on the cot, then another one on the other side, half on, and then another, and another. I then lay down on it and I was wrapped like a mummy, arms and all. My cot was right near a coal-burning heater. This was the first time that I felt warm in months. I was knocked out with something, I think, in that I slept like a log all night. The next morning I was placed in an ambulance with others. We all were ambulatory. I asked where we were going and was told that we were evacuating this hospital and moving to another one further to the east. Then this one would be dismantled and it would leapfrog from this location to beyond the one that we were going to, so that it would be closer to the front lines. There were actually two hospitals, one would leapfrog over the other one.

We arrived at the new tent hospital. It was just like the one we just left, set up right by a great forest, tall trees—peaceful and quiet looking. This forest was large and beautiful, but I do not recall the name of it; however, major battles were raging all around us. The medics told me that they were receiving lots of emergency injury cases of small arms and shrapnel wounds. They were bringing in ambulance-loads of American soldiers, as well as some German POWs, all with severe injuries. The floor of the tent was soil and grass. There were wood or coal-burning stoves set up in the tents that really warmed them. I was cared for wonderfully. Again I was wrapped in these many blankets like a mummy. I couldn't even scratch my nose because my hands were beside me encapsulated in a cocoon of wool blankets.

During the night sometime, I awoke and heard excited whispers by the female nurses and medics, which woke me up. They were rushing around so excited they seemed to be somewhat hysterical. Then suddenly, in came a group of German Wehrmacht officers, armed troops with them carrying automatic assault weapons. I got scared. Is this going to be another Malmedy, another massacre by the Nazis?...I wondered. I could relate to the feelings that my friend Jack Richardson must have had in the last moments of his life standing there in the knee-deep snow in a field at a crossroads at Malmedy, Belgium, when they all had been captured and then gunned down with machine guns.

I felt helpless, scared, and mad as hell really, because I was unable to fight, to defend myself and others form the invasion of this hospital by the enemy. The mere sight of Nazi uniformed troops in battle gear, steel helmets, armed with assault rifles, with potato masher grenades sticking out of their boots, angered me to no end. I had become programmed, I suppose, and couldn't understand anything but to kill them before they killed us. After they left I spoke with a nurse and asked her what they were doing here. She attempted to console me and related to me that this often happened around this area and they were only looking to see if there were any weapons or armed fighting men hiding in the tents, or if it was just camouflaged as a hospital.

She also told me that the doctors in the operating room were operating on two wounded German soldiers. One of the nurses who spoke fluent German took the Germans into the operating room so that they could see for themselves, and she told them that they were treating German as well as American soldiers equally. I had trouble going back to sleep. She gave me a shot of something that knocked me out and then I got a long night's sleep, waking up about midmorning. I really needed that rest.

The following morning I spoke with a doctor and I told him I felt better and that I wanted to return to my outfit, and I didn't like for Nazis armed with submachine guns to come through our hospital with me more or less strapped in a cot, where I couldn't defend myself. I told him that I preferred to be where I had a weapon and could fight. I begged him to discharge me and let me get back to my outfit. He promised that just as soon as my fever subsided that he would send me back to my organization—maybe tomorrow, he told me. He said that I had a terrible sinus infection, which I wasn't surprised to hear after breathing all of that putrefied air in Saarlautern cellars where there was nothing but thick, smoke-filled air, with lots of pollution from rotting potatoes, human waste, and dead bodies, as well as a lot of dust from the destruction of concrete buildings. The smell of burnt gunpowder had been everywhere there. Being enclosed in a cellar for days and nights on end, smelling those rotting potatoes and feces of our men who were suffering from terrible diarrhea could infect anything.

Two days later I was discharged and an ambulance took me to my outfit. I arrived at my Battalion Aid Station at some farmhouse where I retrieved my rifle, cartridge belt, and grenades. I then caught a ride on a jeep to the company CP, wherever it was, in this fast-moving war.

I had talked a medic at the hospital into giving me a new shirt, pants, and field jacket, as well as socks and underwear. He told me he would have my old clothes laundered and wear them himself and I could have his new ones. When I returned to my unit I was embarrassed to no end. I was clean-shaven, wearing clean clothes and they were wearing the same old clothes they had in Saarlautern. I had rubbed and scrubbed my feet to remove all of the dead skin that causes trench foot. I had dried out my suede boots at the hospital, by that heater. One of the nurses had told me how necessary it was to rub the dead skin off of your feet and put on a dry, clean pair of socks if you possibly could, to prevent your feet from rotting from what was called trench foot. My company was now somewhere between Saarlautern and Mainz, Germany, our supposed next objective.

CHAPTER 15

"Patton's Raiders" on the Tanks

"There is only one tactical principle which is not subject to change. It is: 'To use the means at hand to inflict the maximum amount of wounds, death, and destruction on the enemy, in the minimum time.'"

—GENERAL GEORGE S. PATTON (1885–1945)

Very early, before daybreak the following morning after returning from that field hospital, I was told by a sergeant that I would be riding shotgun on tanks, along with several others from my platoon. He never said for how long. It was very early, at the crack of dawn, when I was awakened from my sleep on the floor of this farmhouse. I was told that my tank was waiting for me to hop on it. I had lost my gloves, my hands were already freezing cold. I had slept on the floor of this farmhouse, little to cover with and no heat, but at least there were windows that were intact. It was just getting daylight when the tankers woke us up. We went outside and there were the new tanks that I had heard about; we called them "Patton's Pride." These were tanks that had just recently arrived from the States. They were Pershing Tanks, named after General John "Black Jack" Pershing who commanded American Troops in France in WWI, and who had commanded General Patton, a tanker in that war. I also learned that they had been designed and built to General Patton's specifications and they were really something special to General Patton. In fact, it was said that they were his pride and joy. Only a few of these new-type tanks had been sent to Europe and only ten of them were assigned to the 3rd Army. Two of them were disabled and we had only eight that were assigned to our Division and were operated by the 6th Armored Division.

I jumped up on the tread of this tank, hoping that the tanker with his head sticking out of the turret wouldn't let the tank take off until I had gotten off of that track. I grabbed a steel U-bolt welded onto the turret and pulled myself up onto the tank. I couldn't let go of this handhold—my hand had stuck to it like glue. I didn't realize that it was that cold, but my hand was frozen to this piece of steel. I had never seen weather that cold. I was fearful that the tank driver would take off with my feet still on the track, so I tore my hand from the steel bar and pulled the skin off of it. As I did, I left a layer of the skin off my hand stuck to that steel bar. I closed my bloody fist, put my bloody hand in my new field jacket pocket, and sat down behind the turret. Ken and I were the only two men on the tank that morning.

These new Pershing M-26 tanks had two Ford V-8, air-cooled, gasoline engines in them. I sat over one of the two air intakes, which was right behind the turret. It had a big fan just underneath the grillwork that I had to sit, kneel, or squat down on. These large fans pulled the air in from the top where we had to sit, with the force of a hurricane and blew the hot air out in the back. These tanks had a considerable amount of room on them, behind and beside the turret where we hung on.

As the tank's engines revved up as it started off, I felt the frigid air being sucked from around my body like I had no clothes on at all, frigid air traveling at a very high rate of speed. I was cold, colder than I had ever been in my life. I felt as though I was standing naked in a freezing blizzard. My buddy was right beside me sitting on the other fan that cooled the adjacent engine. There were only the two of us on this tank riding shotgun on this day. Well, the faster the tank traveled, the colder we got.

"This is General Patton's Pride and Joy, these big heavy tanks. I heard that they sent two hundred of them over from the States. I will bring you up-to-date on what has happened while you were in the hospital. They have five inches of armor on them, and let me tell you this, that cannon up there is a 90mm and it is bigger than the Krauts' 88s, not just in diameter, but the chamber is larger giving the shell more velocity, and the barrel is longer and the projectile is larger and more powerful. We are supposed to be headed for Mainz on the Rhine and we are supposed to cross it somewhere near there, I hear. Patton wants us to be in Berlin right away, which is the reason we are out here on the point leading the attack. They say that we guys, us, who are all men from our outfit riding these tanks, are further east than any other Allied troops and we are going to be in Berlin in a few days. Even with this freezing air flowing all over us, it's better than those damned cellars back there in Saarlautern. These are new tanks and we are on the point going to Berlin, right now. We have got to protect them from snipers with rifles trying to knock us off, and also snipers with Panzerfausts trying to knock this tank out, and anything else that we might see. We are to look out for ambush situations, like one of those big Tiger, or Panther tanks that the Krauts have, or an 88 hiding in the bushes or behind a barn somewhere, just waiting for us to come along." Ken told me, shaking; his lips were blue and quivering in the cold, too.

"How long do you think that it will take us to get there?" I asked Ken, as I was shaking and quivering from the cold.

"It won't be long now, that is if we don't freeze to death trying to make it. Do you think that you will be able to hit a Kraut if you see one with a Panzerfaust, if you even see him before he fires that thing at us, the way we are moving and bouncing around?" he asked.

"I don't know, but I am sure going to give it my best shot, or shots, if I have time to get them off before he fires at us. I am going to try to kill his ass before he kills us. These tankers can't see outside very well through those periscopes, so I guess we are their eyes and ears. You know this reminds me of back home deer hunting. I have a pretty keen eye. I grew up in the country, nothing but fields and woods for many miles. Being part Cherokee Indian, I feel perfectly at home in the woods and outdoors. I would come home from school when I was a kid, get my rifle and go down in the field, just hide at the edge of the woods and wait until dusk dark when the deer came out of hiding. They would jump into our fields to eat our crops and I would bring down a big fat buck almost every time. Getting him back home was the big job. I learned quite a bit about having a keen eye and ear. I would hear a twig break and then start looking for my buck. When they jumped into the field, the big buck was the first one to come in, and then he would wiggle his tail if he felt that all was clear and the does would follow him into the field. That was when I would bring down that big buck. So, there ain't much difference, except this time it ain't bucks that we are hunting, it's these damned Nazis with those Panzerfausts. Keep your eyes open, my dad used to tell me when we were hunting, 'Keep your eyeballs peeled.'" I related to my buddy above the roar of the engines as we sped eastward down a narrow country road.

Ken told me, "Did you know that you and I and the other men riding on these big new tanks are now in a special outfit called 'Patton's Raiders'?"

"No, I didn't know that. What does that mean?" I asked Ken.

"Well, it means that you and I and all of the others on these tanks have been handpicked as per General Patton's orders. He told our commanders that he only wanted men riding on, and protecting these tanks that were well disciplined and who had some good judgment and a lot of courage. He told them that he didn't want anything to happen to his tanks, and that he wanted the best men to be put on them that would protect them. There aren't but a few of these tanks over here in Europe, I hear. I have never heard how many of them are operational. The Krauts want these tanks badly and they are going to do everything in their power to destroy them. They would like to destroy all of them as well as we men riding on them. It would be a psychological victory for Hitler if they destroyed any or all of these tanks. Then, that would make General Patton awfully mad. That is what we have got to worry about. I don't think this is going to be an easy job," Ken told me.

"Well, does that mean that we are going to have to ride these tanks for the remainder of the war?" I asked Ken.

"That is what I have heard. We have been handpicked to do this job. All of the rest of the guys in our outfit are riding trucks and doing mopping up operations behind us, as well as trying to keep up with us while we are out here spearheading out on the point. They will follow us, and when we take a town late in the day, they will come in on trucks and secure it, stand door guard, search out buildings and cellars, do the mopping up, and guard the tanks while we and these tankers get some rest and sleep. At least we won't be standing door guard anymore. These tankers are hard-driving soldiers. I heard that they are not to put these tanks out there on the point where they may get hit when trouble starts, but to let the Sherman and the Chaffee light tanks do the dirty work, because General Patton wouldn't like it at all if one of these got knocked out. Someone's head would roll, wouldn't you think?"

"I would think so. So, now we are called, 'Patton's Raiders,' is that what we are?" I asked Ken.

"You said it. We are going to be right up there on the point all the way, spearheading to Berlin, riding shotgun on these big tanks. Right now we are on the point and further east than any other Allied Force and we are to remain up here on the point. Don't that make you proud? These tankers get up early, they move out before daybreak, and we gotta be on them and go when they are ready. I guess you could say that we are Patton's elite troops. That is what all of the guys are saying," Ken told me, as we both scanned the sides of the road ahead for Krauts hiding in the bushes, as well as any place that Kraut tanks and 88s may be hiding and waiting to knock us out.

Panzerfausts are an antitank weapon the Germans used. They were designed to be carried and fired by only one man, at an armored vehicle. The design is a big explosive head propelled by a pipe-like rocket extension filled with propellant. It is fired from a disposable hollow tube that is thrown away after it is fired. The tube has a flip-up sight on it and is fired from the shoulder, or hip, and they have no recoil because they are rocket propelled. They were very effective if they hit the right spot on a tank, like on the track or on the side, where the wheels and sprockets are. They were very plentiful and were used often by the Krauts, mostly near where their armored vehicles were.

"Yeah, these M-1 rifles aren't any good against anything but another human being, here. They sure won't do any good against a tank, it is a waste of ammo to even fire at a tank with our rifles. We have to protect ourselves and our tanks from snipers, whether they are using a sniper's rifle or a Panzerfaust, we gotta get 'em. You keep a good lookout on that side and I will keep a lookout on this side. You know, you shoot the one on your side and I will get the one on my side, like they taught us back in the States. We sure have to keep a sharp lookout ahead, beside us, as well as to our rear. How's your hand feeling?" Ken asked me.

"It's burning like hell, still bleeding, but I can still pull the trigger on this rifle. I am just worrying about getting frozen by that damned fan sucking this frigid air from all around my body. I feel colder than I ever have been." I told Ken.

I was also aware that we must keep a good lookout beside and behind us, in that the rear of the tank is the most vulnerable of all. So, in effect we had to swivel our necks all of the time in order to cover our rear as well. The tankers often referred to us as "swivel heads" because we had to keep a good lookout to the front and the back all the time. We not only had to keep a sharp lookout for enemy ahead, to the sides, and behind us, as well as watching the sky on sunny days for Messerschmitt fighter planes wanting to strafe us. The planes that we had to worry about were the German Messerschmitt ME-109s that had two machine guns in each wing firing at a target on the ground, which in our case was us men on these tanks that they strafed. We became mesmerized when it came to keeping a lookout for enemy soldiers, by constantly looking in every direction, especially over our shoulders, to the rear more so than to the front.

At that very moment I braced myself, pulled my right hand from my field jacket pocket and already had my rifle to my shoulder with my other hand. I braced myself on the turret and took a sight on an enemy soldier just ahead, aiming his Panzerfaust at us. I could see the Panzerfaust in his arms, since he was down on his knees, partially hidden behind a small pile of dirt on the side of the road ahead, and he was in the process of firing it.

I braced myself quickly and squeezed off a round. My sights were right on the Kraut's chest when I squeezed the trigger. I got off two rounds. We both saw him fall back onto the ground from the impact of my first bullet. His Panzerfaust fell to the ground in front of him. His head and body were partially behind this pile of dirt, but we could see his feet, toes up, straight up. That was all that mattered. The tankers saw what happened through their periscope. A few seconds later we were fired upon by German 88 artillery, apparently from their heavy tanks that were waiting in ambush for us up ahead.

"This is just what I have been expecting. We are in for a tough fight. I don't think that the Kraut that I shot would have been there if there hadn't been a Panzer unit ahead of us that he was trying to protect, hoping to knock us out," I told Ken.

Our tank pulled off the road, took cover behind some hedgerow bushes between two large fields—as did the other tanks in our group—and they all began to fire. We hit the ground, took cover as well as we could on the ground beside the tank. Someone surely had called in for heavy artillery, I hoped. I had a lot of faith in our artillery in observing how accurate they had been when they were firing at that bunker back at Saarlautern. I knew that we were moving too fast for our artillery to be in any position to fire at anything up here where we were. Then, just ahead of us, all hell broke loose. Enemy artillery shells came in, landing very close, really too close for comfort. The tankers were all bottled up inside, except the turret gunner who manned the .50 caliber machine gun mounted on ring mount on top of the turret. He always had his upper body protruding out of the turret in order to man the machine gun, and to observe for targets to fire his 90mm cannon at. When the gunner closed the hatch to the turret you could expect to be strafed, or fired upon by enemy artillery, and when he closed it we needed to find cover in some other place. We couldn't converse with them, but we had a ringside view of a tank battle that was shaping up.

Shells were exploding everywhere. Machine gun fire, both incoming, and outgoing, was so heavy that you couldn't tell where it was coming from, or who was firing at whom. I clung to the ground to avoid incoming machine gun fire. When one is on a tank, or in a similar situation under machine gun fire, he has to worry not only about the direct hit by a bullet but also about those that missed him, then ricocheting off the steel tank and hitting him on the rebound. The fire was very heavy. Machine gun bullets were ricocheting off our tank.

Their infantry were always behind our front lines where we were, and anxious to get a shot at one of our tanks, but the turret gunner with his .50 caliber machine gun kept all of them away, making our job easier in that none of the enemy infantry, or Wehrmacht, got close enough for us to see them, as we were lying there on the cold ground by the tank.

The most important job that we were to do was to keep a sharp lookout for not only snipers, but any kind of an ambush situation where there would be a Kraut tank, or an 88mm cannon sitting off to one side or the other, hidden in the bushes, behind a building, or wherever they wanted to fire on us from. We were acting as the eyes and ears of the tankers who were most always bottled up inside. If our tank got hit by an 88 that meant that the chances of survival of anyone riding in, or on it would be practically nil.

One of our light tanks, a Chaffee near us was hit and began burning. I saw one soldier climb out of the turret, bloody as hell, and he appeared to be pretty badly wounded. He couldn't move very fast to get out and away from the burning tank. I then saw another man trying to pull himself out the top of the turret, bloody and struggling desperately. I ran to the tank, climbed up on it, pulled on him, trying to get him out—he couldn't help much. I feared that the tank's fuel tanks would explode any moment. I pulled on him for all I was worth and got him up some. I then saw his left leg dangling and spinning around. It was bleeding badly. I couldn't get him out with that dangling leg catching on things. He put his arm around my neck to brace himself. I quickly took off my belt and put it tightly around his leg just above his knee. Then I took out my pocketknife and cut his trousers and cut the remaining amount of flesh that was holding his leg on, severing his leg, which fell back down into the tank. I worked frantically. I feared the fuel tanks would explode any moment and burn both of us to death. Since there was a fire inside, I also feared the shells inside would start exploding any second. I then pulled him out of the turret of the burning tank, down behind the turret, and then dragged him off of the tank

123

onto the ground pulling him as far away from it as I could. Then suddenly two medics arrived. They took over. Where they came from I will never know; it was like an act of God that they appeared so timely. I assumed that some of our support was catching up with us, or that the people in the other tanks were talking to someone on the radio.

I ran back to my tank that was now maneuvering around like it was about to go somewhere. I sure didn't want to be left there. They always moved around so that the German 88s couldn't get a sight on them, also searching for better cover and concealment, as well as finding a better position to fire from. As it stopped, finding a new and better position of cover, as well as a place to fire from, I caught up with it. I was as bloody as a stuck pig. No one said anything. In times like these, soldiers don't say anything. I don't really think that there was anything to say. I really didn't know what to say.

We waited to learn what the situation ahead was. The tank beside us was still burning. Ammo was going off inside it with loud explosions and billowing smoke, which added to all of the commotion of the battle going on all around us. Machine gun fire, rifle fire, and the 88s coming in and exploding around us, also the big 90mm on our Pershing was going off almost continuously making a hell of a noise.

Another one of our light tanks ahead of us took a hit from a Tiger tank's 88mm cannon as it maneuvered to find better cover, or to find a better shot at the Tiger. The Tiger had moved up into position from behind some buildings, stopped, and fired a head-on shot directly into one of our tanks. All inside, and the two infantrymen riding shotgun, were killed instantly. Then the Tiger backed up and took cover around the corner that it came from and we never saw it again.

That was their tactic—pull around a corner of a building, stop quickly and fire, then back up around the corner and flee to safety. I called it a hit-and-run tactic. Shellfire was all over the place. You couldn't tell who was shooting at whom unless you saw the muzzle blasts.

The Germans were advancing on us. They had bigger tanks. Their tanks had the widest treads that I had ever seen, and also the longest barrels, except for our Pershing. Also the Tiger and Panther had the lowest profile I had ever seen. It was awesomely frightening to even see one moving around, not to mention the strange rumbling sound that they made when they were moving. We had no close-range support to help us defend ourselves, and were out-manned in men, but not in armament, because the Pershings had 90mm, as opposed to the Tiger that had a 88mm. It is not the two millimeters that make much difference, it is the size of the charge in the shell casing that holds the powder charge that propels the shell at a much higher speed, doing more damage. It is the design of the projectile and the length of the barrel that makes it a more effective weapon. All of that design makes the difference, we soon learned. We had just lost two tanks and didn't know what else to do but to stand and fight till we died.

The tank commander told me, "We have a rule: no retreat. But sometimes we do have to make an orderly, strategic withdrawal, which no one ever wants to do, or even talk about."

I never knew of even one American soldier who was willing to give up one square inch of hard-earned ground that we had taken. I wondered who was in charge of this operation back at headquarters, and if they knew what was really going on up here, and if they were doing something about it. I had utmost faith in all of our commanders, but sometimes things didn't go as planned. We were going to get wiped out if we didn't get some support from somewhere, and soon. This was an ambush situation, which we sometimes called a tank trap. I am sure that the tankers were in radio contact with their command, and back at headquarters they were arranging for support for us, I theorized.

"Think positively and don't ever give up," my mother used to say to me.

We were all going to be annihilated by these Kraut tanks if we don't get some help soon, I thought. I prayed silently.

I asked Ken, "Are you a Christian?"

"Yeah, why do you ask?" He replied.

"Well, I just said a prayer. I asked God Almighty to help us, to save us, to give us the strength, courage, and ability to kick the hell out of these damned Nazis and allow us to win this battle, and this war. Do you think that you could help out by doing the same thing?" I asked him, not knowing him very well. We had been very busy for a while. None of us had the time for any conversation about getting to know very much about our fellow soldiers.

"God in Heaven, save us from these heathen bastards. Help us to kick them all the way back to Berlin. Amen."

He then looked at me and said, "Did I do it right?"

"Yes, I know He heard you. That was a good prayer and I pray that He will answer our Prayers. I know He will. We are all on His side. We will win this damned war with His help, so don't worry anymore, we will win this battle and the war too, but don't stop praying," I told my buddy.

The turret hatch opened and a sergeant pulled himself out and told me, "You did a fine job saving the soldier from that burning tank. Think he will survive? He is my buddy, we went through training together in Texas."

"With the help of God I think that he will. He is strong, he helped all that he could, talked to me most of the time, but he lost a lot of blood. I don't believe that he ever passed out. His leg is back there inside that burning tank. I had to finish cutting his leg off. It was blown almost off, about right at the knee, just some muscle left holding it on. What a bloody mess that was. I couldn't have gotten him out without doing it. His leg was just spinning around. I hated to do it, but there wasn't any other choice. Only two men got out—I suppose the third man died in the explosion or fire."

I told the tanker that the credit goes to the medics who happened to be close by. I later learned that they gave him glucose drip and morphine real soon. "Do you have a clean pair of pants down there anywhere? If you do, I would like to borrow them from you," I asked the rugged looking turret gunner.

"I think I have a pair right in front of you in my knapsack hanging there on the turret. Just flip up the flap and look in there and get them. You can have them—throw those bloody things away." the turret gunner told me.

I was lucky, so I took my boots off and changed pants right there on the rear end of that tank, but my skin, field jacket and long johns were almost covered with blood.

"What the hell happened to your hand, is there something wrong with it? Let me look at it," the gunner asked me.

I told him how my hand stuck to his frozen tank early this morning when I tried to pull myself up on it. I had lost my gloves somewhere. "There on that handle is the skin from the inside of my hand that froze to it." He gave me a large bandage, which didn't stick or stay on my dirty, bloody hand very long.

I heard the sound of more tanks coming up behind us. Soon I could see several Sherman tanks, and one Tank Destroyer, called a TD, which was a light-armored, faster tank, but with a big 105mm Howitzer mounted on an open-top turret. They pulled along by us, passing us by and then all hell broke loose just ahead as the Sherman and the Tank Destroyer battled it out with the Panzer unit at close range up ahead. They were firing head-on at each other. Tigers, I think they were, or Panthers—I couldn't tell the difference unless I got a very good look. The Tiger is the biggest, a big boxed and squared-off front end with awfully wide tracks, and a hell of a long cannon barrel. It had an 88 on it, which was longer than the Panther's that had a 75mm cannon on it.

It takes a lot of guts to fire any weapon head-on into another on-coming tank while it is firing at your tank. One of their tanks, a Tiger, was hit on the track by the TD, disabling the Tiger. The crew jumped out and ran. Then trucks loaded with infantry pulled up behind us, the infantry unloaded and spread out on each side of the road. This was some of my infantry outfit, all spread out on foot searching out the area for enemy foot soldiers that were protecting those Tiger tanks. The other Panzer heavy tanks had retreated and were now nowhere to be seen. Our men on the ground came in from the flank and ended all of the fighting in that town. They took a lot of prisoners.

We stayed in that location for a while and when the firing ceased a little, we sped past the Sherman and the knocked-out Tiger, firing our machine guns and the 90mm cannon artillery piece at some 88s and other vehicles up ahead. We knocked out several German half-tracks and Volkswagens that are equivalent to our jeeps, which the Krauts called a Kuppelwagen, as well as trucks and other small vehicles, as we sped down the road beyond the village.

Several German 88 millimeter artillery pieces were hit by our tanks and knocked out. Why they didn't fire at us up close I will never know, but it appeared that their crews had abandoned them or were in the process of doing so. Enemy soldiers were standing by the road with their hands over their heads. I don't think that their gunners wanted to have a face-to-face showdown with our Pershings, Shermans, and light, but fast, Chaffee tanks bearing down on them. The Chaffee tanks are fast and could go forty miles an hour. The Pershing could only go twenty-five miles per hour, probably because they had all of that heavy armor, which was five inches of steel, plus a hell of a long cannon barrel.

It was as if the enemy also knew that our infantry was coming for them, so they just abandoned their 88s and other weapons and fled, or surrendered. I had experiences before, back in Saarlautern with those 88s. They are long barreled, high velocity, flat trajectory, artillery pieces that they would sometimes fire at only one man and they are extremely accurate. They fired armor piercing shells at tanks and also high-explosive fragmentation shells at everything else. I saw many that were just abandoned rapidly when our infantry and tanks bore down on them. We did the mopping up operation for that little battle, with the help of my infantry outfit. I would have traded places with those men on the ground anytime and let one of them ride this motorized bunker.

Later that evening we stopped at a small village where white flags were flying from almost every window. It was a quiet and peaceful looking little place. We searched out the area, put out perimeter guards, and found a very comfortable place to sleep. I found a feather comforter to cover with and slept very warm.

The following morning the tankers were up before daylight, yelling to wake us up, "Lets hit the road." We followed them to the tanks, and this day we had about six or eight riflemen riding shotgun on this big Pershing tank. We had no breakfast, coffee, or anything; it was just wake up and go outside and climb on a tank, and move out. Again, it was just another day of moving out before daybreak, all day on the tanks, watching, observing, hanging on for dear life, fighting our way in to take a town or village at the end of the day, where there was always heavy resistance. It was always, it seemed, in the late afternoon when the hardest fighting started and it was always the most frightening. We fought hard to take those towns so that we could have a decent and safe place to sleep. It was always a fight from before daylight until into the night, day after day.

CHAPTER 16

Deep in Enemy Territory, Inside Germany

"Battles are won by a few brave men who refuse to fear, who push on."

—GENERAL GEORGE S. PATTON (1885–1945)

Now we were pretty deep into enemy territory, it seemed. According to the tanker, our intelligence section didn't know what we would face ahead. The weather was so cold, cloudy and snowy-looking; the observations planes couldn't see anything, so we were just flying blind on those tanks, deep into enemy territory. The enemy has scattered and become disorganized, and had been routed out of their strongholds in that immediate area, at least for now.

As we advanced many enemy soldiers had decided to surrender and were standing by the road with their hands in the air. Some had a white piece of cloth in their hand waving it overhead. I learned they were forbidden by their command and were subject to be shot, if they even possessed a white piece of cloth. We waved them on toward the rear echelon with their hands on top of their heads. They were more tired and dirty-looking than we were. When we stopped they would ask for something to eat, saying, *"Abense essen, bitta?"* (Do you have anything to eat, please?)

We continued down this road at high speed so as to make it difficult for the German artillery to hit us. We were alone again, just us Raiders on a few tanks out on the point, spearheading to our next objective, but I didn't even know what the next objective was, except that our main objective was Berlin. Nor did I ever know what time of day it was, or what day of the month, or even the day of the week it was. We were too busy for such trivialities. Our tanks always moved at their top speed. One reason was that they tried to cover as much territory as possible, and second, they had to move fast to avoid being hit by enemy artillery. Even though the Pershing tanks could only move at twenty-five miles per hour, it really felt like they were going sixty miles per hour.

Where we were is still a mystery. Map reading had been one of my great interests and I always wanted to know where we were and where we were going. I had never been lost before and always was able to stay oriented. Only the people in the command, the tankers, scouts, and reconnaissance units had maps and knew where we were and where we were going. We had been traveling in remote areas on country roads, and off of the main thoroughfares. I could never remember the names of any of the towns and cities we took—they flew by us so fast, then the next one—so it was a waste of time to try to keep up with where we were.

On the point, as we were then, you don't see all of the support personnel that are behind you. You have a tendency to believe that you are the only few soldiers anywhere out there on the point and you are all alone out there in no man's land. You get the feeling of loneliness and abandonment when you are not in contact with, or can't see, any of your support.

Our orders obviously were to just go full speed ahead. That we did for most of the morning. It was a little warmer now but still cold. The weather was getting a little more clear now. Ahead, I could see a small farm village. I told my buddy, "I bet we are in for another battle up ahead. I see a small village; they are not going to want to give it up, either. Little villages are a good cover for enemy 88s and Panzer units, like the ones that escaped us back there yesterday."

As we approached this small cluster of farmhouses ahead, we received some incoming enemy artillery fire that was very close. No direct hits, but the tank drivers sped up. Some went into the fields on the side of the road, probably suspecting mines in the road, or just scattering out to make themselves a difficult target or to make a flanking action against any opposition ahead.

The artillery fire got heavier and closer to us. We couldn't stop; they would hit us for sure. We were hanging on for dear life. There was no way that we could have fired on, much less hit, a sniper, nor could I or my buddy hit one of these Krauts who had a Panzerfaust. Suddenly the lead tank, a Chaffee, was hit on the tread by a shell from an artillery piece or an enemy tank. It was knocked out, but not much damage. The shelling got worse. Shrapnel from the shells was hitting the tank and making a hell of a ricocheting noise. All of us got down as low as we could behind the turret to take cover from the flying shrapnel. Suddenly all of our tanks pulled to the side of the road, near this farm village, dispersed, and took cover behind farm buildings, trees and hedgerows. These were not like those in France where there were very old dirt roads with old tree lines along fences that were very ancient, but here there were just rows of trees and bushes separating different fields.

Then our artillery began again. Our tank took cover behind some bushes and killed their engines. It was quiet now. I could hear our heavy artillery shells passing overhead. I assumed that they were the big 155mm cannons that had about a twenty-mile range, and were very accurate. They carried a hell of a wallop. We could not hear the artillery that fired them, nor hear the shells when they hit their targets, because of the long distance they were shelling. The sound of the shells flying above was an eerie sound, a whirring, swishing, deadly sound overhead, many of them, dozens of them passing overhead. This was a familiar sound by now. It was a reassuring sound, which was even more spine-tingling when you heard them passing overhead at nighttime. It was a sound that gave you faith and courage that the guys behind the lines in artillery units were doing a fine job, as they were always doing and we riflemen riding shotgun on these tanks knew we were not alone, or unsupported, or forgotten. When we were on the point heading for a sizable target we could always hear these heavy artillery shells going over, if the engines were not running. They would be shelling and softening up our next objective.

"This ain't just a village, it's a small town that is up ahead. It sure looks bigger now. Hey, keep looking behind to see if the Shermans and TDs are coming on up here where we need them. Must be something big ahead, we need some big guns up here to help us take this place," my buddy said to the tanker, whose upper body was sticking out of the turret.

"What is that town ahead up there, Sarge?" I asked.

We never got an answer. Who cared? We never knew where we were. What difference did it make anyway? We will have forgotten it by tomorrow, even if we did know.

"Now that small village just ahead is what we want to take before dark," the tank turret gunner explained to us.

"How are we going to take that town up there, Sarge?" Ken asked.

"That is a good question. I don't think anyone has figured it out yet how we are going to do it. It ain't gonna be no piece of cake," he replied.

"Speaking of a piece of cake, Sarge, you don't have any spare K, or C rations with you, do you, that you can spare? We haven't had anything to eat all day. I am absolutely starved. I think that my buddy here is, too. We are out of water in our canteens, as well," I said to the tanker.

"Me too, I ain't never been so damned hungry and thirsty," my friend said, and by this time I had a short conversation with him and the gunner, and as we introduced ourselves. I learned that the gunner's name was Larry Clements, as I recall.

Feeling sorry for us, I guess, he gave us each a K Ration and told us to get our water from the Jerry can strapped onto the side of the tank.

While we were stopped, behind cover, during a lull in the fighting, presumably waiting for some heavy support to arrive, we got off the tank, sat down on the ground, leaned up against a tree and ate our rations. I ate the can of meat, stuck the small roll of toilet paper, the four cigarettes, sugar cubes, coffee packet, and paper matches into my field jacket pocket, and then munched away on the fruit bar. The fruit bar was a candy-bar-sized bar of compressed dried fruit, figs, apricots, raisins, and other fruit pressed hard into a bar. You would have to take your time to eat it, but you would get some energy from eating them.

One needs a lot of water to drink when eating a fruit bar, because they swell up in your belly. I felt a little better, under the circumstances.

We all felt that this was a lull before the battle. It was quiet now for a change, not a soul to be seen, no rear echelon personnel behind us, nothing moving anywhere. The quietness was frightening. It seemed that when we were on the point for a long time, we began to believe we few were the only Americans in Germany, and were lost and all alone.

It was now midafternoon or later. Something just had to happen before dark. It seemed that the tank battles happened in the early morning and late afternoon. The Germans didn't like to fight at night, but they often did. We had to get entrenched under some sort of cover before dark, I thought, but no need to try to predict the future in this situation right now. We had both drunk a canteen full of water, so we filled our canteens again from the Jerry can on the tank. It was getting to be that safe drinking water was as valuable as gasoline, and just as hard to get. We talked of the impending battle before dark and did a little talking on how we were ever going to take this town ahead and get some sleep tonight. This was always the situation in the evening: Were we going to be able to get any sleep and when and where, and if there would be a bed that we could sleep in, rather than on the floor, and would we be able to keep warm?

Sure enough, late in the afternoon they started shelling the hell out of us. All hell suddenly broke loose. Those 88s were hitting all around us. I don't think that they could see us, but they had a damned good idea where we were. About five or six of our tanks spearheading out ahead, now were all stopped, waiting for something. One never knew what the command back there was doing or planning. We foot soldiers never knew what was taking place; we just went where we were told to—and didn't ask any questions.

I quickly became aware that the tanks don't just rush into any situation where there may be an ambush set for them, like a big Tiger, a Panther, a TD with a 105 Howitzer on it, or just one of their 88mm cannons sitting around a corner waiting for one of our tanks to come by. The infantry is most always sent in first to solve this problem. It didn't sound reasonable at first, but this is the way it is done and it works. It was apparent that we couldn't just risk one of those big new

Pershings, or any kind in fact, by allowing them to go right into a trap where they would be knocked out. It was the job of the infantry, working in conjunction with our armor, to solve this situation and protect the tanks.

Our heavy artillery began again. We could hear the shells passing overhead, many of them, hundreds of them, but couldn't hear them hit their targets, wherever that was. All we knew was that some place was getting the living hell bombarded out of it. It's a good feeling to know that you are not alone and that there are others in this fight also. It is also a very frightening sound, because you know that some heavy damage is being done up ahead. Many times you feel lonely, lost and abandoned, because you don't see all of the support groups following behind you. Sometimes I refused to believe that there was anyone back there behind us.

Our Chaffee light tanks were faster and more maneuverable, yet they were not so light either. They are the fast ones with light artillery on them, a 75mm cannon, lighter steel plating of about two-and-one-half inches of armor protecting them, limited in what they could do, but fast. They were the tanks that seemed to be more on the point. They were the scouts, it seemed, for the larger and newer Pershings. Oftentimes I was assigned to ride these Chaffee tanks, and you had to hang on for dear life, or fall off.

The Germans seemed to always know just where these Pershing tanks were, and it was obvious that they wanted desperately to knock them out. We knew that they wanted to wipe them all out as soon as possible. We soon learned that the Nazis knew exactly where each one of these big new Pershings were and they concentrated on trying to knock them out. It seemed that the Krauts were using their 88s, hidden in an ambush situation, waiting for us to come along.

The German Tiger tanks had five inches of armor plate on them, plus an 88mm cannon, compared to our Sherman's 76mm cannon and three-and-one-half inches of armor. Even though it is only one millimeter larger than the cannon on the light tank, it has a larger breach, larger charge of powder in the shell casing, all of which gives it a higher velocity—which I learned, helped the armor-piercing shell penetrate the heavy armor of the Panzers. Our Pershings were kind of held in reserve and let the others do the little jobs.

It was now about time for the heavy stuff again. I thought the heavy armor of the Shermans ought to be getting here by now, along with the TDs and a lot of infantry.

"Sarge, what have we got out there ahead of us? What are these Shermans coming up here for—another heavy battle? God, I am scared now, more scared than yesterday. What do you think is going to happen?" Ken asked the tanker.

"Ken, there ain't no telling," the tanker told him. "We will just have to wait and see. I know that we have lots of resistance up ahead. The Krauts don't want us to take the village just ahead or that city further on up, and they are determined to stop us before we get to the Rhine. I hear that the Krauts are trying to delay us so that they can get all of their vehicles across the Rhine and then blow the bridge there so we can't get across. But we have to take this place ahead of us now."

"It is going to be a foot soldier's job to take this little village before dark. We can take it but we can't hold it and protect it from German infantry through the night. These tanks don't do much good in a city, especially at night. We need some infantry to help us protect them while all of us get a little shut-eye."

The tank gunner continued to tell us what the situation was ahead; "There are just too may gun emplacements. They have maps of this whole area and have artillery spotters everywhere with radios to tell them where we are, and they give their artillery our coordinates and then zero in on us. Watch out for them damned 88s; they are deadly if they hit anything close-up. It would take a direct hit up close for them to destroy this Pershing, which has five inches of armor, but they fire lots of rounds with those 88s. It is a deadly artillery piece. I saw them in a village back there recently, hit every intersection with 88 fires. Just like clockwork. We can't go much further today."

The tank gunner continued, "We don't do any night fighting and it is getting too close to dark to do much more today, plus all of our tanks are about out of fuel. I don't know what we are going to do with you guys tonight if the infantry don't show up. We will just come back to some out-of-the-way building and try to take turns standing guard while others sleep. Just any small out-of-the-way place that we few can defend all night will be the best that we can do without the infantry. We will put you guys outside as perimeter guards while we get some sleep; you will be able to get a little, too, we will relieve you. You can expect some foot soldiers to arrive in a little, I hope. We can't hold ground with these tanks. You ground pounders are the only ones who can take it and hold it. So, look to your rear and soon you should be able to see some tanks and trucks loaded with infantry—or they may be on foot."

"We also need to refuel, and there should be some fuel trucks arriving tonight. We ain't retreating, we ain't going to give up one damned inch of this ground, we will hold it at all cost. But we should have some support here soon, so keep a lookout for them. You guys will then get a little rest, I hope. I know you are tired. Hope you will be on here with us tomorrow. Never know for sure who will be riding shotgun on this tank." Sergeant Clements told us.

Here, there were no living beings to be seen anywhere, not even a chicken, dog, or cat. Just us and the enemy. Just about an hour before dark we saw a column of Sherman tanks and TDs coming up from the rear. Behind them were trucks loaded with infantry, behind them I could see over the fields, ambulances, heavy equipment, and supply trucks for miles and miles. It was a relief seeing the support coming up behind us, which was something that we seldom ever saw.

All of us had a fear of being cut off, surrounded, without the help of any infantry and armor during the night. All of us, including the tankers had that fear of us being cut off and surrounded, and no support being able to get up to us. It was a true but frightening thought. Being too far out on the point and getting surrounded and cut off by the Krauts, was our worse fear. Now we had help coming and plenty of it, coming up fast. So, we could feel a little more secure.

The Germans must know that we are coming and that we have a lot of support. We watched as the Sherman tanks scattered out and pulled into strategic positions on each flank, where they took cover behind bushes and trees. They took up positions on the sides of the road, behind bushes, shacks, and anywhere to take cover.

My captain at Camp Blanding used to say, "If they can't see you, they can't hit you."

I felt better, more secure than I did when it was just us few against a lot of enemy. I knew that the Sherman tanks had plenty of supplies on them, so I went over to one and asked for some rations, if they had any to spare, hopefully some C rations.

"Sure, soldier, you look tired and hungry. How many do you want? I have got some cans of meatballs and spaghetti here, but it ain't hot. I put a can on the engine sometimes to heat it up, but these are cold. Do you want them?"

"You bet I do, I am starved and so is my buddy here, too. Do you have some water? We need to fill our canteens," I asked the turret gunner—remembering what my father had told me what he had heard about the drinking water in WWI: "If you drink the water from these shallow farm wells in Europe, you will get dysentery."

"Take all you want. There is a Jerry can of water strapped on there on the side of the tank, you will have to unstrap it and take it down, but get all you want, and tell your buddy to get some too."

I thanked the gunner in the turret of the Sherman, we got our canteens filled with some good fresh-tasting water, and each of us got a can of spaghetti and meatballs. Even though they were cold it was a feast for us. It was terrible having to bum something to eat all of the time.

It was just we "Raiders," as we were called, up front, riding on these tanks that were having to scrounge for a bite to eat all the time. So, I asked the tank commander, "Why can't our command back there somewhere get us some chow up here so we won't be starving to death all of the time and having to bum from you guys?"

The tanker replied, "If you only knew how congested all of the roads are back there behind us, you would understand. Every vehicle has to have a priority to get on any road. Your chow truck is about a hundred miles back there behind us. This is about the best that you can expect. They won't ever be able to catch up with us the way we are moving. We get our fuel, ammo, and rations that are sent up on a special truck from our outfit, and your outfit is supposed to provide yours. But they can't get it up here to you guys because they probably don't have the priority on the roads. So you are just out of luck, it seems. I guess that you would say that it is a logistical problem. On the other hand, they may be sending your rations up to your platoon that is back there somewhere riding trucks and they may be eating them for you, thinking that they are just some extras. It's pretty lonesome up here on the point, ain't it, soldier?"

While talking to the Sherman tank gunner I asked him what our objective was.

He replied, "It's that town just ahead, for tonight. The more tanks and infantry we have with us when we stop at night like this, the less likely that we will be overrun. We sure don't like it when the infantry don't get up here to us in the evenings. We are really way up front, on our own, in the middle of enemy territory, until the infantry catches up with us to hold what we take."

I told him that I knew that some place was getting the hell knocked out of it by our artillery. I asked him, "Did all of this shelling mean that we were going to have to fight in a pile of rubble again?"

Soon the infantry arrived. I saw some of my buddies that I hadn't gotten to know very well and hadn't seen since I had been riding on tanks. I felt like an orphan, fighting in one outfit in Saarlautern, and then regrouped with my assigned platoon, then here I am with a bunch of hell-bent-for-leather tankers riding shotgun on these new Pershings. Everyone was apprehensive, quiet, deadly serious, and on guard. Then, suddenly I saw our lieutenant who came walking up as usual, when most unexpected, and out of nowhere.

"God, I am glad to see you, Lieutenant. I have been riding these damned tanks, half-frozen, the skin peeled off my hand when I grabbed the frozen handle on that turret yesterday morning, to pull myself up on that tank and the skin of my hand stuck to the frozen steel and peeled the skin right off when I tried to let go of it. It's O.K. though. I just am concerned about where I am going to find a place for my tired body tonight to get a little rest, and get out of the cold as much as I can," I told him, as I briefed him on the day's action.

"Here, take my gloves. I will get some more. Go over there to that truck and there are some blankets in the back. Get you a couple, hang on to them, a couple for Ken too, and team up with some of our other men and find a comfortable place to sleep tonight, that is, if you can. Bring a blanket with you when you get on the tank in the morning. If you don't have any gloves, use the blanket to grab hold of a cleat on the tank to pull yourself up with.

"Just as soon as everyone is in place we are going to take that little village up ahead, so we can have a decent place to sleep. We have enough infantry up here now to take and hold it, with the help of all of these tanks. Then we will deploy perimeter guards and you guys can all get some rest. We are going to have a tough fight tomorrow. Things are getting tougher. The Germans are going to defend this city ahead, probably to the last man. They are highly skilled soldiers, so be on your guard and tell all your buddies to do the same. Be smart, alert, clever—protect yourself, don't try to be a hero, you aren't any good to your country when you are dead. You know the rest. By the way, the tanker that you pulled out of that knocked-out tank, and you had to cut his leg off to get him out, well, I just heard on the radio that he is doing O.K. and is expected to recover, thanks to you. The medics told me to tell you that you did a great job, and saved his life," Lieutenant Anderson related to me.

"Appreciate the compliment, Lieutenant, just another day's work. Glad to do it for the guy. I just hope that some GI would do the same for me. You know, here is my knife that I did it with. When I came into the Army my father who is a livestock man—we raise lots of cattle, sheep, horses, and so forth—well, he went to New Orleans to a store where he buys his stock knives, and he bought this and gave it to me when I left and told me that I would need it. It is made of prewar German steel that sharpens real well and will hold an edge very good. Can you imagine that? The metal in it was probably smelted right back there in the Saarlautern area. It comes in handy for lots of things, like opening C ration cans, when I can get one. I didn't know I would ever have to cut a man's leg off with it, though. If I hadn't had this knife, we both would probably have been killed when that tank exploded, because I would have still been there trying to get him out. I am sure glad to see you again, Lieutenant. Hope I will be back with you guys soon. I don't like riding these damned tanks. I would rather be down on the ground where I can shoot, hide, and maneuver, whatever it takes though to get the job done, that is all that counts. You know we have got to stop that insane man up there in Berlin. I really hope that I am the one that captures him."

"Stick with these tankers until further orders. These guys need some good men for their protection, as well as for the protection of those tanks, otherwise they wouldn't get very far if it wasn't for guys like you. It looks like you men on these tanks are spearheading on them, further out on the point into enemy territory than any others in the Allied Forces. You men on these tanks are now part of what is called, 'Patton's Raiders.' All of you men riding on these tanks have been selected according to General Patton's special order. He only wants men on them who have three qualities, which are intelligence, discipline, and courage. All of these tanks are very special to General Patton and he demands that the best men only be put on them to protect them. You men are lucky, you have been handpicked for this job. You are making history, you are leading the way, so don't let these tankers down—General Patton, either. They need men like you, so keep up the good work. I hear also that you got a Kraut who was about to fire a Panzerfaust at your tank," he told me.

"Well, I did yesterday morning. How did you hear about it?" I asked.

"I heard about it from a tank commander on the radio. I heard that you got him with the first shot. You saved your tank, the crew, you, and Ken. The tankers liked what you did. That is good soldiering," he said.

Suddenly all hell broke loose. The orders came down to take the village ahead, a large group of farmhouses clustered together. Everything seemed in place to do it. All of the tanks spread out across the fields on each side of the road, and we bore down on this village with infantry right along beside the tanks. The TDs, and the Shermans took the lead; the smaller, faster Chaffee tanks took up the flanks. All spread out and as we bore down on that village. We took artillery fire from every direction it seemed.

Our infantry was right along with us on foot. They did the cleanup operation after our Pershings and Shermans did their job of knocking out all of their tanks and field artillery pieces that weren't able to flee the area. We had the whole town surrounded with tanks and infantry. We knocked out vehicles of all kinds, killed or captured all of their infantry; it was like shooting ducks in a pond after we knocked out their big tanks. We killed, captured, and wounded their soldiers, destroyed all of their equipment, with only a few of our troops either killed or wounded. The village was ours. We were getting real good at this kind of thing. The infantry surrounded it and then moved in for the kill, to kill any holdouts who hadn't surrendered or fled and offered no resistance.

I met up with some of the men from my company; we found a comfortable place to sleep and notified the tank crew where we could be located the next morning. We couldn't build a fire to get dry and warm because if the enemy saw the smoke, which they would, they would probably shell the hell out of us. They were everywhere, it seemed, watching where we were and how many of us there were. They knew all of the time just where each of these big Pershings was located because of the civilian intelligence network that they had. We learned that the civilians were instructed to provide the German command with vital information about our whereabouts. The Krauts knew exactly when and where to expect us.

I found a hand-operated water pump, got enough water to shave, as well as washed lots of dried blood off of my skin, using my steel helmet as a washbasin. I felt like a different person. I was amazed at what I could carry in the pockets of my field jacket, shirt, and pants. I had several little can openers that come with rations but don't work very well, candy bars, cigarettes, which I didn't smoke, but bartered for chocolate bars. I also had fruit bars, small packets of toilet paper that came in the rations, cubes of sugar, packets of Postum coffee, my wallet, a comb, a toothbrush, razor, and various and sundry articles—and of course, my pocketknife. I could not conceive of an infantryman in combat not having a knife of some kind. There wasn't much that I had that wasn't an actual necessity. I also had my Bible that my dear mother gave me. I carried it in my shirt pocket over my heart. I had not had an opportunity to read it, but knowing that it was there was a great comfort.

I found a bunk bed built into the wall of one of the houses and I claimed it as mine for the night. With the two blankets the lieutenant had given me, I slept rather warm that night in my bloody field jacket, helmet, and boots, holding onto my rifle. I didn't even have to pull guard duty any that night—thanks to Lieutenant Anderson.

CHAPTER 17

Crossing the Rhine River

"Brad, for God's Sake, tell the world that
we are across the Rhine. I want the whole
world to know that we made it before
Montgomery started across. I have looked
forward to this for a long time."

—GENERAL GEORGE S. PATTON (1885–1945)

There was heavy fighting—mostly enemy foot soldiers and not too many armored vehicles, that now offered little or no resistance as we approached the river. All of the enemy tanks seemed to have already crossed the river on the old steel bridge to the safety of the east side. After the Germans got all of their heavy equipment across they blew up the old steel bridge, which was somewhere between Mainz and Oppenheim.

An infantry group had crossed in boats before the bridge was commenced and established a bridgehead on the other side to prevent enemy machine guns, snipers, and mortars from firing on the engineers who were beginning to construct the bridge. We had been traveling in somewhat out-of-the-way routes to the Rhine. As we got close to it, we saw many vehicles that were moving up, bringing all kinds of equipment and other material and supplies.

Near that bridgehead was a madhouse of engineers, antiaircraft batteries, and other combat units that were there to help build the bridge and to protect the bridgehead. The big steel bridge nearby, to the south, which had been blown up by the Germans, lay partly submerged in the river just to the south of the pontoon bridge under construction. We were told that the antiaircraft gun emplacements around the bridgehead had shot down more than thirty German Luftwaffe planes that strafed them during the construction of that pontoon bridge.

We had stopped near there and were waiting our turn to cross. When we moved up to the Rhine River there was a bottleneck of tanks and vehicles of every description waiting to cross this big river. We learned that it took priority to go across and we were considered top priority. The engineers had just finished the bridge when we crossed. It was raining, misting, and heavily overcast that morning. We got near the big pontoon bridge, called a treadway bridge, newly constructed, and we had to wait. There was a jeep stopped up ahead, about midway of the bridge, holding up traffic. Finally the jeep moved on across, as well as some other vehicles following it. The jeep stopped on the far side. We learned that General Patton was in that jeep. It was soon our turn to cross; we followed some other tanks across.

Riding the tank across that pontoon bridge, I looked down at the pontoons and the water and I would have sworn that we were going to sink. The tank had to speed up its engines to get across the bridge, in that its weight made it go down in the water so much that it was an uphill climb all the way across. I was convinced that the bridge would not hold this heavy tank and it would come apart and we would sink and drown with all of our equipment on, but it didn't and we made it across quickly at high speed.

We learned later that General Patton had his jeep driver to stop midway across the bridge. He got out of the jeep and stood on one of the treadways of the pontoon bridge and urinated in Hitler's largest river and had his picture taken doing it. He did it on the left, or downstream side. One of General Patton's stature would never "piss into the wind," or "upstream into a river." He made sure that the Army Signal Corps photographers were there to take his picture doing it, too.

We maneuvered our way through the narrow backstreets of this town where we came off of the bridge until we got on a main thoroughfare. This was someplace south of Mainz, or a suburb of Mainz. We sped to the northeast as fast as those tanks could go. About noon the weather cleared up considerably, and at one point I could see the city of Frankfurt off to the south of us. We continued all that day without hardly any resistance, but there were many Nazi soldiers standing by the road with their hands over their heads, surrendering. I notice one thing that made me curious and that was that everywhere along the roads that we were on, you could see thousands of Kraut fuel cans. They looked kind of like our five-gallon Jerry cans that we used for water and fuel. They were everywhere. I assumed that fuel came in them, that they refueled their tanks and other vehicles, and just threw the cans away, having no further need for them.

The bottleneck formed by the pontoon bridge had delayed our supplies and support from the rear from getting up to us quickly. Fuel, ammo, and rations were in very short supply. Everyone was concerned about us getting enough fuel, ammo, and rations, in order to make the maximum progress. We were expected to average forty mile advance per day deep into enemy territory. We also realized that it was very dangerous to be out of fuel and supplies, spearheading into a town and being cut off and not being able to fight our way out of a pocket, and at the same time being out of supplies. This made everyone apprehensive. It was our greatest concern. It was because we were moving so fast and in uncharted territory, not knowing what kind of enemy resistance there was ahead of us. We all realized that we were very vulnerable to a counterattack, or being cut off and surrounded, in that we were now so far out ahead of all of our support.

The following morning it was "up and at 'em" by daybreak. I got on the same tank again today, the lead tank that I always seemed to be on. Ken stuck close by and was with me that cold and rainy early morning. There were no special assignments as to which tank we could ride. In the mornings we just grabbed a tank, or usually the tank commander would yell at me to come on and get aboard. Sergeant Clements was glad to see all of us; some men from my squad were on his tank that morning. When he saw us climbing up onto the tank he said, "Man, I am glad to see all of you guys again today. You guys have brought us good luck, hope today will be much better than what it has been, though."

Just as we were getting on that tank Sergeant Lars Agneberg came up and handed me his poncho that he had taken off to give to me. This was a large square piece of lightweight waterproof material with a hole in the center that you put over your head. It had a drawstring on it to tighten around your neck. I really needed it badly, and I appreciated him doing this for me greatly. I had never felt so tired, sleepy, cold, and hungry and I guess he could see that. Also at that time I had two bandoleers of ammo around my neck that were getting awfully heavy to carry. The bandoleers were nothing more than a cotton cloth material that held about eight clips of ammo, with a strap that soon twisted into a narrow string that was cutting into my shoulder. I gave these two bandoleers to Sergeant Lars and told him that they were cutting into my shoulder, and I couldn't carry them anymore. I had even slept with them around my neck each night. I also had about eight clips in my cartridge belt, so I didn't think I needed to carry that much. I kept the poncho for a few days and lost it in all of the activities that we were engaged in at that time.

We rode tanks all that day, capturing quite a few prisoners who were disorganized and indicating that they wanted to surrender. I believed that if they still had food and fuel that they would still be fighting. The road was littered with abandoned German war machinery, either damaged by our artillery or tank fire, out of fuel, or broken down, and it lay there useless with its crewmembers holding their hands over their heads. We just waved them to the rear for the men on the trucks to deal with.

As we approached this large forest, the tanks were no longer very useful, so we were ordered off of them and we joined our units of infantry on the ground to search out some pockets of resistance in the forest area ahead. We found many pockets of resistance that were very strategically located, like well-positioned machine gun nests, artillery positions that were set up just around the bend of a small road through this big forest, just waiting for one of our tanks to come along. We were able to capture quite a few Krauts after we attacked them on foot, firing and maneuvering until we got the upper hand. We usually came upon their pockets of resistance from all three sides, so they usually surrendered when they realized that they were surrounded. We killed quite a few of them with our rifle fire. Many surrendered.

On one occasion, we got off of the tanks so that they could pull back while we searched the area ahead of us for an ambush site. We walked along, reconnoitering some woods along a hilltop and found nothing but some Panzer tank tracks. As I walked alone, back toward the rear, searching for my tank, I was walking down this two-trail woods road, in some bushes, and walked right upon one of our Sherman tanks just sitting there facing me. It was very well camouflaged. It shocked me, in that I didn't know we had any other tanks that far up. The tanker stuck his head out of the turret and asked me what I had seen up ahead. I was continuously amazed at how very cautious and particular all of these tankers were. They were all as rough and tumble as one could be, but still they were as particular and precise in their actions and movements as a ballet dancer. I finally found my tank and we moved out again.

On one occasion we were walking down this road with trees on both sides. It was so quiet and deserted that you felt like something was about to happen. It did. We were walking on each side of this narrow road, men on each side, several paces apart, when suddenly we were fired upon by machine guns. We all hit the ground in the ditches on each side of the road. Mortar shells and screaming meemies were fired by the dozens from their launchers at us. All of this stuff started coming in all around. The ditches were muddy, but we gladly hit them belly down. Then, in came some 88 shells landing all around us. Some of the shells exploded when they hit the treetops above us, spewing shrapnel every which way. We were totally pinned down.

This continued for almost an hour. Then some of our tanks came down the road right in the face of the machine gun fire and began firing like all hell was breaking loose. One of our tanks knocked out an 88 down the road, which had fired on our tank but had missed it, in that it was moving so fast. Our tank then knocked out several strategically located machine gun nests that had us pinned down and cleared the whole area in a very short while. We now could take our faces out of the mud and come out of the ditches. We boarded our tank and as we passed by where the machine gun nests had been, dead German soldiers were lying sprawled around everywhere. It was the 90mm cannon, the .30 and .50 caliber machine guns on it, that did all the damage. They quickly came to our rescue. The tanks led the way to the next village with us riding on them, hanging on for dear life—there were so many of us riding on them. We occupied this village for the remainder of that day and night.

The following day most all of us in my platoon rode shotgun on those tanks again. The weather had cleared somewhat and just as the tank commander told me, "Expect some Messerschmitts to come over and strafe us when we have clear weather like this. The cloud cover has so far kept them from doing that, but keep a good lookout and when you see or hear one, we will stop and you guys just jump off and take cover in a ditch, or behind the tank, if they come at us from the front, or somewhere, wherever you can find a place out of the way of their bullets."

Sure enough it wasn't long before we were riding along on this column of tanks—all of them were Pershings—down this narrow dirt road in a forest of tall trees. There were about eight of us riflemen on each tank. We saw and heard overhead, coming right at us, one, two, three Messerschmitt ME-109 fighter planes, one right after the other, coming straight for us from the front. They were coming right at us, from right out of the sun in the early morning, making it hard for us to see them. All of the tank commanders had their hatches open and were all on the lookout for them. I imagined that they were, or had been, in radio contact with other units who had told them what to expect. All of the tanks came to a sudden stop and the turret hatches were quickly closed. All of us jumped off and piled into ditches on each side of the road. The ditches had mud in them and we just buried our faces in that mud as the planes flew right over us, spewing bullet everywhere. Miraculously no one was wounded.

CHAPTER 18

The Sleeping Enemy Soldier

"Those who expect to reap the blessings of freedom, must, like men, undergo the fatigue of supporting it."

—THOMAS PAYNE (1737–1809)

Another day, and day after day, all of them were getting to be about the same thing over and over, each day being like the previous one. Time flew by. We never knew what time it was. I didn't have a watch or a calendar. Even though if I would have had them, I would never have had the time to even look at them, so I guess I was just as well off without them. I had acquired a built-in clock and always seemed to know approximately what time it was. It was pretty accurate, too.

We hardly ever knew the names of any of the towns and cities that we came to. We had no time to do this sort of thing, like make a log of where we were and what we were doing on a certain day. None of us ever even knew the day of the week it was, not to mention the day of the month, or even what month it was. Not only that, our hands were tied, so to speak, holding on to that tank, carrying your rifle at all times, never letting go of it. To say the least, we were awfully busy. Not only were we awfully busy looking out for Krauts and clinging to that turret, but also we were always hungry, sleepy, and very tired. There were only certain events that stand out in my mind. Many of the worst and more frightening things I have never been able to remember, even to the next day. I am thankful that I have not been able to recall all that happened, in that it would have been too heavy a burden to bear.

On one occasion, a most frightening thing happened that escapes my memory as to time and location. Three others and I were asleep late at night in an old partly damaged building with no glass in the windows. I was asleep on the floor. Suddenly I was awakened by the loud noise of a Kraut machine gun firing just outside this broken-out window. There was no doubt about it being a Kraut machine gun, in that it was firing so fast, it was easy to identify. It was awfully dark. The other men and I jumped up, ran to the window, and peeped outside. At first I was so startled that I thought that I was dreaming. I was so terrified that I thought that the Krauts were firing at us through the window. I had to compose myself to determine if I was dreaming or if this was real. I quickly knew it was for real and the other men were coming awake fast. We all peeped over the windowsill and just outside we saw this Kraut machine gun in the dim light from the muzzle blast and we could see three Kraut helmets behind the blazing machine gun. They were firing at something or someone to our left on a street or road. The next thing that I recall is that we fired on the machine gunners, at their helmets, which is all that we could see in the dark. We eliminated all three of them and silenced the machine gun. We then got some rifle fire coming in through the window. That was when we decided that it was time to get out of there, which we did. We went out a door on the other side of the building and ran to where there were other men that were with us. I have been unable to determine where this was, or any events just prior to, or after, that incident. I was so frightened when I awoke from my sleep by the machine gun noise, that it has been indelibly ingrained in my mind ever since, trying to determine events just prior thereto and thereafter. The noise, the sudden fright, the cold, all in the middle of the night is still in my mind. I recall that event often. It was a shock I have been unable to erase from my mind.

Our days were like, being awakened early in the morning at the crack of dawn, from where we were sleeping, usually on the floor of some house or building of some sort, run out the door, jump on a tank and take off toward the east like a bat out of hell just before the sun comes up. We had to stay constantly alert, looking for enemy resistance even though we were hungry, tired, and very short on sleep. We went through town after town, countryside after countryside, and farm villages galore. Not to mention, skirmish after skirmish and battle after battle. There is no possible way on earth that I, or any of the other men, could recollect everything that happened, where, when, and how it happened. Had I, or any of the others, been able to recall each and every such event, our psyche would not be able to deal with it and I, or any other such persons in that situation, would probably be in a psychiatric ward somewhere.

I would ride tanks for long hours without ever stopping, keeping a very close watch all around us for snipers and Nazis with Panzerfausts, as well as the Krauts who had rifles with scopes on them, who were trying to fire at us on the tanks. In addition to that we had to scrutinize every wooded area, every building, as well as any places of cover that would possibly be a place for an ambush site. As we men on the tanks discussed events that had occurred we would refer to them as "before the Rhine" or "after the Rhine," that is if we could remember which it was and where it was, which was quite difficult to recall when and where something occurred. Recalling the events that occurred each day and the sequence in which they occurred was impossible. I know that it was the loss of sleep, hunger, and exhaustion that made us groggy, drowsy, and mentally sluggish. It was difficult to remain alert all the time.

I would often spot huge rabbits out in the fields grazing like deer. They were so big I didn't know what they were until someone told me that they were rabbits. I still didn't know if someone owned them or if they ran wild like deer. Al Sperl told me one day when we saw some of them in a field grazing like cattle, that he had heard that we were forbidden to shoot any of them. I didn't ever know why. I wouldn't have done it anyway, but I wondered why. I assumed it was because they were of some rare, almost extinct species.

Going through the many big forests of northern Germany, particularly in the big forest areas, I noticed that almost all of the tall forest trees had what looked like Christmas tree decorations on them. They were small, narrow, but long strips of silver-looking foil hanging all over them, even high up in the tops of all of the tall trees. It was what I called Christmas tree tinsel. I asked many people what it was, what it was for, and how it got there up in the tops of tall trees. No one knew the answer. I asked the lieutenant about it one day, and he told me that it was "chaff" dropped by our Allied planes as they flew to their targets, to jam the Nazi radar as it fell to the ground.

At some point in time along the way through Germany, Easter Sunday came upon us. On this Easter Sunday a cessation of hostilities had been, I supposed, unofficially declared in celebration of Christ's Resurrection. We stopped in a clean, undamaged town for that important occasion. I have no recollection of whether this was before the Rhine crossing or after. It was quiet and peaceful that day; the sun came out for a change. I enjoyed sleeping late; I needed it badly, as did the other six or seven men with us. I recall someone telling me that there would be Easter church services held in the wooded area right near this house. I was the only GI that attended. All of the other men, I felt sure, wanted to attend, but they were so exhausted that no one other than I showed up.

Nearby in a beautiful wooded area, a chaplain had gotten this far up on the point and braved his way up through the maddening web of chaotic traffic jams and priorities on the roads in the rear to bring us his message on this Easter Sunday. I felt badly about it and I wanted to apologize to the chaplain about no one else appearing, but I said nothing. I sat down on the grass, in front of his jeep. He had placed a GI blanket over the hood and it served as an alter. The chaplain conducted his service, which was for me only, and it was very impressive and very inspirational. After he finished, he said a prayer that I will always remember and which gave me great faith, hope and courage for the battles that would commence again tomorrow.

We came upon this huge forest of tall trees that had been planted in rows many years ago. They were so tall and so close together that if one went into that forest you would not be able to even see the sky, or to even see the sunlight. It was like darkness inside these huge forests even during daylight. I assumed that is how it got its name, Black Forest, as some said it was called, but I wasn't so sure about that. The real Black Forest is in southwestern Germany. I never really learned by what name it was officially called. Many small farms and farmhouses were scattered in and around this big forest. There were now many of us on each tank.

151

As we got near a huge forest we encountered much enemy resistance. It was mostly 88mm artillery and Wehrmacht troops, most of whom were riding on half-tracks and trucks with machine guns and mortar crews on them. As we went through this huge forest we encountered much enemy resistance that was scattered, but which was always there, as they continuously tried to stop us. There were small arms fire, machine guns, and of course those deadly accurate 88s—they were always shooting at us, it seemed. We would be riding the tanks and encounter enemy resistance where we would have to return fire from the tanks, and with rifle fire to eliminate these many pockets of resistance. This became routine.

When the weather was clear we could expect to be strafed by Messerschmitts. However, there was not much clear sunny weather during this period of time. Things seemed awful gloomy, depressing, and out of the ordinary from anything that we had thus far encountered.

We had little difficulty in eliminating the pockets of resistance that we encountered, comparatively speaking. At night we would stop at one of these many large farmhouses where we would spend the night. Some of the men found some smoked hams and sausages hidden in the farmhouses. Those who found them usually kept the fact that they had them a secret and kept them hidden inside their field jackets. They shared it with only their old-time close buddies. Anytime that I had something to eat I always shared it.

One day in the Black Forest region we were told to get off of the tanks and stay at a large farmhouse there. I never learned why, or what was taking place ahead, but for some reason they didn't want any of us on the tanks. There were about six of us riding on this one Pershing at this time. None of our infantry on trucks came up to where we were. I was afraid that we were cut off from our support and supply lines. I never learned what the problem was, but we were told to stay at this farmhouse on a hill, which overlooked miles and miles of fields in every direction. This house was near some small village. We waited most of the day before our tank returned, then we moved out again.

While there, I found an old emery wheel grindstone used to sharpen farm tools. It was almost like the one we had back home on the farm that we sharpened knives and sheep shears with, which was always my job to do. It was a big round concrete emery wheel with pedals on it that you pedal like a bicycle, and with a homemade seat on it. So, I sharpened my knife and bayonet with it. I was able to get a real good, razor-sharp edge on both.

Also, we didn't have any rations and we were starved, so I found these beehives. I thought that the bees would have enough honey left over from the winter in them for us starved infantrymen to have some, too. I found some cotton cloth, rolled it up tightly, tied it up, and lit it to make a smoke to settle the bees down with. I opened the hives and sure enough there was a good bit of honey left in there, so I took some of it, leaving enough for the bees to have until they could make some more. We enjoyed the honey and it really gave us lots of energy. It was a real break having the most part of a day off of the tanks, and nothing to do but rest and eat honey. We were never told why we were just left there, but I did learn that there was some action up ahead and there were quite a few snipers ahead, who were ready to shoot all of us off of the tanks, so the tankers took care of this situation, without us. I never learned anything further about it. We seldom ever had any time to talk with the tankers. They didn't talk much anyway. When we did have time to talk with them, they would talk about anything but fighting. Oftentimes a tanker would refer to us in a joking manner as hitchhikers, or as swivel heads.

We began searching out more areas of this large Black Forest area where we encountered more and more resistance. We walked through these forest areas for miles, fighting, killing anyone that offered any resistance, capturing prisoners by the dozens. This area was no place for tanks, because there were natural tank ambush situations nearly everywhere, which we had to clear before the tanks would dare to come up.

Some of the forests were young trees planted in very long rows. Snow was still on the ground in one young forest where all of the trees were in long rows. It was a beautiful forest area. The aluminum foil strips were on the trees everywhere, and with this tinsel on them, with the snow on the ground underneath, it looked like Christmas.

We captured more Krauts than we killed, unlike Saarlautern, where we never captured any, just killed them. One day that I recall, we had crossed a river, not very wide, but so cold you couldn't stand it. We had to wade across it. It was almost waist deep. We held our rifles above the water, then had to sleep in a barn that night on a pile of hay with wet clothes on, and our feet wet and our suede boots soaked like a sponge.

The following morning early, we moved along this river, walking and came upon this big farmhouse that we were to take, search out as usual and then go on to the next one. I went into the main entrance, which was a big hallway; the barn with the cows in it was on the left side and the dwelling part on the other side of the big wide entrance. There were no cows or people there, as far as we could determine. I went into this house to search it out and the other GI with me went into some other part of it. I went into a bedroom and there in the bed was a fully dressed, very large, mean, and ugly-looking German soldier with boots and all on, snoring like a buzz saw. There was an automatic burp gun lying on the bed beside him, along beside his steel helmet. I had my rifle drawn on him. I nudged him on his boot with the barrel of my rifle, expecting him to surrender. He awoke suddenly, startled, then he frantically reached under his pillow for something, I believed it to be a pistol or some other kind of a handgun weapon, to shoot me with. Just as he did this, I put a bullet through his heart.

I had learned long ago not to take any chances with an armed enemy. One thing that you never do is to let any enemy get the drop on you. When I nudged him with the end of my barrel, I meant for him to surrender, which meant putting his hands in the air and saying something like *"Kommerad,"* like all of the others had done. I thought surely that I would now find me a souvenir and it would be a pistol—a Luger or a P-38. I looked under his pillow to see what he was grabbing for, expecting to find a Luger, and found only a white piece of cloth. Many enemy soldiers secretly carried a piece of white cloth, which was against Hitler's orders to even have on their person.

Hitler had ordered that any soldier who was even carrying a white piece of cloth would be shot. Many of them would wave it in the air when they wanted to surrender. I was sorry about it later, but I was in no mood to baby-sit any heavily armed Nazi soldier, fully dressed and armed with an automatic rifle, no matter whether he was awake or asleep, especially after I had walked for so long in still-wet suede boots. I was very hungry and completely exhausted, considering it being early in the morning. Any negotiations were just not in order at that time. I had tried to wake him up to get him to surrender. I figured that such a seasoned and experienced soldier that he appeared to be, he would at least know how to surrender. I had already learned the Nazi soldiers had many tricks up their sleeves and we could not trust them to any extent.

It was somewhere in the vicinity of this area where one of our units had gotten pinned down by the Krauts who had them covered with machine gun, mortar, and 88 fire. They were totally pinned down, isolated and had been for quite some time. It was related to me by one of our men who were at a point where two truckloads of ammo, food, water, and other supplies had been loaded on two trucks to be delivered to them, in that they had just about completely run out of all kinds of supplies, including ammo. GIs who were in a trucking outfit drove these two supply trucks. The man on the first truck was courageous and ready to deliver his truckload of supplies to our men up ahead, who needed them so badly. The driver of the second truck was refusing to go. He held up the delivery by just sitting there and doing nothing but refusing to make this trip.

He told a sergeant who had asked him what his holdup was, "I ain't going to go up there and get my ass killed."

He refused the sergeant's order to do so, who then reported it to a lieutenant colonel who had appeared at that point. The colonel gave a direct order to the driver to take off and to deliver his supplies.

His remark to the colonel was, "I ain't going up there and get my ass killed."

The colonel then said to the driver, "Get out of the vehicle."

As the driver got out and stood on the ground by the truck, the colonel pulled out his .45 caliber automatic pistol and put a .45 caliber bullet right between the driver's eyes, and then ordered another driver to continue on with the delivery of the supplies.

The driver had disobeyed a direct order on the front lines in combat. This action was totally and completely justified. Things really are that serious up there. There are no excuses accepted for cowardice or disobeying an order in combat. But for those supplies being delivered, many more of our men's lives would have been lost. By experience, we all had learned that it is not minutes, but that it is seconds that count in many such situations.

CHAPTER 19

Trench Foot

> *"If ye have faith as small as a mustard seed,...nothing shall be impossible unto you."*
>
> —MATTHEW 17:20

We walked many miles each day through this huge forest where there were no roads for tanks to travel. My shoes were wet and seemed they would never dry out. Once you got them wet they stayed wet. My feet began to get raw. I had no time to take my shoes off; I had no clean socks, just the old dirty ones that I was wearing and unable to wash very clean. We were not on tanks all of the time in this area. We had to go ahead of them and clean out Kraut antitank defenses. We spent lots of time searching out woods and villages on foot, where no tanks were involved. It was a slow go. My combat boots and socks were wet all the time. We were in the middle of this large forest one day near noon; I felt that I couldn't make it any further. We were miles ahead of any of our support that was coming up from the rear. My feet were now killing me. I took my boots off and what I saw, I didn't like seeing. I called the medic over and asked him about the skin coming off of my feet. I showed him my feet; the skin was peeling off in thick layers of white dead flesh leaving only raw, bloody tissue underneath. It was raw flesh beneath the thick layer of peeling dead skin. The medic told me to go to the nearest farmhouse, one that we could see in the distance nearly a mile away, and get some rest, clean my feet, administer first aid. Soon there would be ambulances and other support groups coming along the road by that house, later in the evening; he said to flag down an ambulance and they would care for me.

I didn't want any more ambulances or hospital care at all. I could see this small farmhouse in the distance. I put my socks and boots back on and painfully hobbled to it. There was an old man and woman there and a teenage girl. I searched the house out for any enemy, as well as keeping a lookout for any enemy that may be approaching the house. They were cooking rabbit stew and very kindly served me a large bowl of the stew that was about the best stew I had ever eaten. They had a hot fire burning in a big wood-burning stove. I removed my shoes and socks. The old lady and the girl knew immediately what to do for me.

The woman heated a large pot of water to wash my feet with and another one to boil my socks in. The girl got a pan of hot water and I put my feet in it and soaked them. She washed my feet well and rubbed all of the layers of dead skin off very gently. It is this dead skin that rots and infects the underlying tissue and this is trench foot, a common condition in combat where you are unable to keep your feet clean and dry and free of dead skin. If it is untreated one can loose a foot or even a part of a foot, which has to be amputated. She washed my socks then boiled them in a pan of water on the stove to thoroughly clean them. She then dried them and my boots in front of the stove. During this time I was eating a large bowl of that delicious stew they gave me, with some very good pumpernickel bread. The young girl got some clean white cloth and tore it in strips. I helped her and showed her how to bandage my feet with it. Then she put my clean dry socks on for me. I lay down and had a nice, well-needed rest while my wet suede boots were drying in front of the oven. When I left I gave the girl a chocolate bar and the mother a fruit bar. I gave the grandfather a pack of four cigarettes that came in a K Ration. This was all that I had that was of any value that I could give them for being so kind to me. I was most appreciative of what this family did to help me. I thanked them and they acknowledged my gratitude.

It was about late afternoon, almost dark, when I heard American vehicles, a column of them passing by outside. The first of the vehicles were light tanks, many of them. I didn't want any more tanks if I could help it, however I couldn't walk very much. I walked out beside the road and just stood there waiting for a vehicle with "Co. G" written on the bumper, hoping that I may be able to regroup with the men that I had been with that day. When I saw one I flagged it down and crawled aboard. I had to explain how I was able to be up that far on the point when they had just arrived. They thought that they were the only ones out on the point. I think they thought at first that I was a German spy. I convinced them that I was not and informed them that I was one of Patton's Raiders. My Southern accent let them know where I was from. That night I rendezvoused with my squad again. They were billeted in a large farmhouse further down the road.

The medic saw me and come over to where I was and said, "I thought you would be back there at a hospital."

I assured him that I didn't want any more hospitals if it could be helped and I told him about the wonderful care that I had received at that farmhouse, as well as the big bowl of rabbit stew that they gave me. The next morning the tanks arrived at this house, we climbed aboard, and again I was riding shotgun on a Pershing tank.

As we went outside to get on the tanks, I ran upon Al Sperl whom I hadn't seen in some time. We talked for a moment. Al was a very good soldier, as well as a good friend. I always liked to have him with me when things got tough. He was sharp, had a lot of guts, and was a very polite, kind, and loyal friend. I liked to have him with me because, first, he had a lot of firepower with that BAR. Second, he was a very religious man, kind and caring. We also enjoyed talking to each other, which was something that many of the other men on the tanks never seemed to want to do. Many of the men never wanted to talk to anyone. I assumed that the reason so many of the Raiders didn't talk to each other was that they were too apprehensive, and also that conditions were not conducive to being sociable. I knew if I got hit that Sperl would not go off and leave me just lying there. Also, I knew that he knew that I would not go off and leave him lying there either. It was a matter of mutual trust and respect. So, it was great running into someone that you could relate to and completely trust and rightly call your friend.

I took one look at Sperl and recognized him quickly. He had a pair of Kraut binoculars hanging around one shoulder, a Leica camera hanging around the other shoulder, an SS Troopers dagger sticking in his cartridge belt on one side, and a German Luger pistol sticking out of the other side of his belt. He also had two wristwatches on each wrist. Not only that, he had the partial remains of a Black Forest smoke cured ham in one side of his field jacket, and half of a large round loaf of pumpernickel bread in the other side, inside his jacket. This was my friend Al Sperl. I wished that I had been able to get a photograph of this GI at that time. It would have been very picturesque. It was seldom that we encountered each other. Al always had something friendly, uplifting, and encouraging to say to everyone. Always when things got tough, I wished for him and his BAR. When we were together on the big Pershings, his favorite position riding on that tank was up in front of the turret, straddle of the big 90mm cannon barrel, holding his BAR in a ready position to fire at anything that moved. It was always a pleasant experience running into him.

We never knew where we were going to end up at the end of each day. Oftentimes we would be in the territory of another regiment or even another division. I would see people at the end of a day that came up to occupy the town that we had taken, and they would be people that were in some totally different organization. We never knew where our own outfit was. Since I had not trained with the 65th Division at Camp Shelby, I did not know many of the men in my company. It was just us few from my company that were one of us Raiders. None of us knew those that were from other companies very well. We didn't have time to talk with each other, in that we were always moving so fast into enemy territory.

We stopped in a small town in the late afternoon that was some miles off of the Autobahn that lead from Frankfurt to Berlin. You could feel the hostility in the air, it seemed to me. Things just seemed different where there were enemy still around offering resistance. We had no infantry to arrive to assist in securing this village that night. It was just we few men, two men on each tank, and this was all of the infantry that was up there with us. We heard Luftwaffe planes flying over early in the night, as well as early the next morning. We doubled our security guards around the tanks and the houses. We got only a few hours of sleep. We had no infantry, other than we few riding shotgun on the tanks, nor did we have any artillery or other support to call on, because they were slow in getting enough supplies and personnel across the Rhine River pontoon bridge, we assumed. All of the roads and highways leading east from the Rhine area of Mainz were so crowded that support traffic was moving very slowly behind us. We were moving as fast as those tanks could go, and we were moving as far as our fuel supply would allow us to go.

That night I asked a buddy to stand his watch first, then for me to stand the next watch so that I could use his BAR, just in case we had a counterattack that night. Luckily nothing major occurred, but we never felt so uneasy and apprehensive. The following morning, the sun came up, we were riding tanks as usual. It was very early, just at the crack of dawn, traveling on the tanks through this forest when several German fighter planes strafed us. The tanks had time to stop, after seeing them coming in from the front of our column of tanks and right out of the early morning sun. We jumped off and lay in a mud-filled ditch until it was over. I found out that the tankers learned from other tanks, or someone on the radio, that there was strafing taking place in the vicinity. The tankers were always on the alert for Messerschmitts when the weather was clear, especially when the sun was shining. It was only when the weather was clear and visibility goo, that we could expect to be strafed by Messerschmitts. This got to be a common practice for the Krauts to strafe our column of tanks. They obviously wanted to destroy these new Pershing tanks, as well as us infantrymen on them, very badly, but they couldn't.

The following day we went down this wide Autobahn toward Berlin. German soldiers were surrendering in large numbers all along the Autobahn, so the only thing that we could do was to wave them to the rear.

We stopped for the night again. Finally we got some rations and fuel for the tanks, as the troops came up in trucks. The tankers got rations from the trucks that brought up fuel for them, but there was never enough for all of us guys on the tanks, too. It is beyond my memory to know how far we traveled, or for how many days, or what we encountered. Each day was like a whirlwind. We took off again early the following morning.

There are more beautiful forest and countryside in north central Germany than anyone could ever imagine. It was like a dream, fighting in this most beautiful God-given natural setting. It was totally different from the war-torn city of Saarlautern. We met considerable resistance from Wehrmacht ground troops, as well as from Panzer armor, as well as the Luftwaffe, daily. On one occasion, we were riding the Pershing tanks with about ten of us on each tank. On this occasion we had many more men on these tanks than we had ever had previously. These tanks had much more room for us to ride on them than any of the other tanks. For some reason there were about eight of these tanks, with about four to eight men on each one and we were moving through these big forests with only dirt roads in them. We had never had this many men riding on these tanks.

Suddenly, on this beautiful early sunny morning we saw Messerschmitts coming at us from a direction right ahead of us, coming right at us, with the sun behind them, as our line of tanks moved down this dirt road through a big forest as fast as they could go, going to the east and right into the rising sun. The turret gunners were observing for all of the drivers. As soon as they appeared, the tanks stopped quickly so that we could jump off and take cover in the ditches. All of the turret gunners closed their hatches as we jumped off. We had been traveling at top speed, about twenty-five miles per hour. We jumped off on one side or the other and plunged into a ditch on the sides of the road; we were really packed into those shallow and muddy ditches. Just as we hit the ditches, the planes came over strafing us with their machine guns, spraying bullets everywhere. It was a miracle no one was hit. The bullets hit the tanks, making a hell of a noise as they ricocheted off of them.

After they left, we jumped back up on the tanks and sped away down the road again. It was no more than maybe ten to twenty minutes that they, or other Messerschmitts just like them, returned. So, we had the same thing to do all over again, jump into those ditches and get wet and muddy all over again, time after time, that day. After about three or four of these passes, we were able to continue on without any more interruptions from Messerschmitts. I felt certain that the Krauts were after these tanks. We had been told that they were one of the Germans' prime targets and they wanted to try to destroy all of them if they could. We also felt that they were intent on killing all of the infantry on these tanks, which would make the tanks more vulnerable further down the road, if they were able to accomplish that.

That night we pulled into a small farm village and found a large farmhouse where we could find a place indoors to sleep. Some grabbed a bed, the rest of us piled down on the floor. This time the farm family, husband and wife, remained in the house. The next morning as we were getting on our tank, the very nice and intelligent-acting farm wife came outside with a big tray of small dishes of scrambled eggs and gave each one of us one of them, which had about two eggs in it. This was a real treat and it was appreciated by all of us. The civilians there in this big farmhouse were very nice—I couldn't believe it. However, I had not had too much experience with civilians in that we seldom ever saw very many. It seemed that every farmhouse that we came to, all of the citizens had already departed and taken with them all of their animals, as well as all of their food, because I never saw hardly any livestock, just those big rabbits.

Many German citizens whom I spoke with called us infantrymen riding on these tanks, "Patton's SS Storm Troopers." Some, who couldn't speak any English, said that we were "Patton's SS Truppen," as they called troopers. The Nazi radio stations were telling all of the citizens that we were cruel and vicious like their own SS troops, in an obvious attempt to get them to offer as much resistance as they could against us.

The SS troops in Germany were to be greatly feared, so the Nazis tried to instill in all citizens that we were also to be feared, but this was far from the truth. I wondered why, and I asked them. I learned that the Nazi radio was telling the people that we combat infantrymen riding on Patton's fast-moving tanks spearheading into Germany, were the equivalency of the German SS Storm Troopers that all Germans feared. So, these misinformed German civilians that were accustomed to being lied to by their government thought that we were brutal, barbaric, and uncivilized. They were actually afraid of us until they learned that the Nazi propaganda was not to be believed in anything that it told their people. The Nazis were experts in telling lies and using psychological warfare, too. If they wanted to destroy someone, they just labeled them. This was just another of their dirty thug-like tactics.

One early morning as we left a big farmhouse where we had spent the night, the weather moved in and it was very cloudy and overcast for the following several days. This meant that we didn't have to look out for any Messerschmitts strafing us, so we only had to look all around ahead, beside, and behind us. We made good headway and were far out ahead of our command, supply, and troop trucks that were way back yonder somewhere.

Early one morning our tanks were moving through this farm village on a narrow blacktop road. We turned a sharp corner right at the corner of a building, and there was a wagon that the farmers used to haul the liquid manure from their barns to the fields to use as fertilizer. These wagons had a large wooden tank made of wood staves, like a wine barrel. It was built onto a wagon frame and horses pulled it. The farmer would pump the liquid horse and cow urine and drainage from the barnyard, which had drained into an underground cistern, then pump it into these tanks and haul it to the fields, open a valve, and spray it on the soil.

Just around this corner ahead, a farmer had abandoned his liquid manure wagon and fled. Our tank almost hit it after we turned the corner. I looked back and there was a Chaffee light tank following us. The Chaffee tanker couldn't avoid hitting this wagon in that he was going so fast when he turned that corner. When he hit this wagonload of liquid cow and horse manure, it spewed all over the tank as well as drenching the two GIs on the tank. I wanted to laugh but I had long ago lost my sense of humor. I felt great sympathy for those two men. I thanked God that it wasn't me on that light tank, with no place to bathe, and no clean clothes to change into.

We continued our spearhead attack deep into Germany. The weather was cold and cloudy, and we didn't get strafed. We had a little less resistance now, since we had gotten out of the forest area. We moved rapidly to the east where there were miles and miles of farmland. We were taking so many farm villages and small towns we thought that the Germans should be ready to capitulate, but they weren't. In this farm country we could see for long distances ahead, making it easier to spot where Kraut antitank defenses may be. We could therefore relax a little and not have to be so apprehensive about spotting ambush situations ahead.

One evening we took this small farm village and were waiting for the infantry to arrive to search out the rest of the town and stand guard while we slept. There were only three of us from the 2nd Platoon of G Company who were part of the Raiders—Al Sperl, a man named Ted Sullivan from the Bronx, New York, and me. So, to kill a little time we had a bull session. The three of us seldom ever met up and were able to sit down and talk for a while. I asked Ted—a real fine fighting man with a whole lot of guts and a great sense of humor—how he liked Camp Shelby, Mississippi. I told him that I grew up near there. He began by telling me about a beautiful girlfriend that he knew in Biloxi, and he tried to visit her every weekend. The last weekend that he was there, just before shipping out to Europe, he failed an inspection and was denied a weekend pass. So, he went to see her anyway. It was easy getting off base without a pass, but getting back on was almost impossible. So, he told us how he devised a way to get back on the base. He had the driver of the car he was riding in let him out before it got to the main gate where the military police were. He had heard about two men from the camp stockade escaping, so he ran up to the gate and told the MPs that he saw two men run into some bushes back there as he was walking up to the gate and thought it was probably the escapees. So, more MPs were called and a search of the area ensued, but no one was found. The MPs gave him a ride to his barracks and took him right to it without asking him any questions. They also thanked him for his help. Ted was not a bad boy; he was smart, with a lot of guts and a hell of a fighting soldier. He always caught the bull by the horns and was never afraid of anything. Al and I were always glad to run into him and were pleased that he was selected by the captain as one of us, up here riding on these tanks.

Ted then told Al and me about one day at Camp Shelby when in a class on infantry tactics he was asked by a lieutenant what he thought about a flank attack on an enemy position.

Ted stood up and said, "Sir, I am Private Ted Sullivan, a private in the rear ranks. I make fifty dollars per month and I ain't getting paid to think, and what I think don't amount to a damn anyway, sir." He then sat back down. He got a lot of laughs and applause.

It was very seldom that we encountered anyone riding on those tanks that we knew and seldom ever the same person again. Ted was always very humorous under any kind of circumstance, and it was always good to meet up with him and have a few moments to relate to each other and exchange jokes and ideas. Al always complained to me that none of the others riding these tanks would talk to him. I told him that it was because they were afraid, under a lot of stress and anxiety—fear, it is called. We all experienced a lot of it, and there were many times that I didn't want to talk to anyone either. Not only that, I was always too busy eyeballing the countryside to see if I could see any enemy resistance sitting out there someplace waiting to ambush us. If we didn't find them first and knock them out, we were finished, so we always had to be alert. Each of us on those tanks felt that it was necessary for us to stay alive and not become a casualty, otherwise we could loose our lives and the war. Our motto amongst us Patton's Raiders that I told everyone that was on the tank with me—and I told them all to tell it to everyone else—was, "Fight like hell to stay alive today, so that we can fight again tomorrow." This reminded me of the story I read once about what Napoleon said: "For the want of a horseshoe nail, a horseshoe was lost, for the loss of a horseshoe, a horse was lost, for the loss of a horse, a rider was lost, for the want of a rider, a message was lost, for the want of the message, a battle was lost, for the loss of a battle, a war was lost, all for the want of a horseshoe nail."

One bright sunshiny day our tanks suddenly stopped as we were traveling down a dirt road on a ridge, with fields on each side and woods beyond on each side of the fields. We dismounted our tanks and they pulled back, leaving us there. I looked ahead and saw a part of the woods extended out near the dirt road we were traveling on. I knew immediately there must be an 88mm cannon hiding in those woods and there was an ambush situation at that location. The tankers had told us nothing, we had to figure things out ourselves.

There were about ten or twelve of us off of the several tanks and we spread out across this field and on each side of the road. We were just standing there, wondering what we were to do now, so we just waited. Sometime later a truck with infantry on it arrived behind us, unloaded, and a group of about twenty infantrymen came walking up this road to where our line of men were. When they got to where our line was, they just stopped there in a group, not spread out at all and making themselves a perfect target for an 88 shell to knock them all out, and us too. We just held our positions. Soon a rubber-tired armored car arrived and stopped right up where this group of infantry was standing. I moved closer to see what this was all about. A two-star general popped out of the turret and yelled, "Who in the hell is in charge of this group?"

I then saw a major run up to the general's vehicle, salute and say, "I am, sir."

The general told the major, "Get these men dispersed now, before they all get killed by one shell. You should know better than to let this happen." The General then got back into his armored car and it drove away.

This major yelled, "You men disperse now. That is an order, do it now." So the men dispersed.

The next thing I observed, a ways ahead at that growth of trees extending out into the field and nearer to the road, was a small white handkerchief being waved by someone who was still invisible in the woods. I slung my rifle over my shoulder and with my left arm motioned for whoever it was—Kraut soldiers, I was sure, who were at this very obvious ambush point ahead—to come to us. Slowly some of the Kraut soldiers moved out of the woods with more of them waving white flags. Then, more of us were motioning them to come on to us. Then a group of about twenty or thirty enemy soldiers came walking to where we were, all with their hands over their heads, with no weapons or helmets. When they arrived at where we were, I and two or three others escorted them back to the rear a piece, to where some trucks had come and were parked. When we took the prisoners up to where the trucks were, two of the truck drivers began to take their wedding bands, rings, and watches off of them. I went to where this was taking place and I told the drivers to stop. They told me that they were not going to, this was their gold and it was none of my damned business. After I decided that talking wouldn't stop them from robbing the prisoners that I considered to be in my custody, I put the end of my rifle barrel to the throat of one of the drivers and made him give back their wedding rings, telling him that this was a sacrilegious and a wrong thing to do, and these were my prisoners now and I was not going to let this happen to them. So the drivers gave back the wedding rings.

We grouped up and walked down this ridge road through these large fields where these prisoners had come from, and when we arrived at this group of trees there was an 88 sitting amongst the trees, with two machine gun emplacements around nearby.

We didn't have any white phosphorous grenades to toss down into the barrel of the 88, so we left that to the men in the rear. We rendezvoused later that evening with our tanks.

On another occasion, we had gotten off of our tanks early one sunny morning when there was lots of dew on the ground. We were searching out an area of a suspected ambush site ahead of us. It was a rural area and some of our men on the trucks came up to assist us. My squad leader, Sergeant Willie Graybeal was with us as we went up a worn path. It was like being in a ditch, with a bank on each side, about five feet high. Sergeant Graybeal was ahead of me in this path. Suddenly I observed ahead of him a string, or fine wire, that was stretched across this pathway about chest-high. The reason that I saw it was that back on the farm I would go out to the barn early every morning and there would be lots of spiderwebs across paths and at gates. I hated to get tangled up in these spiderwebs, and too, I didn't like spiders anyway. So, on the farm I became acutely aware of spiderwebs. I could see them and knock them away if there was an early morning dew with the sun shining.

I saw the fine dew drops sparkling like diamonds that were on this fine piece of wire stretched across our path just ahead of Sergeant Graybeal. I immediately grabbed his field jacket and pulled him back just as he was about to walk right into this trip wire. I then pointed out to him this fine wire with the dew drops sparkling on it. Others with us came up and observed the situation where we almost all got killed by this booby trap. On the right side of the pathway, hidden in the bank of the path, was a fragmentation grenade with the pin pulled and it had been placed back into the box that it came in, to keep the firing pin down, with this wire attached to it and strung across our path. By anyone just touching the trip wire it would pull the grenade out and it would have exploded, probably killing all of us on that patrol. We disarmed the grenade and disposed of it. I was glad to know that my experiences as a farm boy was now paying off and had just saved my squad leader's life, as well as me and all of the others there with us.

I was learning fast that danger lurked everywhere all of the time and one could not be too alert at any time or place. It was a twenty-four-hour-a-day job of just trying to stay alive. One could never assume that anything would be all right, and no danger lurked there, because it was lurking everywhere, all the time.

We had also learned long ago that to enter a village or town riding on the tanks that one had best not assume that there was no resistance there. Each time that we rode through a village or town on those tanks we had to look in every direction, quickly, precisely and be as alert as anyone could possibly be for resistance in the buildings, on top of them, and in all upstairs windows, both ahead of us and behind us. All of us had to be alert and on guard all of the time to the numerous dangers that existed constantly, everywhere.

CHAPTER 20

Struth, Germany, Panzer Counterattack

> *"Tanks should advance by bounds, from cover to cover, in the rear of the infantry. They will only be exposed when the situation demands their intervention. In such cases they will attack in close association with the infantry."*
>
> —GENERAL GEORGE S. PATTON (1885–1945)

In our rapid thrust through north central Germany, riding shotgun on the new Pershing tanks operated by the 6th Armored Division, we stopped in this small farm village, or town, miles off of the Autobahn, late one evening—as we were getting near Mulhausen, which was not too far from Nordhausen and right on the heading to Berlin. One or more of these places were on our route to Berlin. We had departed from some town very early that morning, without having even a bite to eat and traveled as fast as those tanks would go, all day. The weather had been overcast and dreary all day. We were totally exhausted and hungry when we pulled into this town of Struth just before it got dark.

We were far, too far, out on the point, we were soon to learn. We had expected heavy resistance in this area because of the facilities ahead of us, Nordhausen Concentration Camp and the underground V-2 rocket factory operated by slave laborers. There was also the city of Mulhausen where there was a big bridge right in the center of the city that we had orders to seize control of, to prevent it from being blown up, so that it would not slow down the advance of Patton's tanks and troops. We were expecting a last-ditch defense of Berlin in this area, in that Berlin was only 120 kilometers away, which had been our objective from the very beginning.

I had read about the huge concentration camp at Nordhausen, which was only about ten miles away from Struth, before I ever came into the service. Also, we were near this large underground factory where V-2 rockets were built, which the Nazis still expected to turn the tide of the war with. We had always anticipated heavy resistance anywhere near major military and industrial installations. These installations were the biggest and the most important that Hitler had. We never knew exactly where we were or where our next objective was, except that we knew generally we were on a direct route to Berlin, which was no secret to anyone.

I knew all along that we were heading for Berlin and not too far ahead of us were those two cities, Mulhausen and Langensalza, which were also our objectives. I knew the concentration camp at Nordhausen was one of our prime objectives. We had been told this since we left the Rhine. These two cities were our next objective, then to Berlin.

How we found ourselves in such a rural, remote area and off of the beaten path as this, I was unable to understand; however we had to trust the people in command, in the rear, who had all of the facts and who kept up with every movement by radio. Our intelligence section seemed to always know what was going on, from intelligence information they received from plane observations, from POWs who were interrogated, and other innumerable resources of intelligence information. I am sure it wasn't by chance we found ourselves in this out-of-the-way town.

This was really a remote rural town, or village. It was almost dark when we arrived there in Struth. It was late in the afternoon, getting dark quickly. We all were famished and didn't have one bite of food to eat, nor any water to drink. None of the tankers had any rations with them, that we were aware of.

This was a rather large rural town, and immediately upon arriving here the tankers went directly to the northeast edge of the town where they stopped. All of the tanks were spread out, nearly a block apart, and took cover, which was very unusual. There were miles and miles of open fields as far as one could see, in every direction from this town, or from that part where we stopped.

Our tank was the first to enter the town and immediately took cover inside a big barn right on the northwest corner of the town. The barn had large double doors that were open on each side; one of the double doors was facing the open fields to the northeast, the other facing the houses to the south. As we arrived I noticed the tankers were quite nervous. They wouldn't talk to me, or anyone else.

I, and the other men riding the tank—four of us on our tank— went into the house just across the street from the barn to see if we could find a place to sleep and find something to fix to eat. There was nothing there to eat, not even one potato, but it was a clean farmhouse with nice beds where we then thought we would be able to get a good night's sleep. We rested a few minutes, talked for a while, and sometime later went back to the barn to see what the tankers were doing. We saw our other tanks, before they ever stopped their engines, had also moved into a combat-ready position, as well, further down the street, and they all were facing the open fields to the northeast, too.

Some of the men on those other tanks were also from my platoon and were men that I knew. Ted Sullivan came to the house just as it got dark. Ted was one of our infantrymen on another tank, from my squad. He came over to where we were in that house on the corner of town by our tank before it got dark. Ted was a fine fighting man, as courageous as they came. Al and I knew what a ladies man he was, but this was an unusual situation we were in and no one had any time to fraternize, but he told us that he met this girl there and he had a date with her. I thought that he was just joking with us. I was afraid he would be captured if he began fraternizing with any civilians that were there, if any were there. Things just weren't right in this town that night. Ted pulled from the pocket of his field jacket a handful of coffee packets and sugar cubes that he had saved from K rations. There, in the kitchen of the house, Ted told Al and me, "I have been saving this coffee and sugar so I can have a cup of coffee with you two guys. You two are the only ones that will talk to me; nobody seems to want to talk with me these days except you two. Heat some water and we will drink some coffee together."

We all took out our canteens and none of us had any water, not even a drop in them. There was no water supply in the house that we could find. The tankers carried a can of water strapped onto the tank, but I checked and there was no water in it. Ted then put his coffee and sugar back into his pocket and after talking for a while, all of us then went back to the barn. Later Ted left.

After this, we didn't see Ted for quite a while, and we worried about him having been captured there.

Ted was too clever to ever be captured, and if he ever was he would certainly figure out a way to escape. I thought for a while he had been killed by the troops that I knew were hiding there in that town. It concerned me, but he survived and showed up later.

There were about four of our infantrymen riding on each of these other tanks, about six or eight tanks. Some of the men from the other tanks joined us and we talked about the present situation of not having any food or water and no infantry support having arrived. At that time none of us infantrymen were really aware of the seriousness of the situation, except for the fact we were aware that none of our infantry had arrived, and this really spelled trouble to me. Also, we had no rations, fuel, ammo, or other supplies, which either meant that we were cut off or they were late getting up to us for some unknown reason. That didn't seem right. I had heard many tankers say they could take a town, but they couldn't hold it. The infantry has to hold it. There aren't enough tankers to do it, they would always say. Urban fighting was certainly no place for a tank to be, because the enemy could fire at it with Panzerfausts, or any other kind of weapon, up close, and destroy it. That was our job, making certain that no enemy got even close to our tanks, which would be impossible to do in a town or city. The tankers never wanted to have to pull guard duty on their tanks at night, so they expected the infantry to come up and do it, as well as to stand door guard where we slept. We also expected someone back there to send us men on these tanks some rations to eat and water to drink up to where we were, but it seldom ever happened. Al Sperl believed that the men riding trucks were eating our rations.

As it got later in the evening, just after it was getting dark, no infantry in trucks had yet arrived. I knew right away this spelled trouble for us. This was the first time they failed to come up to where we were, when we took or began to take a town, as I could recall, except for maybe one or two occasions.

No supplies arrived. The town seemed deserted—but yet it didn't, to me. I felt something very eerie and strange about this place. Maybe it was because we were so alone, since no infantry support had arrived. It was also the suspicious actions of the tankers that made me worry. The totally deserted look of this town also made me very suspicious.

I had a rather strange and eerie feeling because it was very unusual for this kind of situation to be happening, because we needed infantry to help guard the perimeter, as well as to search out the houses for enemy troops, and to guard the tanks as well as to stand door guard so the tankers, as well as we men riding on them, could get a few winks. We had never taken a town and slept there, when there were no infantry that came up and cleared the entire town of any enemy. This was a very serious matter. What excited me more than anything else was that when the tanks pulled into town they went directly to the north edge of town and took cover in a combat-ready, defensive position, which was unusual. I had never seen this happen before. The tanks always before just parked in the street right in front of the building where we were going to sleep, or pulled back to the edge of town to be refueled at a motor pool that was set up and secured by guards. Never had I seen them take up a defensive position when we pulled into a town at night. Now, the more I thought about this situation, I became really worried. It didn't take someone with two stars on their shoulders to realize that we were in a very perilous situation.

When our infantry was not up with us, as it got dark, I got very concerned, especially when your common sense tells you that you have been cut off, and this is the reason you don't have any infantry and supplies. I also realized that we were way out into enemy territory. We had never been in a situation like this before, with no support, not for any more than a few hours anyway. I had many times been very apprehensive about this happening, especially when our support failed to arrive before it got dark. However, there had been evenings when we took a town or city, the infantry didn't arrive until after dark. This was also the first town or village I can recall where we entered late in the day and spent the night and no one was there to search out the buildings. This was very unusual to be occurring.

There were lots of things that we needed—ammo, fuel, water, and especially some rations, as well as a lot of infantry soldiers to secure this town. For all we knew there could have been a big Wehrmacht, or Waffen SS contingency hiding there somewhere. But, this time it was just the tankers and we few infantry on these seven or eight big tanks, riding shotgun, and we obviously were the only GIs in this rather large farm town.

Things were different with the tankers this time. No one talked; no one would say why we stopped, or why our tanks immediately took cover in barns and between buildings with all of them facing in the same direction, when the tankers were working hard to put hay all over them. The tankers had never before taken up a ready, or defensive position just after arriving in a town where we were to spend the night. All of the other tanks were well dispersed down the way, all facing in the same direction, toward these open fields to the northeast. It was very quiet in this big farm village. Nothing moved; none of us saw any civilians, or anyone else, to my knowledge. It was just too quiet there. There were no white flags flying from any windows, as you usually saw when there were civilians but no enemy soldiers there.

I noted that none of the tankers ever came into this house, which was unusual. This house we started to stay in by the barn was right on the corner of the town, the northwest corner. So, this house was just across the street from the large barn that our tank was sitting in. This house and barn were bordered by large fields on two sides, right at the northwest corner of this farm town.

I told Al we were not going to stay in this house tonight, even though it was very comfortable, with beds to sleep on. We had no one with us to stand guard while we slept. Nor were there any of our infantry troops there to search out the houses and to defend against an attack, so we may be in real serious danger. Not one building, except the one next to the barn where our tank was, had been searched and I searched it. For all I knew that night there could have been a whole battalion of Wehrmacht infantry, or Waffen SS Troops hiding in the cellars of those houses, who would pop out suddenly at the right time and destroy all of us and our tanks.

Al Sperl, my closest buddy whom I had known the longest and trusted the most, asked me why I didn't want to stay in the house. I told him that it was just a feeling that I had, things just didn't look right or feel right to me, nor did it all make sense, except to say we were cut off and surrounded by Krauts, and I suspected there were enemy troops hiding in this town. I now well knew that one would be a fool to enter into enemy territory without searching out and clearing all of the houses of any enemy resistance before letting your guard down and going to sleep.

I asked Al what would prevent a Kraut from coming in the house that night while we were asleep and blowing our brains out and blowing up our tank with a Panzerfaust? That made him think and be more on guard. It was the Cherokee Indian in me, one-eighth to be exact, which makes me sense things when they are not right. I had a strong feeling, even though we were alone and couldn't see anyone, there were enemy soldiers around there somewhere. Things were just too quiet. I had one of those strange feelings of insecurity, and I told Al that.

I, Al, and the others, decided not to stay in the house that night, so we stayed at the barn and tried talking to the tankers. We stayed in the barn by the tank and we slept on the hay, but slept very little. The men from the other tanks down the way went back to their tanks, but later that night some of them came up to the barn where our tank was and we talked more, more than any of us had ever talked before. I learned that none of the men on the other tanks were sleeping in any of the houses either. In fact, I don't think that any of us on those tanks got any sleep that night. I had become impervious to the cold. I lay on the hay and after midnight I began to get a little cold and pulled some hay over me, which helped me keep warm. I later learned that there was a freeze that night.

Our tanks were assigned to General Patton's Third Army and were part of the 6th Armored Division and assigned to our regiment, and we were assigned to ride shotgun on them to protect them. If the Krauts wanted to destroy these tanks, which we knew that they did and tried hard all of the time to do, well, then this was the time and the place for them to try to do it.

What we were doing was making history. We didn't know it then, though. Riding on these fine tanks was the hardest thing I, or any other combat infantryman could ever be called upon to do. It was hard-driving combat in its truest sense, from before daylight till after dark, day after day. Little or no food, sleep, or rest, plus all of the fear and anxiety that goes with it, made it a killing job, both literally and figuratively. We were then, and had been all along, far out on the point for the Third Army.

The tankers stayed constantly, all night, right by the tank with a driver or gunner inside all of the time. I am sure that not any of them got any sleep that night, except maybe a few winks, one at a time there on the hay. I suspected these tankers knew more than what they were telling us. Just as a precaution, I kept an almost constant lookout to our rear in that village for any enemy who may be there and decide to try to destroy us.

It was getting dark fast. We were deep in enemy territory where we were obviously cut off from our support, back there somewhere, and were surrounded by enemy. It was now obvious that our supply and support lines were cut, taken, and captured by the enemy and we were on our own.

I was only twenty years old, but I had some college and ROTC before I came in, and I had more military training than these younger men. I was always kind, helpful, and considerate to everyone, just always trying to help every person survive and help win the war. Al, age nineteen, said I was the ranking private, because I was older, had grown up on a farm, and was more mature than any of the other kids, all of whom were about eighteen and nineteen years old, and all were city guys. Al often reminded me that I didn't have any "street smarts" but he did, and I was more knowledgeable than he was, and this was why we made a good team.

The next thing that I saw about midnight, was Al Sperl, a city boy from Pittsburgh, out in the front of our tank trying to make some hay stay on that long barrel cannon that had new slick paint on it and the hay just kept sliding off of the barrel. He, however, helped the tankers put a lot of hay on the tank. To me it sure wasn't properly camouflaged, with that long cannon barrel sticking out from what looked like a big pile of hay sitting right in the center of the open double doors of the big barn.

I spoke with one of the tankers about our camouflage of the tank and I told him it looked strange to me, this pile of hay just sitting in the middle of the door of the barn and I was afraid that it wouldn't fool anyone who saw it, because a farmer never blocks the entrance to his barn with a big pile of hay.

The tank commander said he was just following the book. He related to me how one day he was alert for enemy tanks and he suddenly saw this big pile of hay moving slowly across a field. He fired on it, hit a Panzer Mk IV tank and destroyed it.

All that night I would keep a watch for enemy soldiers by looking out the barn door facing the fields to the north and also to the south, where I could see some of the town's buildings, just looking and watching, not wanting to be caught napping and attacked by Krauts. I saw nothing that would indicate there were enemy soldiers or civilians in this town.

The following morning the tankers got us awake and alert early as usual at the break of dawn, before the sun came up. I noticed that the tankers were not on the move at daylight like they had been all times previously. They are always up early, and I was afraid because I had been able to realize the situation we were in. No one was saying anything about anything. Not only that, when I asked the tank commander when we were pulling out, he told me that their fuel tanks were practically empty and there was no where that we could go. Yet, the tank commander got us up early but didn't tell us anything. I already knew that all of the tanks were just about out of fuel and there were no rations or water. We had nothing to eat and I was hungrier than I had ever been. There was a foul-up somewhere about feeding us men up on the point. I assumed that it was because we moved so fast. Al Sperl told me that he believed that the men on trucks in our outfit ate our rations, and this was the reason we never were able to get any. Sperl never lost his sense of humor and he told me, "The reason we aren't getting our rations is these rear echelon guys back there are sitting down somewhere eating our rations." We found out later that he was absolutely correct.

It was obvious that the tankers were just waiting for something to happen, and I didn't know what it was they were keeping from us. I knew that something serious was about to happen. I was getting very anxious. There was an eerie feeling in the air and it was most obvious to all of us.

Al and I, along with the other men on our tank, were by the tank in the barn, watching, early that morning. The sun was very bright today, but yesterday there had been a heavy overcast of clouds. We hadn't gotten strafed yesterday, as we usually had, because of the overcast. The tankers just wouldn't talk at all, no matter how much I bugged them. I not only sensed that we were in big trouble, I now knew it. There was no other conclusion one could draw. We just started looking in the direction they were looking, hoping to see or learn something about our situation here.

Early that morning as the sun came up, all I could see nothing but the rolling fields, beautiful farmland for miles and miles, peaceful looking, it appeared, but it did not feel that way to me. Everything seemed so peaceful and quiet, yet eerie and foreboding.

Suddenly, all at once, coming over these rolling hills of large open fields, we saw tanks coming, big tanks, many tanks, and the ones with the very wide tracks, low profile, and long cannon barrels. They were about two miles away or less. I knew that the Tigers had those deadly 88mms on them and the Panthers and the Mark IVs had 75mms on them. I am certain that they had some tank destroyers mixed in the group, at the rear of the column of tanks. They had the lethal 105mm cannons on them, which were just about like ours. The tanks in this column were dispersed and were in several rows with about three or four of them in a row, with about four or five rows deep and in a staggered formation. That big Tiger was out in front ahead of the others and was leading the group.

Looking closer, behind them and alongside were German infantry on foot, lots of them, hundreds of them, all coming right at us at a slow, menacing, walking pace, at the speed of soldiers walking. It was obvious we were terribly outnumbered and too. They had more firepower than we did, plus they had fuel and could maneuver, but we couldn't, at least not very far.

I knew this must be the end, and we had a terrible fight on our hands to the bitter end, a fight to the finish, unless a miracle happened or some kind of divine intervention occurred. One of the tankers looking through his field glasses said he counted them and there were seventeen tanks, and the infantry were too many to count. I am sure there were at least three hundred of them, if not more. I also surmised that many of them were also carrying Panzerfausts.

We just waited, terribly apprehensive and very scared, as we watched the approach of this column of Panzer armor and Wehrmacht troops—or the fierce fighting Waffen SS Troops, or both—slowly but surely moving directly toward us.

To make things worse, while we watched this deadly Panzer unit approach us, one of the tankers told me that we had gone too far out front and we were now cut off and surrounded. He told me we had no help, no supplies could get to us, and all of our tanks there were about out of gasoline, with only a few gallons left in each.

I knew then unless a miracle happened we were doomed. Never had I seen so many enemy soldiers in an attack, along with so many large tanks. I had gotten to recognize the Tigers and Panthers and the medium-sized Mark IVs, even though there wasn't much difference in the silhouette of the Tiger and Panther. Both were very low profile, a low and flat turret where the cannon was mounted, and the tracks were extremely wide, making them ideal for wet, soft dirt, like in the fields in front of us, as opposed to the narrower treads of our Pershings and Chaffees.

Not one civilian, so far as I could still determine, was in this town, a small town, in that I had yet to see even one. If they were, they sure kept out of sight. I was beginning to realize that all of the Nazi armed forces and civilians alike were all well coordinated and were kept well informed about where we were and what our strength was. I believed the Krauts had gotten all of the civilians moved out of this town, in that in the past, if there were civilians there we would see them. Nor could I imagine the Krauts attacking a town with this much armor and troops with their own people still there, unless they had troops there, too, that would attack us from the rear at the appropriate time. I also believed just as strongly, the Krauts had brought into this town some troops hidden there in cellars. I was certain that the Krauts wanted to eliminate our tanks. But to attack them in this small town, I reasoned that there had to be Kraut troops in the town to attack us from the rear. I feared we were really in a trap.

All of our tanks were under cover, hidden, we thought. But I wasn't too sure we were so well camouflaged, because I grew up on a farm, and

I know that no farmer places a big pile of hay right in the center of the big double doors of the barn, with them wide open and with a big cannon barrel sticking out of the center of the haystack. This really bothered me. We knew that the enemy knew we were there, how many of us there were, and how many tanks, as well as where they were located, since this was kind of hard to hide. This Panzer and Wehrmacht outfit was coming directly toward us, getting closer by the second.

There was nothing to do but to just wait and fight it out, in a very short while, which wouldn't be very much longer. I did learn from one of our men riding on a tank down the way that their tankers also told them they were not only out of gas, but were also out of water and rations. Also, they were told that we had gotten too far out on the point and we were cut off, surrounded. No one could get up to where we were, with our supplies or support. That made me more afraid, knowing that there were only a few gallons of gas in all of the tanks, and I knew that if they tried to move to find better cover that they might run out of gas and be caught sitting out in the open, broadside, as a perfect target. I also knew I didn't want to be on it, or near it, when the shelling started.

There seemed no other way out but to fight to the finish, right where we were. Somehow, I was convinced the lead Tiger knew just where we were, there in this barn with the big doors open, with a pile of hay sitting right in the middle of the doors, with the big barrel sticking out of it. I also knew the German soldiers, especially the Panzer soldiers, weren't stupid and hay over the tank was not very convincing, even to me. Even they had used that same ploy many times.

We just had to wait and handle the situation the best we could, but I felt our tank would be the first target to be fired upon. Our tank was the lead tank and the first one to take up a position there. So, we waited as the Panzer units got closer and closer. I could also see that we few infantrymen, consisting of about 45 men, were terribly outnumbered by these foot soldiers coming at us along with tanks. I could see the automatic assault weapons the Wehrmacht soldiers were carrying in the ready position, as they walked straight toward us.

I borrowed the tanker's field glasses and I could clearly see their ground troops with weapons in their hands, walking briskly alongside in front of and behind all of those tanks. It was a menacing sight, to say the least. I don't know of anything ever that was such a deadly threat to all of us. I was too shaken up to count them, but there were an awful lot of enemy soldiers. I also got a good look at the lead tank: a big Tiger with the long 88 barrel I was certain was aimed right at where our tank was located. I reasoned that since our tank was the first one to arrive in this town and we took up the position on the northwest corner of the town in this barn, it was apparent their observers had seen us arrive and assumed we were the lead tank, which we were. I also believed our tank was the one that they wanted to get first, more than the others, most likely believing it contained a high-ranking officer, which it didn't. I felt sure they had observers hidden there in a church steeple, most likely, that kept up with where we were and what we were doing.

The tank commander of the Tiger, which was their lead tank, had his upper body protruding out of the turret and was looking right at us with his field glasses. As I looked at him with our field glasses, I could see him looking directly at where we were, looking right at me, through his large field glasses—as I knelt down between our tank and the edge of the door opening, only partly concealed by hay. I am sure that he could see me clearly. I could certainly see him good and see his goggles hanging around his neck. I took a good look at the end of the barrel of the 88 on his tank. It was aimed right at our tank, and I could see a perfect circle as I looked into the end of that barrel.

It was a most frightening and threatening sight, to say the least. I was counting the seconds until they opened fire on us with those 88s on the Tigers and the 75s the others had. In the rear of this mass of tanks I could see very well that there were several of their tank destroyers that had 105mm cannons on them that could knock out any tank. They were called Hetzers. I knew that this was going to be a test of the qualities of the Panzer tanks and these Pershings. Our Pershings tanks had about four-and-one-half to five inches of armor; the Tigers had five inches. I had seen the Panzers fire at us before and they always came to a complete stop just before they fired, supposedly to properly sight their cannon. However, when up close, I had seen them fire while they moved very slowly. I told Al and the tank commander, at the moment just before we figure they would start firing, we infantry should move to one side or the other and away from the tank to avoid getting hit by shrapnel, in the event shells hit our tank. The tanker didn't like the way I described it.

We were like a sitting duck. Chills were running up and down my spine, and I know everyone else was feeling the same. We all knew we only had a few minutes, or maybe seconds, to decide what we were going to do in defending ourselves and our tanks. We needed to decide soon what defensive action we should take and let all of the other men down the way know what to do. We all knew that we were outnumbered, greatly. The best Panzers the Germans had were approaching us, more rapidly now, moving at a faster walking pace.

Things were very tense. I believed we were doomed. I spoke quickly to Al and all of our other men there, as well as some men from the other tanks down the way, and we planned our strategy. We agreed to stick by the tanks there in the barns, and when the Kraut tanks stopped to fire or after the first shot was fired at us, or when they got in closer range, we would disperse into the surrounding area where we could protect our tank from the foot soldiers and just kill all of them we could, as fast as we could. We would stay together but dispersed out, take cover behind something solid, move away from the tank to avoid being hit by the shrapnel from the armor-piercing shells these big tanks would fire at our tanks.

Everyone agreed to this plan and prepared to do it by looking for a safe place to take cover and fire from, right then. I told all of our men there to pass it on down to all of the men on the other tanks to follow this plan of action, and they did. We had no foxholes to take cover in and no time to dig any. We had very few things that were strong enough to give us protection from bullets and shrapnel, to take cover behind.

We knew being on the ground beside these tanks, when they were being fired upon, we would surely be killed by flying shrapnel and bullets ricocheting off the tank. I knew when heavy armor was hit by an armor-piercing shell, it heats the metal instantaneously, burning a hole through it and small white hot fragments spew everywhere—not only inside the tank, but out into a cone-shaped area, forward from the point of impact. No one was safe around a tank that has been hit by an armor-piercing shell. Also, we could do no good by being near the tanks when they were under attack, and I told this to all of our men.

We could accomplish more by firing on their foot soldiers from a safe distance on either side of the tank, where we could move to a new location from time to time to take cover. I told all of the men there, what we needed to do was to take cover away from the tanks and concentrate on killing their ground troops just as fast as we could. That was the plan that I suggested that was conveyed down the line of tanks to all of the other men there. This is what everyone agreed to do, plus some very sincere prayers.

All of the other men with us were depending on Al and me to tell them what to do and they listened to us. All of us knew this was the end—or at least we believe it was the end—for all of us, but all of us intended to make the most of it. I told Al I wanted the tank commander in the lead Tiger, and he belonged to me.

Al said, "No, no, he is mine!"

I closed my eyes and said a prayer. I asked my Almighty God to somehow bring about a miracle to save us from this enemy and to grant us victory, to bless and take care of my family and bless them all, and for us to win this battle.

The Panzer units were getting closer by the second. The tanks looked larger and wider, the infantry more menacing, and we felt more helpless each second. I could see they were still moving directly toward our tank in as straight a line as you could see. I had not seen how our other tanks were positioned and camouflaged to know if any of the others were visible to the approaching Panzers. But I now knew the tank commander of the lead tank was moving, as well as looking directly toward our tank. I also knew, considering the odds, that we would surely be killed by enemy fire quickly after it started. It was very clear to see that in just a few minutes, or seconds, we would have a lot of fire thrown at us. I knew we had to prepare for it the best we could.

As we waited, everything was deadly quiet. I could only hear the motors and gears moving as our cannon was sighted, as well as seeing the big barrel moving in precise minute increments, up and down, as the column of tanks got closer.

All of the tankers were now down in the tank and the turret hatch was closed. We men on the outside of the tank were now on our own. We were totally outnumbered in men, firepower, and armament. There were only eight of our tanks to their seventeen. There were about forty or fifty of our men to their several hundred.

I told Al my rifle was more accurate than their automatic weapons and I would find a good position I could take cover behind to fire from, and I could pick off lots of them before they got me, but I needed a secure place to fire from. I told him to not waste his ammunition for his BAR and to make every round count. I had about seventy-five rounds for my rifle. I hoped to bring down at least this many Krauts before I ran out of ammo. When it was used up, I didn't know what I would do, unless I would use my bayonet.

Also, I considered should we be taken prisoner, which was not very likely under these kinds of battlefield conditions, they would just kill us on the spot. I also reasoned that even if they did capture us, they would soon be on the run again, and they would not ever be burdened by having to guard us as prisoners. They would not free us and would most definitely just shoot us rather than release us. I told all of our men there that we would not surrender.

Things looked extremely unlikely for us being victorious in this battle. I told Al we should just fight to the finish, kill as many as we could before they killed us, which was inevitable. We were completely outnumbered and the situation looked absolutely hopeless.

Sometime later a few inexperienced combat people asked me, "Where were your captain, your lieutenant, your sergeants?"

My response to these people was that we men who were Patton's Raiders were furthermost out on the point all of the time and, "We knew what to do, how to do it, and when to do it, and we had the guts to do it, and we did it." Had General Patton himself been up there with us it wouldn't have made any difference, he would have done the same thing that we did. We Raiders were a chosen few, handpicked by our company commanders, as per General Patton's requirements, for this job. All we needed to be told was to, "Go do it!"

All of us Raiders were a special kind of soldier. We were kind and considerate of each other; we looked after the best interest of each other in the best way we could. We were cooperative, protective, and concerned about each other. If anyone needed any advise, we gave it, if we knew; and we accepted it if it was sincere and reasonable. We certainly didn't need anyone giving us orders, not up there. On the point, we always gave the orders. It was simply a matter of fighting to survive.

I also feared that the Germans most likely, considering what I was seeing, had many soldiers hiding in the cellars of the buildings in this town, and would come out when the shooting started and would shoot us in the back. Not one cellar had been searched in that town. I told Al that if these Krauts were good and seasoned soldiers as they were supposed to be, surely they had planted troops in the cellars there, as they set their trap to cut off our supply and support lines in the rear and then attack us with a large column of tanks.

I recalled reading the news of the Spanish Civil War when Generalissimo Franco was marching on Madrid with only four columns. A column was comparable to one of our battalions. He was asked how he intended taking the city with only four columns. His reply was that he had four columns marching on Madrid and a fifth column within the city that would rise up at the opportune time and take the city from within. Thus, the term "fifth column" was coined. I truly believed that the Krauts had a fifth column in this town and I told this to Al and also to the tankers. I also recalled that Hitler had entered the Spanish Civil War in the mid-1930s to test his war machine there.

Now the column of tanks and troops was very close, about one quarter of a mile, or a little further, approximately five hundred yards or so. I knew that the commander of that lead Tiger tank would want to get up to at least about two hundred yards before he started firing at our Pershings, so his 88 would be more effective against the armor of our tanks. I knew we could expect fire just any second now.

I had already told the tankers I was going to tell all of our men who were riding on these tanks to disperse and find a safe position to fire from, away from the tanks and out of the way of any flying shrapnel. He had agreed with me. I explained we were not abandoning them in the tank, but were only trying to protect ourselves, so we could fight again tomorrow— and we would never abandon them, but that we could be more effective away, a few yards apart, all spread out on each side of the tank so we could kill their infantry. I told all of the other GIs there, this was the most sensible plan, to locate a good position to fire from and let's get into that position right now. I knew how much fire-power Al liked to lay down with that automatic BAR, so I cautioned him about firing so much and using up all of his ammo. I told him to fire it single shot and not automatic and after the ammo he had for his BAR was gone, "there ain't gonna be no more." I also told him to fire only one shot at one soldier, to make his ammo last because that was all we had.

Just as the situation became more tense, when the Panzers were about three hundred yards from us, right out in front of us and at about the very moment all of us expected the Panzer unit to start firing on us, suddenly I heard airplanes. They were very loud and low and came from a southerly direction, right over this town and along the east side of this armada of armor.

I looked up and there to my profound surprise—as well as in an-swer to my prayers for a miracle, or divine intervention—there were four P-51 Mustang "tank buster" fighter planes. They came in from the flank of the enemy tank column at a very low altitude. One plane peeled off out of formation and fired his rockets at the Tiger, the one I had just seen the tank commander protruding from the turret of, which was the lead tank. I saw the first shot hit this most forward Tiger and set it afire. Its fuel tanks exploded. I didn't see anyone escape from this burning tank.

I had never heard of our fighter planes using rockets against enemy armor and I had to look close, in that at first I assumed they were drop-ping bombs, because I didn't know that they now had rockets to fire at tanks. Then I saw the rockets with the exhaust flaming out of them as they went to their targets, just like a bazooka being fired. They were not bombs, as some thought they were; they were rockets and they hit their target on the first run.

The tank commander I had just been observing through my field glasses was now only a statistic. One plane at the time would peel off and come in for an attack, it would return to the formation, and an-other one would peel off and attack. They also fired machine guns at the ground soldiers accompanying the tanks and we could see them falling to the ground. After about several minutes of this attack we could see there were about six or eight big Panzer tanks burning and exploding. All of this took place two or three hundred yards directly in front of us. It was a ringside seat for an air and tank battle, the likes of which I would never ever dream.

The planes kept coming, another group of four of them, then more, and in a few minutes the infantry and the remaining tanks suddenly turned around and began to run back the way that they came from. The infantry were all running this time, not walking, trying to keep up with the fleeing tanks that were now going off and leaving them behind. What a beautiful sight this was. It was beyond anyone's wildest imagination.

There was no place for any of the Wehrmacht soldiers to take cover out there in those open fields; they had a long way to run to find a place to hide. The P-51 "tank busters," as we called them, kept coming. It was the most breathtaking sight I have ever seen. Our prayers had been miraculously answered. This was definitely a divine intervention, if there ever was one.

It made me feel very proud to be an American combat soldier. It also gave me great faith in our leaders back there behind the lines, who really knew what they were doing. We knew now full well that they had our interest in mind and hadn't forgotten about us. Some of our command had, most obviously, been up all night preparing for this defense, I felt sure. I no longer had that feeling that we got up on the point, believing we were lost, abandoned, and all alone.

I, and my combat buddies, who I knew well, especially Al Sperl, had total, and complete faith in our Almighty God and Jesus Christ, our Savior. I knew that my Almighty God would not forsake us. The many whispered prayers that I had heard that night on the hay in that barn attested to the religious faith of our men who were all Patton's Raiders, as well as a few tankers.

I wondered what would have happened to us if the weather this day was like it was yesterday, cloudy, cold and overcast, where our planes couldn't fly or see the ground. I wondered whether the Nazi commander of this operation was counting on the weather still being overcast today, like it was yesterday, so as to not be attacked by our planes, that would not have the visibility to make this attack. There were just an awful lot of factors that were working in our favor.

This was the most beautiful sunshiny day I had ever experienced. We learned a little later these rockets fired from under the wings of these P-51 Mustang fighter planes were the first rockets of this kind that were ever used in this war, in actual combat against tanks. I can accurately attest to their efficiency and precision, as well as to the skill of the pilots, not to mention all of the officers in our outfit back there somewhere who brought about all of this counteroffensive support. Someone back there was really on the ball, in a very serious way. I feared to think if our planes had gotten there only a few minutes later, it would have been in the heat of one hell of a tank battle, with no telling what the consequence would be.

It is so lonesome up on the point, it makes you often wonder if our command is on the ball doing their job and this time I knew what great leadership we had, and they were highly skilled and dedicated. I was so thankful I was a member of such a great organization and too, our division commander, General Reinhart; our regimental commander, Colonel Frank Dunkley; and all of the others, including General Patton, as well as our XXth Corps Commander, General Walton H. Walker, who all were riding herd on all of their field commanders and looking after these tanks, as well as each and every one of us combat infantrymen of Patton's Raiders that were riding on them.

Our tankers got out of their tanks and were shouting, screaming, jumping up and down, slapping Al and me on the back, and everyone was hugging everyone else. I told all of our men there, I was happy and thankful to be alive. Never had I seen anyone so excited, which included myself and Al and all of the others with us, as well. It was as though all of us had been given a new lease on life. I asked the tank commander, what now? He told me we just had to wait.

Suddenly, some of our twin engine DC-3s appeared in the sky flying low and they opened their side doors and large flats of supplies were pushed out and they parachuted to the ground right out there in the field directly in front of us. I don't know what the supplies were, some said cans of gasoline, ammo, water, and rations. I had never seen a drop like this. It was food and water, I am sure. I spoke to the tank commander about us infantrymen going out there and retrieving them. He told me not to do anything, to wait right there with them for further orders. He told me a few minutes later that he got a message on his radio that some trucks had gotten through and were coming up there to get us infantrymen out of this place, quickly, in that this battle wasn't over yet. He related that this place would very shortly be under attack by our own infantry. Now I was thoroughly confused, of course, unless it meant that they were intending to attack enemy soldiers hidden in the buildings there, which I truly believed all of the time there were.

Things happened so fast; the trucks arrived, we said goodbye to the tankers wishing them well, and all of us infantrymen left riding trucks in a southerly direction as fast as the trucks could go. When we left the tankers, the supplies that had been dropped by DC-3s were still just sitting out there in the field in front of us and between the burning tanks and us.

Al had told me daily that the 65th Division was the greatest division in the whole of Europe. I always replied that our 2nd Squad, 2nd Platoon of Company G, 260th Infantry Regiment, 65th Division, was the greatest outfit in the whole division, as well as in the entire European Theater of Operations. It later turned out to be true. There was no question in anyone's mind that all of the people in our command were really on the ball, were highly skilled and dedicated to the fullest. We really had some fine people leading our troops. We also had some of the finest troops to be found anywhere. Our 65th Division was known thereafter as the "Spearhead Division." We in the Raiders were getting pretty well known by men in other divisions in the area, as well as in the entire European Theater of Operations. We were also getting a lot of publicity in Germany, that was being broadcast on the Nazi radios about "Patton's Raiders." The Nazi Propaganda Ministry was telling the German people that we were comparable to the Nazis' own SS troops. So they called us "Patton's SS Truppen."

Whoever it was back there that was running this operation was wide awake, and knew what they were doing and we thanked God for that. We now trusted explicitly our commanders, whoever and wherever they were, back there somewhere. But this was one very frightening close call. I heard one of the tankers ask the other one, "Do they give medals for being scared half to death?" These guys were the greatest tankers that there ever were, but they didn't talk very much.

I learned later that men from our and other regiments had attacked this town after we left and a battle raged there for the remainder of that day, all that night, and all of the next day. There were three hundred German soldiers—a Battalion of Pioneers, which was what the Germans called their combat engineers, who were some of the Germans' best fighting men—who had been hiding in the cellars in that town. They came out fighting soon after our infantry arrived there, sometime after we had left, and a fierce battle commenced. The battalion headquarters for these Pioneers was there at Struth. There was serious fighting right out in the streets of Struth, including hand-to-hand fighting. Many American and German soldiers, as well as many civilians, died there in that battle.

The men of our 260th Regiment of our division, as well as part of the 261st Regiment, entered Struth just after we were taken out of there about midmorning, and the heavy fighting then began. Our men used rifle fire, machine guns, mortars, and other weapons to finally defeat the Krauts. When it finally ended, our men captured all of the surviving German troops there. I was glad that they captured the surviving enemy soldiers. I knew that they were there from the very beginning—not that I am a psychic or anything like that, but it just took an application of common sense, as well as a sensible analysis of what we knew, to realize that. At about the same time as this attack was taking place, another of our battalions had taken the city of Mulhausen. Our men came riding into town late after dark, at night, on the day that we left Struth, on two-and-one-half tons trucks, shooting up the town as they sped through it to hurriedly put down any resistance there and take the river bridge in the center of the city before the Germans blew it up—so Patton's tanks would not be delayed. They took the bridge and then occupied the city that was full of German troops hidden in cellars there, too. After a bloody street battle they captured about three hundred of them that night and the next morning.

Also at about the same time, one of our battalions had set up their headquarters in the nearby town of Langensalza and soon afterwards, just at daylight the next day, a lone Panzer tank destroyer moved right up to the front entrance of our battalion headquarters and fired its 105mm howitzer point blank, directly into the front door, killing all of our men inside. I am convinced that the Nazis thought that this would be their day to turn the tide of the war and stop our attack on these very important targets, that the whole world was listening to and waiting to learn about on their radios.

It appeared General Patton's fast thrust toward Berlin had been stopped, and we were now headed in a different direction. I assumed

190

that our tanks had pulled back from this extended point pocket we had gotten trapped in, or that support had broken through the enemy lines behind us and our command was bringing in much needed help, with a new outfit that may be taking our place with the tankers.

I did learn later that these trucks were sent to Struth to rescue us from that town because our command had learned through intelligence information there were about three hundred or more German troops hidden in the cellars there who had instructions to destroy us and our tanks at the right moment. I knew that I was right; there were Trojan Horses in that town. You could also say that the Krauts had a Fifth Column there that was to come out of those cellars at the opportune time and destroy all of us. This was the reason that we were so quickly removed from that town; it was to save our lives. We would have been killed in the crossfire. The tankers could get in their tanks and defend themselves, but we couldn't. Little did we know at that time that parts of two of our regiments were poised on the outskirts of Struth to make an attack on the town and seize it, and take on the Nazi troops they had learned were hiding in the cellars there. We men who had been riding on the tanks would be put at great risk unless we were quickly removed before this attack commenced, which did occur just after we left. We would have certainly been caught in the crossfire.

This convoy of trucks loaded with us infantrymen that had been with the tanks back there, were moving fast on a narrow road in a valley as we traveled in a southerly direction away from Struth. Soon we saw some of our own bombers overhead. They were B-26, twin-engine bombers. They came in from the front of our column of trucks at no more than two to three thousand feet altitude and made one pass over us with their bomb bay doors open. Everyone waved excitedly, then I saw them making a big circle and heading back toward us. I wondered why they were coming back again with their bomb bay doors still open. I saw that they had made their turn and were coming in a very straight line on their final approach, directly toward the head of our column of trucks, just like they were lining up for a bombing run again.

I just knew that now we were going to be mistakenly bombed by our own planes. I then realized that I didn't see any color panels displayed on the trucks, as there should have been, which was a signal to our aircraft that we were friendly. I wondered why no one had sense enough to know that we needed those color panels displayed. They are about the size of a single bed sheet with a fluorescent orange color on one side and yellow on the other. They are used to identify our vehicles from the air. I knew that all of our vehicles were supposed to display them so our planes could identify them. We had too many fine fighting men on these trucks who had just endured an ordeal beyond belief. I quickly realized that this was no time to be just fooling around, afraid to say or do something. It was not my nature to remain quiet when I saw some impending danger that needed to be dealt with. Someone had to make a decision about this situation and do something quickly.

It flashed into my mind what my mother always told me; "If you see something that is needed to be done, don't wait for someone else to tell you to do it, just do it and do it good. Never be a slacker, always meet all of your obligations and responsibilities, to yourself and to others as well."

I asked the dumb-ass driver why he didn't have his color panel out and he replied that he didn't know. I asked him where in the hell it was and he said the assistant driver was sitting on it. I made him get off of it and give it to me. I got it out, unfolded it, and we held it up and waved it in the air. Just as we did the bombers saw it, apparently just in time, and they closed their bomb bay doors immediately, dipped their wings, and flew on directly over us and away toward Struth behind us. What a relief that was.

I shuddered to think of how close we came to being torn to shreds by our own bombs. This was a close call, so close that split seconds mattered. I am certain that they were looking for the fleeing enemy tanks and soldiers that we had confronted back there in Struth. It had to be who they were after, and they flew off in that direction. I asked my buddy Al, "How many more of these kind of close calls can we take today?"

Al told me, "I owe you my life. If you hadn't had the intelligence to get that color panel out, I, you, and all of us would now be dead."

I had my own life to think about saving, as well as the lives of all of the other men in this convoy, and I certainly had no intentions of just sitting there and doing nothing about getting the signal panels displayed.

We continued traveling down this road at a high speed in a convoy of about four or five trucks when suddenly two German Messerschmitts came over a hill from behind us. They came from the east. I looked back when I heard them; I was almost blinded by the midmorning sun. They strafed the whole column with machine gun fire, killing two or three of our men and injuring several, some on almost every truck. They disappeared about as fast as they came, over the hills. We hardly had time to look up before they were gone. These trucks all had an open cab with a .50 caliber machine gun mounted on a ring turret over the assistant driver's seat, but these drivers, this day, didn't seem very alert—maybe they got no sleep last night, coming up there to get us. I was beginning to learn that it takes some soldiers quite a while, and others maybe just a few minutes after they have been under fire up on the point, to realize that this is war and that you have to think and then act—and do it quickly if you want to survive.

Al told me that these truck drivers and their assistants were inexperienced, as well as scared to death. I knew that no one else was going to do your thinking for you up on the point. If you wanted to survive, one had to take control of the situation, decide what should be done about it, and then make the most of it. Every man on the truck that I was on was highly nervous and agitated. Having to experience what we all had on this day, was enough to unnerve anyone. As I looked my fellow soldiers in the face there on the truck as it was moving down this road at a very high speed, I could see in their faces fright, hunger, sleeplessness, and exhaustion. It was very apparent from the blank expressionless look on all of their faces.

After we left Struth was when the heavy street fighting took place between our men of both the 260th and the 261st Regiments, who had moved in to take the town and the enemy soldiers that came out of the cellars to defend the place.

All of the resistance back there in that town was done to stop our advance to Nordhausen Concentration Camp and the V2 rocket factory, which we thought would be our next objectives, and then on to Berlin. The *Stars and Stripes*, the American forces newspaper, had been saying that Patton was headed for Berlin—and we had been—but something changed that.

We traveled south where there was less enemy resistance. Late that evening we stopped at a small village where we spent the night and waited for further orders. We were pleasantly surprised when the next afternoon our tanks arrived at this farmhouse where we had pulled into the evening before. We were excited to see them, to say the least. It was these same tanks and crews that we fought with all the way from across the Rhine and then to Struth—and would be with on into Austria at the end of the war.

I observed also that the *Stars and Stripes* so far as I know, never printed anything about us being cut off from all of our support and supply lines and being under attack by a huge Panzer column. Maybe they thought that it would be embarrassing to our command for these tanks and men to be allowed to be too far out ahead of their support and supply lines and allowing themselves to be cut off. On the other hand, they should have printed it, because it was a great work of strategy and logistics for whomever it was that saved our lives by sending in the P-51s and then dropping the supplies to us, as well as sending in the trucks to pick us up—all of which saved us from annihilation.

We learned that Patton's Third Army was now being diverted to the south to head for Nuremberg, Regensburg, and then to Linz, Austria. The purpose being, according to the *Stars and Stripes*, that the Allied Command wanted Patton to go to the south so that he could search that area in the mountains of southern Germany and Austria to find the German war criminals thought to be hiding in the Redoubt Region. We also learned that the 101st Airborne Division was right on our right flanks all of the way and that their objective was Hitler's Eagle's Nest at Berchesgarten in Bavaria and part of southern Austria. The 10th Armored Division was also on our right flank, and their objective was Munich and Dachau Concentration Camp, which they liberated.

General Patton had stated many times that he intended to take Berlin. General Eisenhower had made the statement that he couldn't conceive of anyone wanting to take Berlin, because it was so devastated.

We seldom got a copy of the *Stars and Stripes* up on the point, but it was always welcome reading when we did get one. The Germans thought that we were headed to Berlin, not expecting us to go in any other direction. We all wondered whether this redirecting of General Patton's Third Army from Berlin to Austria and Bavaria was a result of our being cut off and surrounded.

Something went terribly wrong and a catastrophe almost occurred. We shouldn't have been so far out on the point, where we could have gotten cut off from our support and supply lines. Being in that kind of a situation had always been my greatest fear. I thanked God for saving us and for having such great leadership that kept up with the situation, was aware of the predicament that we were in, and sent help—those fighter planes, the DC-3s, and the trucks that retrieved us just in time. Another two minutes or less would have been too late for all of us.

The Battle of Struth was much more than what is described here and which has been heretofore described by anyone. We infantrymen who were Patton's Raiders riding shotgun on tanks and were there, only experienced a small part of the total Battle of Struth, which had not really begun when we were pulled out. After we departed on trucks, the battle was just beginning between a Panzer tank that had been hidden in Struth, along with a lot of German infantry. Our infantry that were already in a nearby area, came in to take Struth from the enemy soldiers hiding in the cellars there. When the two battalions of our infantry came into Struth, I don't believe that they were really aware of the danger that they were walking into. After one group came in, someone began to ring the church bell continuously, which obviously was a signal to the enemy hiding in the cellars there to come out and attack our units that had come in to take the town. Our infantry and one of the 6th Armored tank destroyers eliminated the Panzer tank that was in Struth and at the end of a long and fierce street battle that lasted through the following day, our men had captured all of the remaining German troops that had been hiding in the cellars there, that came out to fight.

It was obvious that someone in our command, through their intelligence efforts, knew that those enemy troops were there in the cellars. We forty or so combat infantrymen there with those tanks were no match for an indeterminate number of enemy troops there with automatic weapons. At least the tankers could button up in them and use their machine guns and their cannons to do some damage to the Kraut troops. We Raiders on the ground, would not have stood a chance of surviving if we had not been taken out of there when we were. Our tanks got out of there soon after we did, in that they would have been destroyed quickly by the Krauts who had lots of Panzerfausts, as well as other antitank weapons.

This counterattack offensive action by the Nazis at Struth, Langensalza, Mulhausen and the surrounding area was under the command of German Field Marshall Kesselring, and the offense was under the direct command of German General Hitzfeld, commander of the German 1ˢᵗ Army who had over 2,200 infantry troops in the area, that fought in the battles there. There was much street fighting as well as other tank attacks the following morning. Fierce fighting took place in Struth and in the surrounding towns, after we had left, and the town of Struth was in almost total ruins.

It was over fifty years later that I learned that this column of Nazi Panzer armor that attacked us there that day at Struth, was under the command of a Colonel Worgitski. The second-in-command of that column of tanks was a Panzer Captain Carl Peter Dirk. Captain Dirk related to me that he had tried to talk his commander, Colonel Worgitski, out of making this attack on Struth where he had a battalion of over three hundred Pioneer Troops hiding in the cellars there, but that the colonel refused to follow his recommendation. Captain Dirk related that he then took command and after other tanks were knocked out, he gave the order to withdraw. All of this that he described occurred right in front of me, about two or three hundred yards away. When we departed Struth this big Tiger tank and others were still burning.

It was related by men of our 261ˢᵗ Regiment that two of their men were on a reconnaissance patrol north of Struth the following day after we were taken out of Struth, or the day after that. They were in their jeep and had stopped when they observed a large column of enemy troops marching toward them in formation, down this road. They were marching just as they would on a parade ground. Their officer in command came ahead, carrying a white flag, and talked to our men in the jeep and told them that these German soldiers were unarmed and wanted to surrender. They were the men that were the ground troops who supported the tank column that attacked us with that column of tanks there at Struth, the previous day. The men in the jeep radioed for support, which arrived, and accepted the surrender of these surviving three hundred Kraut troops that had attacked us yesterday, and took them into custody.

We also found out that parts of our own 260th Infantry Regiment participated in the fighting at Struth, as well as parts of the 261st Regiment, all of which was after we had left on the trucks, regrettably. I would love to have engaged the enemy that day, on a level playing field, with adequate support by our troops, and not being so outnumbered and having been caught in a trap. However, our small group of Patton's Raiders were in no condition to fight that day, not having had any rest, sleep, food, or water in a very long time. None of us had even one sip of water in our canteen.

Those who have written about and recounted the Battle of Struth have been obviously unaware that we men on the tanks that first entered Struth that night were totally and completely cut off from all of our support. They have also failed to recognize that we remained in Struth all that night and until nearly midmorning on the following day, when we were taken out on trucks after the attack by the armada of Panzer armor. Our tanks got out just after we left. During this period of time we were totally surrounded and outnumbered by Nazi troops in Struth who could have annihilated us in a matter of minutes. Nor did anyone ever relate to anyone else about the column of tanks and ground troops that were attacking us, which were repelled by the P-51s, or about the supplies that were dropped for us. Some of our troops who attack Struth after we departed assumed that no other American soldiers had ever been there prior to their arrival. Many of the men apparently assumed that the town had been cleared of enemy resistance before they arrived, which caused them to be caught off guard when the attack by the Nazis started. This was a mistake that was often made, even on one occasion by us on the tanks. One could never assume that any town or building was free of enemy soldiers unless they first searched it out completely.

We also learned that when our men came into Struth, just after we rode out of there on trucks, that one GI saw some movement in a haystack in a field right beside the town, fired on it, and killed a few Krauts. Then all of the others hiding in the haystacks came out and surrendered. There were fifty Nazi paratroopers hiding in the hay waiting for the word to attack us there in Struth.

When we infantrymen, Patton's Raiders, rode shotgun on tanks, we never knew what infantry unit was supporting us or where our own battalion, regiment, or division was. We rode the tanks wherever they were directed to go. We were supported by whatever unit was nearest to us at the time, and seldom ever by anyone in our own company.

Commentary of German Panzer Captain Carl Peter Dirk

Fifty five years after this battle I have been in communication with German Panzer Captain Carl Peter Dirk and he has related to me events that occurred prior to and up to the time of the Struth battle, which I will quote:

"...Before the tanks became available [new Tiger 4 Type built by Mercedes] Patton headed for Kassel and instead of defending Berlin, we were ordered to Kassel and arrived there on April 2nd. My function was that of a shooting instructor for the Tiger Two, but on leaving Berlin we had only three or four Mark IV tanks left. From the eastern front, actually the Sudeten Area, we received three antitank companies, each having 12 Hetzer, and 16 tank destroyers. On top of that all other small tank units in the area were added. We were told to join an attack to free the German Army Group B in the Ruhr area, but we didn't get off.

"In April 4th or 5th we learned that a counterattack to the southwest was imminent to attack Patton's North-eastern flank in the Eschwege-Eisenach area, but we were delayed and could only start on the 7th of April at 2 o'clock A.M., to arrive north of Struth by 4 A.M. Then we were to pass Struth in the West and head for Eisenach. There were 2,200 men in Oberst I.G. [Colonel] Worgitski's task force, one infantry brigade, and one Pioneer Brigade to take Struth, supported in the west by a total of 50 to 60 tanks and tank destroyers.

"The first wave of about 18 to 21 tanks and tank destroyers soon got stuck, the Pioneers had only two or three companies earmarked to "infiltrate" Struth after 2 A.M., but they were largely untrained and noisy and the element of surprise got lost. My function after April 1st was that of a liaison officer for Tank Destroyer No. One. When the Struth attack got stuck, I went to pick up Colonel Worgitski so he could come to the center of the battle and see for himself. There was a young Captain who almost despaired in view of high losses and he insisted to have the first wave of tanks re-directed and join his efforts in the center of Struth. I had to go and connect with our signal car and the first wave began to withdraw in the west.

"On the eastern flank two infantry battalions didn't get started either, they were held up by one company ordered to join the Struth fighters. To my knowledge there were 6 to 15 GIs holding out in the east until relief troops arrived about 11 P.M.

"Tank wave No. 2 and 3 never got started, in that wave No. One lost between 12 and 16 tanks and tank destroyers, mainly by air attack. Late in the afternoon I escaped to the north and joined wave No. 2 and 3 heading for the west of the Harz Mountains. There were two Tiger II tanks left behind by Field Marshal Kesselring, who had his headquarters near Braunlage for about a week.

"When Patton headed for Kassel, it transpired that by or around the 4th or 5th of April that the last German gold reserves and bank notes had been brought from Berlin to West of Eisenach to the Merker Potash mine. Part of our mission was to reconnect with the German 7th Army in that area and then jointly advance to Merker, but without an 'umbrella' of fighters this was asking too much. Tanks had become vulnerable to air attacks, infantrymen were largely untrained youngsters, or old aged or disabled men. When there was a need of a new tank commander I had no choice but to do what I was ordered.

"The Struth battle was in command of Kampfgruppe Oberst I.G. Worgitski and Lt. Colonel Stockhausen, Lt. Colonel Bremm, Major Lamberts, Major Reden, Major Hirschfeld, and I.G. Fberst.

"On April 6th these officers were assembled at Worgitskis Headquarters with Stockhausen as Chief of Staff. There were heavy disputes with Reden and Hirschfeld, who wanted to infiltrate, whereas Worgitski insisted men were not trained well enough for that. Reden and Hirschfeld kept behind and did not accompany their troops.

"Out of 2,200 men only two Pioneer companies attacked Struth, with the wrongly displayed tanks, wave number one. Lamberts also kept in the back, the second and third waves of tanks never ever got started.

"Hirschfelds two companies in front were held down at the eastern flank, he, like Lamberts never appeared on the battle field.

"Worgitski appeared around 09-15 hours, I took him to Struth, where one of Redens battalions had their headquarters. With the absence of all 6 Staff Officers, except Worgitski, the whole thing was bound to fail.

"Out of the 2,200 men, a maximum of 100 tanks came into action, and out of 600 to 800 Pioneers only 300 to 400 came into Struth, Hirschfeld's two companies were held down, his three reserve companies did not see action. Rumors have it that there were 250 of our men dead in Struth, plus almost 30 to 40 civilians and probably up to 40 or more American soldiers lost their lives there."

Again, that day, we were saved from being annihilated by our own B-26 bombers when we had no color panels displayed on the trucks that we were riding on, until I displayed the panels to the bombers. It was my getting the panel displayed at the very last moment, as a signal to the bombers that we were friendly troops, that saved us from all being killed. This also was a split-second action that could only be defined as divine intervention at the very last moment. I realized that there were no panels out and I became seriously concerned about myself and all of the others there, and I didn't wait for orders to come down through channels to do something about this situation. I later spoke to my cousin who flew B-26s, and I related to him about the bombardiers closing their bomb bay doors so quickly upon seeing our color panel. He informed me that the bombardiers scrutinize a target very carefully through their Norden bombsight as they approach it and that the very second that they saw that color panel, they would instantly close the bomb bay door, and that they were the only person on the plane that could close it.

We all knew that day, the point was a very lonely, as well as a extremely dangerous place for Patton's Raiders to be. By the Grace of God, sheer guts, and great faith and courage, as well as belief in God Almighty, we were saved from annihilation. It was due to the great faith and courage of all of our troops everywhere who participated in that operation, including all of our leaders. We were winning, and this was a rewarding feeling.

Letters

The following are excerpts from some of
my letters to my family.

Somewhere in Germany
15 April 1945
Dear Mom and all,

How is everyone by now? I haven't had any mail in
so long, I feel totally isolated from the rest of the
world. This morning we had five minutes of silence in
Honor of President Roosevelt's Death. I hear there was
a write up in Time Magazine about what we did in
Saarlautern, and broke the Siegfried line. That makes
me think of what someone told me the other day. When
I was in Camp Blanding I read an article in PIC Magazine about what we would do after the war, and I sat
down and wrote them and gave them a piece of my
mind about what I thought about it, and they printed
it, and this person found the magazine over here on
the road and read it and told me about it, and it was in
either the December, January or February issue. I wish
you would try to find it for me. I bet I have something
on you, I had deer steak again last night. We have been
sleeping in houses lately, and I hate to think where we
will be sleeping in the next few nights. Yesterday a
French woman here in Germany gave me a bottle of
Apricot Cognac that she had been saving for Americans. She was the first black haired woman I have
seen in Germany. I knew at first she was French, then
she said, "Parle vous France?" Don't worry about me

making a pig of myself, there are always too many other fellows who want a drink. I sure wish I could get some mail from you, don't worry about me. Take care of yourselves. Lots of love, Oscar Jr.

Germany
April 26, 1945
Dear Mom and all,

I got a letter from you today and enjoyed it very much. I am pretty tired and worn out, but caught up with my sleep this morning. All we have had to eat was K Rations. The other night we slept in an old barn and I like to have froze. It snowed a little that morning and sleeted all of the rest of the day. It is fairly warm though, today. Last night we put up in this old hotel with all of the conveniences you ever saw, I slept until 12:45 this morning. One boy killed a deer and I dressed it and cut it up and the whole platoon had steak for dinner with French fries, pickles, noodles and huckleberries. We do our own cooking in these kitchens. I wish you could see the messes we make sometimes.

We have been spearheading for the whole Division all of this week and have really covered some ground. We recently took a prisoner of war camp where the Germans had 5,000 English and Australian prisoners. They were swarming over the countryside like a bunch of chickens that had been shut up for a long time. We see news correspondents right up here on the line with us. I know that Dad keeps up with every bit of it. I wish I could tell him more about what is going on, but the censers won't let it go through. The artillery is going off so fast now that you can hardly hear your own self talk. Our Company is to establish a beachhead across the Danube tonight, so I had better close and get a little sleep. Take care of yourselves, lots of love,
Oscar Junior

Germany
April 29, 1945
Dear Mom and all,

I am getting along fine, but kind of worn out. I got three letters from you yesterday. I was glad to get them. We have been pushing forward every day, and eating nothing but K Rations, and I am so sick of them, I can hardly stand to look at them. There is lots that I could tell you about what we are doing. It is in the headlines back home by now, but I will have to wait till later, I have a German Generals uniform I am going to try to send home. I hope I can. I heard yesterday about the Germans in Italy surrendering. I sure hated to hear about Newton Ladner getting wounded. I had better close, will write more later. Lots of love to all, Jr.

Some of the 2nd Platoon, Co. G, 260th Infantry Regiment, 65th Division.

Mauthausen Concentration Camp
May 9, 1945
Dear Mom and all,

Well, we moved out here day before yesterday and are living in nice houses that were used by the SS Officers who ran Mauthausen and Camp Gussen Concentration camps. You have probably seen pictures of it and read about it. It is about thirty miles from Linz. I will have to wait and tell you how horrible it was here and what they did to the prisoners, it is too much to write about. Tell Dad to get some help there on the farm, it is too much for him. But thank God you have something to work with, and it is not all destroyed by bombs and shells.

Well, it is 10:15 and I must close and get some sleep, we are on guard for two hours and off for four for 24 hours, then we are off for 48 hours. Please take care of yourselves and write often.

Lots of love to all, Oscar Jr.

My squad at the end of the fighting, in Linz, Austria. I am far right on the back row. Sgt. Willie Graybeal is front row, center.

Austria
May 10, 1945
Dear Mom and all,

How is everyone today? I am fine. I guarded prisoners last night till 12:00 and I am kind of sleepy this morning. I was talking to a prisoner, 19 years old, and a Lieutenant. I asked him if he was glad the was over and he said "No." He told me that when he heard the war was over he wished that someone had shot him. I asked him who started the war and he said, "Poland, England and America. I asked him why Germany attacked so many countries and he told me, "You don't understand that Germany is so small with so many people they had to have more room." He could not understand that Germany was imposing on the rights of other countries. I asked him if it wouldn't be much better for everyone if we were friends from now on, and to forget about war, but he didn't think much of the idea. He said that Germany had fought so bravely for six years, and yet lost the war. He said that their leader, Hitler, fought to the last bit of ammunition. He said that Hitler was a little man, yet he was so great. As he talked you could see his hatred for all of the Allies. He seemed to think that it was our fault that all was lost for them. He said that we unnecessarily and unmercifully bombed Germany cities. I asked him if he knew what Germany did to London? I asked him if he knew that the Germans destroyed Amsterdam even after they had surrendered? He said that they started it and asked for it. I told him that now that Germany was defeated, we were going to set up a new and better government for them and make sure that they didn't start another war. He didn't think much of the idea and said, "You can't give us a better government that what we had."

He told me that every person in Germany had a job, and that in America we had millions of unemployed. He could not understand that in Germany they were building war materials and pillboxes and fortifications, and doing this with forced labor and money they had taken from the Jews and with money borrowed on credit from other countries and never paid it back.

He said the we Americans were fair in war compared to the Russians. He said that for every shell they fired at us they got back fifteen in exchange.

If you could only see the slave laborers here in this city, and see how undernourished and how poorly clothed they are, you would have some idea of the brutality of these people, yet, to hear them talk they are so cunning and innocent, you would think that they were a bunch of Angels. They shave the heads of the Russians and cut it short and shave a streak down the center for the Greeks. The citizens here are praying that we will not move out and turn it over to the Russians. It is not that the Russians are so cruel and are barbarians, but they give back to the Germans the same medicine they have been taking from them.

The Germans know that we are kind hearted and easy going, and they take advantage of it, and at our backs, they say we are stupid and will fall for anything. These peoples minds are warped and revenge through warfare is welded into their minds. It is these people that we are going to have to deal with and we must keep a close watch on them, not for a few months or years, but for generations. The war may be over here, but peace is not yet won and guaranteed.

Well that is a load off my mind, and I feel better having told it to someone. Tell every one hello and lots of love to you all. Love, Oscar Jr.

Austria
May 11, 1945
Dear Mom and all,

It has been mighty peaceful lately, no noise, nothing to worry about, no rush, you can just feel that the war is over. Walking down the streets on guard at night with the lights on and lights coming out of the windows makes one feel that they are back in the States. Mom, I know that you have been worrying about me, but you don't have anything at all to worry about now. Well, tomorrow we parade for the Russians, they are just across the river from us, and also we are going to be inspected by General Patton. We don't have to do anything but eat, sleep and pull guard. We just got a letter today from a boy who is back in the hospital with a cerebral hemorrhage that he got after we crossed the Danube when the Jerries threw 88 shells at us. I was just a few feet from him when he was wounded by the concussion. He is a real great guy and was a great help when our moral was running low. He is the man that the Major fined $25.00 for eating two eggs from these poor old innocent Germans, but we had a good laugh about it, just the same. Tell Mildred not to feed those kittens too much and to not let anyone slam a door on them. Sure wish I could see every, I will close now, with lots of love,
Oscar Jr.

Austria
May 12, 1945
Dear Mom and all,

Today I witnessed the greatest event of my life. I was an honor guard for General Patton today as he met several Russian Generals at the airport here in Linz. We went out to the airport in trucks and after awhile General Patton's plane arrived and taxied right up close to where we were. General Patton got out and was met by some of our Generals. It was a very formal occasion. There were more Generals than you could shake a stick at. General Patton inspected us and paid us a very nice compliment. After awhile the Russian Generals arrived and you have never seen so much hand shaking and saluting. The whole place was swarming with photographers and news cameramen taking news reels. After the Russians arrived, we were inspected again by General Patton and the Russian General. Just before that Patton pinned a medal on the Russian. I think his name was Molonofsky. All of this time flying fortresses were landing and taking off. The sky was full of them and it was thrilling to see them land and take off again. Two P-51s taxied up and parked right behind us. They were escorts for General Patton's plane. His plane flew the red flag with four silver stars on it.

Well, I wouldn't have taken anything for having been there. Maybe my picture will be in the news reels, and you will probably see pictures of the meeting in Life magazine.

I guess I had better close. Please take care of yourselves and don't do too much work. Lots of love to all, Jr.

General Patton meets Russial General at Linz, Austria when the Author and other of Patton's Raiders served as his Honor Guard.

Austria
May 21, 1945
Dear Mom,

No more censorship rules. Now I can begin to tell you something about what I have seen and done. I am in Linz, Austria, one of the largest cities in Europe, and on the Danube River. On May 12, General Patton met a Russian General, head of the 3rd Ukrainian Army. I don't know what his name is, but they met here at the airport, and I for one was one of the few in the company chosen as an Honor Guard for Patton. That day I wrote you a letter telling all about it, but the censors gave it back to me, so I will mail it now with this letter. But today they called for the same men that were Guards for General Patton to go out to the airport as Guards for General Walton H. Walker, Commander of the XX Corps. He complimented us very highly. As you know I am getting $74.60 per month and I was awarded the Combat Infantry Badge which raised my pay $10.00 per month and I also have the E.T.O. (European Theatre of Operations) ribbon with two campaign stars on it, Rhineland and Central Europe, as well as the Bronze Star Medal.

I don't know if we will be here for the occupation or not. It is rumored that we will be here for six more months before going to the States. I just have four hours of guard duty per day with the rest of the time off. Give my love to all, Jr.

Linz, Austria
May 23, 1945
Dear Mom and all,

Yesterday I got nine letters, all mailed in March, except one from Grandpa Baker and it sure was a nice letter. I was out at the airport today and there were five thousand French slave laborers there waiting for a plane back to France. You have heard of Hitler's mass murders and his mass extermination plan, well, this morning I was unfortunate enough to see this plan under way. On this side of the airport is one of his concentration camps filled with Poles, Russians, Czechs, French and dozens of other nationalities who could not withstand the exposure, beatings and under-nourishment that were imposed on these slave laborers, so now that they couldn't work, they put them here to await their turn to be exterminated. Before we arrived there were 800 a day dying. They could only cremate eighty per day. So the rest of them were thrown in huge holes and were only partly covered.

This morning while I was guarding prisoners, the Engineers came after 900 prisoners to work in cemeteries, and they had to make the prisoners go. All other times they were only too eager to work. I asked one of the Engineers what it was all about and he told me, and I didn't believe it was so, and I went out and saw for myself. The prisoners were made to dig graves and bury these exterminated people.

I talked with some of the slave laborers in the camp and they begged for cigarettes. I took some pictures of them. Their bones was almost cut through their skin. They had been waiting their turn to die, now they had a little hope. They are eating American food and gaining weight. The death rate has been cut in half. I remember reading about things like this that the Nazis were doing, but I didn't think much of it. I have heard people say that they didn't believe all that stuff they read, but they were just joking with themselves and didn't know it. Give the kids a big hug for me and tell Christine that I sure enjoy hearing from her and she writes such interesting letters. Take good care of yourselves and don't work too hard.
Lots of love to all, Oscar Jr.

Linz, Austria
May 25, 1945
Dear Mom and all,

I just got a letter from you, and it only took nine days to get it. I am getting along fine and I wonder how everyone is at home. You can't realize what a hard life it was over here. For almost a month we ate only K Rations which was just enough to keep you going. You get no rest at all and fight like hell all day and stand guard nearly all night, you keep going through rain and snow. I can tell you what it is like to be soaking wet and crawling up a little narrow ditch full of mud, with bullets flying a few inches above your head and 88 shells bursting a few yards from you and you keep digging your head a little deeper in the mud and just wait for that unlucky moment, it never came to me, but I have seen others who were less fortunate than I. I don't know if I told you that I got a letter from Grandpa, I sure was glad to hear from him.

This morning we discharged 300 prisoners, I had to sign a Captains name to the discharges and give it to them. Some looked very sad and some looked very happy. We were leading the attack for the 3rd Army for thirty days is the reason you haven't heard much from me, and I couldn't tell all that happened, they would send it back. Write often, Love, Jr.

Linz, Austria
June 12, 1945
Dear Mom and all,

I just received a letter from you and was sure glad to get it. It seemed that you were feeling good when you wrote it, I am sure glad that you are getting along fine. I just heard that the 3rd Army is going to be the Army of Occupation, and if it is so, we will be here, and in Germany all winter. It is not so bad now, and I don't mind it much, but I sure would like to be back home. We are sure getting plenty to eat now as I have told you before, we pull guard at this hospital and are on duty for one day and are off for two. When we are there we eat four meals a day and we can eat all we want.

I am glad that you kept up with the Third Army as it came across Germany. Our Division lead the attack for it nearly all the way. Our Regiment was always spearheading for the Division, and our company was most always spearheading for the Regiment. At one time our company was closer to Berlin than any other outfit, but in a few days we were relieved and started south and were just hitting it in the high places until we got to the Danube and were slowed down considerably, but we were a happy bunch when our company was the first ones into Regensburg. I found a little map of Germany and I will try to trace the way we came, most of the places are not on it, but most of the big ones are.

I will close until later, so take good care of yourselves, and tell the kids to be good and to write often, you don't know how much a letter means. Good night to all of you and with all of my love. Love, Oscar Jr.

Linz, Austria
16 June 1945
Dear Mom and all,

 I wonder how every one is tonight. I am fine and tired as can be, I just got back off a cruise down the Danube. Our Special Service Officer arranged it for us. It was a nice excursion boat built to carry people up and down the Danube. We ate dinner and supper on it, we had all of the fried chicken we could eat. It sure is beautiful country along the Danube and it was such a nice sunny day, too. When we got back to the company the Lieutenant told us that there was ice cream in the dining room and I mean I really filled up on it. I am kind of tired so I had better go to bed. By the way, I can speak quite a bid of German, am learning more every day, they say slafen for sleep. I am hoping I can be home soon so I can eat some of your good cooking, there is none that can beat it.
All my love, Oscar Jr.

Linz, Austria
July 11, 1945
Dear Mom and all,

I am fine and wish I could see everyone there. Yesterday about forty men from our outfit were shipped out to the States. We hear that our division will be broken up, but you can't ever tell. Four of the men were from my squad and they really hated to leave. After you have fought alongside a fellow, and went through the same hardships that he had, and see your buddies left behind, some wounded and some you will never see again, you develop a kind of brotherly love for each other that will remain in your mind forever. You know that they won't ever let you down, because when the going was the roughest, they were right there with you.

When I got up this morning I looked out the window and I could clearly see the snow capped Alps mountains good and clear. I told several men that it was going to rain, and it did this afternoon. That is the way these people know when not to cut hay. Take care of yourselves and lots of love, Oscar Jr.

Waizenkirchen, Germany
August 12, 1945
Dear Mom and all,

Well today is Sunday and I have nothing at all to do. I won't be in the 65th much longer.

We are leaving Wednesday for the 10th Armored Division which is in Partenkirchen, Germany, south of Munich in the Bavarian Alps. It is rumored that it is getting ready to go back to the States, which I hope is very true. These Armored outfits are pretty good outfits and all of the men ride in half-tracks. I now have all of the names and addresses of the men in my outfit and am enclosing them. I can't think of anything else to write, so I will close for now. Lots of love, Oscar Jr.

Fursstenfeldbruck, Germany
October 19, 1945
Dear Mom and all,
    I had to get up this morning at 2:30 and go on
guard. About daylight the GI with me said that if we
were at home, what would he and I like to have for
breakfast. He said that he would have one and one-half
dozen fried eggs with smoked ham and hot biscuits. I
told him I would like a big pot of oatmeal, a pot of hot
cocoa, two dozen hot buttered biscuits and some good
smoked sausage. It was fun just talking about it, but I
can't wait until it can come true. Tell the girls to write
and to study their music. Tell Grandpa Baker hello for
me. Lost of love to all, Oscar Jr.

My combat buddy Al Sperl, the "BAR" man, and me, on a cruise boat up the
Danube River on a Sunday after the war ended. The Captain was trying to
teach us the days of the week again.

CHAPTER 21

Reunited with our Tanks

> *"Government is a trust, and the officers of the Government are Trustees; and both the trust and the Trustees are created for the benefit of the people."*
>
> —HENRY CLAY (1777–1852)

We traveled on the trucks until late that night after we left Struth, which was very unusual for us to be doing—and in fact it was the first time that we Raiders had ridden on trucks since right after we crossed the Siegfried Line. We stopped at a small farm village and searched it out for enemy troops. The village was abandoned by civilians, and we slept in beds for the first time in a long time. How the civilians were able to know we were coming, and to disappear so fast, was something that I was never able to understand.

The sun was high in the sky when we awoke the following morning. It was very quiet and peaceful there. I was in need of a lot of rest, which I got that night, even with all of my clothes, boots, and helmet on, and my rifle in my arms. I always slept with my rifle against my chest, with the butt between my legs. My rifle had become an integral part of my body. The only time that my rifle was not in my hands at all times, was when I was in the hospital.

Little did we know at this time that soon after we left Struth, units of the 261st Regiment of our division, as well as units of our own 260th Regiment moved into Struth and fierce fighting took place there, with many Germans as well as Americans being killed and injured, fighting in the streets. Nor did we know that it continued all during the day yesterday, and into the night last night, and was still raging this morning. So, what I told Al Sperl and the others about there being German troops in cellars there, was certainly correct. When we heard about what happened, I hated to tell all of the other men, "I told you so"—but I did. I told them all, it was easy to understand—just put yourself in their places and what would you have done there, then?

One of our men who went in to fight the Krauts that had been hiding there in Struth was in the barn, the same barn that our tank had been in, on that frightful night, when a Kraut mortar shell landed near him and a piece of shrapnel hit him in the chest, penetrating a lung, causing him severe pain, loss of blood, a lot of which he was spitting up as bloody foam. A Kraut soldier came to him to help stop the bleeding, but the GI waived him on and refused his help. Soon, medical help arrived and the GI there in that same barn that we and our tank had been in, survived. This indicated to me that our tanks had already left there when the fierce fighting commenced the day after we first arrived there.

Our tanks wouldn't have had a chance of surviving that battle without lots of infantry supporting them and protecting them from such things as Panzerfausts, and even Molotov cocktails. Tanks are not suited for urban fighting at all. They must have plenty of room in which to maneuver, and enemy troops must be kept quite a distance away from them. They are very defenseless in an urban area in that lots of things can be done to knock them out, such as Molotov cocktails, Panzerfausts, as well as mortar shells tossed from an upstairs window onto the tank.

One thing that I learned in basic training was that one can knock out a tank from an upstairs window if you only have one mortar shell. The fuse in the nose cone of those shells is armed by the momentum of its being fired from the mortar. Another way to arm the shell so that it will explode on contact is to point the shell up and pound the base of it hard on a solid flat wooden surface, similar to it being fired, which dislodges the safety pin in the nose; one can then throw it nose-down onto the rear portion of a tank where the engines are and it will explode on contact and knock the tank out. Always when we went through a town or city where there were buildings higher than one story, I always looked up toward the rooftops and upper-story windows for enemy soldiers trying to do this to our tanks. In such a case we always fired at anything that moved in upper-story windows and on the roofs. I was delighted to learn that our tanks had gotten out before the Krauts there could knock them out.

We later learned that just as our troops arrived in Struth, there were obviously Kraut observers in the church steeple, they always were, and they rang the church bell incessantly, which was a signal to the enemy troops to come out of their cellar hiding places and fight the Americans, which they then did. When the Krauts came out to fight, they used small arms, mortars, Panzerfausts and machine guns to kill Americans with. The Kraut soldiers had many Panzerfausts with them that they intended to fire at the rear end of our tanks to knock them out, but our tanks had already left the area before the fighting commenced. It was no place for a tank there. It was not until the following day, day three, that our men got the situation under control and our troops captured the remainder of those that had not already been killed or wounded.

None of us ever really learned all of the many other complexities of the Battle of Struth. However, it was later reported that there were eighty-one enlisted men and nine officers wounded, and nineteen enlisted men and one officer killed in action there.

It was as though we had now gotten out of the battle zones, for a while, anyway. We waited. I found some stationery in the house and wrote my family a letter. It didn't make much sense, because we could not write about things that were sensitive, like where we were, or what we were doing—and if we did, the censors would return it to us.

Later that evening our tanks arrived. They were our very same Pershing Tanks that we were with at Struth. We again boarded these tanks, four to six men to a tank, the following morning. It was quite a reunion when we realized first, that these were the same tanks; and second, that the crews were the same, all part of the 6th Armored Division. All of us were awfully glad to see these same tankers. These tank crewmen were highly skilled and the most dedicated men that I had seen—other than us Raiders. They knew how to fight with those tanks. They knew tactics, maneuverability, and could seemingly sense danger, usually just before it happened—with our help, of course. The tank crewmen were rugged, tough, and had an awful lot of guts and endurance. They were always able to wake up and get going early in the morning before the sun came up, apparently without any problem. They were courageous, but took no unnecessary chances at all. We all were very glad to be back with them, and all of us felt that we would fight with them anywhere, anytime. It was this kind of teamwork and camaraderie that won this war. We all looked out for each other, and no one ever hesitated to stand up and speak out about anything. It was the honorable and noble thing to do. We all were a great team—patriotic Americans, fighters for freedom.

It was not quite as cold now; a little sunshine made thing a lot better as we left that farm village riding on our tanks again. We took enemy strongholds, one after the other. We had a little more time—less rush—more time to shave, brush our teeth, less destruction, more buildings that were intact, and most of all, there were beds in these buildings.

Struth had been a turning point for us. We spoke of things that happened as being either before or after Struth. It seemed like a different kind of combat now, than it did before Struth. One thing that I noticed was that we all felt more courageous, unconquerable, and indestructible than ever before.

We stopped in a small town the next night. We moved so fast I didn't ever know where we were, in that the towns and cities flew by us so fast it was impossible to remember any of them. Just as soon as we got settled in this town, late in the evening, just before dark, we heard Messerschmitts overhead, close, low, like they were going to do some strafing. The noise that they made was easily identifiable. The sound of their engines had a high-pitched, whirring sound, while our planes had a deep-sounding roar. They flew just above the rooftops. I believe that they were just doing a reconnaissance to determine where our Pershing tanks were now located, as well as to learn if there were any, or how many, foot soldiers that had come up to where we were. Only a few infantry had reached us. It was pretty nerve-racking, and it interfered with my sleep on a very nice featherbed that I found.

A few men of some infantry unit that I had never heard of, arrived on one truck and helped us search out and occupy this town for the night. These were men that I had never seen before. I never knew what organization any of them were in; we just didn't have time to discuss specifics with anyone. On that occasion, I do recall a soldier who had arrived on one truck. He was a short fat guy who wore the two stripes of a corporal's rank on his sleeve. He was carrying a clipboard with him everywhere, as he sprinted from house to house, writing down everyone's name. One of our men remarked, "How many Krauts does he think that he is going to kill with that clipboard?"

He came to the house where about four of us were billeted and asked for everyone's name, which he wrote on his clipboard. He was so gung-ho, everyone laughed at him and called him, "Corporal, sir." He loved it. He was the kind of person that we detested up on the point. I really had some doubts at first about him, and I thought that he may be a Kraut in disguise because he just didn't act like any other American soldier. One man remarked that basic training was behind us, and that this was now real war, and that he should learn that. We never knew what outfit he was in, and we didn't care. He asked me who was standing door guard now, and I told him that I was, but since he rode in on a truck that he would be, in just a few minutes, if he hung around much longer. He left and we never saw him again. He was a disgrace to all noncommissioned officers in that this guy obviously was the only noncommissioned officer in the entire European Theater of Operations that wore his rank on his sleeve. He apparently had never learned that his two strips didn't amount to a hill of beans up where we were. In fact, he had never learned that rank didn't count here, but what did matter was guts, discipline, and intelligence, none of which he seemed to possess. He must have not been in the 65th Infantry Division.

You would think that by now the Nazi Regime would have surrendered, but they were still fiercely fighting. We learned that Hitler had given an order that any soldier who surrendered would be shot, and that his family would be sent to a concentration camp and exterminated. Also, that any German soldier caught carrying a white flag on his person would be summarily shot. What a pity, I thought, that some farsighted, patriotic German hadn't shot his brains out long ago. It seemed strange to me that some tyrant dictator could gain power and control over citizens, commit atrocities upon atrocities, and not expect to be gunned down by honest, dedicated citizens who believed in what was right and were willing to fight and die for it.

We departed on the same tanks the next morning after I had gotten a fairly good night's sleep in a featherbed with a feather comforter to cover with. We were on the point again, on the lead tank, out in the middle of nowhere again, it seemed.

That afternoon we took this small town. There were white flags flying out of the windows of many of the buildings there, which was supposed to mean there was no resistance and no enemy soldiers there, and the town was surrendering and there would be no resistance there.

The tanks had pulled back for some reason, probably because command learned of antitank defenses of some kind ahead. Any pulling back was only until we could make clear these big tanks—that the Nazis wanted to destroy so badly—would not move right into the muzzle of some hidden 88mm cannon on a big Tiger tank hiding around some corner. Our job was to make sure it would be safe for them to move on ahead without being ambushed, especially with us on them. This is not to imply that these tanks were not to engage the enemy, but no one walks into a trap unless he is stupid.

We stayed there for the night. The next morning we could see the next town ahead, and could also see through field glasses that there were many white flags flying there, as well. Nevertheless, for some unknown reason, the lieutenant sent his jeep with a scout, a private who was a member of our platoon, in it with the driver, to this next town to reconnoiter it. The obvious reason being to make sure that there was no resistance there, before we approached it. We did not know his reason or suspicion for doing this. Any of us would have just walked right up to that town and occupied it, or we would have counted upon doing that. Of course the lieutenant had intelligence information that we were not given. Suddenly, after the lieutenant's jeep had left, we heard artillery fire from that town. We could see that the jeep that had just reached the edge of the village had been hit by a shell, and it was demolished, burning, the two men obviously killed.

The lieutenant called up a tank destroyer that could knock out about anything. I think that there were two of them; they passed us by and went, hell bent for leather, to this town. A lot of firing took place, then they radioed us that it was safe to come on in. We rode the light tanks that came up into that town. A Mark IV German medium tank was sitting in the middle of the main street of that town, smoking, burning, and the shells in it were exploding. The white flags were still flying, the civilians were there in the village and had never left. I wondered it they thought that we were just a bunch of fools. Any German troops that had been there were now dead or had fled.

We hit the ground off of those tanks and were told to round up every civilian, search out every house, bring all of the civilians out into the main street, and we did. We then marched them down the road to where the bodies of our two men lay beside their demolished jeep, and forced them to view their mangled bodies. We then went back into this town and were told to take cans of gasoline and torch every building in that town. This was orders from headquarters, which we carried out.

The civilians were crying and screaming. I spoke with some of the townspeople who spoke good English. I told those that I talked to that they had it coming to them, that they were responsible for what their government did, that in fact they were the government and they should have controlled what it did, and if they had done that, this sort of thing wouldn't be happening.

I further explained to several that could speak English, that when a government does some evil, criminal, illegal things, like that which the Nazi Party did, the citizens were considered to be a part and parcel of the entire operation, consenting and agreeing to what was being done by their representatives, and were therefore responsible for what their government did. I told them if they didn't like what their government did, then they should eliminate those creating the problem, and it would have saved a war.

I tried to explain that they were to be held responsible and account-able for what their government and what their leaders did, and of course, they had to pay the price for their own failure to correct their political failures. I further told them when they learned what Hitler was doing, it was their duty to eliminate him, get rid of him, any way they could, and the fact they didn't do it, they were therefore responsible for all he had caused. I explained that if they had done this, none of this death and de-struction would ever happen, and they would be peacefully occupying their homes there, and our two men in that jeep would still be alive.

On the other hand, I thought to myself, these people are slaves of a tyrant dictator and their freedom of participation in their government has long been taken from them. I felt very badly about having to destroy their homes. I believed they were as much a slave of their tyrant dictator and his goons as those in his concentration camps were.

I further explained that they, the citizens, had set a trap for us by flying those white flags; or, they had allowed, permitted, and cooperated with some Nazi radical extremist nuts who used them to set us up in a trap, by flying the white flags when they well knew that there was a large tank there that would kill any of our troops who were deceived, and enticed, by these white flags, to come in. In fact, they were demonstrating that there was no resistance, which was a big lie, and they were setting a trap, a deception, contrary to the rules of war, of mankind, and of the common laws of a civilized society.

I told this one intelligent woman, "You people are on the verge of capitulation and you don't need to be doing crazy things like just happened here. How would anyone ever think they could do something like this and get away with it, scot-free?"

Therefore, they had now paid for their deception, lies, deceit, and destruction, which was the cause of these two dead American soldiers, who in essence, had taken them for their word that there was no resistance there.

I further explained to them that a lot of German soldiers were surrendering, waving white flags, and we now could not trust them. Maybe now we would have to shoot all of them, not knowing if they were actually surrendering, or setting a trap to try to kill us, like what just happened right here.

Of course, they didn't appear to understand and would not agree with me. I think that the message got around, in that there was no more of this kind of dirty tricks played on us, and if there were, they well knew what would happen to them. I thanked God for a leader like Lieutenant Anderson. Had he not sent these two men into that town, and if we had gone walking into it, we all would have been annihilated by the one single Mark IV Panzer tank, and one lone, crazed, fanatical Nazi tank crew. One angry woman called us "Patton's SS Truppen." I told her that she had been listening to too much of Herr Goebbels' Nazi propaganda lies on her radio.

CHAPTER 22

Capture of Ohrdruf Concentration Camp

"Another improvement that we have made is that we have built our gas chambers to accommodate two thousand people at one time."

—RUDOLPH HESS, HITLER'S SECOND
IN COMMAND (1874–1987)

Near this place, and a little further ahead, was Ohrdruf Concentration Camp, one of the most gruesome death camps operated by the Nazis. Our tanks we were riding came to this camp, and we took it without any resistance. The Krauts had already fled. We didn't stay there very long. We were looking for the fleeing SS troops that had operated this camp. We moved on and left the occupation of this horrible place to support groups behind us.

The foul odor from the dead, decaying, and those dying in filth, permeated the entire area for miles around it. We learned later that the conditions there were so horrible that it was visited by General Dwight Eisenhower; General Patton; General Bradley; our XXth Corps Commander, Major General Walton H. "Bull Dog" Walker; and others in the high command. We learned through the grapevine that Eisenhower became sick, dizzy, and had to be carried out. Also, that General Patton became so ill that he vomited right on the spot, inside this horrible death camp, soiling his shiny boots as he regurgitated.

The Burgermeister of the town of Ohrdruf, and his wife were brought there by orders of General Patton and they were made to view the horrors of this most horrible of all extermination camps. After they left, they returned to their home and both hanged themselves. I and the other Raiders riding our tanks were grateful that we on tanks that always kept moving, and we left the occupying of such things to the infantry and other groups behind us, riding on trucks.

CHAPTER 23

Liberation of a Canadian and Australian Prisoner of War Camp

> *"Our mortars and artillery are superb weapons when they are firing. When silent, they are junk—keep them firing. They should fire at these targets with high explosives, or white phosphorous, because if the enemy receives such fire, he will consider himself discovered and reply at a range so as to render him ineffective."*
>
> —GENERAL GEORGE S. PATTON (1885–1945)

We came upon a farmhouse where we stayed that night and got only a few hours of much needed rest, but no sleep. The following morning the lieutenant was up early briefing us on conditions ahead. We were told of heavy resistance up ahead. The tanks had withdrawn, to somewhere behind us. This appears to be a job only for the foot soldiers. We had gotten off of the tanks some distance back, late last night, and walked up to this real fine farmhouse. Some of our infantry came up to help us clear the area. There were lots of enemy infantry and armor in the area just ahead of us attempting to stop us from taking a prison camp not too far ahead. This was a job for us in the infantry—to clear a village—before the tanks were allowed into it, for fear that they would just run right into an antitank trap of some kind. We were told that there were lots of Wehrmacht along with Nazi Panzer units, including antitank weapons, defending the area ahead.

In such a situation, I knew that it would be suicidal for tanks to just go into an area where there are antitank traps set for them. We didn't know exactly where the tank traps were, which usually consisted of 88s, or a Tiger tank hidden somewhere out in a wooded area, about several hundred yards to our flank.

It seemed that this was a job for us infantrymen, in that if the tanks went in, there was a good likelihood they would be surrounded and cut off, or completely annihilated by antitank weapons hidden and waiting for us. We sure didn't want that to happen again. In such a case, the tanks usually pulled back a piece, and waited until we infantry could clear the area and we could move forward again. Always while this was taking place, our support behind us piled up back there somewhere, creating congestion and turmoil in the rear. Some of the men of our platoon came up to help us clean out this area. We started out early that rainy morning and moved up from this first farmhouse to the far edge of the woods. From there we could see what we had to do.

We took up a position beyond this very fine farmhouse, on the edge of a wooded area with fields beyond it, which overlooked another big farmhouse out in the middle of this extremely large field with a village beyond it, early that rainy morning. There was a church nearby at the edge of the woods, just ahead of us, and further on beyond the church was this large farmhouse. Beyond the large farmhouse was this small village. This one, lone, large farmhouse with very large fields around it was ahead of us about a half mile. We were told that this big farmhouse out in the middle of a very large field was our objective for the day. It was now occupied by Krauts, which we could see through field glasses. It was still early in the morning and we were near this dirt farm road that ran along the edge of these trees where we were holding up, keeping a sharp lookout for Kraut infantry and armor up ahead. None of us that were riding the tanks had anything to eat that day, and only one K Ration yesterday.

Suddenly, I saw a jeep coming from our right flank on this dirt road along the edge of the woods. There just were not supposed to be any American jeeps up there then, at that time. For this to happen would certainly draw fire from the enemy and cause a lot of casualties. They had to be lost—or they were the enemy impersonating Americans. Nothing like this was supposed to be happening.

As this jeep approached where I and another man were waiting, I let the driver see me and flagged him to halt. I told my buddy to cover me, in that I didn't know who these clowns were. I had my rifle to my shoulder and was drawing a bead on them. He came to an abrupt halt. I made both of them get out of the jeep and put their hands up. I spoke with the driver and the other sergeant in the jeep, and asked them what in the hell they were doing up there. The driver did the talking and told me that his general had sent them out into the countryside to get him some fresh eggs for his breakfast, and told them not to come back until they had his eggs. I was mad as hell at hearing this. I was pretty ill tempered that morning, not having had any sleep that night or any food that day, and very little yesterday. I am always a very nice and a polite person when the circumstances warrant it. I was rapidly getting soaked by the rain. I felt that they should not put my, and my buddies lives in jeopardy by hunting eggs for their general in the face of the enemy.

I told these two rear echelon jeep jockeys, "General George Washington never ate until all of his men had eaten. None of us have had even one bite to eat this morning, and nothing to eat that we can so far foresee getting anytime soon."

I told the two GIs in the jeep I hadn't even had not even a K Ration, and I didn't even get one wink of sleep last night. I told him that there were some 88s up in the woods ahead of us and some tanks, half-tracks, and German infantry defending this area just ahead, and at that big house ahead there were some Kraut vehicles there. I explained that the Krauts there were obviously trying to stop us from capturing a prison camp up ahead. I told these two sergeants that if they didn't get the hell out of there now, they would draw enemy fire and would most likely never get to see their general, or anyone else again. I told these two rear echelon jeep jockeys that we all were going to get wiped out by the tanks and the 88s, just because they were out there exposing themselves to them, drawing fire—not just on themselves, but on all of us here on the point.

Just so that they would be convinced I was telling it like it was, I told them to take a close look at that big farmhouse over there in the field about a half mile away, and they could see a Kraut half-track and other vehicles there at that house. They took a good look and then they asked me, as they got back into their jeep, "Sir, can we leave now?"

I told them, "You don't have to say "sir" to me—I am just a buck private. But I am in command of this situation, right here on the point, right now and, yes, you most definitely can leave now."

They turned their jeep around, and sped back the way that they came from, as fast as that jeep would carry them.

It began to rain harder that day, a heavy drizzle, cold, and very hazy. We all began to get soaking wet. This is the kind of weather I knew the Krauts liked, when they were going to use their armor, in that visibility would be bad and none of our tank-busting P-51 fighter planes could attack them.

We were ordered by the lieutenant to move forward across this very large field. He pointed out this large farmhouse and told us that we were to take that house before dark. There were Kraut armored units at this farmhouse, and also beyond the house, in the woods, as well as in the village on the other side of the farmhouse.

He told us to be careful on approaching it, and to send out scouts ahead if need be, to make sure we were not running into an ambush situation. He told us that the Krauts were occupying this farmhouse, and if it looked like they might be leaving soon, to just wait and let them leave, then to move in and occupy it, because we would have an observation post there, in the event the Krauts intended to counterattack that night. Otherwise, we were now on our own.

I sure didn't like hearing that word about Krauts making a counterattack, and at night, and just us few men up there on the point being their first targets. I could see what was developing, and I figured that I'd better start using my head again, like I did that day at Struth, otherwise we would all get wiped out.

All of our tanks were holed up back there somewhere until we could clear out the antitank defenses here. The lieutenant had also told us that since we had to stop in order to clear out these Krauts ahead of us, that all kinds of rear echelon units had queued up back there behind us and the traffic back there was a nightmare. He said they even had a kitchen set up back there in a field and many men were going there to eat some hot food. We weren't that lucky.

It rained all the way, all day. On the way we searched out the large church that was near where we left the wooded area, and I climbed up into the steeple and found where the enemy soldiers had been there in the church steeple recently. There was mud from their boots in the church that was recent. The Krauts loved to use these church steeples as observation posts for their artillery observers. There was no shortage of church steeples in Germany. We knew we were close on their heels, but I would have liked for them to take all the time that they needed to move on out before we got to this big farmhouse, even though we would be waiting in the rain for them to leave.

When we got within several hundred yards from this house, as it got later, we saw a motorcycle, a half-track, and a Volkswagen—a jeep-like vehicle—by this house.

They could see all of us, which was about a whole squad, maybe a few more men, all spread out across this huge field in the rain, just standing there several hundred yards from the farmhouse. I am sure that they thought that we few men looked menacing to them, just standing there in the rain. I know we surely must have looked damned determined to take that farmhouse.

We stopped, just standing out in this large field, all spread out, and dispersed. Sergeant Graybeal was alongside me, a great guy, kind, helpful, and a fine soldier, but today he was dead on his feet. He didn't get any sleep last night either, nor had he had anything to eat that day. While we were stopped, standing out there in the middle of this field, all dispersed in the rain, waiting for the Krauts to vacate that house, so we could occupy it for the night. Sergeant Graybeal had the butt of his rifle on the ground between his feet, holding on to the barrel with both hands, and he went sound asleep, just standing there in the rain, snoring.

I moved close to him, watched him, and when we saw the Kraut vehicles leave this house, I woke him up and held him as he woke up. He appeared right ready to just fall over.

We moved in, took the big house late in the evening, just before dark, immediately after the Krauts moved out of it. Everyone went into this house, except myself, and the radioman who the lieutenant had sent up there with us. Some of the men built a fire in the stove, heated some hot water for our Postum artificial coffee, heated some hog lard, and began cooking potatoes. While the radioman waited in the barn, I went in the house for a moment and spoke to Sergeant Graybeal and explained to him the situation as I saw it. He told me to go back out there and to take care of the situation, that he was too exhausted to do anything else. He told me that he was glad that I was there to help him out, and he knew that I would do the right thing. I assured him that he could count on me.

With everyone trying to get dry and get warm, I was outside, soaking wet, worrying about what enemy forces were out there in the edge of those woods and in that village up ahead, that were most likely going to counterattack us that night and try to wipe us out. I wondered, why else would they still be there? It didn't seem that anyone else there with us was consciously aware of the dangerous situation that we were now in. Several of our men seemed to be in the frame of mind that this was just a house that we took, and we were to get dried out, eat, and spend the night here. I knew that there was more to it than that. I knew that something had to be done before it got too dark, to insure our safety during the night.

I certainly didn't like the idea of the Krauts just sitting out there, like they were ready to attack us, and we men all up there alone, assuming that everything was going to be all right, and not doing anything about it. Something had to be done, and done soon if we wanted to prevent a counterattack that night and not become a casualty.

I was determined that there would not be another Struth situation here that night, or the next morning, if there was anything that I could do about it. We didn't worry about making any smoke, because they knew we were here. They saw us arrive—so what? Let them come on. We were ready for them with all of our support piled up back there behind us. That was just the way that I felt. Now, we had plenty of artillery and mortar support with which we could wipe them all out quickly, but we couldn't wait until they wiped us out to try to do something about it. It was getting dark fast. I wanted to do whatever had to be done, now, and get it over with so that I could dry my clothes and get a little sound sleep—which I hadn't had in an awful long time—and hopefully find a bite to eat, without having to worry about being overrun and killed that night. I knew that none of us would get any sleep, and probably not be alive in the morning, unless this situation was dealt with right now, and before dark set in. No one else could deal with this situation, but just us men here.

Because of the delay caused by our having to leave our tanks and do this mopping up on foot, to eliminate antitank defenses and traps, lots of our support had arrived back there behind us, such as artillery, mortars, and other support weapons. So I figured, if the Krauts wanted to do battle, we could do it too, this time on a more even footing. Now, it was going to be done my way.

I had been in such a trap up at Struth and I would be damned if I was going to let anything else happen like that if I could help it. The lieutenant had sent his radioman up with us. There were about eight to maybe twelve of us at this house. There were only a few of us men there that rode tanks. No one wanted to stay outside and observe what the Krauts were doing, so it left just the radioman and myself standing out in that barn, out of the rain, observing and contemplating what should be done. The radioman had field glasses, which I borrowed, and I used them to observe the Krauts that had moved to the far corner of the field into the edge of the woods there, as well as across a small bridge at the edge of a village up ahead of us. It was getting dark very fast.

Me and the radio operator, a sharp guy, and a good soldier, were out across the road at the barn, just right in front of the house, as it was getting dark. I took the field glasses and observed the village ahead and the corner of the woods to our left front. I could see half-tracks and other vehicles, as well as Kraut soldiers in the edge of the woods at the corner of the field, as well as in the village ahead, just beyond a bridge that led from the village out toward us. Their armor was stopped, but headed toward us, just beyond the bridge.

This armor, and these troops up there in the corner of the field convinced me that we could expect a counterattack soon that night. The only way for them to get out of that corner of the field was to come toward us, or along the edge of the woods to the village ahead of us. If they hadn't planned to attack us, they would have stayed on a road and not in the corner of the field, in the woods trying to stay out of view from us. It was now apparent to me that these troops off to our left front, in the woods at the corner of the field, probably had an 88 hidden there, and it was this thing they planned to use on our tanks, had we come down this road this morning. This was a perfect ambush situation.

My first thought, as I told the radioman, was that these vehicles were going to attack us just as soon as it got dark and try to wipe us out right here. They knew that there were only a few of us here, about eight, ten, or twelve men. They saw us come in just after they left. Now, we had occupied the house that they just left, and I knew that they were mad as hell for having to give up this farmhouse, especially when it is raining. Now they were out in the rain and our men were in there with a fire in the stove, getting dry.

I told the radioman that I didn't intend to just leave these Krauts alone tonight, and leave them there to attack us. "I am going to do everything that I can to teach them a lesson, and that is, that we ain't taking any counterattack from them tonight," I said. I reasoned that a good offense is better than any defense, anytime. This was something that I knew that I had to do, if we were to survive the night.

The radioman agreed with me. He and I were standing out in front of the farmhouse, just inside the big barn, trying to stay out of the rain, as we observed the Kraut armor through his field glasses.

"Can you get our artillery gunner back there in the rear on your radio?" I asked the radioman.

"I sure can, that is why I am up here. They, the command back there, are expecting a counterattack tonight. I was told to come up here with you men, so that if you were attacked that I could let them know. There is a prison camp not too far from here where they have five thousand Canadian and Australian prisoners of war, and the Krauts don't want us to take it until they are able to evacuate all of their guards and other things out of there."

I told him that for us up here to let anyone in the command back there in the rear know when we were getting a counterattack, we would be wiped out before anyone ever knew it.

I told him, "If we get attacked during the night, it is going to be too late for us to do anything about it. So, if we do let command know about it, it will be all over for us by then. We will all just be wiped out by the time that happens. So, it is imminent that we are going to be attacked. I don't know when, but if we can't do something now to stop it, we all had better pull back immediately, and I damned sure don't want to do that. Can you get our artillery on that radio?"

"Do you need to talk to the artillery gunner now?" the radioman asked.

"I sure do—now, not after we are wiped out, that is if we plan to be alive in the morning. I don't like what I see, and I don't want to be overrun by these Krauts during the night and wake up dead in the morning, do you? I sure don't want to wait until they attack us, to call on help from artillery. It would be a little late to do that, then, wouldn't it?" I asked him. The radioman was now getting very nervous.

"Well, if you want some artillery fire, you can sure get all you want; that is why I am up here. I had rather be back yonder, you know, and artillery don't mind giving you all the support that you want. They are all set up and ready to fire. There is all kinds of support piled up back there just behind us. All you have to do is ask for it, it's your judgment call. But, I sure won't be able to get any sleep up here tonight, with all of those Krauts out there," he said to me.

"Well, since Sergeant Graybeal is drying out and resting inside, he told me to do whatever I think should be done. He is totally exhausted, even went to sleep in the rain, standing up holding onto his rifle; he is inside now, drying out and resting. I have a lot of trust and faith in him, and he has the same for me. So, I want to teach these damned Krauts who in the hell they are fooling with, and do it quickly, so you and I can get in there and get dry, and hopefully get a bite to eat before all of those guys in there eat up all of the potatoes. Get me the artillery gunner on the radio," I told the radioman. It was now dark, too dark to see any of the Krauts in the edge of the woods, or at the village up ahead.

I looked at the map that he gave me. There was a big apple tree out in the center of the field between us and the corner of the woods. I gave the artillery gunner the description of where we were, and where the apple tree was, and told him to zero in on the apple tree, and to fire one round there as a point of reference. I told the gunner that it was about two hundred yards beyond, or over, and three hundred yards to the left from where we were at this barn. The artillery gunner told me that he knew where the house and barn and apple tree were, that he had it on his map.

I told the gunner to put me a shell right on that apple tree, for a point of reference.

It was our big 155mm artillery pieces back there that were doing the shelling. The first round hit just about two yards over from the apple tree. I then told him to fire some white phosphorous shells about two hundred yards over from that point of reference, and about three hundred yards to the left, where the corner of the field was at the edge of the woods. They did.

The white phosphorous shells hit right at the corner of the field, lit up the whole wooded area where these vehicles were stopped. When the shell burst and the chunks of burning white phosphorus flew upward and then came raining down on the Krauts there, the pieces of glowing white phosphorous rained down like fireworks and illuminated the area with white bright light. We could see the Krauts running every which way in the bright light from the explosion of the white phosphorus shells as the brightly glowing chunks came down on them. They were trying to find cover from the white-hot phosphorous that was raining down on them. I saw some of them running into each other trying to find shelter from the rain of white phosphorous. Some of the shells were tree-bursts that really lit up the entire area very well.

There were many half-tracks at the edge of the woods that we could see. I couldn't determine if there were any tanks there or not. I definitely could see the outline of an 88mm cannon right at the edge of the woods. Always when I see a halftrack, I then look for machine gun sites and for an 88mm cannon, in that they carry all of the crews, haul the machine guns in them, and tow the 88. I was now convinced that a counterattack that night was, or had been inevitable. I know that they had planned a counterattack that night, but I just blew it for them. I told the gunner to fire at will with both white phosphorous and high explosives, and he did. Shells landed in that area, high explosives, and white phosphorus mixed in, and saturated the whole area with artillery fire as we watched.

Next, I asked him to do the same for the village up ahead, and right in the road, just beyond the bridge up there at that village. I informed the gunner that there was a line of armored vehicles facing in our direction on the other side of the bridge, or had been, just before dark. The artillery gunner commenced firing white phosphorus and high explosives in that area. The white phosphorus shells lit up the area beyond the bridge so I could see what was there. I related to the gunner that there were several tanks, half-tracks, and other vehicles in the street, facing toward us, just beyond the bridge, in the edge of this town. I could see people scampering every which way, trying to escape from the pieces of white phosphorous falling on them. I thought about that observer back at Saarlautern that I encountered. I thought also that they had to be pretty cocky to still be there after their units in the corner of the woods had just been wiped out by this GI artillery observer. I hoped that they didn't think that I would overlook them. Now it was my turn to call in some artillery shells on some Kraut positions.

Then I directed him to lay down a barrage of high explosives in that same location, which he did. I could see vehicles burning and shells exploding in the burning vehicles. I told the artillery gunner to fire at will with high explosives, as well as white phosphorus. I wanted to be able to see what kind of a job our artillery was doing. I must say that in every instance when our artillery were putting down fire up front, they were so accurate that it would absolutely amaze you. They had to be the best in the entire Allied Forces. They always laid it down precisely where it was supposed to be.

I had learned that it takes a lot of aggressiveness if you want to survive and win. You have got to get them before they get you, which I learned early back in Saarlautern.

The artillery gunner peppered the hell out of both sites that I had given him, and the shelling continued for about half an hour. I watched the show that I had directed until I was sure that they were no longer a threat to our safety for the night. I told the gunner to hold the fire, and if these Krauts still wanted to attack us, that I would let him know and we could do it all over again until we got all of them.

After this bombardment, I didn't think that they wanted to make a counterattack that night. They didn't. However, I hate to think what would have happened to us men in this house that night if no one would have taken the action that I did. I am certain that we would not have had a chance of surviving.

We shut down the radio for the time being and had a man from inside to come out and stand watch, while I and the radioman went in and enjoyed a little warmth and hot food, like fried potatoes cooked in hog lard. The heat from that hot stove was a most welcome feeling. I finally got dried out, but was now totally exhausted and awfully sleepy.

I was wet, tired, cold, and hungry. As I dried out in front of that stove, I told Sergeant Graybeal what took place. He heard all of the shelling and I recounted to him all I had done, and he complimented me greatly. I was proud of what I had done to save our lives, for that night at least. We kept two men on guard in shifts all night, as observers out by the barn and at the back side of the house. One man said that he was too scared to stay out there and I had to replace him. He refused to stay out there under any condition. He was not one of us Raiders; he rode trucks. He was a coward, and I was too tired and weary to discuss it with him, but I let him know what I thought about him and then I found a bed and fell soundly to sleep.

The next morning just at daylight, our Pershing tanks arrived right at the front door of this large farmhouse. As I and one other man in the Raiders crawled up on our tank, the tank commander stuck his head out of the turret and said, "Hey Ladner, I hear that last night you eliminated a few obstacles that were in our way up ahead."

I told the tanker, "Sarge, I did my best. If I hadn't done it, we wouldn't be here this morning, and you guys would be fighting a bloody tank battle today right out there in this field, without any of us being here to help you. How did you learn about it, anyway?"

"I heard all of it on the radio. So did your lieutenant, captain, and everyone else that had a radio. Everyone was very anxious last night to see what was going to happen up here. They were listening in on your conversation with the artillery gunner."

"What did the lieutenant say when he heard what I was doing?" I asked the tank commander.

"He said that you sounded pissed off. I also heard him say, 'Leave it to Ladner. You can always count on him and you don't have to tell him what to do."

"Have you got an extra K Ration that you can spare? We haven't had anything to eat except some greasy potatoes last night."

"Here, take a couple of these K rations. They had a kitchen set up back there last night and we went through the chow line and ate a lot of good hot food. Sorry you were too busy to join us."

There were only three or four of us Raiders that were there, who got on our tanks. The other men had to wait for a truck to come for them so that they could return to the rear, as we headed out into the unknown on the point again.

I was thrilled to no end, in seeing the blown-up tanks, half-tracks, Volkswagens—or Kuppelwagens, as the Krauts called the jeep-like vehicles that they used. Several 88s and other vehicles torn apart by the artillery were still burning. We moved on up forward as fast as we could to liberate that POW camp.

Some miles ahead we came upon this very crude prison camp with a big barbed wire fence around it, and outside the gate were quite a lot of skinny, half-starved inmates—Australian and Canadian prisoners of war that had been captured by the Germans, either after the invasion, or in Africa, Italy, or somewhere, maybe at Dunkirk, I surmised. It was obvious that they had been imprisoned for a long time.

We stopped at the gate of the prison and talked to many of them who were just standing there. They were cold, hungry, and ragged, asking for something to eat. The tankers had previously told me to never give any prisoners that we liberate anything to eat, in that it would be too rich for their system and they could die from it.

No guards were to be seen anywhere. I asked them when the guards left and was told by a Canadian that about midnight last night they all got in vehicles and just left them all there. No more guards or locks. The men there looked pitiful. Their minds seemed sluggish and they didn't seem to think, or react very well. They just were not right; they were undernourished more than I was.

I asked some of them where they were from and none of them seemed to comprehend what I was asking. One of the tankers said that one of the Australians told him that they had given us, their liberators, a name, which was "Patton's Flyers," meaning that we got there so fast that we must have flown. They also said that their guards had called us "Patton's SS Truppen."

One of the prisoners told me that when the guards left last night, one of them told him they had to leave now because *"Patton's SS Truppen ist kommen."* We didn't stay very long there talking to those men. The tankers never lost a minute in making advances.

I don't recall much after that, what, or where our next objective was. I was so tired, hungry, and sleepy that everything was foggy. There were many times that I had blackouts of memory as to what occurred. It was as though hunger, exhaustion, and anxiety, coupled with loss of a lot of sleep, just did something to me. The next few days somehow have been blacked out of my memory. I learned that sometimes when I was extremely exhausted and stressed out, and had very little food or sleep, it was like I was in a fog or daze, and everything seemed vague to me, as though I was in a daze. At times some of our men had to tell me what we did yesterday, which I could not recall. I was getting to where I had trouble concentrating. I was just not as alert as I should be. I was not the only man that was having this kind of trouble; all of us were the same way. What one man couldn't remember, someone else sometimes could.

CHAPTER 24

Capture of the Big Luftwaffe Base and Strafed Again

"What is faith, unless it is to believe what you do not see."

—ST. AUGUSTINE (354–430)

"I believe in Angels because the Bible says that there are Angels; And I believe the Bible to be the true word of God."

—BILLY GRAHAM, *ANGELS: GOD'S SECRET AGENTS* (B. 1918)

Several days after the liberation of the POW camp, very early in the morning, we bore down on a Luftwaffe air base, a big facility, with lots of fine, large modern buildings. It was a very elaborate air base. I do not know the name of the base, or the very old and beautiful city where it was located. We only had one man on each tank this day. I was told by a sergeant they could afford only one man for each tank, for some unknown reason. There had not previously been a time when only one man was riding on one of these tanks. I couldn't understand the reason

241

for just one man on each tank. I surmised that just having one man, especially when we captured a Luftwaffe fighter base, that it would reduce casualties to do so. I wondered if that was the reason for having only one man per tank.

When we first arrived at this Luftwaffe base, I was the only man riding shotgun on the tank, and there was just one other tank with us that took this big air base. At that time, these two tanks just bore down on the headquarters buildings, as if they knew where to go, and we stopped there.

We were very short of men—we and the tankers were told—so the tankers had to make do with only one rifleman on each tank that morning, which they didn't like to do. I have never been able to determine why there was a shortage of men on these tanks for that one day only. Our two tanks had stopped right in the front of this apparently recently abandoned, modern headquarters building. I had a strange feeling about that place from the moment that we arrived.

I got the impression that everything was intact, but that there were no people there anywhere. I and the soldier off of the other tank that stopped there with us, were standing in front of the entrance of this big beautiful building, just stretching our legs. I never knew this man's name or what outfit he was from. It never seemed to matter; we were all brothers in a way, anyhow. But he was a very outstanding soldier. We never knew what was taking place strategically. None of the tankers got out of the tanks. In a few moments a jeep and one or two other vehicles, one of which was an ambulance, arrived. An American colonel got out of the first jeep, and was entering the building alone. He was anxious to get in there for some reason. He was a tall lanky man with a lot of presence. He was determined in his demeanor, and obviously knew what he was there for. He smiled as he spoke to me, and asked how I was doing. I was standing near the entrance. Our two tanks were stopped right in front of the entrance.

The colonel started into the building, and I told him that we had just arrived and that the buildings had not been cleared. I told him, "Sir, there may be enemy soldiers in there. We haven't cleared it yet, we just arrived."

"That's O.K., soldier. This is going to be my headquarters. I am taking it over right now," the colonel said, as he walked right into the elaborate-looking, undamaged headquarters building. I followed right behind him, simply to protect him in the event there were some enemy resistance left in the place. I noticed that he had a .45 caliber pistol in a fast-draw holster hanging low on his pistol belt. You would think that a place this elaborate would be defended to the last man, and I had one of those eerie feelings about it.

The colonel walked into the lobby, turned to the left, and started down the long hall with me following behind him. Suddenly, I saw a German soldier with a submachine gun in his hands come out of one of the rooms, into the hall, just ahead of us. The Kraut didn't seem to be aware of who we were, or what the situation was, or even that we were there. I really believe from observing him for just a moment, that he had been asleep and had just woke up. Nevertheless, he was heavily armed and dangerous.

I saw the colonel abruptly draw his .45 from his fast-draw holster and fire it at the armed Kraut who fell dead instantly. I was about to get a round off at the time he fired, but he was faster.

His jeep driver and another soldier with him came running in and looked stunned when they saw their colonel standing there with a smoking .45 caliber pistol in his hand, and a dead German soldier lying on the floor right in front of us.

The colonel looked at me and said, "These damned Nazis have got to learn that this is my damned territory now and they need to get the hell out of town when I arrive."

I had to wholeheartedly agree with him. I said, "Yes, sir, I can see that."

He continued down the hallway looking the building over as if nothing ever happened, as I followed behind covering him with my M-1. I often wondered if there was a reason for an ambulance following his jeep.

Soon, more jeeps arrived, ambulances, trucks with supplies, a lot of headquarters people of my division. While we waited, I and the man on the other tank went into an adjacent building and found piles of rabbit fur jackets and vests. We got us a sleeveless vest and put it on, the fur side inside, underneath our field jackets. We needed more warmth and this seemed the way to stay warmer.

When we got back to the tanks, I showed it to the commander of my tank and he quickly said, "You need to take that damned thing off now, because if you get hit by shrapnel or a bullet, it will take lots of rabbit hair right into your body, and the medics will never be able to get all of that rabbit hair out of you."

So, I and my buddy on the other tank took them off and threw them away. After a short time, we were instructed to leave on the tanks again. We had to take the nearby town.

I don't recall the name of it. However, I believe it to be Erfurt, or some city to the south of or near there. We left the air base and headed for the city, which was at a lower elevation and a short distance away. We could see the city from the base, which was at a higher elevation, on kind of like a plateau. We went to the city below us and stopped at an intersection in the center of the city, just our two tanks. It was a wonderful sunny day and the sun felt very warm and good.

It was a beautiful old city, clean, and undamaged. I was the only person riding on my tank, and also there was only one man on the other tank. I felt kind of all alone by myself. I and the man from the other tank got off and looked around at some of the stores, all of which were closed and their shelves empty. The city didn't seem to be damaged from artillery or bombs and looked very quiet and peaceful, but deserted. I think that we were waiting there for other tanks to arrive, so that we could regroup. Soon, more of our tanks arrived from different directions and we all rendezvoused in the center of the city at this intersection. These tanks also had only one man on each of them. When the other tanks arrived, about six or eight all totaled, I would estimate, the tankers signaled to me to get aboard.

We moved slowly off of the main street, down this long, very narrow, old, cobblestoned street with old, but very fine dwelling buildings about three floors tall on each side. I now realize that the tankers pulled down this very narrow cobblestoned street in an attempt to avoid being seen by Messerschmitts, that they obviously had gotten a report that they were in the area doing some strafing.

Suddenly, all of the tanks in our column stopped. My tank stopped on this very narrow cobblestoned street, which was so narrow there was only about three feet of room on each side, between it and the walls. To my left there were big, tall, double entrance doors, and one of them was being opened by a very old lady in a long dress. I assumed that she lived there and wanted to see what all of the tanks were doing outside her door.

Just at the very moment that I observed her standing there in that doorway right beside me, opening one of those big tall double doors, I heard the whirring sound of Messerschmitts flying low, coming in from behind us.

Just as soon as I heard that plane, I instantaneously looked to the rear and saw a Messerschmitt with its machine guns in its wings firing right down this street where all of our tanks were stopped, and it was coming at us fast.

There were four machine guns in the wings, and all were spewing fire. It was coming right down this street, right at me. I had only a split second to take cover.

Immediately upon seeing this plane coming at us, I then looked back at this door, and the old lady was then motioning with her arm for me to come in. I immediately leaped off of the tank with my rifle in my right hand, and propelled myself toward this open door with her standing right in the middle of it.

As I leaped into the doorway, with her standing there in the middle of that open doorway, I knew that I was going to hit her with my body, knock her down, and probably injure her, I was moving so fast. There was no way to slow down to avoid it, so I grabbed her as I went down with both of my arms, with my rifle in my right hand and behind her, carrying her down on the floor with me. I twisted myself as I fell, so that she would land on top of me, to cushion the fall for her. It was a real flying tackle.

Just as we hit the floor, and as we were lying right inside the doorway; just at that very moment, outside the bullets from the Messerschmitt were hitting the tanks, the cobblestones in the street, and ricocheting in every direction, making a very frightening and deadly noise. I heard the bullets ricocheting off the tanks and off of the cobblestoned street at about the very second that we hit the floor, just inside the doorway. This plane was just above the rooftops and sprayed everything in the street with machine gun fire. Suddenly it was quiet, except for the ringing in my ears.

There we lay, this very old woman lying on top of me, in my arms, with my rifle still in my hand, and behind her, with my helmet lying on the floor over there somewhere.

My thoughts were also about the safety of the other men on the other tanks. It scared me to think that the other men on the tanks may not have had time to get off in time and had not been able to take cover somewhere, as I had been able to do, due to this little old lady opening her door with split second timing, which saved my life. All of the other men on the tanks were right in the line of fire from this fighter plane. I hoped that they had gotten off and taken cover somewhere, somehow. The plane's four machine guns in its wings fired about fifteen hundred rounds a minute, each. The sound of the plane's engine and its machine guns was deafening, as well as very terrifying.

I looked at the sweet face of this little old lady, her lying there on top of me. She had a very frightened look on her face. I squeezed her as though she was my own grandmother and kissed her on the cheek. I got up, lifted this wonderful little old lady up to her feet and placed her hand on the door latch for her to hold on to. She was about 85 years old and had miraculously saved my life in the matter of a split second. I held onto her for a moment, to make sure that she was not hurt in any way and was able to stand. I was so thankful for being alive, I hugged her and gave the old lady another big kiss on the cheek as a token of my appreciation for opening that door right in the nick of time to save my life. I was so grateful for her kindness and concern. I tried to cheer her up by smiling at her, and hugging and squeezing her.

I quickly grabbed my helmet from the floor and got back up on my tank. Just as soon as I got on the tank, all of them started up and we moved out, fast. I looked at the tanks ahead of and behind me. I saw that the one man on the tank ahead had been hit by the machine gun fire from the Messerschmitt, and was lying dead or wounded behind the turret. One injured or dead soldier fell off the tank behind me onto the side of the street as his tank started to move. There was nothing that

I could do for him and I felt very badly about not being able to give some assistance, even though he most likely was dead, as he appeared to be. He was the man that was with me back there at that air base that we had just taken. I had never seen him before. However that was nothing unusual—I never hardly ever knew anyone on these tanks with me, in that there were different men from different outfits on them. Hardly ever were any of us together on the same tank. Nevertheless we were all close and concerned about each other all the time, even though I didn't know their names, which wasn't that important. We were all brothers, anyway.

Heretofore, when we were strafed we would jump off and lie in a ditch, or something like that. It had always been where we had places to run to for cover, like away from the tanks. But not here on this cobblestoned street that was very narrow and ancient, with nowhere to run to, unless an angel opened a door for you to take cover just in the split second of time. No one should ever remain on a tank when it was being strafed, if there is any other place to go, and time to get out of the way of the rain of bullets.

The remainder of that day and for days thereafter, I have little memory. This incident did something to me, to my psyche. It hurt me, it broke my heart, it made me angry, as well. I felt humble and thankful to be alive, yet I was very angry and I wanted to fight harder so that we could hurriedly finish this dirty war. I wanted to kill more and more of the enemy in order to successfully end this war as quickly as possible. I was now convinced that not all of the German citizens were our enemies.

I was in a daze the remainder of that day, and for days thereafter. I frequently thought, as everyone else that I had talked to felt, "How many more close calls can I survive without being killed?" I said a prayer and thanked God for having saved my life and I asked him, "My God, my God, why me, why was it just me that survived?" It came into my mind the promise I made to my God in Saarlautern: If He would return me home safe and sound, and in one piece, that I would continue to fight tyranny and oppression as long as I lived. Was this His answer to me? Was He letting me know that He was keeping his promise, and we had a binding agreement? I wondered an awful lot about things that had occurred, and my life was saved in a fraction of a second.

As we left that town that bright and sunny day on that tank, things appeared to be very foggy to me, and I felt like a zombie or a robot and in a daze. I was very hungry and tired all of the time. We were not able to get nearly enough food or sleep. I felt weak and groggy, like I was in a fog. There are times that something just seems to snap, and I could not recall at all any events that occurred, like where I was or what we were doing at certain times, especially when I had been without sleep and food for a long time, and when I was enduring an intensely stressful situation. I was terribly afraid that I was getting that "mile-long stare," which was a stress syndrome that many GIs developed. I believed that I could endure the stress, but not the stress and a great loss of sleep, extreme exhaustion, and the lack of nourishment, too. I had lost so much weight that my clothes no longer fit me. I was tired, weak, and was very skinny. So was every other Raider.

Soon thereafter I found some paper and a pen and wrote to my mother and told her that we had won the war, but the enemy wouldn't quit fighting, and that there was still a lot of killing going on. I told her that I was tired of all of this unnecessary killing and that it should stop, in that it was now becoming awfully senseless.

CHAPTER 25

Setting Up Our Own
Military Government

*"It is courage that the world needs, not
infallibility...courage is always the surest
wisdom."*

—SIR WILFRED GRENFELL (1865–1940)

I recall sometime later—I don't know how long afterwards—that I and
my buddy Sperl were riding on a tank. We'd had an exhausting day and
it was late at night when the tanks stopped in this small village. I only
recall this night because I was so tired, mentally and physically, but we
got some good sleep that night. Sperl and I had found a rather nice bed
in a house where the tankers also slept that night. The only thing that I
recall was the next day I awoke about midmorning, the sun was shining, it was as quiet as a mouse everywhere. I looked around and there
were no tankers in the house. I rushed outside and there were no tanks
out there, where they had stopped the night before. It was now only Al
and I. It was still as quiet as a mouse. I wished that the war would just
go away and it would always be this way, just peaceful and quiet. I was
fully aware that I was much in need of some real rest. I believe that if I
had not gotten that extra amount of sleep, as a result of the tankers not
being able to wake us up and leaving us there in that house, that I
would have passed out or cracked up from sheer exhaustion.

The tankers had left us there. I often wondered if they felt sorry for us and didn't want to awaken us, or felt that they didn't need us, or that they couldn't wake us up. I could only conclude that we were so exhausted that they were unable to wake us up, so they just left us there.

Only a very few civilians were around anywhere in that village. Since Sperl spoke fluent German, he found the Burgermeister, the mayor of the village, who came quickly. We had no rations with us, not even a fruit bar in my field jacket pocket where I usually carried one as a reserve. Sperl ordered the mayor to have a dinner cooked for us right away—a chicken, or a goose, or duck, with dumplings, and all else that goes with it. Soon it was served. We had a delicious meal of roasted duck, dumplings, boiled potatoes, and pumpernickel bread.

We heard a Messerschmitt circling overhead. We went out to see what was taking place. It kept circling low, and Sperl fired a clip or two at the circling low-flying plane. It began to smoke, and it made a wheels-up landing in a field. We ran to where it crashed, and the pilot had gotten out and run into a nearby barn. Sperl spoke to him in German and told him that if he didn't come out with his hands up, that we would burn the barn down. So, the pilot came out and surrendered with his hands up.

The pilot, we learned, was only nineteen years old. He stated that he was surrendering, coming home, and that he lived in that town. I looked at his plane and there was a small clock on the instrument panel that I was able to salvage and bring home with me, which I still have.

We talked with the pilot for some time. I asked him if he would try to answer a question for me. He was agreeable and kind-acting, and stated what I had heard dozens of other prisoners say: They didn't want to fight us Americans, but they had to. He was aware of Hitler's order that any soldier surrendering would be shot, and his family put into a concentration camp and exterminated. I told him not to let that worry him, because we Patton's Raiders were in charge here now. He told me that all of them knew of "Patton's Raiders." He told us that none of the German citizens, or even the German military ever trusted anyone in the SS. He also related that the German radio said ugly things about us Patton's Raiders, such as that we were cruel, vicious, malicious, barbarous, and brutal. This was sure news to us.

I asked him why someone didn't overthrow Hitler or kill him long ago. That they all should know that he was insane, a criminal, a mass murderer, and was destroying Germany, its people, and in fact he had already destroyed almost all of Europe. That, if he was so bad, as we all knew he was, why have the people tolerated him and allowed him to live, to kill so many people, and destroy most all of Europe? Further, that he had destroyed Germany and its people, and most of the rest of the world, so why hadn't someone gotten rid of him, killed him, or eliminated him, in some form, or fashion? I reasoned that it would not be a crime, in that it would be just self-defense, and in defense of many people.

The pilot's reply was that Hitler gained too much power and control over the people before the people were aware of his terrorist, mean, and hateful nature, that the citizens were unable to do anything about it, mainly because no one but the military and his group of criminals that he surrounded himself with, had any weapons to fight him. He also told us that Hitler controlled the German people with his propaganda and no one ever knew the truth about what was taking place in Germany.

I further asked him if he did not realize that by allowing Hitler to continue in power, that they were in fact, condoning and being in a conspiracy with him to commit the acts and atrocities that we all now know that he committed. I was unable to get a sensible answer and concluded the conversation. I told Al that all of the German people should have to take the course of Civics 101 that is taught in American schools and colleges. Sperl sent him on his way to find civilian clothes and to go to his family here in this town where he grew up.

Sperl had the mayor, or Burgermeister, stand guard at our door that night. We had none of our troops to pull door guard while we slept. So, the mayor did a good job. I checked on him frequently throughout the night, and he was standing his watch, dutifully, in a chair in the hallway outside of our door. After we awoke, we sent the mayor to get breakfast for us. He had some women to prepare us some eggs and potato pancakes, which were very good, and we both ate like we were starved. It seemed that it was the best breakfast I had ever eaten. We also had some ersatz, or imitation coffee that was not very good.

Late that afternoon American vehicles, trucks, and all kinds of support vehicles arrived, but were just passing through. Some major was very curious about how we were ever able to be that far up front. As usual he had the feeling that they were the furthermost troops up front. He inquired of us how long we had been there, how we had gotten there, and all about us. We told him that we had gotten separated from our outfit, and had set up our own military government there for the past two days, in that we had no transportation to catch up with our tanks, and it was as simple as that. We hitchhiked on these trucks to our unit, which took about two days to catch up to. It was hard to go back to K and C rations after eating the good cooking in that village.

The day we arrived back with our unit we told everyone what had taken place, but no one wanted to believe us. They really thought we were fabricating it and had only goofed off somewhere. I really made their mouths water by telling them about the eggs and potato pancakes.

CHAPTER 26

The Danube River Crossing and Capture of Regensburg

> *"The decision of whether the assault should be led by the infantry, or the armored vehicles, depends on circumstances. When operating against known anti-tank guns, or extensive anti-tank mine fields, or when it is necessary to force a river crossing, or a defile, the infantry must lead, and the tanks follow, as, and when the situation is cleared."*
>
> —GENERAL GEORGE S. PATTON (1885–1945)

We were on the tanks and had been moving fast all day on dirt roads through beautiful country. All along the way civilians had left the area and were no where to be seen. However, we were under a constant strain to observe for snipers, tanks, 88s, and other antitank defenses along the way, on both sides of the roads, as well as behind us and overhead too. Often the tank would stop, we on the back of the turret didn't know why, and never did the tankers say to us what kind of danger we were approaching. I was always suspicious of there being an 88 or a Panzer of some kind out there behind a barn or in some woods somewhere, so I was constantly on the alert. On one occasion that day our tank stopped on this narrow dirt road. The tank commander put his head out of the turret and said that there was some loose dirt in the road up ahead and we should check for a mine. I had not noticed it because I was too busy looking for Kraut snipers with Panzerfausts, 88s, and hidden armor. Sperl and I got off and probed for land mines with our bayonets ahead in the dirt road where the dirt was loose and had been disturbed by someone, but we found nothing but some disturbed dirt that appeared to be where someone had dug a hole, making it look as though a mine had been planted there. I assumed that the Krauts did it to slow us down.

Soon thereafter we, our column of two or three tanks, ours being the lead one, came upon two of our trucks stopped on the side of this road that ran alongside a small river that was swift but not very wide, about 50 feet or so. The tank commander approached the stopped vehicles ahead of us very slowly; we saw no one around anywhere. Then, it was obvious that the trucks ahead of us had been ambushed. We found one American soldier, the driver, dead in the front seat of one truck, another dead American soldier in the back of the other truck. The windshields of both trucks were full of bullet holes.

It was obvious that they were ambushed from this tall rocky hill just ahead of us. As one approached that hill, you faced it head-on, then you went around it, to the right of it, and very close to the river, between it and the river. It was a perfect ambush site. We went up onto the hill hoping to find some enemy who did this, but found only where machine gun nests had been, and some spent rounds of ammo. The Germans usually retrieved all of their spent rounds of ammunition, but in a night operation they never got all of them. We returned to the tank, went around the disabled vehicles, which belonged to one of our combat engineer units. I asked one of our tankers how these vehicles got so far ahead of us.

I learned from him that there was a river, a bigger river up ahead that we were supposed to cross, and the engineers had passed us last night with a group of our own 65th Division's Reconnaissance troops accompanying them up to their objective. This Recon. troop is a very tough, rugged, highly skilled outfit that was often called upon to handle extremely tedious and highly skilled, strategic operations, kind of like a special forces unit. Any situation that we ran into, where it was expected to be a tough technical job, you could count on them being there, doing the tricky, hard-hitting job of whatever it took to outsmart and defeat the enemy. They were with the engineers to help them, so that they could get near this river with their equipment, to get us across, and make a bridgehead there in preparation of taking Regensburg. It was beginning to make sense to me that there was a big operation in the making up ahead somewhere, to have all of these other units coming up ahead of us and passing us by in the nighttime. It appeared that they planned to do some sort of highly technical job up ahead. I had assumed that they were just going up ahead to throw a Bailey bridge, a portable steel bridge, across this stream so our tanks could cross it up ahead. But I learned that was not the case.

After we had gotten around this ambush mountain, our tank and two or three other tanks we had rendezvoused with, stopped in a group, which was not the safest thing to do. We had never put ourselves in a congested area where one shell could knock out lots of our own men and materiel. The tankers with their radio communication always seemed to know what the situation was, but we infantrymen on the rear of it didn't know anything, except to protect that tank, regardless of the situation.

Someone built a small fire to heat some C rations. A tanker gave me a can of C Ration spaghetti and meatballs, since I had not had one mouthful of food all day. I cut a slit in the center of the lid and then cut it half off of the can, put my bayonet through the slit, and held it over the fire. It was heating just fine when suddenly the tankers yelled to get aboard and let's go. As I attempted to climb upon the tank with my bayonet holding my sizzling can of spaghetti in one hand, as well as holding my rifle with my other hand, the can of spaghetti slipped off of my bayonet into the dirt, just as the tank lunged forward and just before I could grab a handhold. It was a sad occasion for me. No one thought it was funny, either, because getting some food in the first place was so hard to do, then losing it in the dirt was no laughing matter.

Before dark we stopped at a small but very nice, recently abandoned hotel, clean and nice, where we apparently and hopefully were going to spend the night, or at least thought we would, in that I'd had very little sleep or food in a long time. I was just living on nerves alone. I had already burned up what little body fat that was on my body and I was now as skinny as a rail.

The tankers told us that this was as far as they were to go, they were to pull back, which they did, leaving us at this small resort hotel, which really wasn't anything unusual for them to do. No civilians were anywhere to be seen. More men soon arrived; they walked there from somewhere they had unloaded off of trucks. Some had come in on other roads from different directions, riding tanks also. We didn't have any vehicles up there with us at all now. All of them had pulled back to some place in the rear. I had heard from the tanker that there was to be a big river crossing to take place up ahead, but I just thought that it would be a minor operation where the engineers would throw a steel Bailey bridge across this fifty foot stream we had seen. Soon after we arrived at this location, some more men who had been riding trucks came in, walking from the point where they had unloaded off the trucks. We all then knew something big was about to take place.

While waiting there at this hotel, I found a room that I and another GI occupied. There was a typewriter in there and I sat down and typed a letter to my mother. It was somewhat vague, in that we could not write about very much we were doing. If you did, the censor would return it to you. I carried this letter for about a week before I was able to give it to someone who could put in the mailbag.

The lieutenant asked me to accompany him, the captain, and two or three others on a Reconnaissance mission before it got too dark. We walked to a hilltop overlooking the Danube River, which was about two or three miles from this hotel. I really didn't know what the situation was, except that this was a big, wide, fast-flowing river. I was just a guard for the captain, the lieutenant and some others that I didn't know, but as usual, I was curious about what was going to take place, as well as when.

As we arrived at that location, which was a hill top that overlooked the Danube River, we could hear machine gun fire down below this hill, near the water's edge, on our side of the river. I knew that they were ours. I could also hear Kraut machine guns across the river, firing back at our machine guns, down below us near the river. There is a distinct difference in the sound of each. I didn't know we had any infantrymen up there doing that. So, I asked the lieutenant who they were and if they were some of our men. He told me that they were ours, on this side, and that they were part of the division Reconnaissance troops that had come up here with the engineers when they brought the assault boats up last night, that we were going to use to make the river crossing. He never said when and I knew not to ask.

It seemed that our machine guns were firing across the river at the Krauts, and they were firing back at our Recon. troops. This firing was almost continuous.

Our mission was to cross the river, take the ground beyond, establishing a bridgehead for other troops to go across safely, and then take the tree-lined hill beyond the fields that were just beyond the big field. We were to then take the city of Regensburg later, possibly the following day, which was about five miles farther to the east. That was the plan that I heard discussed. Some sergeant that I knew gave me an Army map of the entire area—which I still have—which showed the exact location of where we were to cross.

We got into position up on this hill where we could see, with field glasses, across the river. It was just before getting dark. We could see German soldiers digging foxholes in the large field across the river, and they were digging like hell, too. We could see them placing their big machine guns in these foxholes, which were U-shaped, with the machine gun in the bend of the U, all facing toward the location on the river, just below us where the machine gun skirmish was going on.

I knew from previous experience that the Germans always had three men in a machine gun crew: the gunner, the ammunition bearer on the left side of the machine gun, and the man who carried the tripod and collected the spent rounds on the right side of the machine gun. So, this U-shaped foxhole was ideal for them. They were digging lots of them as fast as they could dig.

I had read where General Patton had remarked about German machine guns and their foxholes, and he had said, "The enemy are great diggers." Their foxholes always were very neat, and well dug. I observed that the foxholes that the Krauts were digging all faced to the north, toward the point of the river where we were standing right now, up on this hill that overlooked the river. However, the Krauts didn't know that we were up there observing them while they were firing at our Recon. troops down below us.

Below us were our Reconnaissance troops, men who had gotten ahead of us last night and had come up with the engineers to protect them, but to my surprise, they were deliberately and purposefully engaging the enemy across the river. They were making it appear to the Krauts across the river that we were going to try to cross there. At that time I never saw any of the engineers or any of the men in the Recon. unit either, who obviously were well dug in just below us.

Our Recon. troops had set up machine gun nests down below this hill near the water's edge and they were firing at the Krauts across the river, and the Krauts were firing back at them. The machine guns were doing battle with each other, making a lot of noise.

We could see down below us, across the river, enemy machine guns firing across the river, and we could see their muzzle blasts. It sounded as though there were a dozen or so German machine guns firing across the river at our Recon. troops below the hill, who were returning fire.

The Krauts were using the sleeves on the barrel of their machine guns to make one machine gun sound like several guns were firing, but there were many of them that were firing. I had become so used to this in Saarlautern that I could readily identify that deception.

Also, I could see and hear our Recon. troops' machine guns firing from on our side of the river, just below us, unendingly. So, it appeared that this was a diversion action, and that the Recon. troops were down there drawing enemy fire, making them believe that this is the point where we are going to cross the river. They were also burning up an awful lot of ammo, too.

Our Recon. troops did not know that we were on the hill above them. Nor did the Krauts know that we were up there looking down on them. Our job was to observe what the situation was, as well as the lay of the land. There was a large field across the river and beyond this field was a ridge of trees that ran alongside the far side of the fields, parallel to the river. This ridge of trees was about two hundred and fifty yards from the river. We could also see the Krauts up in the edge of these woods, on the ridge, digging in and setting up machine gun emplacements higher up, at the edge of the woods.

I learned that the Recon. troop unit who had accompanied the engineers up there, had set up machine gun nests downriver from where we were to cross. This was a ploy that they were using so as to fool the Germans into believing that we would cross there, where all the firing was taking place. It was a very good deception and it was working extremely well.

The Krauts across the river were digging in their machine gun emplacements that faced toward where the firing was taking place. So, I assumed where we were to cross was upriver and to our right, beyond where all of these machine gun nests were. This would allow us to cross the river and come in behind their machine gun emplacements that they were digging out there in that field.

I also learned authoritatively that we were to cross the river down below this area, further south, but this was not to be spoken about, to anyone. I still was not able to learn when we were going to make the crossing. Hopefully not tonight—I was exhausted and so hungry that my stomach wouldn't quit growling. I really worried about getting back to this little hotel, I was so exhausted. It was now nerves alone that was keeping me going.

All of the foxholes that we saw being dug by the Krauts across the river, as well as up in the edge of the ridge, were for machine guns, and all of them were facing downriver toward where the machine gun battle was going on, down below us. As we faced the river, it was flowing from our right, to our left at seven miles per hour.

The Danube River had a bank on the opposite side, about eight or ten feet high, almost straight up, with about three or four feet of land between the water and the bank. The bank on this side was low and sloping right to the water's edge, making it easy to get the boats in the water. Across the river from the point we were to cross were fields along a flat area beside the river, then beyond the fields were hills, trees, and small brush. We had to take the flat fields and also to go into the hills and take control of the woods beyond. In order to wipe out any opposition in the hills that could fire down on our troops continuing to cross the river, we had to first go to our left and clear out the fields, then go up into the woods and come in on those up there from the flank and wipe them out. This would have to be done under cover of darkness, otherwise the machine guns up in the hills would cut us down if it would be light enough for them to see us.

We saw from our observation point, through our field glasses, the German soldiers up in the edge of the woods on this ridge were digging foxholes, putting machine guns in place in them, lots of them. They were digging very fast. All of the foxholes the Krauts dug were always very neat and precisely done. Our Recon. troops were below us, near the water's edge, engaging in a machine gun battle with the Krauts that didn't seem to cease. I never could determine how they were so close to the Krauts across the river and could not be hit by their machine gun bullets. They had to have been behind some kind of a ridge or defile. This was a continuous and ongoing battle that had been going on for some time, probably since their arrival last night. I couldn't help but feel sorry for the men of the Recon. unit. It was obvious that the Krauts really were convinced that we were going to make our crossing right there, and they were just going to gun us down as we came across the river. I don't know what other kind of ploys that the Recon. unit used to further convince the Krauts that we were going to cross there.

We could now see our engineers to the south of us, putting their equipment in place, unloading aluminum assault boats from trucks near the river, but they were out of sight of the enemy soldiers across the river and were hidden by trees.

As we left the hill, we got closer to where the engineers were working, to the south of us, and south of where the machine guns were firing. They were unloading their equipment off of trucks, behind trees where they could not be seen, quite some distance from the river. They were carrying the assault boats to a point behind trees nearer to the river. I also observed that the trucks carrying the assault boats and other equipment had killed their engines and had rolled down a long hill to get close to the river, behind the trees, so that they couldn't be heard or seen. I was more than impressed with the knowledge and skill of the men of our 65th Division who planned and were executing this operation. This planning was the work of a military genius.

Also, it was obvious that the Recon. troops firing those machine guns, not only were carrying on a diversion, but also were making a lot of noise where the Kraut machine gunners across the river couldn't hear our engineers working. This whole operation was a great fascination to me, as well as being one of the best battle strategies I had ever seen or heard of, and I was lucky enough to be participating in it.

I had read of great military battles in history, but whoever conceived this operation was in the class of Caesar, Napoleon, Peter the Great, and General Robert E. Lee, not to mention General Patton, and our own XXth Corps Commander, General Walton "Bull Dog" Walker, who was so tough and pudgy that he reminded one of a bulldog.

I am sure that our division commander, Major General Stanley Reinhart, and our own regimental commander, Colonel Frank Dunkley, as well as a lot of other courageous leaders of the 65th Division, had a lot to do with this operation as well. Who all it was that planned and carried out this operation, at this location and in this manner, was a genius. I now was so excited that I forgot about being exhausted, sleepy, and hungry.

The deception was working. All of their machine guns in the foxholes were facing in the direction of where the Recon. unit was firing from. I couldn't help but get a big laugh seeing those Krauts over there across the river, working their tails off digging, when it all was going to be in vain. For tomorrow, they all would be our prisoners, or dead.

Soon we returned to our little hotel several miles to the rear, hoping and expecting to get some sleep, at least a few hours, which I needed very badly. There was little hope for that now, but I still didn't know when we would make the crossing. I couldn't conceive of us crossing that night, as tired and hungry as all of us were. I just wouldn't let myself believe that we would make that crossing tonight. However, I wondered how long our Recon. unit down there could keep up their deception before we were to cross. It had to be tonight, I thought to myself. I sure didn't want anything to go wrong with and upset this splendid operation.

By the time we returned to this little two-story hotel, I was about to lay down on the nice bed there, to go to sleep, when a man in our squad came in with a deer that he had shot. Since I was the only person in my whole company who knew how to dress a deer, I dressed it, cut out the loin, sliced and cooked it on a stove just for my buddy Sperl and me. While we were eating that venison, I whispered to Sperl that we had a big job to do tonight, to clean out some Krauts out of their foxholes, but, I told him not to mention it to anyone, since it is going to be a real big operation. I told him we needed to stick close to each other, and we needed each other's help to do this job, later. Each of us knew when we fought together we could accomplish more than with anyone else. We also knew we both had a better chance of surviving when we were fighting together.

All of the others cooked their own venison, after I cut it up for them to cook. One of our men put together some potato pancakes, which went well with the venison steaks. At least we had some food for that day, which I desperately needed. Before my stomach could settle enough to go to sleep, a sergeant came by and said, "Lets move 'em out." We were just getting comfortable and enjoying a few moments of much needed rest. It was about 1:00 A.M.

We moved out and walked, in staggered formation, the two or three miles to the river. As we walked quietly in the darkness of the very early hours of the morning, we heard hundreds of 155mm shells soaring overhead. We were so quiet walking to the river that it was almost totally silent. This silence was only broken by the swishing sound of the spinning big cannon shells flying overhead. It was the heaviest of artillery, well, really not our heaviest but big enough. We couldn't even hear the sound of the guns that fired them, nor could we hear the shells explode when they arrived at their destination at or near Regensburg. This artillery had about a twenty-mile range or more. It was a reassuring sound. It was one that I had heard many times before when we were walking at night, when everything was quiet, and there was no noise of tank engines. I am sure that the Krauts in those foxholes down there across the river also heard all of these artillery shells going overhead toward the city they were supposed to be defending. I wondered just what was going through their minds.

I had learned that the largest Messerschmitt factory in Germany was in Regensburg, as well as some large ammo and chemical factories. The rumor going around was that the chemical factories there were making some very dangerous, either biological, or chemical warfare agents. I was fearful of the artillery hitting one of the factories, and those things escaping into the air and killing everyone. As we left the hotel, someone was passing out K rations and I put one in my jacket.

We walked on to the river. Just as we got there, the engineers who apparently saw us coming, were putting the first boats into the water, which wasn't a coincidence. Their operation was just like precision clockwork. Sperl and I were the first ones in the first boat that went across. It was all extremely well orchestrated. We just walked up to the edge of the water and stepped right into the boats that had just been placed in the water seconds before we got to the edge of the water. These engineers were real heroes in my opinion, in getting all of us across safely and bringing their boats back, with just two of them in it. These were some of the best trained and most efficient soldiers that I had seen. They did one heroic job, working very hard all night and into the next day, doing a very difficult job and doing it extremely well.

We piled in, about ten men to a boat, plus the two engineers. There were wooden paddles that each of us had. We were two abreast, with a paddle. We had to either be on our knees or squat down in the boats. I talked in whispers to the engineer who sat right behind me as we paddled as hard as we could.

Fifty-four years later I met this man and talked with him at the 65th Division Convention at the Imperial Palace Hotel, in Biloxi, Mississippi, and he remembered me. He also related to me that many of the men lost the paddles into the water. Later that night as other men were crossing, they had no paddles to use, so they used their steel helmets and rifle buts to paddle the boats with. He also told me that on one trip coming back across the river that the current carried them too far downriver, and they came ashore too close to where the machine gun battle was raging and had to tow the boat along the water's edge, back upstream to the starting point.

We had so much equipment strapped to us, if the boat sank or overturned, we would go right to the bottom. We had only a few inches of freeboard, distance between the water and the rail of the boat. So, everyone paddled like crazy to get across in a hurry. We carried bandoleers of ammo, plus our ammo belt that held about ten clips, four hand grenades, bayonet, canteen full of water, and all of the other things that one carries.

When we got across and out of the boats, the two engineers paddled the empty boat back to the other side for another load of soldiers. We clung to the bank waiting for orders to go over it. We waited for a sufficient number of our troops to get across before going over the top of the bank. The lieutenant told us to fix bayonets and to keep very quiet, in that we expected to take lots of prisoners by surprise, by coming up behind them there in their foxholes and if no one fired a shot and kept quiet, it would save lots of our men's lives. Everyone knew to pass the word that was given to us, on down the line to all of the other men, which everyone did in a whispered voice. His whispered command that was passed down the way was that there were machine gun nests up in the tree-lined hill, beyond the river, but they couldn't see any of us now in the darkness, and therefore wouldn't be able to fire on us until it got lighter, nearer to daylight. This meant that we had to clear this field, then get up beyond this tree line and clear it out before it got light enough for them to see rest of our troops down below that would be still coming across. We would be taking those machine gun emplacements up in the hill from the flank and also by surprise, I hoped. I whispered to Sperl and told him that this would be our job—to clean out those machine gun nests up on that ridge.

This crossing officially took place at 2:00 A.M. The lieutenant instructed us, after we went over the bank, to move away from the river, crawling for some distance as far away from the river as necessary, toward the hills and then, as more troops got across, to stand up and move to our left, to go downriver in a sweeping action and clear out the flat fields as far as to where the machine gun battle was raging, or until we had cleared the entire flat area. The strategy in every river crossing is to get as many men across as quickly as possible, to keep dispersed, and to be concealed as much as possible, so that as many other men as possible, can get across before commencing any offensive action. We did just that.

He further instructed us that the first ones moving to the north, and nearest to the ridge, would then go up into the woods, come back to the south along the edge of the woods, and clear out the machine gun nests along the edge of the woods on that ridge. He warned that most likely the Krauts would then be firing down on our troops as they crossed, when it got light enough for them to see—unless we worked fast. Our troops would still be coming across in that flat area once it got to be daylight and we should go up in the hills at a point beyond where they were, and come back along the edge of the woods from their flank, and clean them out. Of course that meant Sperl, the BAR man and I would be going up in the woods and cleaning them out.

We clung to the steep muddy bank, as we waited for orders to go over the top. It was now getting very crowded there between the water's edge, and the steep bank. There was only about three or four feet of land between the water's edge and the bank for us to stand, while waiting to go over. I thought that maybe the whole company was now here, clinging to this bank, it got so crowded. I just couldn't believe that our engineers were able to get this many men across that fast-flowing river this quickly.

Since Al and I were in the first boatload—I was closest to the bank—I got two men to clinch their wrists together so I could use them for a step, and I climbed up and peered over to see what we could expect when we got the word to go over the top. I wanted to know if, when we went over the top, whether or not there would be a machine gun nest or foxholes to our right, that we may be right in front of and if that were so, we were finished unless we did something about it now. I stuck my head over the bank and took a long hard look to our right to make sure that we were not going to come over that bank right in front of a machine gun nest, but I didn't see any Krauts in that direction. However, I could see their helmets and their machine guns sticking out of the foxholes to my left, a very short distance to our left.

Soon the whispered order came and was instantly passed down the line to "Let's go." We moved out over the top of that steep bank, our feet slipping and sliding as we crawled up it. Al, and I were the first men over the top. We crawled over the bank on our bellies, quietly, then crawled as fast and as quietly as we could to get away from the river edge so that no one would be bunched up together after the men came across; and also so no one would be seen before we got enough men across to hold the area. When enough of our men had gotten over the bank with bayonets fixed, we crawled away from the river as far as possible, and then turned to our left toward the machine gun fire. We then stood up and were in a sweeping line between the river and the hill. We now were in a line from the river, across this field, as we moved to our left, making a sweep across the field toward downriver where the machine guns were still firing at each other. The night was very dark and we were just walking into the darkness, searching for those machine gun nests.

We began to come upon those foxholes from behind. In each were three German soldiers with their machine guns set up and ready for action. As I expected, I noticed that all of the machine gun nest foxholes we came upon were facing to the north, just as I had seen them digging them from up on the hill earlier, through field glasses.

The machine gun battle between the Recon. troops and the Krauts across the river was still raging on. I just couldn't believe this deception was still working; it was getting to be kind of comical. If we had crossed up there, we would have been cut down with grazing fire from all of their machine gun nests that were well dug in, and all facing in that direction.

We surprised them. We came up from behind them. When I came upon the first foxhole, I was right behind the men in it before they realized what was taking place, and when they turned around and looked at me, with my bayonet right in their faces, all three of them quietly put their hands up, crawled out of their foxholes, and said, *"Kommarad."* They began to surrender as fast as we came upon them. It would not be very easy for them to reposition their machine guns, to turn them around and fire them in the opposite direction at us, very quickly. Some were not willing to leave the safety of their foxholes, for some unknown reason.

As I approached the second foxhole I came upon, two German soldiers came out with their hands up saying quietly, *"Kommarad."* I motioned them to the rear where we had just crossed. I looked in the hole and there was another one in there, the gunner, bent over forward and squatting down right behind that big fast machine gun. He did not have his helmet on, obviously trying to be inconspicuous, which provoked me more. I spoke to him in German quietly for him to "Come here." I said, *"Kommarad, Kommen sie hier."* He did not move at all. I pondered what next. I knew that I just couldn't leave him here, nor could I fire on him, but he wasn't moving. Neither was I! Maybe that is why we were ordered to fix bayonets, I thought to myself. It also went through my mind that this was a Kraut that would rather die than surrender. If that was the way he thought, I could definitely accommodate him.

I looked to my right, and there right beside me was my company commander, Captain Graham.

He whispered to me and said, "Are you going to leave that son of a bitch there, and let him kill all of us with that machine gun after we pass by? I know that you know what to do, so what are you waiting for?"

My captain then walked on ahead with the other men, just as though he was a private like me, and away from and directly in front of this machine gun. Now, this Kraut machine gun was pointing right at the back of my company commander, as well as several of my buddies, with this Kraut gunner right behind it in the foxhole.

His walking on ahead with me facing this situation meant to me that he trusted my judgment and my ability to handle the situation, believing that I would do my job right. I appreciated his faith in my ability to do my job well and not let a catastrophe happen that would kill or endanger his and all of the other men's lives, as well as my own. There was never any doubt in my mind that I would hesitate for one moment to do whatever was necessary to help win the battle, and my captain well knew that by now.

I understood what the Captain was saying to me, and there was only one thing left for me to do, and that was to bayonet the son of a bitch. I instantaneously recalled all of my training and experience, knowing that he had on a thick coat and other clothing, and a bayonet don't go in or out all that easy. I also recalled that I had sharpened my bayonet on an old-fashioned emery wheel at a farmhouse, days before Struth, and it was very sharp, with a sharp point on it. Lots of things went through my mind in a split second. One thing that I thought was, this Kraut was a diehard fanatic Nazi and was following Hitler's order not to surrender. Little did he realize that I would quickly oblige him. I also contemplated that this Kraut machine gunner was playing possum with me, and was planning to gun us all down if I ignored him and left him there. Regardless what may have been going on inside his head, he had one of two choices: Come out with his hands up or die now.

I had to do it quickly and get it over with, because all of our other men were walking on ahead of me, leaving me there alone to deal with this Kraut who refused to surrender. I had to do it quickly so that I could catch up with them ahead of me. I really wanted to be one of the first men to go up in that hill and wipe out those machine gun nests that I had seen them digging up there that evening. I hoped Sperl would be with me to help me do it. I was not about to let this Kraut blow that opportunity.

So, to make sure I did a good job, with my captain right ahead of me, and in a direct line of fire from this machine gun, I put the butt of my rifle firmly against my shoulder, stiffened my elbow as I held it very firmly, leaped in the air, came down with all my weight and strength, and plunged my bayonet right through his back between his shoulders. I heard a gurgling and moaning sound.

I had trouble pulling my bayonet out of him, so the only other thing for me to do was to jump in the hole on him and put both of my feet on his back, which I did, and pull my bayonet out of him. I was certain that he wouldn't be able to ever operate a machine gun again when I walked away from that foxhole and went on ahead to catch up with the other men. I didn't realize until later in the day that I had blood all over my suede boots, and I was never able to get it all off.

We moved on upriver in the pitch-black darkness of the night, spread out, taking prisoners, clearing the field of Krauts as we went. As I walked away from that foxhole, everyone else was ahead of me and they were taking lots of prisoners. The prisoners were passing by me with their hands over their heads. Some looked at me and others ignored me. I motioned all of them in the direction that we wanted them to go. I quickly caught up with my group. I glanced back, and our men were still coming over the bank by the dozens, not that I could see them, but there were many of them coming behind me.

We went as far to the left and downriver from where we crossed as we could, where we ran out of foxholes and Krauts. As we got near where the machine guns had been firing at each other across the river, they suddenly stopped firing at each other. They stopped their firing right at the proper time to prevent any of us being hit by their fire. I have never been able to determine who and how it was communicated to our Recon. troops over there across the river to stop firing over toward us, but they did quit firing in our direction at the proper time, so that we would not be in their line of fire.

When I got to the end of where the machine gun emplacements were, there was a wide path that went up the hill into the wooded ridge. I looked up into the woods and it was as dark as pitch up there. I saw Captain Graham, Technical Sergeant Lars Agneberg, and First Sergeant Leo Menard from Falls River, Massachusetts, and they were talking. I walked up to them and asked about the machine gun nests I saw the Krauts digging while we were up in this hilly wooded area that afternoon. Captain Graham agreed with me that it was still too dark to go up into those woods, but in a very short while it would be light enough to see. We just talked and waited there for a little daylight to arrive. Sperl was there also, just waiting for us to go up in this wooded ridge.

As a little early-morning light began to break, Captain Graham told me, "Ladner, take a man with you and go up this path and clean that wooded ridge out, all the way down, then get into a holding position along the east edge of the wooded ridge, and hold up there until further orders." I looked at Sperl, he appeared ready. We hurriedly went up into the tree line and started back south along the edge of the tree line, going in the opposite direction from which we had just come, to clean out all of the machine guns and any resistance that was up in this hill. The Krauts there were now beginning to be able to see down in the field below, toward the river where our men were still coming across.

The Kraut machine gunners had just now commenced firing down on Fox Company as they were coming across the river and over the bank. We didn't have to look for them now, they all were busy firing toward our men that were still coming across the river and moving up. We could now hear them and find them easily. Daylight was rapidly approaching now and we knew that we had to rush to prevent the enemy machine gunners from killing our troops that were still crossing the river and coming over the bank.

Sperl was right beside me with his BAR. Al Sperl was a real fighter and most of all, he carried a lot of firepower, more than any of the other infantryman armed with only a rifle. We worked so well together, we understood each other, and worked like a team; we were more like brothers, and looked out for each other. I always tried to pair up with him. We thought alike and fought together well. We both knew exactly what to do in every situation and we always did it.

Our job was to wipe out these machine gun nests up in these woods. We knew what needed to be done and we agreed, volunteered to do it, and we did it, without having to be told.

We heard machine gun fire coming from up ahead of us all along the tree line that faced the river, and we had to search them out and eliminate them, very quick. They were killing our men. We could see our men still coming over the banks, and away from where they had crossed the river, from where we were up in the hills.

We then heard and saw an enemy machine gun nest that was just ahead of us along the edge of the wooded area, that was firing on the men of Fox Company down below, as they were attempting to come over the side of the riverbank, and were moving away from it. We crept up close to the foxhole. We heard and could see their machine gun spurting away as fast as it would fire. We could see our men down below in the flat field, falling, as it fired. This of course was not the only fire that they were receiving. There were more machine guns going off further on down the tree line.

Sperl was a gutsy soldier and a fine guy to get along with. He was a hard-fighting and a determined soldier, one of the best that I had ever encountered. We signaled each other to let's crawl and creep up on that machine gun nest and give them some hand grenades. I always liked to use them up quickly when I had them, because they were heavy to carry. I carried them by hanging them on my field jacket chest pockets, and also hanging some on my cartridge belt.

The Krauts in this machine gun nest didn't have any idea in the world that we were coming up behind them. Their machine gun was making so much noise they were not able to hear us coming up on them. However, we crept up close to the nest and we each threw two grenades in on that foxhole. We silenced that machine gun and eliminated the gunners. We worked as hard and as fast as we possibly could in trying to save as many of our men's lives as possible.

Quickly, we continued on down the tree-lined ridge to clean out the other machine gun nests that we could hear firing. We heard this other one, closer now. We rush up on it, got up very close to where they were operating that machine gun. When we got close enough that we knew that we could just fire on them with our rifles and not miss killing any of them quickly, we opened fire, killing all three of them. It was like shooting ducks in a pond.

Then, further down the tree line, we heard another machine gun firing continuously. As we crept up near it, we saw that they were leaving their foxhole and were running through the woods, just ahead of us, toward the east side of the woods that faced a large area of fields of farmland. They were running from our right to our left. One man was running ahead carrying the machine gun, another behind him was carrying the tripod, and another carrying two boxes of ammo. All were running from their foxhole through the woods to the east away from the position that they had been firing from. All of them were running in a row, one behind the other, about twenty feet apart. Sperl got the first one who had the machine gun. I got the man with the tripod and, simultaneously, we both got the other one, just like precision work. We went to them to make sure they were dead, so they wouldn't fire on us and shoot us in the back as we went past them to search out the remainder of the wooded ridge.

We continued moving south, clearing out the woods as we went. Many of the machine gunners had abandoned their foxholes and machine guns as they ran to the east, toward the open fields where there were many piles of what appeared to be wheat straw, before we could get them. We did not find any other opposition in the woods, but we did come upon abandoned machine gun nests where they had left too hastily to take their weapons.

We continued south until the wooded area ended. We went down a path, along a steep bank to near the edge of the river, and searched out some caves in the riverbank where the citizens kept their foods cool, and they had large blocks of ice in them. While there, some 88 shells landed all around us. Al and I ran into one of the cellars, or caves, that had been dug into the side of the hill beside the riverbank to store food in, until the firing ceased. We came out soon after the shelling stopped. There was a woman who had been just standing out in the open while the shelling was going on. She was holding a small baby in her arms who had been killed by the shrapnel from one of the Kraut 88 shells that had hit near her. We tried to console her, but to no avail. She was very hysterical. We tried to take the dead baby from her to see if there

was anything that we could for it, but she refused. She was still screaming hysterically when we left, going back up this narrow path.

We started up this same path back into the hill and as we did, an 88
shell landed right beside us, about five feet from us in the dirt, kicking
up some dirt as it hit, but it didn't explode. If it had exploded, it was so
close to us that it would have killed both of us. I wondered where there
could be a Kraut artillery spotter that could see us down there. I wanted
to find out where he was positioned so that I could find him and eliminate him. I looked every which way trying to find him but I couldn't. I
don't have any fondness for Kraut artillery spotters. We then moved
fast, running up this very steep hill to the east edge of the woods facing
the open fields on the east side of the wooded ridge. The fields there
had many big piles of wheat straw piled high.

Now, other men from our platoon were coming through the woods
that we had just cleared out and we were assembling along the east edge
of this tree-lined ridge facing these fields of piles of wheat straw. I was
the last, or the end man on the south part of this ridge.

We found foxholes already dug; often it was the case, where the
citizens would dig fortifications for their own soldiers' use. It was a
mystery to me why they were located at the edge of the woods, facing to
the east. It was as though they had prepared them for us, for some
unknown reason. Maybe they planned it that way so we could be ambushed by snipers from behind the stacks of straw piled into many piles
out in the fields to the east of the hilly woods. We had time to spare, we
had no place to go, and the word was passed down for us to just hold
our position there, until further orders.

These foxholes were already dug and were facing the wheatfield to
the east, along the east edge of the tree-laden ridge. I sat down on the
edge of this foxhole, as did Sperl and others in foxholes to my left. It
was a good feeling to finally be able to sit down and get my breath and
rest for a few minutes. I was now more than totally and completely
exhausted. A few other of our men were now catching up with Al and
me. I observed to the east and there were big fields with many hay or
straw piles in them, also an awful lot of church steeples that one could
see in the distance, over the rolling hills of farmland. The whole situa-

tion looked dangerously suspicious to me. I was certain that there were spotters in each of those church steeples.

I had a K Ration in my field jacket and I sat on the edge of the foxhole, leaned up against a small tree, and ate it. As I was eating, I heard a loud crack of a rifle bullet pass near my head, right by my right ear, which almost deafened me in that ear. The trunk of the small tree that I was leaning against was hit by a rifle bullet and the bark had splintered off and struck me on the neck, causing it to bleed. I thought that I was hit at first; then, upon examining the situation, it was the splinter from the tree that had hit me and cut my neck. I suddenly sank down into the foxhole to be out of the sniper's view. I yelled at Sperl in the next foxhole down about thirty feet away and told him what happened and to be cautious. I also told him to pass on down the line what I said to the other men as well, that I bet there was a sniper behind each one of those piles of hay or straw out there in the fields in front of us, and that I believed that these foxholes in this location were a trap for snipers out there in that wheatfield to pick us off. Sperl passed the word on down the line that there was a sniper behind every haystack out there and then he and the other men opened up and fired on many of the haystacks.

Since the snipers weren't able to get any of our men, I was fearful of 88s coming in and hitting the treetops above us and getting aerial bursts of shrapnel coming down on us, even though we were in a foxhole, the shrapnel from a tree-burst comes down on you, and a foxhole is no protection. Even though you are in a foxhole it don't protect you from shrapnel from these tree or aerial bursts.

We could see for miles and miles over the hills of farmland and over each crest was a church steeple. As usual, the steeples had observers in them and they knew every move that we made and they also directed artillery and mortar fire on us.

As darkness approached, we moved along the tree line of the east side of the hills and assembled in a small farmhouse down the hill and to the north. I don't know where the captain came from, but he was there, doing a great job as always, a great commander if there ever was one. It was getting very dark when I entered that farmhouse. In there was every sergeant in the company; they were all there.

The captain told me to take a man with me and to go out to the barn where he had seen a shovel, to get it, and go down the dirt farm road about two hundred yards to where it intersected another farm road, and to dig a foxhole, set up a perimeter defense and observation post there. Others were doing the same in different directions. I took a man with me that I hardly knew, since Sperl had fallen asleep on the floor with two bricks under his helmet to hold his head up. He was already snoring up a storm.

We all were exhausted. It had now been over forty hours since I had any sleep and only a few hours before then. I got the shovel from the barnyard and we went down this dirt road in the direction of the hayfields and came to where this dirt road intersected with another dirt road, a wagon trail, and I told my buddy Billy, we will dig our foxhole right here. He wanted to know "Why there?" I told him that this was a road intersection and that anyone coming to this farmhouse, we were to protect from either direction; they would have to pass us. Also, there was a pile of cow manure there. I wanted to put this foxhole right in front of it so that it would be a black backdrop for us, so that it would help camouflage us, so we would not be a silhouette out in the open and could not be easily seen by anyone approaching from either direction. We did just that. We dug our foxhole, not a very good one—we were too tired to make it deep. We dug it just deep enough for us to sit in, facing each other, and we both were in this hole, a narrow slit trench that we sat down in, facing each other with our legs overlapping, each of us looking in the opposite direction.

Soon I saw Billy look startled, I spun around to see what it was behind me, and there was a German soldier with a rifle in his hands approaching us, walking very fast, coming down the road from the field where the stacks of straw were. I twisted my body to my left where I could see and also get a bead on the Kraut coming at us. I yelled *"Halt."* He did not halt, or slow down. I am sure that he heard me, but he obviously never saw us. I immediately threw off my safety as I drew a bead on him. As I was squeezing my trigger, he evidently heard the click of my safety. He was then only about fifteen feet away. He stopped suddenly, dropped his rifle, put his hands up, and said, *"Kommarad!"* He was a good Nazi and knew how to surrender. Nevertheless, I feel certain that if he had seen us before he heard the click of my safety, he would have shot us.

I sent Billy after help while I kept my rifle on him. As Sergeant Agneberg came and took him away, I picked up his rifle and found that it was a sniper's rifle, the safety was off, and it was ready to fire. It had a fine-looking telescope sight on it and would have made a great deer rifle.

I knew immediately that this had to be the sniper that fired that shot at me as I sat on the edge of my foxhole this morning eating a K Ration. He was coming from the field where the piles of straw were. He had to be the one that shot at me, and he had waited until it got dark to leave that field, under cover of darkness, so he wouldn't be seen, he thought. He was going to this farmhouse, which the night before was occupied by enemy soldiers. Also, he had no way of knowing that we had already taken over the farmhouse. I took the bolt out of his rifle and buried it deep in the pile of cow manure and smashed the telescope sight with the butt of my rifle.

Soon the captain sent a replacement for just me, and I got a few hours of sleep. When I got to the farmhouse where the captain was, I was told that the prisoner was being interrogated and he had already given the captain some valuable information about Kraut gun emplacements, as well as how many soldiers they had in that area. He definitely had been the sniper that was firing at me from one of those haystacks that afternoon.

I am certain that if I had not positioned our foxhole in front of that pile of cow manure, that this sniper would have seen us, and most likely would have shot us before we would have ever known he was there. I got a few hours of sleep that night. I was so exhausted, every muscle in my body ached. I just passed out on the floor. It had now been over forty hours since I had any sleep.

Somewhere in the area the following day, one of our men in my squad somehow got two eggs from a farmhouse, cooked them and was eating them when in comes some major. Now, majors are in a class by themselves. They always seemed to be out of place and out of character for a combat leader. So, this major slaps a twenty-five dollar fine on this real great fighting man, a good friend of mine who was more hungry than I was, for eating two of this farmer's eggs.

This same GI had also received a concussion when an 88 landed right near him, earlier that day. Later, just after the war ended, while we were in Linz, Austria, his post traumatic concussion symptoms became worse and he had to be evacuated to Stateside for treatment at a neurological hospital. I wanted to say something about his unfair and unjust fine, in light of the fact that I had recently stopped two sergeants who were sent out by their general and told not to return until they had found him some eggs for his breakfast. That was not equal justice for all by any stretch of the imagination. I thought that was what we were fighting about. I never did encounter a major that I liked. They always seemed to be some kind of an out of place misfit—or was this just a run of bad luck that we were experiencing? This was most likely the same major that I had encountered in Saarlautern.

We learned that the 261st Regiment had crossed further downriver from us where it made a bend and turned to the east. This regiment got an awful lot of resistance from the Krauts and many of their men were killed. We heard they took a group of prisoners and as they were being escorted back to the rear; there was a lieutenant colonel there and one of the Nazi prisoners saw him and suddenly took a pistol from underneath his coat and killed the lieutenant colonel.

That early morning, after the crossing, we left this farmhouse to continue our push to Regensburg. We searched out houses and villages, and found a wooded area of tall pine trees that contained huge piles of artillery shells, stacked high under these trees and they were barely visible in this big forest, which had a small railroad running all through the ammo dump. I walked through this ammo dump and I saw 88 shells stacked very high in big stacks, each stack at least one hundred yards long. Never had I seen so much artillery ammunition. Uncle Adolph must really be on a dedicated killing rampage, I thought, but he wouldn't ever get the opportunity to use this ammo.

As the afternoon approached, we got near the city. As we approached, we were on the main route for the center of the city. We walked down this long street, from the south, for miles into the city. It seemed as though we would never get there. Not one civilian was to be seen anywhere, nor did we see any white flags flying from the windows of homes and businesses, as was the case in many towns and cities that we took.

Our job was to clear the city of enemy resistance before the top brass came in to accept the surrender of Regensburg. As our small platoon of tired and weary soldiers approached the center of the city, we saw a welcome sight. There was a big table out in the street, with a white sheet on it, in front of the Rathaus, or city hall. Behind the table there rigidly stood Nazi admirals, generals, as well as the Burgermeister and other dignitaries, surrendering to us and saluting. I recall Sperl telling them in fluent German, "You guys are just going to have to be patient until all of the big brass gets here. They are the ones that you will have to surrender to."

Soon, our assistant division commander, General John Copeland, and our regimental commander, Colonel Frank Dunkley, and other officers arrived and formally accepted the surrender of Regensburg. We learned then that one of the German generals that had been there, and who was the commander of Regensburg, had suddenly decided that he wasn't going to surrender, and he left just before the formal surrender. Rumors were that he knew about Hitler's order that any military person who surrendered would be shot and his family exterminated in a concentration camp. Al, upon hearing this, asked me, "I wonder if the general's family would have a choice of which concentration camp that they would like to be exterminated in?"

I replied, "Such as this will happen in any country, if the citizens don't keep the gangsters out of their government."

Sperl then went to the mayor, the Burgermeister, and asked, "Where are the closest luxury dwellings in the center of the city?" The mayor pointed out an area where we could find some quality living quarters, very near there. We stood by until the jeeps arrived carrying our officers who accepted the surrender. The Signal Corps people of our division also arrived to photograph the surrender. We then left and found some of the most luxurious living quarters that we had yet seen. There was no food in this elegant house. One man went into the weed-infested yard and gathered some dandelions, and we put some vinegar and oil on them and ate them as a salad. That is all that we had to eat that day.

There was a large library in the house and I looked through some of the books to see if I was familiar with anything that the owner read. Behind some books I found a .38 caliber pistol. I examined it and found it to be loaded. I put it back where I found it, believing that soon the owner would need it to protect himself, his family, and his property from looters, as well as people starving for food that would come to steal it. It was obvious that there would be a lot of postwar crime in Germany, until real law and order was restored. We only stayed there one night and then on to the next objective.

We left Regensburg the following morning, riding trucks loaded with our infantry. This was the second occasion since I first started riding tanks that I rode a truck. We were still hungry as a wolf. We had a difficult time getting rations up to the front, in that the supply lines were so long and the front was moving so fast. As the trucks sped east from Regensburg, the men on the truck ahead of us had a big can of Kraut sauerkraut that the guys were eating away on by grabbing handfuls of it and eating it. We wanted some of it terribly bad, so we sent a message to have the drivers of both trucks to hold their speed steady and allow our truck to pull up close behind the truck with the sauerkraut on it, and a man got on the front bumper and he was handed the large canister of the stuff and then passed it on back to where everyone got all they wanted. We then passed it on back to the truck behind us.

These drivers were very good at their job, and did a great job of driving that day. They were from our own division. As we sped down the highway at top speed, one man on the truck grabbed a handful of the sauerkraut and before he took a bite, he looked over both shoulders and remarked, "I just was looking around to see if there was a major around anywhere looking at me eat this sauerkraut." Soon that evening we regrouped with our tanks.

One day soon after that, I was getting on Al's case about using up so much ammo so fast and for wasting it when he should fire that BAR as a single shot to conserve ammo, but he didn't like to do that. He liked to fire that thing so much he couldn't carry enough ammo for it, as big as he was. So I said to Al, "I wish that I was your company commander. I would chew your ass out all the time."

Al replied, "I wish that you were, too. We would win this damned war a hell of a lot quicker."

CHAPTER 27

The Half-Cooked Chicken

"An army marches on its stomach."

—NAPOLEON BONAPARTE (1751–1836)

The next thing that I recall is that we unloaded off the tanks and set out on foot. We stopped in this village that was abandoned by the civilians, so we took over one house late in the day, thinking that we would stay there that night. There was nothing in the house to eat, and we had no rations. We all were half-starved. I looked around and saw only one lonely chicken in the backyard. I built a fire in the stove and put on a large pot of water to use to pluck her feathers and another to cook her in. I caught the chicken, dressed it, plucked all of the feathers off after I scalded it, and put it in a pot to cook. For some reason I left the feet on that chicken, presumably thinking that I may have to transport here to another location. It was soon after that, just as my chicken was about half-done, when we were ordered to leave and in a staggered formation take off down this country road. The expedient thing for me to do with the chicken was to carry her with me, since I had never been so hungry in my life. I was also determined to not be defeated in my effort to scrounge something to eat. Not being able to devise any other way of carrying this chicken, I tied the feet together and hung it on my bayonet on the left side of my cartridge belt.

I was walking on the right side of the road about 10:00 P.M., on this very dark night, when a colonel in a jeep came by. I think that it was our regimental commander. His jeep slowed down to my speed, right beside me. I could tell that he was a colonel, because I could see the eagle on his collar underneath his jacket. No officer in his right mind on the front, would wear his rank exposed, like on his helmet.

The colonel's jeep slowed down to my pace. He was right beside me as I walked along. He asked me what I was going to do with that chicken. I explained about attempting to cook it, but we got called out to do this maneuver, so I decided to take it along to where I hoped that I could find another stove and a pot to finish cooking it, and then eat that chicken.

So, I also told the colonel, "Sir, you are not feeding us well enough. I am starved for some food—we all are. I have lost a lot of weight and I and all of the other men here are actually starving to death, sir. Napoleon said that an army marches on its stomach, but this army don't feed too well."

He smiled real big, waved at me, and motioned his jeep driver to move on. I felt good that I had been able to get my message across; maybe it would get some results and we would receive some food. By daylight, after walking all night, we came upon this very modern-appearing small town, beautiful to no end. We stopped for some rest and I went to this real neat cottage where an old man was dressed in a suit, vest, tie, and all. He greeted me and invited me in. I had my chicken with me and they seemed to understand, so the lady of the house put a pot on the stove and finished cooking my hen, and she did an excellent job. She made some dumplings and put them in the pot to cook with this chicken. That chicken and dumplings was real good. I shared her with the elderly couple who seemed about as hungry as me, as well as with some of the men with me who wanted some of her. Not everyone did. I assumed that they were men that rode the trucks and had been eating our rations. I was glad that the colonel didn't have this major in the jeep with him when he saw this chicken hanging on my cartridge belt, I would have gotten, probably a hundred-dollar fine for cooking a hen.

The very next day we were still searching out woods and farm villages for tank traps and any resistance groups that still wanted to fight. We came upon this old farmhouse that afternoon. Some women were out in the yard beside the house at an outdoor stone oven, baking bread. It smelled wonderful. There were just a few of us men in this patrol. I stopped and tried talking to the women, but no one could speak any English. One woman pulled out a big round loaf of black pumpernickel bread from the oven. My mouth watered an awful lot as I smelled its wonderful aroma. I knew that this woman knew that I was as hungry as one could be, and she smiled. I pulled out my wallet and found a five-dollar bill in it, which was all of the money that I had; I got it out, showed it to her, and gave it to this woman. She accepted it with a smile and gave me the big loaf of hot, fresh bread. I took out my pocketknife and cut off a piece of it immediately, and began eating it. I caught up with the other men and cut each of them a big piece of this wonderful bread. This made my day.

CHAPTER 28

Are We a Bunch of Uncivilized Heathens and Barbarians?

"God grants liberty only to those who love it, and who are always ready to guard and defend it."

—DANIEL WEBSTER (1752–1852)

The next incident that I recall was in a large city that we took. We arrived there late at night on tanks. It was almost dark when our tank pulled up in front of this large, expensive dwelling building near the center of the city. Never had I been so tired and irritable, as well as totally exhausted, and also being awfully hungry. We had started out on our tanks early that morning just before the crack of day. We had ridden all day, and one frightening incident after the other occurred, as we came closer to this very large city. I didn't have the faintest idea what the name of it was. It was almost dark when we came into this city, riding tanks, ours the lead one as it always was.

We took the area that was near the center of the city, which were large, expensive, old, but very luxurious residential buildings. Our tank stopped in the front of this building, others stopped in front of other such buildings. Soon the trucks came in, loaded with our infantry, and they began searching out the cellars of all the other buildings. I had already searched out the cellar of the building where our tank stopped, expecting to spend the night there. The men on my tank and the tankers had all congregated in the big living room of this fine home and were there when I came out of the gigantic cellar from searching it out.

It is not easy for one to go into a strange building late, with hardly any light or any kind of flashlight or anything to help one see in one of these big cellars. I had learned to smell, take several whiffs of air at the top of the stairs, to see if you can sniff out the body odors of people who may be in a cellar. If there were people in there, you could sure smell them, as well as feel the heat from their bodies. I knew from my college chemistry that an average body gives off two hundred watts of heat. If the air smells cool and there is an absence of any body odors then you can be pretty well certain that there are no enemy troops in there. This was my theory and practice and it worked. If you feel the heat of bodies, smell the odor of bodies and dirty clothes, then you should call for help before going into that cellar, as I had told the other men on the tanks.

I recall once that I was very frightened that there may be enemy troops in this other cellar. I felt the heat of bodies and I smelled the odor of people. Before I started down into it, I took a grenade, pulled the pin, put the pin in my pants pocket, held the grenade in my left hand, with my rifle in my right hand, and began saying in German for them to *"Kommen sie heir."* (Come here.) All the time, holding the grenade out in front of me, so they could see it in the faint light.

If there had been enemy troops in there and if they had shot me, I would have dropped the grenade, and in so doing I would have taken a few of them with me. Luckily there were no troops in there, just some old folks and lots of older women. I then put the pin back in the grenade.

I searched out the large cellar of this very large and luxurious dwelling first, then we all assembled in the big living room of this house. I recall the tall ceilings, large windows, and spaciousness of the rooms, as well as the massive elegant furnishings and decor.

It was getting so dark that we could only see the image of each other in this room. There were no utilities, as usual. The group of us that had been riding this Pershing tank were in the room and were just standing around in a circle by a large table, not knowing what to do next, but try to find a bite to eat and a place to sleep, as usual. Then, in comes Tony, who had ridden in on a truck. I don't know how he found where we were, he just appeared. He had a middle-aged, well-dressed, very sophisticated, and refined-appearing woman with him who was crying. He was leading her by her hand. Tony tells all of us in the room, about six or eight men, "I just screwed this bitch. Anyone want some of her?"

No one said one word. I looked at this poor woman who was shaking, trembling, silently crying, with tears pouring down her cheeks as she stood there beside Tony, motionless.

I said to Tony, "So, did she give you her consent to do that?"

His reply was, "Hell no, she didn't have any choice in it. It was a good piece of ass. Anybody want some?"

No one said anything. The silence was deafening, the light in the room, late that evening, was very dim. Everyone seemed to be just frozen, in that no one even moved or said one word. I became extremely angry. I asked one of the men who spoke German to ask her if he had raped her or forced her to have sex with him, and if this was her house. She nodded her head in the affirmative, and the GI interpreter stated that she said he had, she hadn't consented, and this was her house. I blew my top.

I looked at Tony and told him, "You little sorry, sawed-off, low-life, no-good son of a bitch, you raped this woman. You low-life piece of crap, I am ashamed to be in the same outfit with someone as depraved as you are. Do you know that the penalty for rape is death by a firing squad, and that our military is executing soldiers all the time for rape and murder? I will volunteer for the firing squad. You ought to be took out and shot. You are a sick son of a bitch, and a disgrace to America, the Army, and everyone else in it. You ain't nothing but a piece of scum. I hope that they put your ass before a firing squad for doing this. We are not a bunch of uncivilized barbarians, as you are trying to make us look like; we are Americans, if you know what that means, you sick, no-good, low-life, trashy son of a bitch. The German radio and the citizens are saying that we are "Patton's SS Troops" and now you make it a reality, you make it come true. You are the worst enemy that we have. How in the hell did you find us here, in the first place, where did your sorry ass come from anyway? I don't want to ever even look at you, or even to be in the same room with you, ever again. You ain't nothing but trouble going somewhere to happen. Get your sorry ass out of here now, and don't you ever speak to me again. I hate your low-life guts, you are sicker than sick, you son of a bitch. Get your sorry, no-good ass out of here now." He left in a big hurry.

The German-speaking GI told Tony to get the hell out of there, and not let either him or me have to look at his sorry ass again. He went running down the street and told someone that Ladner threatened to kill him, but when he was asked what it was all about, he refused to tell them why.

I took this woman to the next room, which was her bedroom, and she was told by the man with us that could speak German that she would be safe, that no one else would bother her, and to go to sleep and not to worry about anyone bothering her again. He told her to lock her door.

I never saw that no-account piece of fecal material again. I did learn that the true facts were related to the captain by all of the other men who were there. All of us that came in on the tank moved out of this house and went to another one down the street, searched out its cellar using the faint light from paper matches to see in there, and we slept in this house for the night. We needed trash like Tony like we needed a hole in the head. I never saw that piece of rubbish again.

The next thing that I recall is that we were searching out some woods, a large forest and were walking along this road. I was extremely tired when someone from the company CP told us that President Roosevelt had died. We all were very saddened. We then came upon a small resort area in a forest about noon and stayed there the remainder of the afternoon and that night, which was very comfortable, and we somehow acquired some food. I don't know how it happened but someone brought up some cases of ten-in-one rations in a jeep. They were very tasty in the cool mountainous air. I often wondered if our colonel sent those rations up there for us. It was in a beautiful mountainous area and very cold that night, so I got some much needed rest in a very comfortable bed.

We got off the tanks late one evening at the edge of a city, expecting to stay there for the night but that was not the case. The engineers came up with truckloads of assault boats. The Krauts had blown up a bridge across the Enns River, and we had to cross it to get to Linz, Austria. We went into this house near where we were to cross and I found a clean pair of what may be called crude, homemade boxer shorts, bloomers, or whatever one wanted to call them, and I changed from my filthy long johns that I had been wearing since I was in the hospital. I changed right there, throwing my filthy long johns away. I felt a whole lot cleaner.

That night we paddled across the river in assault boats with little or no resistance, walked right through the middle of the city in the wee hours of the night and on into the countryside down the river, putting down any enemy resistance that we met. We walked all night and finally at daylight we came upon a farmhouse and I told someone that I was just about totally exhausted and that there was a nice bed in this farmhouse and that I was going to sleep. So, I did and had a good nap until about noon when I was awakened by a sergeant, and we moved out again.

Thereafter, days later, we came to an area near Linz, Austria, where the German soldiers were surrendering by the hundreds, if not thousands. It was late at night when our tanks suddenly stopped in front of a large contingent of German soldiers who were standing in the middle of the road, and all of them had their hands over their heads waving white flags and asking to surrender. They told us that they were coming from the eastern front, fleeing from the Russians and they didn't want to surrender to the Russians because they would send them to Russia to rebuild what they had destroyed there, or kill them. Many of them told us that they wanted to volunteer to join us and fight the Russians. They had many vehicles of all kinds. Their weapons and ammunition had been abandoned previously. It was late at night and difficult to deal with the situation at that hour, but we managed to place all of them in a field on the side of the road where they either pitched their pup tents, or just lay on the ground. We directed traffic, directing all of their vehicles into an adjacent field. There were just a few of us American soldiers, so we found ourselves surrounded with these thousand or more Krauts wanting to surrender. We were kept busy getting them organized into these fields and off of the road. We few GIs were right in the middle of hundreds of them, telling them where to park their trucks, where to assemble and pitch their pup tents for the night. It was a very strange feeling, we few Patton's Raiders on the side of the road, late at night, surrounded by thousands of Kraut soldiers begging to surrender. They were friendly and caused no trouble. We spent the entire night trying to put some order in all of this chaos.

We got no sleep that night at all, trying to manage all of those surrendering enemy troops. They just kept coming by the thousands, in all kinds of vehicles, but no fighting vehicles like tanks or half-tracks. All of their combat vehicles had been abandoned. Many of the trucks had food supplies in them, so we corralled all of their vehicles into one area of an open field and all of the POWs in another part. We did this all night long.

The next day, on May 5, 1945, at about 5:00 P.M., we went into the City of Linz, Austria, and occupied it. It is a very old, large, and beautiful city on the Danube, and it had been declared an open city. The bridge across the river is right on the main thoroughfare through the city with a large city square right at the end of the big Danube River bridge.

We billeted in some nice residential buildings in the downtown area—the address was 3 Bischofstrube. The following day we searched out the city, searching for German soldiers, and there were many of them hiding in the buildings, but none of them were armed or offered any resistance. We took so many prisoners that we had a difficult time dealing with them. We filled up some sort of a sports arena, a large athletic field, until it was overflowing, so it was decided that we take the overflow to the Linz Airport where they could be placed in a fenced compound there until they could be processed out into civilian life. We had the German soldiers take their own trucks and haul these POWs to a compound by the Linz Airport. We patrolled the city for anyone who may be looting or otherwise committing any crimes.

The city was full of German troops who were begging to surrender to us, and trying to avoid having to surrender to the Russians who were just beyond the city to the east. German soldiers were continuously coming from the east to surrender to us, rather than to the Russians. This situation created a monumental problem for us to have to deal with.

CHAPTER 29

Unconditional Surrender of German Forces and Cessation of Hostilities

"We here highly resolve that these dead shall not have died in vain; that this nation under God shall have a new birth of freedom; and that government of the people, by the people, for the people shall not perish from the earth."

—ABRAHAM LINCOLN (1809–1865)

We men in combat were informed that on 7 May 1945 the German High Command had signed an unconditional surrender agreement, the terms of which were to become effective at 0001 hours on 9 May 1945.

Our division commander, Major General Stanley E. Reinhart; assistant division commander, Brigadier John E. Copeland; and chief of staff, Colonel William J. Epes, traveled that night to Erlauf, Austria, where they met with the Russian general who was in command of the Soviet forces, the 7th Guard Parachute Division, that met our forces there, which was 45 miles east of Linz.

Since there had now been a cessation of hostilities, our duties occupying and policing Linz was almost as difficult as combat. We had to maintain law and order, get the citizens there to return to their jobs, such as restoring utilities, and otherwise try to get the city returned to normal operation again. Our biggest job was dealing with the surrendering Nazi troops, housing and feeding them, and then discharging them and organizing their transportation to their homes. We hastily commenced dealing with these prisoners so as to get them back into civilian life, and helping to commence restoring Austria to a peaceful postwar condition. Their minds were so militarized and so disciplined to a military order that it was not easy. It seemed to me that none of them would do anything unless they were given an order to do it; no matter who it was, they just had to be ordered to do something, in order to get them to do it.

CHAPTER 30

Linz, Austria, Memorial Service for the Honored Dead

> *"You have a right to be proud of these accomplishments, for each has given of his effort, energy and strength, to say nothing of heroic courage, to the common cause, that you and I and our families shall be secure to live in our American way, free from the threat of the enemy domination which has caused such human misery and suffering as the world has never known before."*
>
> —MAJOR GENERAL STANLEY E. REINHART,
> COMMANDER, 65TH INFANTRY DIVISION

On May 30, 1945, our 260th Infantry Regiment of the 65th Infantry Division held a Memorial Day Service for the Honored Dead, in the City Square at Linz, honoring the men of our regiment who died in the service of their country, in combat.

All the men of our regiment attended, except those who had duty that they could not leave. We all were still dressed in combat gear. It was a warm and sunny day, one that I shall never forget, as we stood there in formation for this formal service honoring our fellow soldiers who died in combat.

A processional was played by the division band. There was an invocation given by Chaplain Thomas Bailey. Our regimental commander, Colonel Frank Dunkley, gave the memorial address.

A Roster of the Honored Dead was read by Captain William E. O'Neal, regimental adjutant.

The flower ceremony was conducted by our three battalion commanders: Lieutenant Colonel Lucien F. Keller, 1st Battalion; Lieutenant Colonel Clarence J. Stewart, 2nd Battalion; and Lieutenant Colonel Elmer H. Walker, 3rd Battalion.

A prayer was offered by Chaplain Francis F. Salzman, and the firing squad played "Taps."

Benediction was given by Chaplain Walter K. Maud, then the division band played the National Anthem.

Standing at attention for so long, many soldiers fainted and fell to the ground while standing there at attention. I attributed it to malnutrition, exhaustion, and stress, because that was the way that I felt, weak and tired all of the time. In fact, many times I felt so very lightheaded and dizzy I thought that I too, may pass out. General Reinhart made a speech, in which he stated, "…you men have a *right to be proud.*" His remark, "Right to Be Proud," became our division motto.

Soon we were assigned such duties as guarding and discharging POWs. For a few nights I and another soldier drove around the city of Linz on patrol in a jeep. One of the most unusual things was that many of the inmates from the Mauthausen Concentration Camp—which was located across the Danube River, downriver from Linz, and to the north—had just walked away when the Nazis left the camp and before American troops arrived. These deranged, emaciated inmates were walking around everywhere, it seemed. They acted like zombies, in a daze, hysterical, and insane-acting.

One night on patrol in Linz, I heard some horrible sounding screams near the city hall, or Rathaus, at the foot of the bridge, and by the large city square in front of it. We went to where we heard the screams and found this deranged, former inmate just standing alongside a column of the main building screaming his head off, making the most frightening sounds I had ever heard. We couldn't handle him; he was afraid of us. I caught him and had to subdue him. He was dressed in the usual concentration camp uniform—striped pants and shirt—filthy, nasty and wild-acting. His clothes smelled so foul that I could hardly stand it. We tied his feet and hands, put him in the jeep and carried him to a hospital that our medics had set up for sick concentration camp inmates and the displaced persons, at the Linz Airport. He screamed at the top of his voice all the way there. We had to restrain him to get him there, to prevent him from jumping out of the jeep. There were an awful lot of former inmates from the concentration camps and work camps that were mentally deranged as a result of the cruel and abusive treatment they had received while confined. I again swore to my Almighty God that I would fight until I died to prevent violence and brutality from ever being again inflicted upon any person, anywhere, for any reason.

I was then assigned to work at the prison stockade at the airport discharging prisoners, most of whom were Luftwaffe fighter pilots who were the first of the POWs to be discharged. I recall one Messerschmitt fighter pilot I was processing out of service, who was only 17 years old. He, as well as all of the others, denied being in combat in Germany and related that he had only flown in Italy. He tried very hard to convince me that he only fought in Italy and never flew against the Allies in Europe. In fact I found it very difficult to find any of the German POWs who would ever admit that they fought against Americans. It was obvious that none of the POWs wanted us to think badly of them, by their admitting that they had strafed us back there some place. My job was to prepare and record their discharges from the German military forces and to sign one of our officer's name to their discharges and send them on their way home, when we had enough to fill a train that would be going in the direction of their home.

I was amazed at the reactions of many of them. Some were happy that the war was over and glad to be going home. Many had no home or family to go to. Some were arrogant and disillusioned that the war was over and awful sad that they had lost and were no longer in the

German military. Some of them took out their anger on me. I just wasn't in any mood to take any of their horse hockey and I quickly told them that if they wanted to continue to live in those shabby tents in that open field there, for about a year, they would have to start acting like real men. The word got around. I even had a detail of them go to our barracks every day where we lived, which were very nice; in fact, it was the former barracks for Luftwaffe officers. They did the cleaning, making up the beds, mopping floors, taking out garbage, doing our laundry, as well as any other chores there. We also gave them some rations and other amenities, which all of them appreciated. They all soon learned that my acts of kindness were not an indication of weakness.

They were glad to do it, but there were some who were not pilots, who were just Wehrmacht and SS troops. Those who had been in the Waffen SS tried hard to change the fact that they were ever in the SS. This was difficult for them to do, in that all of them had the SS symbol and their serial number tattooed on their forearms, as well as their blood type tattooed under their armpits. There were so many SS troops we found amongst the Wehrmacht and Luftwaffe pilots we had to put them in a separate facility, because not even their own fellow soldiers wanted anything to do with them.

When I began helping to process out the SS troops, I found many of them to be very respectful, cooperative, and helpful, much to my surprise. I didn't know if they were just being manipulative or if this was their true personality. One of them gave me a sterling silver SS ring carved from pure silver in the form of a skull and crossbones, with emeralds in the eyes of the skull.

Behind our barracks was a displaced persons area where the DPs, as we called them, stayed unguarded, doing their own cooking, living in whatever kind of makeshift tent that they could find. They didn't cause anyone any trouble, but they did keep me awake often at night playing sad and lonesome-sounding accordions and guitars, all night long, every single night. They were gypsies, Greeks, Slavs, and Serbs, as well as people from all of the Balkan countries and about everywhere else. They were awaiting their turn to get a train to return to their native country. Little did those from the Soviet bloc countries know that when they returned there that the Soviets would kill all of them upon their arrival.

One morning I was standing at the gate to the compound where we kept the POWs, which was on the road from the airport to Linz, with a German lieutenant POW who was my interpreter. A truckload of Russian displaced persons, slave laborers, drove by. Most all of them were slave laborers from Russia who were being transported to another area because they were so violent and still wanted to kill all of the German prisoners of war that they could find. One of the men on the truck had a pistol and as the truck that he was on passed by us, he shot at my interpreter who was standing right beside me at the gate and hit him in the foot, injuring his foot badly. I had to get him to an aid station. I was very angry in that the shooter almost did and could have hit me with his pistol. Many of our fellow soldiers got the notion that all Russian, or Soviet, DPs, soldiers, as well as anyone from the Soviet countries were mean as hell. I learned and believed that it was the Mongolians who were the ones that got the blame for that, and that the people from Russia, the Caucasians, who looked like we did, were no more mean than anyone else, but they were tough and rugged as anyone could possibly be.

There were so many killings in the German POW camp by the airport that a group of us searched out the whole camp for weapons. It was an open field area where the prisoners had pitched small tents and some were just sleeping on a piece of canvas on the ground. We searched every man's belongings and seized many dozens of weapons, pistols of all kinds, knives, brass knuckles, and daggers of every conceivable description, even pieces of wire with a makeshift handle on each end—a perfect garrote that they could kill someone with, quickly, silently, and bloodlessly.

I could never determine why the German POWs were killing each other. One thing that I was aware of and that was that there were many of the German troops who were professional killers. This consisted mostly of the SS troops, Gestapo agents, and other members of elite Nazi organizations, most of whom were Wehrmacht and SS troops who had seen a lot of action and had been killing people for so long that they had become accustomed to it and apparently just couldn't stop. Also, I learned that the SS troops were violently oppressive against any other German soldier who spoke out against the Nazi regime, in any manner.

I told my interpreter to tell all of the prisoners there that if there were any more killings in this camp that all of them were going to be delivered over to the Russians, to be sent back to Stalingrad in railroad boxcars to rebuild all that they had destroyed there. There were no more killings amongst the POWs after we took all of their weapons from them and after they had all gotten my message. We made them realize that they were now prisoners of war and that the fighting and killing was over.

I spoke with my interpreter, as well as many others who had served in the German armed forces. Many of them told me that in the Nazi armed forces the noncommissioned officers, as well as the officers, were trained to give orders, to be strong disciplinarians, and that they all loved to exercise their rank and authority, give orders, and to punish anyone who disobeyed them and to do it harshly, sadistically, and unmercifully. A quotation from Adolph Hitler explains this, when he stated: "A violently active, dominating, intrepid, brutal youth, that is what I am after."

I was told that if they were being strafed while riding on a vehicle, they were forbidden to get off of it and take cover, without first being given an order to do so. In other words, they were all forbidden in any manner to exercise their own individual judgment and common sense. The officers and the noncommissioned officers loved to give orders and to check passes and papers. No one was allowed to go anywhere without a pass. I assumed that it was all a matter of total and complete control and domination over every individual, whether military or not. It was not so much a matter of military discipline, but a matter of the destruction of a person's individual initiative, liberty, and freedom, as well as the destruction of his ability to think for himself.

I thought about it quite a bit, how we in the American armed forces were able to exercise our own thoughts, ideas, judgment, and expressions—of course, as long as it did not interfere with our main objective. Without our individuality, exercising our common sense and good judgment and respect for each other, as well as our faith in God and our officers and fellow soldiers, we would not have been so successful in winning the war. We were trained to think and then act on what was the best thing to do to win the battle, under the circumstances. I would not have made a very good Nazi.

CHAPTER 31

Honor Guard for Generals Patton and Walker, and Receipt of the Bronze Star Medal

"You damned men have done a damned good job, so far. I am proud of you! The one Honor which is mine, and mine alone, is that of having commanded such an incomparable group of Americans, the record of whose fortitude, audacity and valor will endure as long as history lasts."

—GENERAL GEORGE S. PATTON (1885–1945)

One morning I was told by a sergeant that I and others had been selected to serve as honor guards for General Patton and to get cleaned up as well as we could and to get on this truck that was waiting, with a group of other men of our company, to go to the airport. The men in our company who had been Patton's Raiders, as well as any Bronze Star recipients—I being the only recipient in the company—had been chosen to serve as an Honor Guard for General Patton, who was to arrive at the Linz Airport for a meeting with a Russian general. His name was supposed to be kept secret, as per the request of the Russians, but I learned that his name was General Molonofsky, commanding general of the 3rd Ukrainian Army. I just happened to be one of those lucky few that had the opportunity to be present at this very historical meeting, and to have been an Honor Guard for General Patton, and to have been so close to him and in his presence. I admired and respected him greatly.

It was a great occasion for me on this day, in that my captain had informed me that I had been recommended to receive the Bronze Star Medal. The final approval and award had to come from the War Department in Washington, D.C. This is an award for "heroic or meritorious conduct" in the face of the enemy, where a soldier distinguished himself by "heroic or meritorious achievement in military operations against the enemy." A prerequisite to receiving the Bronze Star is the award of the Combat Infantry Badge, which I had been previously awarded. It was sometime later that I received the actual medal and the certificate of award from the War Department.

We freshened up as well as we could for the General. We arrived at the airport and took our positions with our rifles, steel helmets, cartridge belt, with canteens and bayonets attached to it, just as we were dressed in combat, only a lot cleaner and neater. Across the way from us about a hundred feet, there was a line of Russian solders of the 3rd Ukrainian Army who were the Honor Guard for the Russian General. We were facing each other.

Soon a DC-3 plane taxied up near to where we were standing, and I recall that the first thing that I noticed was that just as the plane came to a stop the pilot opened his window and displayed the four-star flag representing General Patton's rank.

General Patton got out of his plane and was greeted by our division commander, Major General Stanley E. Reinhart, and other generals, and there were many of them. After the greetings, he inspected his Honor Guard and walked closely in front of us. He walked down to the end of the line of the men who were serving as his Honor Guard. I was on the far right end of the first of the three rows. He looked at me, did an about face and walked back to the center of the line, stopped, and faced us all. He spoke to us, and said, "You damned men have done a damned good job, so far. I am proud of you. The one honor which is mine, and mine alone, is having commanded such an incomparable group of Americans, the record of whose fortitude, audacity, and valor will endure as long as history lasts."

He then went over to the Russian side with an entourage of Generals with him, met, saluted, and hugged the Russian General and inspected his Honor Guard, about thirty of them, just the same as our guard. Some of us had been betting a dollar whether or not he would hug and kiss the Russian general, which was a custom in that part of the world. He did, I lost a dollar. He and the Russian general then came over to us and walked down in front of us and they turned around right in front of me and returned to the Russian side where they spoke for a while and the Russian general got into his American made armored car and departed.

During this ceremony there were many newsmen and photographers there who were standing over to the right of me taking movies as well as still photographs of the entire ceremony.

I had noticed that just as General Patton's plane arrived, two P-51 Mustang fighter planes had taxied up and parked right behind us. They were the same kind of planes that saved our lives a short time ago at the battle of Struth. Someone there said to all of the others of us, "Hey, look behind us, there are the P-51 planes that saved our asses at Struth."

I learned that they were escorts for General Patton's plane. Before we left, a colonel told us that General Patton said that the war was over and that we could remove our steel helmets from our helmet liners and just wear the liner and that we could throw the old beat-up steel helmets away, which we did, in a ditch on the way back to Linz. Without that heavy steel helmet on my head I felt much lighter, as well as a little naked. Upon returning to the company and reporting to our captain, we learned that the *Stars and Stripes* newspaper had just reported that General Patton had just volunteered our 65th Division to go to the China-Burma-India Theater of the South Pacific to fight the Japanese.

Now, it made sense what Patton had just told us, "You damned men have done a damned good job, *so far.*" "So far" meaning that we had more fighting to do, in that he had just volunteered us to do it, but he hadn't told us that. Our division had the youngest age average of any

American division. General Patton liked our division and gave us lots of credit for doing a great job.

It was our men, we who were from my squad and my platoon, the 2nd Squad, Second Platoon, of Company G, that was on the point, far ahead, out on the Third Army's main line of attack, out on the point, spearheading across Germany, furthermost to the east, and more so than any other outfit in the entire Allied American Forces. That is the way that it was related to us, as well as the way I experienced it.

General Patton then wrote about us in his diary on 9 May 1945: "The one honor which is mine, and mine alone, is that of having commanded such an incomparable group of Americans, the record of whose fortitude, audacity and valor, will endure as long as history lasts."

When I returned from the airport to our billets in Linz, I sat down and wrote a long letter to my mother detailing all that had happened that day, and told her also about having been awarded the Bronze Star Medal. A few days later my letter to my mother was returned to me by the censor, who stated that the details in my letter would not pass censorship.

A few days later all of us Patton's Raiders, who had been chosen as Honor Guard for General Patton, were again taken to the airport to serve as Honor Guard for General Walton H. "Bull Dog" Walker, Commander of the XXth Corps. The Third Army was made up generally of three Corps, and each Corps consisted of three divisions, usually—it varied. Our division was one of the three divisions that made up the XXth Corps. General Walker later commanded the 8th Army in North Korea.

This ceremony at the Linz Airport was just a repeat performance of what occurred when General Patton had arrived, except that there were no Russians there. General Walker told us that censorship of our mail would end that day, so I wrote my Mom another letter about being an Honor Guard for General Walker and sent this letter and the letter that had been returned to me, both letters in the same envelope, to her.

We were kept awful busy—mostly at the airport, handling civilian matters, prisoners of war, and inmates from the concentration camp, and also the thousands of displaced persons who had been the slave laborers working in ammunition factories, farms, and all industries. Many of the forced laborers told me that they worked in ammo factories that made 88mm shells and that they put everything imaginable from just trash, sand, feces, and anything available, in the shells to prevent them from exploding on impact. This accounted for the many duds that had landed near me for one—as well as a lot of our other men—that never exploded, especially the one that landed right next to me after we crossed the Danube near Regensburg. For all that I know, it could have been one of the duds that this man assembled. I shook the hand of this displaced person and thanked him for what he did to help us quickly end the war, with fewer loss of lives, so they could be released from slavery. This proves that even a displaced person who is a slave laborer can still fight and be instrumental in putting down tyranny and aggression.

We all knew that General Patton was greatly impressed with the performance of our beloved 65th Division during combat. A few days after being Honor Guard for General Patton, our company commander arranged for a large excursion boat on the Danube to take some of us for a cruise, on a trip up and down the scenic Danube River.

My friend Al and I went on this cruise one Sunday. We were about to learn which day of the week that it was again. I observed many of the men on that boat kept inside the cabin, looking out through the glass, and had their helmets on the entire time. I guess that they were still gun-shy, taking cover, concealing themselves, and not realizing in their minds that the war was now over. My friend Al and I sat outside on the deck in the sun and enjoyed the scenic cruise up and down the Danube River. After we returned to our billets in Linz that afternoon, the lieutenant had acquired from somewhere, a large container of ice cream and it was waiting for us when we returned from this cruise on the Danube. Some of the men were so hungry for something sweet they dipped into the container with their bare hands and ate it that way.

We also learned that tension was running high between General Patton and the Russian commander, General Georgi Zhukov, who demanded Patton give him all of the boats on the Danube that were in our zone. We learned through the grapevine what transpired, which directly affected our division.

An officer who was General Patton's aide had related that a Russian came to Patton's headquarters in Bad Tolz, Germany, and demanded that Patton turn over all of the watercraft that was in our zone on the Danube River, to the Russians. Patton said to his aid, "Get this son of a bitch out of here, now! Who in the hell let him in? Don't ever let any more of those Russian bastards into this headquarters again."

Patton then yelled at another staff member and said to him, "Alert the 4th Armored Division, 11th Armored Division, and the 65th Infantry Division for an attack to the east!"

When this word got around in our division, it caused quite a stir. Many of us who had served as Honor Guard for General Patton, jokingly remarked that we should go out the Linz Airport road and try to retrieve our steel helmets that we had thrown away in a ditch when we had returned from serving as his Honor Guard. We would need them when we attacked to the east.

One interesting bit of information that came down to us was that when General Patton met General Zhukov, they were talking, and General Zhukov said to General Patton, "Patton, I have got a new tank that can sling a big shell more than seven miles."

General Patton replied, "Hell, Zhukov, if I had a tank gunner that would even fire on a target that was more than 700 yards away, I would court martial his ass."

CHAPTER 32

Working at Mauthausen Concentration Camp

"Those who have long enjoyed such privileges, as we enjoy, forget in time that men have died to win them."

—FRANKLIN D. ROOSEVELT (1882–1945)

Another division and part of our regiment had liberated Mauthausen Concentration Camp, which was across the Danube and downriver from Linz to the north. It was located near another concentration camp, Camp Gussen at St. Georgen, Austria, only four kilometers away. This unit had to be relieved, in that the horror of the atrocities—as well as the ghastly odor of the camp there—was more than any soldier could take, especially after having been in a combat situation, as we had been. Both Camps were horror camps, extermination camps, in that they used the healthy inmates to quarry stone and to dig a huge tunnel that was about two miles in length, total, in a big hill near the camp. It was used as a Messerschmitt assembly plant. When the inmates became too weak to work, they put them in the gas chambers, then their bodies were cremated in the ovens.

As in most Nazi concentration camps there were satellite camps nearby where prisoners were kept and used to do all kinds of laborious work. At KZ (Concentration Camp) Mauthausen, there was a large stone quarry where prisoners were used to cut stone blocks from, and carry them out. When these prisoners got too weak and exhausted to work they were exterminated. There were fifty steps that led down into the quarry from the barracks. The inmates had to carry these granite stones out of the quarry and up these fifty steps, which were called "the fifty steps of death."

There were two large barbed-wire fences around the compound at Gussen, with guard towers on each corner and in between. Inside were poorly constructed wooden barracks that contained bunks that were made out of rough lumber, about three or four bunks high, with straw on them and a few old worn and filthy blankets scattered around. I went into one of the barracks just to see the conditions, and my body became covered with fleas. There were so many of them that I could grab handfuls of them. The inmates had been removed from all but a few of the barracks where some of them still lived there, refusing to leave, or else they had no place to go that would accept them. So, I assumed that the fleas had no blood to feed upon and they were starved. I had to be sprayed with DDT to kill them and I heard later that it was discovered that the insecticide DDT was a carcinogenic that caused cancer.

We guarded German SS prisoners whom we used to pick up the sick and put them on carts that took the sick to a truck that carried them to Linz Airport, where a field hospital had been set up to care for them. Those deceased were taken on a large cart to a field where our engineers had a bulldozer that was digging mass graves. All of the inmates who could be treated medically were taken to the hospital that we had set up for them at the Linz Airport Luftwaffe Officers Quarters. They were all skin and bones, just walking around in the nude, like zombies. The reason for their being nude was that they had no plumbing or running water of any kind with which to wash their clothes, or their bodies, or their bowls that they ate out of, so their clothes were too filthy to wear and they just discarded them. I saw some of these inmates just walking along and suddenly fall dead. It was nothing unusual to look into the compound and see many emaciated bodies lying on the ground, dead. Many died after receiving ordinary food and eating it, in that it was too rich for their system and they just died almost instantly.

Each morning the SS POWs would pull carts into the compound and pick up the dead and take them to the big ditches. It was a routine thing each morning, there where I worked—in the office just outside the main compound gate—to look out the window and to see SS troops pulling a wagonload of corpses out of the compound. They passed right by the window where I worked and down to the edge of the facility, into a field where the big open ditches were dug with bodies still lying in them, not yet covered. The SS troops would lift them off of the wagon, one holding the feet, another holding the hands of the corpse, and they would throw them into the big ditch. When it was full, the engineers would start their bulldozer and fill it up with dirt and dig another one.

There was one inmate who looked fairly well cared for, who was middle aged and who wore a white coat like a physician. I got to know him. He was a neurosurgeon from Warsaw, Poland. He was a Catholic and had somehow fallen out of grace with the invading Nazis, due to his fighting in resistance movements after the Nazis occupied Poland. Many people from the countries captured by the Nazis really hated them, fought them very hard, and resisted the occupation by them. In retaliation, the Nazis would capture them and send them to one of their death camps, somewhere. They had many of them.

They sent this doctor to Mauthausen Concentration Camp where he worked as a physician, treating both inmates and the Waffen SS personnel there. He refused to leave after the camp was liberated, in that he had no where to go that would accept him. Stalin would not allow anyone in Germany or Austria, especially those in concentration camps, to be returned to any Soviet bloc country. He worked hard daily to help the remaining inmates there, as well as anyone else needing medical attention. He related to me that he could not return to the Soviet-occupied Poland and that if he did, he would be killed by the Soviets.

I asked him why, and he told me that he had learned that this was now the policy of the Soviets. They were not accepting any concentration camp inmates or displaced persons the Nazis had taken from their country, including Soviet Union POWs, back into the Soviet zone. I could not understand this. The Soviets' excuse was that they didn't have facilities, housing, food, clothing, or the personnel or funds to care for them. He further related to me that it was the policy of the Soviets, that anyone who fought against the Nazis was also an enemy of the Soviet Union. It was reasoned that if they fought the occupation by the Nazis, they would also offer the same resistance toward the Soviets, and were therefore automatically an enemy of the Soviet Union. But this was not the real reason for killing so many people. At the least, Stalin was identifying himself with another madman dictator, Hitler. Stalin reasoned, apparently, that anyone that had been subjected to the Nazis in any way, had been indoctrinated against Communism and he would never thereafter trust them, so he had all of them killed. What a tangled web these two psychopathic mental cases, Hitler and Stalin, had woven.

Another rationale they used was they claimed that any person from the Soviet zone who had been in custody of the Nazis, was a security risk, therefore an enemy of the Soviets. The Soviets obviously made up any excuse at hand to avoid taking back these homeless refugees. This doctor told me that he would just stay there, or wherever there was something for him to do, medically, for as long as he could and then, he didn't have the faintest idea as to what would happen to him. He had no property, friends, or relatives, no income, and could be considered to be destitute; yet, he was a great physician and relieved much pain and suffering.

He also informed me that the Soviets were not permitting any concentration camp inmates to return to the Soviet-controlled countries, and they were just killing those who did return when they arrived. I thought that this was maybe wrong, somehow, or some misinformation he had received. I soon was to learn what he told me was entirely correct. He told me that he had no country to return to that would accept him, outside the Soviet bloc of countries. I never had a chance to discuss it with him again, but I did authoritatively learn that he was exactly correct when he told me that the Soviets would kill him if he was returned to one of the Soviet bloc countries that they occupied. I at first found this very hard to believe, after all that these people had suffered and endured in these death camps. I couldn't comprehend how anyone could be so cruel, depraved, and degenerate as to murder masses of helpless, homeless victims of tyranny and oppression.

I learned that the Soviets claimed that all concentration camp inmates were collaborators with the Nazis. This was just an excuse, in that if they were collaborators of the Nazis, they wouldn't be in a Nazi death camp starving to death. I did soon learn, authoritatively, that when any of them were returned to any of the Soviet bloc countries they were immediately killed.

I became convinced that dictator Joseph Stalin was just as big of a cold-blooded murderer as Adolph Hitler—if not bigger. It was very saddening to learn things like this were happening, after fighting as hard and as fast as we had to win the war, to get to these people, to help them, so as to save these people's lives, who Hitler had enslaved. It now appeared that all of them that came from the Soviet Union were doomed to certain death.

CHAPTER 33

Austrian Civilians Forced to Visit Camp Gussen Concentration Camp at Mauthausen

"Our Country, right or wrong, when right, to be kept right; when wrong, to be put right."
—MAJOR GENERAL CARL SCHURZ,
UNION ARMY (1864)

One day, on a Sunday, we got orders to go into the nearby towns and villages and to gather up all of the civilians and put them on our Army trucks and bring them there to view the horrors of Camp Gussen and Mauthausen concentration camps. We had to make them look at the bodies of the poor people who had just died and whose emaciated bodies were thrown into the big ditches dug by our dozers, as well as visit the extermination building with its ovens, large shower room, and the room that held all of the clothing that those who had been exterminated had been wearing. The work of picking up corpses and burying the dead, cooking for and caring for these inmates was done by the German SS troops whom we guarded, and forced them to do it.

Many of the civilians that we brought to Mauthausen cried; some just couldn't convince themselves that this was happening there. We then took them to the extermination building where the gas chamber and ovens were located. All of them were made to visit the large room that was filled to the ceiling with the clothing that the inmates had worn, before they were placed in the "shower room" where they showered, then were gassed. I showed them the clothes, all kinds of clothes, shoes, all kinds of shoes, men's and women's, and children's of all kinds.

We showed all of them the ashes from the cremated corpses piled high in front of the ovens. The ashes contained pieces of bones and joints, like a knee joint, and a piece of a heart that had not been completely incinerated. Some sacks of ashes were still there. They had been bagging them up and selling them to the citizens for fertilizer. The larger pieces of unburned bones were thrown into one special area, in a big pile. I asked many of them if they had used any of these ashes on their vegetable gardens or other crops. Some ignored me, others started crying and shaking, and a few vomited. Many acted disconcerted, some cried hysterically.

Some of the civilians cried terribly and seemed sorrowful. Some appeared hostile and arrogant and I wondered who they were angry at—us American soldiers, or the Nazis. I recall that one of our men asked a brave woman who was brought to the camp, if she knew that Hitler had ordered this done. Her reply was, "No, no, our Fuhrer would never do anything like this, only Goering, and Himmler, maybe. They were the evil ones." I had heard this same kind of statement made by many German and Austrian citizens.

The room where they were given a shower and gassed was adjacent to the room with a row of ovens with a curved steel tray they would place a body on, then slide it into the white-hot oven.

There was a gasoline engine outside the building and its exhaust was piped into the building, as well as other chemicals, to asphyxiate the inmates in the shower room.

They had a shovel, or rake, that was curved just to fit the curved steel trays, to use after the bodies had been turned to ashes; they raked the hot ashes off onto the floor to cool. They were then bagged up and sold to the farmers as fertilizer.

They also had a large pile of hair from the inmates heads that was used to pad airplane cushions with at the nearby underground

Messerschmitt assembly plant. I spoke with some of the inmates that were still there and somewhat healthy, who had worked in the extermination building. They operated the ovens by putting the corpses on the steel trays and then pushing them into the ovens. They were so used to doing it, it didn't seem to bother them. One told me that it was a way to survive and get decent food from the SS guards there.

In the main office of the camp, I saw a large glass jug that was filled with gold teeth, another one filled with gold wedding bands taken from the prisoners before they were cremated. There were also many lampshades there made from the skin of inmates that had tattoos on them.

The wife of the Nazi camp commander used this one inmate, whose job it was to inspect all of the inmates for tattoos when they arrived and to notify her, and then she would have them especially exterminated with her skin tannery man present to take the tattoos off, skin and all, tan it like leather and make this woman lampshades with the skin from these tattooed, exterminated inmates. These teeth, wedding bands, and lampshades were preserved by us to be used in the Nuremberg War Crimes Tribunal where the Nazi criminals were to be tried by an Allied Court in Nuremberg.

While we worked there we lived in houses nearby, in St. Georgen, where the SS troops who guarded the camp lived before the camp was liberated. They were very modern, nice, and comfortable. I recall at nighttime after work, we had to place the clothes we had worn to work at the concentration camp on the outside of the house so as to avoid having to smell the foul odor of the camp.

One thing that I observed while working at Mauthausen Concentration Camp was that we, as well as anyone else, were not allowed to take any pictures of that concentration camp, nor were we allowed to let any photographers into the camp to take photographs. I asked my captain about it and he told me the Allied Command had decided Austria was to be freed and allowed to govern themselves, and not be occupied by Allied Forces and we would soon be leaving. They did not want any adverse publicity about Austria having been a part of the Nazi regime that was responsible for these horrors.

CHAPTER 34

Cleaning Up Man's Inhumanity to Mankind

"There is nothing, absolutely nothing, which needs to be more carefully guarded against, than that one man should be allowed to become more powerful than the people."

—DEMOSTHENES, ANCIENT
GREECE, (384–322 B.C.)

We had to keep all of the DPs, (displaced persons) in some sort of confined, unguarded area so that they would not ramble all over the country creating a problem. We helped to process them to be sent back to their country of origin. For some reason, all of the concentration camp inmates had to be held under guard until they could be processed and returned to their country of origin. I assumed that one of the reasons was some of them, allegedly, were murderers, rapists, and other ordinary criminals who had been confined there with all of the political prisoners. It appeared though, there were only a few such cases of hardened criminals, if any, in the concentration camp. All of them were enemies of the Nazi regime, but not by reason of any crimes that they had committed.

They all were processed to be sent on a special train back to their country of origin. Many of them spoke English and I had conversations with lots of them. It seemed that none of them wanted to return to their native countries in the Soviet controlled bloc of countries, and chose to remain there in the compound of the concentration camp, rather than to return to the Soviet zone. Not one of these inmates had a home, or any place they could call home. Our orders were to just return them to their "country of origin," wherever that was.

Upon inquiry as to why they didn't want to return to their own native lands, I learned that many of them would, as they related to me, be killed or put in prison there for "collaborating with the Nazis," which was a trumped-up false charge concocted by the Communist dictator, Joe Stalin. I was soon to realize that "trumped-up charges" were commonplace in both the Nazi and Soviet dictatorship countries, or in fact, in any country where there is an absence of democracy, and where there is a totalitarian dictatorship. It was the Nazis who put these people here. So, they couldn't have been collaborators with their captors, especially under these circumstances. This was the pretended reason for the Soviets eliminating them when they were sent back. I was unable to understand how a slave laborer of the Nazis could also be a collaborator with the Nazis, especially when so many of them were doing things like assembling 88 shells so they wouldn't explode. Some just stated that their government in the Soviet bloc was so corrupt they refused to return there.

Nevertheless, we processed them to be returned to their country of origin on special trains and we shipped them back, under guard, to their native country. However, as long as I worked there, none were shipped back to the Soviet zone, in that the Soviets firmly refused to accept them. So, those had to be kept there, under guard. They would otherwise have escaped, and just been wandering around in Germany like so many others that we saw, if we hadn't kept them under guard. Also, when the concentration camp was liberated, just after the Germans left and before our forces arrived to take over, all of those strong enough had just taken off down the roads, walking—not knowing where they were going, or how they were going to survive. It was a terribly pathetic situation. It was also an insane and satanically cruel situation these two evil dictators, Stalin and Hitler, intertwined all across Europe and in all of the countries occupied and controlled by the Communist Soviet Union.

I spoke with one very intelligent English-speaking German who told me that many of the slave laborers were labeled as criminals in their native countries occupied by the Soviets, whether it was true or not, and this is the reason they were afraid to return there. I was unable to determine who adjudged them to be criminals in their native country—the Nazi occupation government or their own Communist socialist dictator, or both.

So, one could only conclude that if a person was an enemy of either Communism or Nazism, he was therefore an enemy of both, in that neither wanted any citizens who opposed either; he therefore had to be what we would call a patriot. In any event, Hitler and his Nazi partners in crime, as well as the Communists, just about totally destroyed civilized society in Europe.

CHAPTER 35

Citizens Owning Guns Defend a Country Against Tyranny

"The accumulation of all powers, legislative, executive, and judiciary, in the same hands, whether of one, a few, or many, and whether hereditary, self appointed, or elective, may justly be pronounced the very definition of tyranny."

—JAMES MADISON (1751–1836)

Being an avid deer and turkey hunter, I treasured my guns. Everyone that I ever knew relied upon their guns for hunting and for protection of their person, their homes, family, and property. I was told by German civilians that the first thing that Hitler had done, after all of the citizens had been forced to register their guns, was to then confiscate everyone's weapons. His first act was to require every person who owned a weapon of any kind to register them. Then, after the Nazis knew who owned guns, they burst into their homes in the middle of the night and grabbed them. Anyone caught with a weapon thereafter was sent to the concentration camp to be exterminated. They then asked me, "How do you think that we could have overthrown Hitler, with no weapons available to us civilians to do it with? We were just taken over by a terrorist dictator and were just as much a victim of him and his Nazis as those in the concentration camps."

One German man said to me, "Before you criticize us for not overthrowing Hitler and his regime of fascist criminals, you had better consider what you would do if this happened to you in America and you didn't have any weapons. This could very well be you someday."

All of the citizens of Austria and Germany that I talked with said the same thing, they were overpowered by the Nazis and they were nothing more than slaves of the Nazi government, who controlled everyone's lives, totally.

Anyone disobeying orders given to them by the officers of the terrorist government were summarily sent to the extermination camps without a trial. Every citizen that I talked to said they lived in constant fear of their strong-arm terrorist government and the gangsters who controlled it.

While working with POWs, displaced persons, concentration camp inmates, as well as German and Austrian civilians, I got a great education in political science. Our fighting was finished, there was a cessation of hostilities, as such, but the war still raged on, in getting all of the prisoners and displaced persons settled and relocated in some location that was agreeable to them and the country that they wanted to reside in. Many of them wanted to remain in Germany. They told me that their country was so demolished by the Nazis that they would not return there, to the ruins and destruction, and that Germany was less destroyed than their country was.

They related how their country had been destroyed by the Nazis, which was the killing of all worthwhile citizens and the destruction of every building of any significance. I learned an awful lot about the politics of Europe, about the evils of Communism and Fascism, especially in Germany, in our occupation of Austria and Germany. I could only conclude that there was no difference in either Communism, Fascism, or Nazism, except their political, economic, and social theories. All were ruled by absolute totalitarian dictators who were all evil.

On one occasion we were sent to a beautiful part of Austria where Nazi war criminals were suspected of being in hiding. We lived in this large farmhouse by a small river. It was a mountainous area that was quiet and peaceful, as well as very beautiful. I had much time off during the day and spent lots of it in the mountains around the area, deer hunting. We had lots of deer meat to eat and a good chef to cook it for us. We took shifts manning roadblocks and searching vehicles, but there were very few people using the roads. When a vehicle did come through, we searched it very thoroughly and had to identify all of the occupants to determine who they were and where they were from, and then check their identity papers and examine lists and photographs of wanted war criminals.

I had further discussions with many civilians about these war criminals who were to be tried in a War Crimes Tribunal in Nuremberg. Since their propaganda ministry had been silenced, they were no longer fed lies by the Nazis. They began to learn for the first time, the truth of the entire Nazi regime, as well as about Communism and how evil both of them were. I could see no difference in either, other than in their political ideology. I quickly learned that the Soviets—Joe Stalin and his hit man Beria—killed millions more Russians, or Soviets, than Hitler did in the entire duration of Nazism. One can then draw their own conclusion which they preferred to live under, Communism or Nazism.

We did find quite a few of the lower echelon people in government who were in disguise and had false papers. We could easily tell that they were wanted as war criminals because they were so nervous, shaking, suspicious-acting, and there were conflicts in the answers that they gave to our questioning. We men on guard on the road only brought to the house we were staying in, the ones that acted suspicious. There, we had an interpreter to interrogate them to determine if they should be held and turned over to the military government, or released.

The Military Occupation Forces took very seriously the apprehending of the Nazi war criminals. These people were the criminals who brought about all of the crime, destruction, suffering, and turmoil that had been visited upon all of Europe and its people by one man named Hitler, acting through his criminal psychopathic henchmen and executioners. It was very obvious that they would not go unpunished and that they would now have to answer for their crimes.

We kept up with the preparation of the Nuremberg War Crimes Tribunal in Nuremberg. It was certain that I was not the only person in the U.S. Military that was conscious of the criminal action to be brought against the criminals of the Nazi regime. It was through their greed for power and money, which was the reason that they had just about destroyed civilized society in Europe. Both the Communist dictator of the Soviet Union, Joseph Stalin, and the Fascist dictator of Germany, Adolph Hitler were murderers, thieves, terrorists, and as evil as Satan could possibly create them. Both forms of government, Fascism and Communism, can only be ruled and controlled by one dictator, and only a madman created by the devil can acquire so much absolute power over so many people. I thanked God daily for our ancestors giving us such a great democratic form of government, where hopefully, such as I saw there, then, could never occur in my homeland.

How it could have happened in such a progressive and enterprising country as Germany and Austria, with so many hardworking, intelligent people, I found it terribly hard to believe; but it happened. The only answer was that the people had no voice in their government, in that it was controlled by a large group of totalitarian, terrorist thugs that had gotten the citizens under their total and complete control. Control, total control over all of the people was their secret to total domination.

Many of the German and Austrian people who I talked with told me the same story, that Hitler had confiscated all of the citizens' weapons, hunting rifles, and pistols that they kept for their personal protection. That this left them totally submissive and obedient to the terrorist Nazi government they tried hard to stay in good graces with, in order to keep from being sent to the death camps. That was the threat that Hitler and his henchmen held over the head of every person in all of the countries they occupied and controlled, including Germany and Austria.

Then, there was Dr. Goebbels, Hitler's propaganda minister, who fed the citizens nothing but lies and kept them pumped up with hysterical-type propaganda and patriotic martial music. In addition to that, they blamed the SS Storm Troopers, Hitler's private police force and the Gestapo for keeping the people suppressed and obedient to Hitler and his fanatical group of criminal goons.

They told me that they never were allowed to know the truth about anything, but were only informed as to matters that were presented to them on the radio and in the newspapers, which was all that they were allowed to know—all of which was totally contrived to keep the citizens under control, by the Nazi Party, particularly by Dr. Goebbels.

One prisoner of war who had been in the Wehrmacht fighting far away in Russia, related to me that when they began to lose and suffer greatly from the extreme cold, from the terror and horrors of battle, they were told by their commanders the French were coming to their aid to fight against the Russians and for the Nazis. Also, on other occasions, they were told Hitler had made peace with the Allies who were coming to help them win the war against the Russians. Many believed that we Americans were going to attack the Russians and the Nazis were going to help us. All of this was told to the front line soldiers to build up their moral, so that they would have hope and continue to fight to the last man, believing that help was on the way. After the Nazis attacked Stalingrad, out of 660,000 Nazi troops that made the attack, only 60,000 survived. All of the citizens that I talked with were so brainwashed that they found it difficult to comprehend what had, and was now, occurring in Germany. I believed that they all should somehow be rehabilitated, by being deprogrammed.

My buddy Sperl had an aunt living in Passau, Germany, which was not far from Linz. The captain gave him a jeep and a driver to take him to visit his aunt after the war ended. He related to me when he went to his aunt's home he was warmly greeted, and the first thing that he saw was a big picture of his mother hanging on the wall of the living room. He returned telling me how sad it was that his own relatives were so brainwashed, propagandized, and misinformed and he was terribly shocked. His aunt told him her son had been killed fighting in the German Army.

It was just as difficult for me to comprehend how such intelligent people had allowed some fanatic criminal psychopath to take control of their mind and body, to totally control them, and then engage them in such a horrible and cruel conflict, inflicting so much cruelty and inhumane punishment on so many innocent people.

It was very obvious to see there, then the first thing in their government that went wrong was when Hitler created the propaganda ministry, which indoctrinated the German people, programmed their minds, and kept them from learning the truth about their government and what it was doing. This propaganda controlled their very thinking, which was nothing but mind control.

This is why our forefathers put into our Constitution the First Amendment that is supposed to guarantee freedom of speech in America as an "inalienable right."

He simultaneously confiscated all of their weapons so they couldn't do anything about his corruption, whether they liked it or not, or wanted to, or not give him the power over the people that he sought. This is why our forefathers put the Second Amendment into our Constitution. I then and there learned the meaning of our Constitution and why it is absolute that we protect these amendments to the letter. The rights guaranteed under our Constitution are inalienable, and will not ever be, in any manner, adulterated or eliminated without a fight to the finish.

I also learned what the first thing Hitler did, which was to test how well he was conditioning and programming the minds of the German citizens, and how well he controlled them. He devised a way to determine if he had total and complete, life-and-death control over the citizens, and if they would be totally obedient and submissive to him.

He had all of the deformed, mentally, and physically deficient people in institutions killed by injections. The Nazis then reported to their families that they had died from natural causes. The German citizens knew what their government had done, but they humbly accepted it and did not voice any opposition to it. They were afraid to, because of what most likely would happen to them if they did. They realized that if they voiced an objection, some contrived false charge would be lodged against them and they would be arbitrarily thrown into an extermination camp without any semblance of a hearing or trial. So, they accepted the fact out of fear, that the Nazis had killed their sick children and they did nothing, not even to voice an objection, out of fear, they said.

Hitler then knew that he had the citizens under his total and complete control and they would never object to anything else he did, no matter what it was. They were then seeing the consequence of this control he had over the people. He controlled the entire government so much that no citizen was courageous enough to even question what had happened to their retarded or deformed child in a government institution. No one questioned the Nazi government. So Hitler got away with euthanasia on an awful lot of his own people in Germany. This was a test of how strong his control was over the citizens.

Realizing that he could now do anything he wanted to, no matter how inhumane and cruel it was—now he had their guns, and had silenced their voices, and there was nothing the people could do to stop him—he then built the extermination camps, including the gas chambers and ovens. He quickly filled them up with enemies of the Nazi government, an evil and corrupt government, and even did this faster than they could be built. He then exterminated the inmates faster than they could be cremated.

CHAPTER 36

Learning by Experience, We Must Protect Our Constitution

"I have sworn upon the Altar of God, eternal hostility against every form of tyranny over the mind of man."

—THOMAS JEFFERSON, (1743–1826)

I actually learned through firsthand experience that the two most precious things that we have in this country are the First and Second Amendments. The First Amendment protects our freedom of speech, which not only means a right to speak, but an inalienable right to be informed by the press and media about what is occurring in our country, and not to be misinformed, even by the withholding of any significant information.

The Second Amendment allows us to bear arms to defend ourselves, our property, and our country in times of peril. I recalled the oath that I took upon entering the service. I recall repeating the words: "...I do solemnly swear to uphold and defend the Constitution of the United States against all enemies, both foreign and domestic...so help me God." I often asked my combat buddies if we had sworn to defend our country against both foreign and domestic enemies, how could we do it without any weapons to do it with?

I often reminded all of my friends and combat buddies that there was no time limit or expiration date on this oath, and it was continuous and ongoing for the rest of our lives and we should always live by and uphold this oath.

I thought many times, "Who knows when we may have a president we somehow mistakenly elected, or who came into power by deceit and deception, and we then learned that he was a dishonest, psychopathic criminal—or maybe a communist or fascist who would be bent on the destruction of our government and try to destroy it, and the citizens as well, just as Hitler, and Stalin had done. What if he would then declare himself a dictator, deny us the right to know the truth, take our weapons, subjugate us, and destroy our country, as Hitler had done to Germany, and as Stalin had done to Russia. Who will be there then, that is able and willing to protect us from the human misery I have witnessed being inflicted upon millions of people, and with what weapon?"

It was then and there indelibly imprinted on my mind, if our Constitution was ever denied us, or in any manner perverted and its integrity destroyed, then we would find ourselves in the same condition the German citizens now find themselves in at the end of this tragic war. Then more blood would have to be shed to restore our Constitution to its original meaning and intent. I have faith in the good and responsible citizens of America that they would never let this happen in our great country. I hope and pray.

There was one thing that World War II did for me: it instilled in my mind, indelibly, that no government would ever take my guns from me without killing me first. I strongly felt if anyone in our government ever attempted to take control of our government and its people, as Hitler had done, it would be a sure death sentence for such a tyrant, after what we American soldiers had suffered and endured in putting down gangsters such as Hitler and his strong-armed terrorist henchmen.

I swore to myself, as did many other soldiers, this would never occur in America without much bloodshed. It would be better that way than to die in a concentration camp, freezing, and starving to death, while being inhumanly treated, stripped of all of your human dignity and identity by a bunch of deviate, psychopathic, power-crazed criminals. I vividly recalled what General Patton once said, "I had rather die on my feet than to live for eternity on my knees."

I begged my commander to let me have leave to attend some of the Nuremberg Tribunal Trials. He could not, because we were so overworked in handling German prisoners, displaced persons, and other occupation duties, trying to restore Germany and Austria to a functioning democratic government again, so I was not able to even get a seat there.

One great lesson that I learned was that any corrupt leader of our government would have to be sacrificed long before he would ever be allowed to bring about the crime and corruption we were seeing here. We swore to each other we would never let this happen in America. Not to us, our friends, neighbors, loved ones, or any other American citizen. Never!

CHAPTER 37

Stop That Train!

> *"Never turn your back on a threatened*
> *danger and try to run away from it. If you*
> *do that, you will double the danger. But if*
> *you meet it promptly, and without flinch-*
> *ing, you will reduce the danger by half.*
> *Never run away from anything. Never!"*
>
> —WINSTON CHURCHILL (1874–1965)

One day the lieutenant drove his jeep all the way from Linz to where I was working at the time—about eight miles. He told me to take a man with me and to come with him and get in his jeep. This was in the offices at Camp Gussen Concentration Camp where I worked. I processed records there and arranged for shifts of guards to guard the SS POWs that we had working there, burying the inmates as they continually died from starvation and maltreatment. The only person that didn't seem to be very busy was a young GI who had just arrived from the United States a few days previously, so I told him to accompany me, not having any idea whatsoever what we were needed for.

We got in the lieutenant's jeep and he drove toward Linz for a few miles, turned off onto a dirt road to the Danube River, and drove up to the railroad bridge that came across the Danube from Linz, which then ran northeast into the Soviet zone.

After we arrived at the railroad bridge that crossed the Danube, my instructions from the lieutenant were to go to the other side of this bridge and to stay there until relieved, and while there to stop any train that came from the direction of Linz, and to stop it and not let it cross over the bridge under any circumstances.

I told the lieutenant that I needed to know something about what the situation was. I could always do a better job if I knew what the purpose and reasoning was—not just to stop a train, which didn't mean much to me—and he told me.

The lieutenant told me that this was a serious international matter that had just arisen. There was this train now being loaded with an awful lot of displaced persons down in Linz and it was headed into the Soviet zone—and it must be stopped and not be allowed to enter the Soviet zone. He further explained to me that the Soviets did not want any of the displaced slave laborers, or any of the inmates from the concentrations camps or from POW camps in Germany and Austria, that had been brought by the Nazis from the Soviet bloc countries, to be allowed back into any of the countries that they occupied—under any circumstances.

He further told me that the Soviets were complaining that they had no food, clothes, housing, guards, or any facilities whatsoever to care for them. Also, that they did not trust any of them. He told me that one of the Soviets' claims was that all of the inmates from concentration camps, and all of the displaced persons who were the slave laborers, as well as all of the Russian POWs, were collaborators with the Nazis and were all criminals. This of course was not true at all. The bottom line was that they refused to accept any of them into their territory. They obviously just didn't want to be bothered with them, so let the Americans deal with them. That was the way I saw it, and I told this to the lieutenant. He didn't disagree with me.

As a consequence, there had been a high level agreement that stated that our Occupation Forces would not send any of these people into Soviet territory, and that these orders came from Washington as per an agreement between President Truman and Stalin. He further explained that if this train got through to the Soviet zone—which was only a few miles from us—it would develop into a very serious international incident, with serious implications, in that America would then be in violation of their agreement with the Soviets. It was obvious that all of the prisoners, inmates, slave laborers, and POWs returned would be exterminated immediately upon arrival. He stressed to me the extreme importance of stopping this freight trainload of displaced persons that was just now leaving the rail yards of Linz, heading for this bridge across the Danube and on into the Soviet zone. I appreciated him telling me this information and I thanked him for doing it. I always work better if I know what the circumstances are. I have always taken what I do seriously, especially if I know what I am dealing with.

I had some second thoughts about how I was going to stop a train, especially if the engineer didn't want to stop. I reasoned that if the engineer just ignored me, trying to be too occupied with the operation of his train, how would I stop that train? I knew that these displaced persons—slave laborers is what they really were—had no food or water, and they were desperately trying to return to their homes. I feared that if the train did stop for me, that then the DPs would attack me in order to continue their trip to their homes. The questions in my mind was just how would I stop that train? If I didn't, I would find myself in the middle of a serious international incident, which I didn't want any part of. I asked my lieutenant, "What if the engineer just don't stop?"

His reply was, "You will stop that train! Just make sure that you do! Why do you think that I came all the way up here from Linz to get you to do it? When the captain told me to stop this train, I asked him the same question that you just asked me.

"The captain said to me, 'Go get Ladner. He will stop it, if anyone can.'

"I then asked the Captain, 'What if he can't?'

"The captain then said, 'Tell him to take a man with him.'" This was his famous remark in a time of crisis. He would always say that, which ended the conversation about it. This was Captain Graham's way of letting a person know that he is to use his own head and just do it the best way that he knows how. I have had him tell me that on several previous occasions, and I knew what he meant: Use your own initiative and just go do it. This was one of his great attributes, and I liked him for that.

The lieutenant left in his jeep and told me that he would return for me later. As we were about halfway across the bridge I looked at my buddy who had never seen one day of combat. He now was as scared as he could be, looking at me with a quizzical and frightened look. He asked me, as we walked across the Danube River railroad bridge to the Linz side, "How are you going to stop that train?"

I told this kid, fresh from basic training at Camp Blanding, Florida, "What do you mean, 'How am I going to stop it?' We are going to stop it and don't you leave my side at any time, either!"

I wondered how much help he would be to me.

It was not long, standing there at that bridge, before I saw a very long freight train coming with an awful lot of freight cars filled full with displaced persons. This freight train was going fast; it was so long I couldn't count the cars that it was pulling, there were so many of them. In fact, that train was so long that I couldn't see the end of it. The DPs were all hanging out of the doors of the boxcars. All of them were skinny, shabbily dressed, undernourished, and with shaved heads, and had filthy clothes on. As soon as the train came into sight I started flagging it to stop. I stood by the track at the end of the bridge, at the east edge of the river. I positioned my feet firmly on the ground beside the track. I flagged the train with my left arm, while holding my rifle in my right hand with the butt of it resting on my hip, so the engineer could see it clearly. I could see the engineer in the cab. He put his upper body out of the side window and was attempting to ignore me by smiling and waving a friendly wave toward me as if nothing was happening. It was obvious that he had no intentions of stopping and he just kept coming.

I put my M-1 Rifle to my shoulder and fired one shot into the upper part of the windshield, right over the right side of his head. I now kept my rifle aimed at his head. I was going to fire on him, at his head this time, if that warning shot didn't do the job. There was only one engineer operating the train. Just seconds before I was squeezing off another round at his head, he immediately applied full brakes and came to a screeching halt right at the end of the bridge, right beside me. I motioned him to go back, while I kept my rifle pointed at his head. He then began waving his hands in the air like he wanted to argue with me. I ignored him and aimed my rifle again at his head and began squeezing the trigger. He understood and reversed the train and began backing up, returning to Linz very fast.

After the job was finished, I looked around for my buddy. He was down the bank of the river about thirty feet, at the edge of the water by some bushes with an awfully frightened look on his face.

Soon, the lieutenant received word from someone in Linz that the train was not allowed to cross the Danube and had returned to Linz with its load of human cargo. He came in his jeep and picked us up. He chuckled and told me that I had done a fine job of stopping that train, which he really didn't think I would be able to do. I told him that if the engineer hadn't stopped the train, I would have killed him and there would have been this long trainload of humanity going down the tracks into the Soviet zone with no engineer. What a hell of an international incident that would have been. I was glad that this job was over.

Little did I know then, but I later learned, had I not been able to stop that train and if it had gotten through to the Soviet zone, the Soviet 3rd Ukrainian Army would have slaughtered each and every one of them upon their arrival in the Soviet zone. This then translates into the fact that by my stopping that train, I saved the lives of each and every person on it, approximately two thousand slave laborers, at least temporarily.

I thought about why the lieutenant drove his jeep all the way from Linz, about eight miles, to get me to stop that train and why the captain had him go all the way up to Camp Gussen to get me to do it when there were surely men in Linz who could have done it.

Al Sperl had gone down into the Russian zone on some kind of mission as an interpreter, so when he returned I told him about the lieutenant coming all the way from Linz up there to get me to stop that train. His thinking was that it was such a serious matter, in that if the train got through it could have created hostilities between America and the Russians.

Sperl told me, "Apparently the captain really had to have that train stopped bad. If I had been your captain, I would have gotten a Bronze

Star Medal recipient to have done it, because if he failed, I could say, 'You see, don't blame me. I sent the best man I have up there to do it.' If the man did stop that train, then the captain could write a good report to his command." I also learned later from my platoon sergeant that Sperl was totally correct in his assumption, in that the captain said exactly that. I thanked Sperl for this compliment.

Sperl told me also that he had seen a Russian jeep while he was in the Soviet zone. I asked him what it looked like and if it was made in Detroit. He told me that it was a two-wheel cart that was very crude that looked like it was made in Julius Caesar's time. It had wheels cut out of wooden boards that had been nailed together, and it was pulled by a half starved oxen with a Soviet soldier riding on the cart with a whip that he was beating the ox with.

CHAPTER 38

Underground Messerschmitt Factory at Camp Gussen, Mauthausen

"O God, give me the serenity to accept the things that I cannot change, the courage to change the things that I can, and the wisdom to know the difference."

—ST. FRANCIS OF ASSISI (1182–1226)

After I stopped that train I was assigned to a more pleasant job—no more concentration camp work—which I was thankful for. I was assigned to guard the underground airplane factory near Mauthausen and Camp Gussen, where prisoners there had been used to dig out a huge tunnel in a big hill, two miles of underground tunnels dug out of solid rock. There was only one large entrance and a railroad ran right into this underground factory, which was used as assembly lines for constructing Messerschmitt fighter planes. While I was there a Russian delegation came to inspect this factory. They were always everywhere wanting to inspect everything. I was unable to talk with any of them, but someone took my photograph with some of the Russian soldiers. They were very friendly, but they were tough, not well dressed, in that their uniforms were somewhat inadequate and tattered. None of them were Mongolians. They all looked about like I did at the time, very undernourished, but much more so.

I assume that our command had decided that we GIs had been doing enough work at the concentration camps, working with displaced persons, as well as working hard to discharge Nazi POWs. New kinds of work was found, so we could be frequently rotated from one kind of work to another. It was all very stressful, almost as bad as being in combat again.

We were living in nice homes that had been the residences of the SS troops that had guarded the concentration camp that was located in St. Georgen. It was so comfortable that it was almost like home. We had a large living room and kitchen downstairs and two bedrooms upstairs with twin beds in each. One night we were told that a contingent of Russian troops would come to share our sleeping quarters with us. They were in the area for some kind of inspection, which they always seemed to be doing. So, after dark, a sergeant brought a group of the Russian soldiers into our house. There were about ten or twelve of them. They just came right in, laid down on the floor and went sound to sleep. They did just like we had been accustomed to doing when we were riding tanks on the point, in combat. Not one of the Russians could speak a word of English. So, there wasn't much talking taking place. We just went to sleep, the same as they did. The next morning they quietly left, just at daybreak.

CHAPTER 39

Furlough to Paris

"A God wise enough to create me and the world I live in, is wise enough to watch out for me."

—PHILIP YANCEY, *WHERE IS GOD WHEN IT HURTS?*

One day the captain called me into his office and asked me, "Where would you like to go on an R and R [Rest and Relaxation] leave—to Paris, London, or Switzerland?"

I immediately replied, "I would like to go to all of them, sir."

His reply was, "Well, I can't let you go to all three places right now. How about taking it one at a time?"

"Sure, fine, sir, I will take Paris first, then London, then Switzerland, sir."

Soon, me and a buddy were no longer involved in any of the multitude of activities of cleaning up the messes made by Hitler and Stalin. We were on our way to Paris riding in a very comfortable passenger train. No one was allowed to go anywhere without a buddy, each to look after and protect the other, even though the war was over.

We rode on a very modern train that was quite comfortable and had a dining car. I was so excited about going to Paris that I didn't mind any inconveniences of the trip, even though it was a very long and tiring trip. We went through Salzburg, a quiet, clean, and beautiful city undamaged by the war. It was about the cleanest city that I had yet seen.

331

Next was Munich, which had received quite a bit of damage. The next major city was Strasbourg, France. This city was so severely damaged it looked like a ghost town and as devastated as Saarlautern. The train pulled into this very large rail terminal that had once been glass-covered, but now it had been ravaged by bombs. As far as one could see, there was nothing but rubble. We only stopped there for a few minutes and very few people got on or off. I could not see where anyone would want to go there, in that it was all very devastated.

We were met at the train station in Paris by a beautiful English-speaking French special services girl who was our hostess and guide. She took us to our hotel where we ate some very good food; the next day she took us on a tour to the Eiffel Tower. I stood where my father had stood in 1918 when he had been given leave to Paris. We then walked to Le Invalids, which is where Napoleon's tomb is, then across the Seine River, over the beautiful Alexandria II bridge to the Arc d'Triumph. These were all places that my father also had visited. I began to believe that history really does repeat itself.

We stayed in Paris about ten days and had a fantastic time in this most beautiful and historic city in the entire world. While there our hostess took us almost daily to a fabulous ice cream parlor in the Montmartre area. Ice cream was hard to find there, but we gorged ourselves on it every day. My buddy suggested to me one day that we go to Place Pigalle, a red-light district that Americans GIs called "Pig Alley." We agreed that we should not tell our hostess about it, who was such a refined and beautiful young lady, who was so wonderful, caring, and concerned about us. She was making our vacation there something very special.

Just as we got out of the subway there, at Place Pigalle, we started to go into a bar that was right on the corner of the street where the subway entrance is, to have a drink before we started chasing the beautiful French women. As we started into the bar to get a drink, two gorgeous girls came from the inside of the bar and met us at the door, grabbed each of us by the arm, then led us to a small hotel right around the corner. We didn't even have time to get a glass of wine or cognac. Now, we had something to brag about to our other buddies when we returned to Linz.

Food there was sparse, and one had to eat what they had to serve in the restaurants. In most places you had no choice, just a piece of meat, like chicken or rabbit, two boiled potatoes, snap beans, and a piece of that wonderful French bread, and of course a glass of good wine. We hated having to leave Paris and return to Austria. I vowed to return again someday, and I did.

Soon, after we returned to Austria I got a week's vacation at a resort at a luxurious hotel on a lake, in the mountains south of Linz, that had been, and was a very famous resort hotel on this beautiful lake. There was lots of entertainment that we enjoyed very much, like magicians, jugglers, acrobats, yodelers, and the like, all of which were very good, and they entertained us each night. Each morning I would get into a canoe and row across the lake. The food was fantastic, beautifully served in a elegant dining room. It was a very enjoyable vacation, which greatly helped in relieving the stress that we had acquired in recent months. While there one day, out by the water, I spoke with a small group of men, some of whom were dressed in business suits. They told me that they were American congressmen who were there inspecting the facilities to make sure that we combat veterans were getting proper rest and relaxation. I assured them that they could report to their taxpayer constituents, and tell them that everything was great, and that we were grateful to them for what they were doing to make life enjoyable for us after the ordeal that we had endured. They were greatly pleased to hear this. I also related to them that United States Senator Theodore G. Bilbo was my second cousin, and to please give him my regards when they returned to Washington. They took my name and assured me that they would, and they did.

After we returned to Linz, I had no assignment, in that our much loved 65th Infantry Division was being deactivated. So, the captain told me to get ready to go to London for ten days. I also learned that when I returned from London that I would then be going to Switzerland, then I would go to Munich and to Garmish-Partenkirchen, where the Zugspitze—the highest mountain in Germany—was, for ten days. I also learned that there were other resort rest areas that I would be able to go to in Southern Germany and Austria.

I also learned from the captain that I would be assigned to the 10th Armored Division located near Munich after the deactivation of the 65th Division.

CHAPTER 40

Rest and Relaxation in London

"If people want Peace so much, I think that government should get out of the way and let them have it."

—DWIGHT D. EISENHOWER (1890–1969)

It was not long before it was time to leave for London. On the way there, we changed trains in Paris, then to Le Havre, France. Riding these very nice and comfortable trains was quite a contrast from the forty and eight freight trains that I had ridden form Le Havre to Metz to get to the front lines.

At Le Havre, we were billeted in houses that had been taken over so as to house us while waiting to depart. We slept on folding cots while we waited our turn for a ship across the English Channel. While there awaiting departure of our ship, we had beautiful American Red Cross girls serving us real coffee and doughnuts. The ship we boarded was a rather small English ship, the weather was awfully bad, and the seas were even worse, with high waves. We were not supposed to depart in this weather, but the captain took off anyway. The channel between there and Southampton was so rough that most everyone on the ship was heaving their guts out. The ship was a mess. I found a bunk up high by a porthole that I opened to get some fresh air. I never got seasick, as most all of the others did, and I was quite comfortable. We landed in

Southampton at the same dock where we boarded a ship to cross the English Channel to go fight a war.

From there we took a train to Victoria Station in London. We stayed in a very comfortable hotel near the Odeon Theatre and I had a great time in London, visiting all of the wonderful historic sites there, spending lots of time at the Odeon Theatre seeing movies and listening to the world's largest pipe organ. My favorite thing to do was to buy fish and chips from a street vendor who cooked them right there on the street. You could eat them out of a newspaper that they were served on, right there on the sidewalk. This was the first fish that I'd had since leaving home to go in the service, and I made a point to eat some every day.

I was getting off a bus near my hotel one evening and I ran into my buddy getting on it, and I asked him where he was going. He told me that he was going to Piccadilly Circus to find him a pretty girl. Just as he said that, this pretty girl right behind him heard him, who was also getting on the bus. She grabbed him by the arm and said, "Come on with me, soldier boy, and we will go to my place at Piccadilly Circus." I kidded him about this for some time.

On my return, we again crossed the channel and upon nearing Le Havre, as we got close to the harbor, the wind and waves were calm, the water was as smooth as glass, except for the gentle swells of the tide. There was a large round mine that had broken loose from its mooring somewhere and was sighted floating near our ship. It was about three or four feet in diameter, maybe more, with detonators sticking out from it all over. We stopped dead in the water near the mine. A crewman went up on the bow and fired many shots at the mine and missed each time. It would soon be dark and anything could happen. I was apprehensive. I went up to him and asked if I might try a shot, or two. He said that I could and he gave me the rifle. I told him that now we needed to go up on the bridge in the center of the vessel where there was little or no motion of the ocean waves and I would shoot from there. We went there and I fired twice and on the second shot I hit the mine's detonator and it exploded with a loud explosion that rocked the boat. I got a loud hand of applause from all of the GIs standing on deck. It was just another achievement by another American soldier. We then went on into the harbor and debarked.

CHAPTER 41
The Decommissioning of the 65ᵗʰ Infantry Division and Reassignment

"Peace is an armistice in war that is continuously ongoing."

—THUCYDIDES (471–400 B.C.)

The 65ᵗʰ Division was soon decommissioned, and disbanded in August 1945. This was a very sad day for many of us. All of us in my company had developed so much respect for each other, that we were like blood brothers. I, along with others, was sent to near Munich and assigned to the 10ᵗʰ Armored Division. It was a tearful time for many of us, being split up from most of our buddies we had fought with and trusted with our lives. I really hated to leave the sergeants that I had gotten to know in my company and who were some of the finest men that I ever knew. They were gutsy, courageous, fair-minded ,and they were greatly liked and respected. I must mention their names here out of the great respect that I had for these brave and courageous men.

First Sergeant Leo Manard from Fall River, Massachusetts, was not only a fine leader, but was also my friend.

Also, there was Technical Sergeant Lars Agneberg from South Dakota, one of the finest, most caring and brave men I knew. He gave me his poncho one early cold rainy morning as I was getting on a tank,

336

which probably saved my life in the cold rain. He always looked after his men with great concern for them.

I must mention my squad leader, Sergeant Willie Graybeal, one great guy, kind, caring, concerned, and a man who was always right there where the action was and went the extra mile for all of his men. We all would miss these brave and valiant select few.

Captain Graham would also be greatly missed, as well. He was a courageous leader who had great faith in the men of his company and he was always there when the going got tough. All of his men had great faith and confidence in him. It was not just these great men that I would miss, but all of the other men in our company as well, who made it the distinguished outfit that it had come to be. We truly had a *right to be proud.*

Our first stop in this assignment to our new division was Garmish-Partenkirchen, near the Zugspitze mountain ski resort up high on a mountain that could be reached only by riding a train up a steep mountain railroad, and then through a tunnel to the other side of the mountain. The train was pulled up the steep mountain railroad by a big cog wheel that caught in the grooved center track that pulled it up the mountain. At the top was a large train terminal, a huge lobby, a restaurant, and a hotel. Outside were beautiful ski slopes and you could also catch a cable car to carry you even further up to the very peak of this mountain that was covered with snow year-round. This was the highest point in Germany. These were very exciting times for a country farm boy like me.

We then were assigned to a remote mountainous region northwest of Garmish where we stayed in local small hotels, like a bed and break-fast place. It was very neat and clean. The owners prepared very good meals for us. The mountainous scenery was fascinating. I enjoyed looking out my window and seeing the clouds come down below the level of the window. I never slept so well as I did in that clean, clear, cool mountain air. We set up roadblocks and looked out for big time Nazis who might be using these mountainous roads, but otherwise had very little to do.

The next rest and relaxation trip was when I got a week's leave to Lake Ibsee up in the mountains, on the route up to the Zugspitze nearby. This is a very large and beautiful old hotel; the food was great and the water in the lake was extremely cold. I slept very late every morning and then ate a whale of a breakfast. I was now finally regaining some of my weight and strength. I had now regained ten pounds of the twenty that I had lost in combat.

Vacation in Switzerland

Soon, I was told I had a furlough to go to Switzerland. I and a buddy loaded onto a passenger train in Munich and departed for Switzerland. We stayed in some very luxurious hotels and had some wonderfully delicious food. The Swiss breakfast consisted of still-warm, baked early that morning, flaky hard rolls, honey, fresh homemade butter, and coffee. It was called a continental breakfast and it was great. Breakfast was my favorite meal, the one I enjoyed eating most of all. We could have it served in our room if we chose to. One GI said that the definition of a continental breakfast was, "A roll in bed with honey." This was the second time I had enjoyed some good real coffee since I had left home to go fight a war. I enjoyed my breakfasts in Switzerland more than anywhere. However, one day I was in a store and I saw some Corn Flakes and having seen them I had a craving for some. I bought a box and took them to the hotel with me, and the next morning I asked the waitress to serve them to us. When she returned she brought us a banana to eat with the big bowl of Corn Flakes, with a big pitcher of real whole cream to put on them, just like mom always did back home. We really enjoyed eating that breakfast. It was an awful lot like being home again. We had a wonderful time and life was getting a whole lot better.

The train ride through the mountains of Switzerland was so beautiful, peaceful, and refreshing, it was like a powerful sedative that enthralled me. The quietness and serenity reminded me of our peaceful country home back in Mississippi. The small train that carried us through a picturesque mountainous region reminded me of the comic strip, *Toonerville Trolley.* It consisted of a small engine, one passenger car, and one mail and cargo car. It carried the mail and delivered the groceries and other supplies that the mountain people had ordered the day before. It was slow and quiet, giving its passengers plenty of time to enjoy the beautiful mountain scenery. The beauty of the snowcapped mountains, the clean fresh air, and tranquil landscape was breath taking peace and beauty. We stopped one afternoon and got off of the train in this quiet and peaceful little village that was high in the mountains. We stayed in a small bed and breakfast–type home, two-story, high in the mountains, right beside where the train stopped. I sat in the backyard that afternoon and watched the cows come home, as they followed this mountain trail around the edge of this mountain, coming into the village. When the cows got into the village each one went their separate way, directly to their respective owner's barn. The lead cow for the whole group had a large cowbell around her neck that could be heard from far away. All of the other cows followed the lead cow. It was a beautiful, peaceful, and tranquil sight that did a great deal to set me on a course of healing the terrible stressful trauma that I had endured.

Dinner was served that evening and it was wonderful. I do not think that any five star restaurant could do any better. This lady and her husband had prepared a marvelous dinner of whole fried trout that he had caught that day in a nearby mountain stream. We ate vegetables that were gathered that morning and fresh rolls baked that day, as well as a fascinating and very tasty dessert. It was food that I was not quite used to in the Army, so we enjoyed it to the maximum.

That evening we went to a local bar, the only one in this village. It was quaint, located in the basement of a small building in this tiny village. There my buddy and I met a Swiss soldier who was in uniform. We had a very nice conversation about how army life was. I learned that the Swiss military people have their own weapons and they keep them at home with them, even though they are the property of the government. They are there to protect the home front and were stationed in secret and secluded defense positions hidden in all of the mountain passes. The Swiss soldier wanted to learn all he could from me about what combat was like. I explained a little of it to him, explaining that it was different for each person, in every location, but I chose to change the conversation and have another glass of that great Swiss wine. I had already learned that I could not tolerate reliving the horrors that I and my fellow combat infantrymen had endured. To discuss combat with anyone was like reliving it all over again. Never had I ever met such friendly and wonderful people as I met in Switzerland.

The bedroom of this very small hotel had only about three or four rooms they rented. They were comfortably furnished and there was a feather comforter to cover with, which was very warm when the temperature got down so low that night at this very high altitude. The following morning we had the most wonderful breakfast I think I ever ate. We had eggs, Swiss ham, blueberry jam, coffee, grape juice, those famous hot flaky hard rolls and the most tasty butter I ever ate, which Switzerland is famous for. Soon, our train arrived right outside the little hotel and we boarded it for the most exhilarating ride through the mountains that one could ever imagine. On the way, I saw a young girl in a field with an old man, probably her grandfather. They both had a large scythe they were cutting wheat with. They were tying it into bundles, like they must have done hundreds of years ago. The serenity and peacefulness of the whole mountainous country astounded me. The entire trip was so relaxing I almost forgot that I had just finished fighting a horrible and terrifying war. I really hated to leave Switzerland, it was such a peaceful and tranquil place to be. It was a sad trip back to Garmish-Partenkirchen, Germany.

CHAPTER 42

The Untold Horrors of Dachau Concentration Camp

"Communism is based on the belief that man is so weak and inadequate that he is unable to govern himself, and therefore requires the rule of strong masters."

—HARRY S. TRUMAN (1864–1972)

Next, I was assigned to work at Dachau Concentration Camp, which was near Munich. This was more of the tremendous amount of Nazi gruesomeness that we had to endure in trying to clean up Hitler's dirty sordid mess. It was more stressful, it seemed, than combat was. This camp was so large and with so many inmates in it, we had a monumental job to clear out all of the inmates there and repatriate them to their country of origin. At first I was assigned to work in an office near the main gate of this huge concentration camp where thousands of inmates still were kept, but now better fed and clothed and living in a cleaner environment. But still they were not permitted to leave until they were processed and repatriated to wherever they originated from, assuming that country would accept them. Many of the inmates had to still be fed only potato soup, but with a little more calories in it, because too many calories were deadly to them.

It was my job to help process the inmates as to where they were to be repatriated to, and to arrange for them to be transported by a special train for their use only to a designated destination, supposedly to a city nearest their former places of residence. Most all of them had no place of residence, or family to return to, or homes or property anywhere, especially those from within the Soviet-controlled countries. No citizen in the Soviet Union could own any property anyway, so they were totally at the mercy of the fanatical dictator, Stalin. Many came from ghettos of large cities like Warsaw that had since been totally demolished by the Germans, and then even more so by the Russians. There, when they were interned by the Nazis, all of their family and friends from the ghettos were either killed there or exterminated here, and the ghettos destroyed in the fighting of the war by bombs and artillery, as well as fires that were deliberately set.

The reason that so many were still here was that they had nowhere to go, and no one in the whole world wanted to receive them, care for them, and afford them food and housing. They were just homeless unwanted people, pitiful, emaciated, both mentally and physically deteriorated. All of them had been stripped of their identity, their dignity, family, friends, self-respect, their homes, their heritage, and property, and what was left was just a walking, mindless corpse that didn't even have any clothes to wear.

It was a real problem, in that no one in our command was trained in knowing how to handle such enormous political and sociological problems. We were working hard, and desperately trying to cope with this situation the best that we knew how. Such a situation had never previously occurred in the history of mankind anywhere in the whole world, like it was here. No one knew how to handle such a serious problem as this, especially when now we were having to deal with a terrorist, a sadistic mass murderer, a Communist dictator named Joe Stalin.

Almost all of the GIs here were combat veterans. None of us were trained to handle a situation like a concentration camp, or how to undo all of the trepidations that were attached to it. We could not repatriate people who could not be repatriated. The Soviets definitely didn't want—not even one single one of them—to return to their zone. They had no food, no living space, no medical facilities, no clothing to provide them, no jobs for them, and no rehabilitation to afford them—so they said. Nevertheless, we all felt and sincerely believed that if the Soviets and their dictator, Stalin, had any Christian or otherwise good moral principles about him, he would have found a way to receive and care for them. Few if any had any way of ever earning a living again. It was obvious that their health problems were overwhelming. So many of them were totally bedridden and were unable to even ride a train to Warsaw or Bucharest.

I was provided an interpreter, a young man who was an inmate at Dachau. He was from Poland, had been a college student working on his doctorate in political science and history at a university in Krakow, Poland, where his father was at that time a professor, until he and his wife were killed by the invading Nazis. Their son, this young man, fought hard, resisting the Nazi invaders, was captured, and was told he had a choice of joining the German Army and fighting the Russians—or going to Dachau for extermination, for fighting in the resistance against the Nazis. I could not pronounce his name, so I called him Joe Kowski. I will never be able to forget this intelligent young man. He was kind and friendly, and spoke impeccable English, as well as many other languages. He was extremely well groomed, very neat, and had a good appearance. He was a Christian, a devout Catholic, as well as a person with principles and high moral standards and Christian values. He was very knowledgeable about history, politics, government, the arts, and humanities. He told me that the Nazis and the Communists both, didn't want any such people like him around, in that these were totalitarian governments—one Communist and the other Fascist. He stated that these people in power, in both governments, didn't want to know anything about politics and government or history; nor did they want any citizen to know anything about it. They, the dictators, did only as they pleased and they considered such educated intelligencia as being a threat to their totalitarian dictatorship. So, both the Soviets and the Nazis just killed people like him and his father, considering them to be useless and in the way of their totalitarian reign of terror. Prior to the war his family was fairly wealthy, lived in a fine home in Krakow, enjoyed the finer things of life, and contributed greatly to the betterment of society there. He had been a very good athlete as well as a fierce fighter opposing the Nazis. He told me that after he was captured by the Nazis, their military told him he had one of two choices, to join the German Army and fight the Russians, or go to Dachau. He chose not to join the Nazi Army who had murdered his parents and taken over, and later destroyed, their home. He related to me that it would be just as bad, either way, but that he could not compromise his principles and fight for a government that had murdered his parents and destroyed all that they owned.

Joe Kowski would be with me all day in the office near the entrance of Dachau, as an interpreter and translator. He worked very hard in helping process all of the papers for the inmates to be repatriated to whatever country they chose to return to, assuming that was where they originated. We had to get an approval from their country of origin before we could ever send any of them there. He related to me how horrible the conditions inside the camp were before the American 10th Armored Division arrived and liberated Dachau. His greatest concern was if he would be able to survive—not the imprisonment in Dachau, which he had done, but would he ever be able to return alive to his native land of Poland and live there in peace and happiness, which he told me that he had not seen any of since the Nazi invasion of Poland.

He was a handsome young man with a great smile and personality. He told me that the Nazi SS guards at Dachau liked him and he earned a special status there, doing errands for the guards, using his language ability as an interpreter for them. It was this way that he was able to get enough to eat and maintain his health. He now worked right in the same office, at the same desk, and right beside my desk, that he had worked at before the camp was liberated by the 10th Armored Division. I tried to counsel Joe, but he was much more intelligent about such matters than I was, especially in European political matters.

I related to him about my experience of stopping the trainload of refugees and sending it back to Linz, and not letting them go into the Soviet zone. He well knew that the Soviets didn't have any food, clothing, or housing to provide to refugees, and that the Soviets just didn't want any of the inmates from Dachau or any other concentration camp to come into the Soviet zone. He also knew that the Soviets didn't want any of the other displaced persons to be returned to the Soviet occupied countries, and if and when they did return, they all would be killed immediately and their bodies disposed of in a mass grave.

I also learned that the Soviets—Joe Stalin, the dictator—were not going to accept back into their zone any of the Soviet troops that the Nazis had captured, and who were still imprisoned in Germany and Austria. However, several months after the end of the war in Europe, an agreement had been worked out between Truman, Churchill, and Stalin that those who were originally from a country within the Soviet zone could be returned there. The Soviets had promised that they would accept them, then distribute them to their place of origin, even though there was nothing there to return to but ruins. It was soon learned by everyone that the first trainloads of returning inmates were killed by the Soviets immediately upon arrival.

This quickly became common knowledge, not only amongst us GIs, but to all such DPs, inmates of concentration camps, and all inmates of Soviet POW camps—when they returned to the Soviet zone they would be killed. Not one person in our command seemed to express any great concern for this occurring. It was orders from headquarters, wherever that was, and they, the people in command, behaving like good soldiers, carried them out. It was difficult for me to comprehend that this kind of mass murder was still happening and that no one, not even the media back in the United States, made any mention of this most serious matter.

As I continued to learn about the overwhelming cruelty to human beings that was continuously being carried out by the Soviets, the more angry I became, and I as well as an awful lot of other soldiers that I knew were hoping that General Patton would "attack to the east," as we heard that he intended doing. I would have gladly volunteered to fight the Soviets in order to restore democracy, humanity, sanity, Christianity, and total religious freedom to that evil, atheist, communist country.

I and many others were disgusted with our command, who carried out the orders that came from President Truman to return this mass of people to the Soviets, when we all knew that they would kill them upon arrival. Those in command, particularly General Eisenhower, voiced no objection or complaints about what we all were being made a party to, which was mass murder.

I considered it an illegal and an immoral order to return all of these poor people to the Soviets to be murdered, and so did many other American soldiers. I reasoned that this was mass murder, not only by the Soviets, but also by Americans who knowingly carried out these illegal orders to send these people to their imminent death. We principally blamed President Harry Truman for yielding to Joe Stalin's demands for their return, knowing that they would be killed, and then they were killed. I had many sleepless nights worrying about this situation. I was absolutely sickened by the entire sordid mess.

A buddy from the 65th Infantry Division came by to see me and I learned that he was also in the 10th Armored Division and was working there at Dachau. He and some others from our old division had been assigned to ride trains, guarding the Dachau inmates who were sent back into their countries of origin within the Soviet Union. His trips as a train guard were to deliver inmates into the Soviet zone. I asked him what his work of riding trains loaded with inmates going into the Soviet zone was like.

He told me that as soon as we processed enough inmates there at Dachau to make up a trainload to go to some large city in the Soviet zone near where these inmates wanted to go, or had been taken from, he would ride the train as one of the guards, to deliver them there. They were placed on a train, a long passenger train, and it would go to a designated large city in the Soviet zone and deliver the inmates there, supposedly to be repatriated to the place of their origin.

Theoretically, and in accordance with an agreement worked out between President Truman, Churchill, and Joe Stalin, the inmates from Soviet countries were to then be sent from Dachau, and from other camps in Germany and Austria, to a destination of their choice, or to near their place of origin, in the country that they originated from. We had to communicate with the Soviets to let them know when a train would arrive at certain locations with a load of concentration camp inmates.

It was apparent to many people that Truman and Churchill were aware of what Joe Stalin was doing to these people once they were delivered into the Soviet zone, but they did nothing about it, except to turn their heads and look the other way while Stalin continued his mass murdering. It could not be more barbarian than that. Not even Adolph Hitler had been that crude and gruesome.

I strongly believed that when any country is ruled by a one-man dictator with absolute power, that the citizens of his country are really his victims. I strongly believed that no country should stand for a leader who, without controls and restraints being placed upon him by the citizens, and who did not possess strong Christian or other principled religious and moral values, should be given such power and authority over the citizens. Otherwise, such a man with so much power could be nothing less than a Stalin or a Hitler.

When we got enough inmates to fill the train, the inmates would be loaded on. The guards would lock all of the doors on the train. The train would have one caboose right behind the engine and another one at the end of the train and this is where the guards, all American soldiers who had been combat infantrymen, would stay. They also had to patrol through the passenger cars to make sure that the inmates were not trying to escape and were otherwise all right. They were fed good food that was brought for them to eat and it was served to them on the train. This meal in reality turned out to be their Last Supper.

My friend further related that he had just returned from taking a trainload of these inmates from Dachau to Bucharest, Romania. He told me that when the train arrived at an isolated railyard just outside of Bucharest, all of the inmates rushed to look out the windows to see who the people there to meet them were, who would process them out to be sent to their homeland.

He related that the inmates on the train were expecting the people there who would receive them to be Romanian police and civilians, and not Soviet troops only.

When they looked out the windows and only saw Soviet troops who were members of the 3rd Ukrainian Army they all became extremely upset, agitated, and terribly frightened. As soon as they all realized that the only people there, anywhere around where the train stopped were only Soviet soldiers of the 3rd Ukrainian Army, many began weeping, and all of them had tears pouring down their cheeks. They told my friend that they knew as soon as they saw the Soviet troops outside the train and realized that they were all troops of the 3rd Ukrainian Army, they would all be killed, and soon.

All of the passenger inmates were removed from the train and lined up quickly against a stone retaining wall at the base of a hill, which was in a very isolated area with no other people around except the Soviet Ukrainian troops. There were no vehicles or any other form of transportation by which these inmates could be transported away to any place. They were told to line up against this wall, so they could be processed and then sent back to where they came from. After my GI friend and the other train guards made sure all of the passengers were off of the train, it pulled out to make a circle to return to Dachau, Germany. He further related to me that just after the train pulled off, the GI train guards on the train all went to the rear caboose of the train so that they could try to see and hear what was going to happen to these people that they had delivered to the Soviet Communists.

Just as soon as the train pulled out and was just out of sight, but only a short distance away, machine guns opened fire on these long rows of inmates they had delivered there. They heard many machine guns begin to fire at that location where they had been unloaded. Many of them fired until they stopped, apparently by running out of ammunition, or further killing those that weren't dead yet; then they would start again. All of their passengers were now obviously killed or still dying.

He surmised that the machine guns had been set up on the opposite side of the tracks, emplaced out of view, and that they were also using their automatic weapons they carried on their person. He related to me that this was the only realistic and logical conclusion they or anyone could draw.

My combat buddy related to me that many of them obviously didn't die from the first firing of the machine guns, and as they pulled away the machine guns would stop firing for a minute, then began firing again until they all were obviously dead. This was not only his observable conclusion, but also that of all of the other train guards, all former 65th Infantry Division combat infantrymen who had previously made such deliveries into the Soviet zone.

As the train made a circle, turned around, and came back very close to where they had unloaded their passengers, and only a short distance away, they could still hear the machine guns firing sporadically at the location where they had unloaded the inmates. He talked with other GIs who were on the train as guards, and they told him they saw the bullet holes in the stone wall that the passengers had been lined up against, apparently being there from the previous load of inmates delivered there who had been executed in the same manner.

My friend told me that he also saw the bullet holes in the stone, or cement, retaining wall from the previous trainloads that had been delivered there, and he observed this as the inmates debarked from the train and were told to line up against this wall. He further told me that the inmates knew immediately before they were lined up against this stone wall, they were going to be killed—and many of them related this to him.

The guards for the next trainload of inmates taken there that I talked with, reported that the first thing they saw when the train arrived were the bullet holes in this retaining wall. Other men from our old outfit reported the same thing happened when they rode these trains to many other parts of Soviet-occupied territories, delivering inmates from Dachau to their homeland inside the Soviet occupied countries.

I learned that the Soviets used Soviet Ukrainian troops to do the mass killing of these inmates, who were about seventy percent Jews. The reason related to us for the Soviets using Ukrainian troops from the 3rd Ukrainian Army was that they—the Ukrainians—hated the Jews because they blamed them for killing twenty-six million Ukrainians during the period when the Bolshevik communists were in total control of Russia, under the dictatorship of Marxist Vladimir Lenin, after the revolution.

Reluctantly, I spoke to Joe Kowski about what my friend and the other men I knew had told me about the killing of the trainloads of Dachau inmates when they arrived in the Soviet zone. Joe was quite reluctant to discuss it with me, primarily because I was not that knowledgeable about Soviet politics and he didn't think that I would understand—or that it would be so shocking to me that I would not believe what he told me.

I previously had been telling Joe to look forward to returning to Poland and building a new and better country and government there, in that there would have to be many great opportunities. How wrong, naive, and unenlightened I soon learned that I was.

Joe told me that after Karl Marx, a German Jew, had written the *Communist Manifesto,* that in 1917, and before that, thousands of Jews from all over the world immigrated into Russia to prepare for the overthrow of the Russian government, and the takeover by the Jewish-controlled Marxist Bolshevik (Communist) Revolutionaries. This was at a period of great economic depression and turmoil, not only in Russia, but in Germany and other parts of the world, which left not only Russia, but many other countries, very vulnerable to a revolution. Many of the immigrating Jews dropped their Jewish names and acquired Russian names. Communism was a Jewish philosophy of government where the government owned and controlled every person and all property of all kinds, like the churches, homes, farms, utilities, businesses, etc. There was no private ownership of any kind of property, not even one's own home or farm. All of the churches, except synagogues, were federalized and many were torn down and remodeled and used as warehouses, factories, etc. He related that many wealthy Jews around the world contributed billions of dollars financing the Russian communist revolution.

He further explained that after the Bolsheviks won the revolution and killed the Czar and his family—by first killing off all of their guards, loyal supporters, friends, and relatives, leaving them alone and vulnerable—they were assassinated in the basement of the palace and their bodies were thrown into an old well. The Romanov royal family were devout Christians.

The Marxist communists won the revolution by organizing the low-paid working people who were then in a depression, unemployed, and hungry. They made them believe that they would live in a virtual utopia and that every citizen would earn the same amount of money, and the government would provide them with food, clothes, and living space equal to that of everyone else, including the wealthy business and professional class of people.

Upon the death of Vladimir Lenin, in 1924, Leon Trotsky, a Jew, was to succeed him. However, Stalin set about to kill Trotsky and ran him out of Russia so that he would have no opposition and could gain total control of the Bolshevik government himself, since Lenin had suffered a stroke and had proclaimed Trotsky as his successor. After Stalin gained control over the Marxist party, he had the KGB kill Trotsky in Mexico, rather than in Russia, obviously to direct attention for doing it away from him, so that the Jews who were the ones that actually controlled the Party would not suspect him and retaliate against him.

Joe was convinced that the Jews who fought to overthrow the Russian democratic government were determined to make it a religious war, in that the communist doctrine focused upon the destruction of Christianity and the first thing the communist revolutionaries did was to federalize all of the churches in Russia, and take complete ownership and control of them, and they would harass and intimidate any Russian citizen who attended, other than the very elderly citizens.

Christianity in Russia was almost totally and completely eradicated by Lenin, and then Stalin, who had gained control of the Marxist Bolshevik Party. He related that this was one of the main thrusts of the Bolsheviks who controlled the country during the early years after the Communist takeover—to destroy Christianity, which they were very successful in doing. He reasoned that the mass killing of the Russian citizens now—by the Bolsheviks in all probability—was responsible for all of the cold-blooded killings of all of their citizens, whom we were now trying so hard to get repatriated back into the Soviet-controlled countries. It is to be noted that most all of the Jewish survivors of the Nazi concentration camps who had resided in Germany, had been communist revolutionaries in Germany at the same time that Hitler was making his claim to power.

It was obvious to everyone that the Soviet Marxists were an atheist and Godless nation, with a total and complete absence of any Christian values, moral values, principles, or civilized societal doctrines. It was also obvious to many that the victims of the anti-Christian policies carried out by the Bolsheviks against the Russian people, were now being felt, or just now being known by enlightened people. It was now the Soviets' own people, the Jews in the concentration camps, that were being repatriated back into their own country, who were now the victims of horrendous and atrocious crimes committed by the Bolsheviks upon their own people—in this situation, the Jewish as well as the Christian survivors of Nazi concentration camps.

The Bolshevik Communists had no Christian or other moral values or principles, were now slaughtering their own people by the millions immediately upon their arrival in Soviet territory, under the false promise to them that they were being repatriated.

This mass murder was being carried out willingly by the Ukrainian soldiers in their enthusiastic retaliation against the Jews, who, in the beginning of Communism, carried out similar orders for the mass murder of twenty-six million Ukrainian peasants.

It was during the time that Lenin was dictator that the Marxist Communists went into the Ukraine to communize it, by taking possession of all private-owned property. They dispossessed the peasants of their farms and tried to put them in communes, to work in farms and factories like the slave laborers were treated in Germany by Hitler.

The Ukrainians refused to give up their land and leave their homes, so they were summarily shot—men, women, and children, as well as the elderly members of the families—right there in their own homes, by the millions. The Marxists destroyed all of the heritage, culture, and lifestyles, including the religion of all Soviet citizens. The Ukraine, as well as all of the Soviet Union under Communism, became a wasteland of civilized human values. Once a person's heritage and religion is destroyed, you have only a shell of a human being, a zombie-like, brainless robot.

During the time that Lenin ruled, his troops went into the Ukraine and took all of the food and farm produce from the peasants there, who had owned their own farms that had been handed down to them by their ancestors for centuries. They all had been devout Catholics, or Russian Orthodox before the Communist Revolution; now they were heathen barbarians. Their soldiers were now willingly and cold-bloodily murdering survivors of Nazi concentration camps that were from the Soviet Union, ostensibly in retaliation for their ancestors being murdered by the Marxist Communists.

Many peasants then starved to death after the Marxists took all of their food, and seed to plant. Many others, in fact entire families, were just shot in the head and killed on the spot, in their homes, because they could not produce enough food to feed all of Russia. Many were also shot and killed because they refused to surrender the ownership or possession of their homes and farms to the ownership and control of the Bolshevik government. He explained that the Bolsheviks in control of the government had their troops go into the Ukraine and take all of the food from the peasants. They also took the grain seed, potatoes, and other seeds that the Ukrainians were to use to plant new crops in the spring. The Communists used it for food, leaving nothing for the peasants to eat or plant, thus creating starvation and death to many more millions of Ukrainian peasants as they continuously were robbed of their crops—thereby creating a vicious cycle of starvation throughout the Soviet Union for many years. The Ukraine had been the breadbasket of all of the Soviet Union, but not after the time when the Communists totally destroyed the food-producing ability of the citizens there.

This caused mass starvation of millions of people in the entire Soviet Union. The final toll of those Ukrainian farmers killed by the Bolsheviks was twenty-six million, which is historically well documented. These Soviet Ukrainian troops could not forget how their ancestors and family members had died from killings and starvation, and they were now very vengeful and did not hesitate to kill en masse the returning Jews, as well as the Gentiles accompanying them. They took out their merciless vengeance on the poor emaciated inmates from the concentration camps, that another criminally insane totalitarian dictator had enslaved. This was a vicious cycle of annihilation of a large segment of humanity by barbarian Godless Marxists Communists.

Joe Kowski further related to me that these soldiers of the 3rd Ukrainian Army had no moral or Christian values now, because the Bolsheviks had destroyed their churches by nationalizing them and harassed the citizens who attended them. In reality the Bolsheviks had created this situation that was now resulting in the killings of their own people, who ironically had survived Adolph Hitler's concentration camps. Any criminal element, I have always contended, will sooner or later devour or consume itself and totally self-destruct.

So this, he told me, was why the passengers on the trains got very nervous and started crying when they learned that only the Ukrainian troops were taking control over them when they arrived. Joe related to me that the passengers knew that this was payback time when they saw the Ukrainian troops taking control of them. He also remarked that even though about thirty percent of the inmate population being returned to the Soviet area were non-Jews, the Soviets would not be bothered with separating them, but eliminated all of them.

Joe was a devout Catholic and he further related to me that Jesus Christ told us that "what you sow, ye shall also reap," and this was now more apparent than any other kind of event in the history of the world. These events were kept secret from the American people by the Jewish-owned and controlled media in America who did not want any deprecating remarks made in any way about communism.

Joe Kowski was bitterly against communism, relating to me that it is a totalitarian government consisting of mean, greedy, ignorant, depraved, and immoral people, where the citizens are treated horribly, and that they are nothing more than slaves of the state. He emphasized that the Soviet Union is a country without any Christian values and principles. So, without any freedom of worship of any religion, their moral values became decadent. There was little or no difference between Communism and Fascist Nazism, only, he related to me, that the Soviets were more cruel, inhumane, and devoid of any Christian or other moral values than the Nazis were.

To me, the moral to this piece of history is that one does not go into another country and overthrow their government, murder their Royal Family, and set up their own form of untried, anti-religious, anti-Christian, and untested totalitarian government, without assuming the blame and suffering the retribution for the consequences therefrom, in the event that it fails. It was apparent what this retribution against these Jews who had survived Hitler's concentration camps by the troops of the Ukrainian Army, acting willingly under Stalin's orders, was for: murdering their Czar Nicholas Romanov and his family; the overthrow of the Russian democratic government by the Bolsheviks in order to gain power, control, and ownership over that country and its people; and to institute their own barbaric form of atheistic and heathen government.

I spoke with many other of the men who guarded these trainloads of inmates from Dachau after they returned from some large cities in the Soviet, delivering these inmates back to their country, or city of origin. All of them related that after the inmates were unloaded from the trains, always by the 3rd Ukrainian Army troops, that they were lined up and shot just when the train pulled out of sight, but not out of hearing. It was no different than at all of the other locations where the inmates had been sent to cities inside the Soviet zone to be repatriated.

We in the occupation forces had to make sure that none of them escaped from the train, or escaped from Dachau, so that they could be returned to their country of origin. All of those people that were brought to Dachau by the Nazis from the Soviet zone had to be returned there. This was a high-level agreement that had finally been agreed to by Stalin, Churchill, and President Truman that the Allies would deliver to the Soviets all of the inmates whose place origin was in the Soviet zone.

Many of our soldiers began to blame Truman and Churchill for turning over these inmates knowing what would happen to them, and they began labeling these two great leaders as cowards who had capitulated to a terrorist atheist, Joe Stalin, a psychopathic mass murderer. Stalin apparently did not reveal to Truman and Churchill that he would execute all of the inmates that we returned to the Soviets; nevertheless, everyone in authority of this matter knew what would and did happen to those inmates who were returned to the Soviets.

We had to do our job. Many of my old buddies began to realize what was happening to these inmates they guarded on the trains going into the Soviet zone and they became sickened by it, and complained to their commander who always asked, "Did you actually see the shootings?"

The answer was always, "No, but…"

The GI doing the complaining was then always reassigned to another job and reminded that he had said that he hadn't seen anyone shoot anyone. He was usually given a promotion, as was my combat buddy, after he became repulsed by this situation and complained about what he saw and heard and refused to guard any more trainloads of inmates going into the Soviet zone.

My friend and combat buddy, Al Sperl, made one trip on a train delivering inmates to Bucharest, Romania. He experienced the same things that have been related by other combat men from our 65th Division. He told me that he could not endure to make another trip. Al was very religious and had strong moral and religious teaching as he grew up. I told him to go directly to our regimental commander and tell him because of his religious beliefs he could not endure another such trip on that train now that he knew what was happening to these inmates upon arrival in the Soviet countries. I told him to ask for a transfer. He did as I instructed—and the colonel transferred him to ordnance and promoted him to staff sergeant.

We also had trainloads of inmates that were sent back to France, Italy, Holland, Greece, Belgium, and a few other countries. The GIs guarding these trainloads of inmates reported that always they were greeted and welcomed, were treated very civilly upon their arrival, and were adequately provided for. Good people with Christian values, food, clothes, and other necessities of life met them and afforded them help and relocation to a safe and secure environment.

Soon, there was a trainload of inmates being processed to return to Krakow, Poland, or the vicinity thereof. Then, a few days later, I learned it was Joe's time to be repatriated back to his place of origin. Joe met me at the gate as he was about to board this train; he was extremely sad and there were tears in his eyes. He had no place to go to, to call home. He had no job waiting for him, and of course no money, friends, or relatives to welcome him. I tried to cheer him up, but it was useless. I tried to reassure him that there was always hope. He didn't think so. He told me that the whole world today was an evil, ugly, and a very cruel and anti-Christian place. As he was loaded onto this train like he was some kind of a common criminal, the tears were rolling down his cheeks. I went to him and he grabbed me around the shoulders, hugged me, kissed me on both cheeks, and said to me, "Oscar, you have been a true friend. You are a kind and great guy. I must say goodbye to you now, forever, but I will see you in Paradise." He then got on the train.

After the train returned from Krakow, I asked the guards, many of whom I knew, about what happened when the train arrived there. I was told that it was the same thing as in all of the other places, that it was déjà vu with all of the other trainloads of inmates; they were obviously now all dead. They had been met only by Soviet 3rd Ukrainian Army troops, with no one else present and in an isolated area. I was told by the train guards that even though they didn't actually see the shooting, that all of the circumstances they did see and hear were sufficient to convince them, conclusively, that the people that they delivered were all now dead.

I then went straight to my regimental commander and told him that I could no longer endure the revulsion and horrors that existed here at Dachau, and actually I preferred combat to this kind of gruesomeness and madness that had been brought about by uncivilized, barbaric madmen. I told him that I could not continue to be a party to mass murder, even though it was an order, it most likely was an illegal order, being a party to knowingly sending these people to their death. I told him that it was against my Christian principles and beliefs and in addition to that, I was totally and completely repulsed and sickened by the entire sordid mess. I asked for a transfer.

My colonel told me that he had a position for a regimental recruiting sergeant and that recruiting had now commenced and he needed someone to fill that position, and he asked me if I would like to have that job. I assured him that I would like it very much. I was given an office right next door to his office in the main administration building at Furstenfeldbruck Air Base.

CHAPTER 43

The Annihilation of Soviet POWs by Soviet Soldiers

"I believe that man will not merely endure;
he will prevail, he is immortal, not because
he alone among creatures, has an inex-
haustible voice, but because he has a soul, a
spirit capable of compassion and sacrifice
and endurance."

—WILLIAM FAULKNER, IN HIS NOBEL PRIZE
ACCEPTANCE SPEECH (1897–1962)

It was not just the concentration camp inmates and the displaced slave laborers that the Soviet dictator didn't want back into his country. Stalin grabbed this opportunity as an excuse to put to death all Soviets who had been taken into Germany by the Nazis, regardless of who they were, their conditions, or circumstances. I met some of the men from my 65th Division who were working at Dachau. I discussed this matter with them. They remarked that near Linz, just after the war ended, their unit took control of a POW camp just south of Linz that contained Russian prisoners of war, who were Russian soldiers that had been captured by the Nazis and brought back to Germany and Austria and placed there in this POW camp. After the war, the Soviets at first refused to accept them back into their country under any circumstances.

After the high-level agreement had been reached between Truman—who himself had fought in combat in WWI as a captain in the artillery—Churchill, and Stalin, wherein Stalin agreed to accept his own soldiers like they accepted the concentration camp inmates and displaced person slave laborers, back into the Soviet zone. This acceptance of their own people back into their own country meant that they killed all of them upon arrival in the Soviet zone. So, the Allies agreed to deliver the Russian POWs over to the Soviet authorities, regardless of that fact, but fully aware of the fact that they all would be murdered en masse upon their arrival back into the Soviet zone.

This lieutenant related to me that a special group of American Army 2nd lieutenants in our 65th Division had been specifically chosen to carry out the operation of supposedly repatriating these Russian POWs after this iniquitous agreement had been made. This contingent of especially selected 2nd lieutenants were first told the Russians were refusing to go back to their country, in that they believed that they would be murdered upon arrival into the hands of the Soviets. This specifically trained group of 2nd lieutenants were rehearsed as to how they would carry out this operation of forced repatriation of these Russian soldiers.

They were ordered to go into the Russian POW camp near Linz at 4:30 A.M. in order to catch the Russian POWs off guard, while they were still in bed, in an attempt to prevent them from committing suicide. Most all of them had razor blades or some other sharp object hidden under their pillows with which to cut their wrists and commit suicide, rather than give the madmen controlling the Marxists government the pleasure of killing them. The group of lieutenants were instructed to rout them out of bed, place them on GI trucks, and deliver them to a specified rail sidetrack location in the Soviet zone in Czechoslovakia, just thirty kilometers north of Linz.

Our men, all 2nd lieutenants, were chosen for this job. They rushed into the barracks that early morning and forcibly took them from their beds and herded them into the center of the room in a matter of seconds. Some leaped back toward their bed where they had razor blades hidden under their pillows to kill themselves with, rather than to be delivered over to the Soviets to be murdered by them. All of them exhibited stark terror, and each one had tears streaming down their cheeks.

In addition to that they screamed, shouted, and waved their arms, all in a hopeless protest of being delivered over to the Soviets.

These Russian POWs had fought valiantly for the Soviet Union, endured tremendous hardships, had been captured by the Nazis and held in a POW camp in compliance with the Geneva Convention governing treatment of prisoners of war—even in spite of the fact that the Soviet Union was not a party to the Geneva Convention. We Americans took control of them at the war's end. The Nazis had treated them civilly and humanely while they were being held prisoners. Now they had been liberated by us and we were sending them to their deaths. The Russians had no Red Cross that could visit the Soviet POWs, to collect and deliver to them their mail and distribute food items to them like our Red Cross would do for American POWs held by the Nazis. So, the Soviet POWs had no line of communication with anyone back in their home country they could contact in any manner, because the Soviet Union was not a member of the Geneva Convention governing the treatment of prisoners of war.

A 2nd lieutenant in the 65th Infantry Division, who had been selected to assist in the "repatriation" of these POWs, and who chooses to remain anonymous for purposes of his own personal privacy, describes the situation in his own words as follows:

I Would Rather Have Been Court-Martialed

by Anonym

"The war in Europe ended May 8, 1945. One month later I was ordered to lead my platoon on a short term special assignment. It would be 1952 before I would learn the full significance of the disgraceful task we performed that day in May 1945.

"By virtue of winning the war, the United States Army had inherited the responsibility for masses of displaced people and prisoners of war—because they were in the territory that we now occupied. Our assignment concerned a prison camp right there in Linz, Austria that held Russian soldiers who had been captured and interned by the Germans.

"I am writing about this event more than 50 years after it occurred, so my memory is somewhat hazy. I remember that the day before we were to perform the task, all of us who were in charge of platoons, were given a briefing. Our assignment was to get those Russian prisoners onto trucks and turn them over to the Russian Army. They would resist, and some would even attempt suicide, which we were to guard against. The briefing was short and concise, and concluded without an opportunity to ask questions.

"We arrived at the camp at 4:30 the next morning, very quietly walked through the gate and assembled outside our assigned barracks to await the signal. When it came, we burst through the door, turned on the lights and rushed to the bunks. We had all the prisoners on their feet and into the center of the room within a matter of seconds. When one of them made a lunge back to his bunk, I grabbed his arm and pushed him back with the others. When I lifted up his pillow, sure enough, there was a razor blade, along with a small stack of papers, which I stuck in my pocket.

"There must have been 40 or 50 prisoners in our barracks, all huddled inside the circle of my platoon—with every face exhibiting stark terror. They were pleading with us, using every form of communication except the English language, including hollering, screaming, shouting guttural sounding words and waving their arms around. Their revulsion against what we were doing was so genuine, we were all deeply moved. We were presumably Allies with the Russians, which these men were, yet we were treating them like enemies, which they weren't! It was really a pathetic scene, and by the time we herded, dragged and carried them onto the trucks, there wasn't a dry eye among us.

"Riding in our jeeps with mounted machine guns, we helped escort the convoy through Linz, across the Danube and into Czechoslovakia, which was only a short distance from Linz. The Russians were waiting and the process of turning them over began. The prisoners in each truck were methodically counted and checked off, and signatures were affixed to the documents. Then we watched as they were taken from our trucks and herded into the railroad cattle cars strung out along the tracks. The prisoners had, by now become subdued and offered no resistance, apparently resigned to their fate. We had completed our task. I thought it was over, but the worst was yet to come!

"We were moving along in our jeeps, behind our convoy of empty trucks, on our way back to Linz when we heard the familiar rattle of machine gun fire. We pulled over and stopped. We knew instinctively what was happening, even though the hilly terrain obstructed our view. The rattle of automatic fire continued, on and on. We looked at each other in disbelief. We had been betrayed! We had assumed that those prisoners had just been slaughtered by their own countrymen. We were on Russian occupied territory. There was nothing we could do.

"It was a quiet, somber ride back. I felt anger, disgust, shame! I knew then that following orders, in this case, had been wrong. I felt then, as I do now, that had I known their fate, I would have chosen a court-martial, rather than to have participated.

"Through the years I watched the press reports that would explain this event to the American public. As none appeared I concluded that the United States Government had successfully concealed its complicity."

I also learned from other lieutenants that the Soviets there herded them out of our trucks and into their railroad cattle cars that had been parked in a deserted area on an out-of-the-way rail sidetrack. These cattle cars had planking several inches between them, so that one could clearly see what was inside of the cattle cars. These cattle cars were not connected to any train engine to go anyplace. In fact there was no engine anywhere in sight. These cattle cars served the same purpose as Hitler's gas chambers did, only more brutal and barbaric. This was in an isolated location. The contingent of lieutenants in their trucks and jeeps left with only the Soviet soldiers standing guard at the train cars filled with their fellow soldiers.

Immediately upon leaving the area where the POWs were put into the cattle cars, all of our American soldiers heard incessant machine gun fire at that location. Many American soldiers who participated in this "repatriation" delivery cried and wept profoundly. They told each other that had they known what would happen to these men, they all would have refused to obey an order to do what they had done, which was being an accomplice and an accessory to murder, and that they would have requested a court-martial—as did one of our lieutenants in the 65th Division who was able to record his reasons for refusing to be a party to the mass murder of our allied soldiers, in his court-martial hearing.

Just as they pulled away, a lieutenant related to me that he stopped his jeep over a crest and observed the Soviet soldiers firing machine guns into these freight cars containing their own fellow soldiers, killing all of them, presumably. He could see through his field glasses the blood flowing out of the freight cars in streams as he pulled away and out of sight from this maddeningly gruesome scene. His opinion was that Stalin was more vicious than Hitler ever was. I agreed wholeheartedly. The words "communist" and "communism" became to all of us American soldiers a profane and vulgar word of a hated and despicable nature, without any redeeming values whatsoever. It is nothing more than a satanical form of government, to destroy the goodness of mankind in our civilized social order.

I have often wondered if one man, Stalin, could have been this cold-blooded and heartless, or was he following the orders of those who placed him in office and had ordered him to do it? Or, was this part and parcel of the Marxist doctrine, to eliminate as many white, Christian Caucasians as possible to reduce their numbers. In any event, it took the two elements: Stalin, placed in the totalitarian position by the Communists as a cold-blooded, blood-thirsty murderer; and a government that had no checks and balances, or regulatory agencies with principles, and which was also void of any Christian or otherwise civilized moral values. Any government, in my opinion, that places so much power in only one man with absolute and total power, is extremely evil and should be abolished from the face of the earth as being detrimental, dangerous, and destructive to civilized society. In my opinion, absolute control over any people or government is pure unadulterated tyranny.

Such mass killings of Russians by Russians could only have been deliberately and maliciously done to eliminate a large segment of that country's population. These very intelligent Soviet soldiers were strong and healthy. They were obviously needed to rebuild the country and to otherwise contribute to the betterment of their homeland, but the Communists didn't want any enlightened intelligent citizens with compassion, a heart, and a soul in their evil form of government. Communism became a fighting word amongst us American soldiers.

The reason for the mass murder of these soldiers made no sense, other than to eliminate a large element of young, healthy, and intelligent men who were white Christian Caucasians from the population. These men could have been utilized to rebuild their country and to contribute to the betterment of society. But, whatever the reason, it must be left to your own best educated conjecture and speculation as to the reasons why all of this uncivilized activity occurred in that country and at the end of a long and bloody war.

It was not until June 1952 that any of the American media picked up on this wholesale annihilation of the Soviet Union's own soldiers by Soviet troops and printed anything about it. They then only paid lip service to the matter. The citizens of America needed to know what took place and denying them the knowledge of what had occurred was a dastardly reprehensible act of subversion and anarchy. Without a history that is accurate, how can we keep Americans from making a mistake in the future? For the American media to print and publish to Americans only what some communist wants us to know is nothing less than treason and should be treated as such, with the death penalty carried out. A controlled media is an ongoing and living lie to our citizens who have an inalienable right to know the truth about everything, otherwise we may as well be living under the rule of a mad dictator of communism or Nazism.

An excerpt from an article in the *U.S. News & World Report,* as well as the *Readers Digest,* printed a brief version of these horrors. One such excerpt is as follows:

"…The fate of these liberated Russians, however, was settled, by a directive of the Allied Supreme Command, issued soon after the Yalta Conference, which stated that, 'All Russians Liberated within the area controlled by the Supreme Commander will be transferred to the Russian authorities as soon as possible.' So forced repatriation began on a large scale in May, 1945. It lasted for more than a year. During that period, hundreds of thousands of Russians tried to escape being sent home, and tens of thousands committed suicide in the process. Americans guarding these persons were forced to take part in shipping them off. One Allied Officer underwent court martial when he balked.…Great numbers were herded onto trucks…forcibly transported to Russian held territory. Of these, large numbers were executed on the spot by Russian Secret Police Officials. Others were moved to Moscow for mass trials, then, executed." (The mass trials in Moscow were only mock trials.)

Many people I talked to were of the opinion that this matter had been suppressed by the American Jewish-controlled media, so as not to disparage and discredit their Marxist Communist government that they were still supporting, by stealing and selling American military nuclear secrets to the Soviet Communists. Otherwise, how could such atrocities and barbarism have been so suppressed by our media? Why were only Hitler and his Nazis singled out to be labeled as barbarous and atrocious, and not the Soviets who were even more barbaric?

Many of our GIs involved in this and similar operations, today, still suffer great grief, remorse, and mental anguish for having to participate in the death of these Soviet POWs.

The Soviets were, theoretically, our ally in this war. However, they had been allies of the Nazis immediately prior to the invasion of Poland by the Nazis. These soldiers were allies of ours who had done nothing wrong, except to have been captured and held prisoner by the Nazis, just like our American prisoners were.

In my sincere opinion, America's and England's greatest mistake in handling this "man's inhumanity to man" was to have stopped General George S. Patton from attacking the Soviets and completely annihilating all of these heathens and restoring democracy, Christianity, and other religious freedoms to that once-great country that had suffered self-destruction under the Communistic Marxist form of totalitarian government. Previous to the Marxist Revolution Russia had been one of the leading cultural centers of the world.

An awful lot of knowledgeable people at that time related to me that Stalin was nothing more than a puppet of the Marxist regime that was in total control of Soviet Russia at that time, and was only carrying out orders from the Marxist leaders who had put him in power and who could remove him if they chose to merely by giving an order to Stalin's executioner, Lavrenty Beria.

All of those involved in the operation of that Communist Totalitarian Marxist government were cold-blooded and heartless barbarians, and it was patently evident that Communism was a creation of the devil himself, which every American soldier that I knew had a passionate hatred and contempt for. Stalin himself had absolute power over the lives of each and every person. Not only did he have millions of his own people murdered by his own terrorist government officials, but he also had sixteen of his most brilliant and efficient generals and admirals executed, and their families also murdered and/or terrorized and eventually mercilessly destroyed. In the 1930s alone, Stalin had over ten million (10,000,000) citizens of Russia murdered. All of this was blatantly a direct and proximate result, and a product of the vicious criminal takeover of and the destruction of the legitimate Christian democratic government of Russia by anti-Christian Marxist Revolutionaries, who were obviously intent on destroying the entire Christian religion of the largest country on earth. The official estimate of Soviet citizens slaughtered by the Marxist Communist government during the tenure of Lenin and Stalin was in excess of one hundred and eighty million (180,000,000) citizens of the Soviet Union.

Not only Hitler had concentration camps, but Stalin and his Marxist Communists built gulags in Siberia where the enemies of the state and enemies of the Marxists were sent to their deaths. Those sent there were those who disagreed with the Marxists. Once sent there, no one ever returned from the Siberian wasteland of frozen tundra. The number of those committed to the gulags, and exterminated, until present day is still unknown, because there are no records, but the estimates are many millions, estimated to be in excess of twenty million (20,000,000) Russians. This makes the total number of Russians murdered by their own government to be two hundred million (200,000,000). One did not have to commit a crime to be sent there to those death camps; only those who were disliked by the Marxists were exterminated there.

Stalin's executioner was a Jew named Lavrenty Beria. He is the executioner who executed sixteen of the Soviets' most intelligent and capable admirals and generals that he and Stalin didn't like for some unknown reason, other than that they were more intelligent than he was, which Stalin resented, and distrusted them for being so. It is believed that their motive for this killing of their own intelligencia was because they were highly educated, that the Marxists suspicioned they naturally disliked what the Marxist regime was doing to their country—which was totally destroying it and its people.

At the beginning of the Marxist Revolution, Beria was only a Soviet Marxist police official who rose in rank under Stalin to be head of the Soviet secret police, and it was he who was head of the Soviet concentration camps in Siberia, called gulags. He was responsible for the deaths of millions of Soviets, whom he manufactured false evidence against in order to have them sent to the gulags and killed. He also personally tortured and killed thousands of citizens. In 1946 he, Beria, became a member of the Soviet Politburo. After Stalin's death in March 1953, Gorgy Malenkov succeeded Stalin and had Beria and six of his accomplices arrested, prosecuted, and executed by a firing squad for his crimes against the Soviet citizens. I am reminded that "what you sow, ye shall also reap."

It is to be noted that it was Beria that carried out Stalin's order to execute the concentration camp inmates, the displaced laborers, and Soviet soldiers who had been the prisoners of the Nazis, that were slaughtered when we turned them over to the Soviets.

What a great day it would have been if we could have only kept all of these Soviets in Germany and not returned them until after the death of Stalin and the execution of Lavrenty Beria.

CHAPTER 44

Soon to Return Home

*"The strength of a nation is derived from
the integrity of its homes."*

—CONFUCIUS (551–479 BC)

After all of my vacationing, rest, and relaxation, and partially regaining my weight and strength—and then experiencing the horrors of Mauthausen, Camp Gussen, and Dachau Concentration Camps—I was transferred from working at Dachau and was stationed at a former Luftwaffe air base at Furstenfeldbruck, Germany. As a result of my request for a transfer from Dachau Concentration Camp, I was assigned by my regimental commander in the 10th Armored Division as the regimental recruiting sergeant, while I awaited my return to the States, to be discharged and to enter college. I was given an office in the main administration building at Furstenfeldbruck Air Base, in a room adjoining the regimental commander's office. The work there was very pleasant and free of any stress and anxiety, which I had already endured more than enough of. I was very much tempted to stay in the Army and make a career out of it, but I was terribly anxious to see my parents and pursue a college degree in some field where I could contribute to a greater and better America, and world, for all mankind.

While there, I acquired a puppy, a German shepherd that was a beautiful dog. I wanted very much to bring him home with me, but I was going to college and had no place to take care of him. It hurt me very bad to have to leave him there, where no one wanted to take him and care for him as I had been doing.

The long train ride from Furstenfeldbruck to Bremerhaven, our port of debarkation, was a very tiring train ride, but it was exciting knowing that I was going home, and all in one piece, too. It seemed that on that train I felt a relief, a release from some very frightening and disturbing experiences that I had endured. It was as if I were saying goodbye to all of Europe's troubles and problems—but I was sure that they wouldn't ever go away in my mind.

I then realized, as I watched the beautiful German countryside glide by, that we in America had an awful lot to be thankful for and even more to protect and defend. I hoped that the good people in America would be able to profit from all of the mistakes and shortcomings that had been made in this great conflict, and what had occurred here would never happen to us in the United States of America.

We did not have any concentration camps, no Gestapo agents, no SS troops, and no KGB Soviet Secret Police–types, invading our lives, no one waiting to slaughter our American GIs who had been serving in a POW camp in Germany when they arrived home. We did not have to get a permit from some ignorant goon to go from one town to another. We could worship whatever faith that we chose, in a place of worship that was not owned and controlled by a corrupt and evil totalitarian, anti-Christian, atheist, dictatorial communist government. We had the liberty and freedom to speak out about these kind of things. We could also own and carry weapons to protect not only ourselves, our family, and property, but to protect our government and our Constitution from any intrusion upon its principles. We had none of the manifest problems that the people of Europe had suffered and were forced to endure.

Back on the farm we could go about our daily lives as a free people, dictated to by no one. We had no secret police trying to take our land, our homes, or our crops from us, claiming that they were the property of the state, leaving us with no food to eat, and no seed to plant next spring. We had no kangaroo courts presided over by ignorant, controlled bully thugs. We had no one to tell us that our churches belonged to the government, or that we were forbidden to worship as we chose without being intimidated and terrorized. No one told us that our land belonged to the state and that we had to live in a commune and produce food for the state, controlled by thieves, crooks, and goons. There were no machine guns waiting to cut down our fellow Americans who had been held captive in Nazi POW camps.

No American leader in their right mind would ever commit genocide against returning American veterans. No one would ever take our guns and enslave us, so that we would be unable to unseat a totalitarian terrorist dictator. Guns in the hands of patriotic, loyal American citizens should be enough to make any government officeholder and politician honest, and to uphold their oath of office, and to serve honestly.

We were our own boss—honest, hardworking, Godfearing, caring, loving, friendly, neighborly, and concerned citizens of the Untied States of America. We only did what we sincerely believed was the "right, fair, and honest" as well as the Christian thing to do. I asked myself, "Isn't that enough to be thankful for, and isn't that enough reason to go off and fight a war, in order that those Christian values and principles be protected and preserved?" I swore to my God Almighty, in Saarlautern, that if He would return me home, and in one piece, that I would continue fighting tyranny, oppression, terrorism, political and governmental corruption, thuggery, as well as all injustices, so long as there was a breath left in my body. I meant what I said to my God and I intended to do just that. Never would I ever renege on a promise to my Almighty God.

I also wondered if I would ever be able to recover from all of the fears and hardships that I endured in combat, as well as all of the mental and emotional scars that I endured, both before and after the cessation of hostilities.

Upon arrival at Bremerhaven there were so many troops there waiting to return home that we had to almost continuously stand in a chow line to get something to eat, the lines were so long. We would get in line early in the morning; then after several hours of being in line, we would get served in our mess kits. Then we would return to another long line to receive our second, and only other, meal of the day. One sad part of it was that I had to leave my beautiful German shepherd puppy behind, that I had become so attached to. He was so devoted and loyal to me that it broke my heart.

After several days at Bremmerhaven we boarded the SS West Point and sailed home. We were awakened early one morning as we sailed past the Statue of Liberty; we all went up on the deck to see it as we went by it. Soon we were on a train home. What a wonderful occasion that was, to once again be with my family.

Upon entering college, I joined the ROTC, and when I graduated I received a commission as a 2nd lieutenant, which I had turned down upon completing basic training so that I could fight to help win this war. I served in the reserves for many years.

For too many years I suffered from nightmares in my sleep, where I was unable to awake or be awakened, believing that my left leg had been blown off and that I was bleeding to death and that there was no one there to help me. This disturbed my family deeply, in that my parents would be awakened by my screams and come to me, and place cold towels on my face, working for hours sometimes before they could awaken me. I could vividly feel my bloody stump and the sharp, jagged edges of the broken bone of my leg, as I tried to stop the bleeding that I clearly believed was taking place. I could hear my parents talking to me, but I believed that I was lying on a battlefield with my leg gone, and I was just dreaming that I heard my parents' voices. I felt more sorrow for my mother, father, brother, and sisters than I did for myself, for their having to endure those many ordeals. My college roommates also worked hard to awaken me often, there in the college dormitories. After many years these nightmares subsided, but were replaced by other horrible nightmares about frightening experiences that continued for many more years. This was just a tiny shred of the post-traumatic emotional ills of combat, but it was minute compared to so much that I had witnessed others to have suffered. This was no more than what many other returning combat veterans were also enduring. This was nothing, compared to those who actually lost a limb or were otherwise severely injured in combat. The only thing that I had wrong with me were those terrifying nightmares for many years, flashbacks of frightening experiences, and a bleeding duodenal ulcer. I spent many months in a veterans hospital being treated for this bleeding ulcer that they wanted to cut out, but I wouldn't let them. I considered myself to be extremely lucky.

I returned home fully aware and totally believing, with all of my heart and soul, that had I not had true faith in my Almighty God, my country, as well as faith in all of my fellow combat soldiers, my officers, leaders, and my family, as well as possessing the God-given courage to do my job well, I would not have survived that ordeal. I was also convinced that but for the prayers of my mother and father, praying for my safety, I would not have returned safe and sound.

Give the Gift of

A Test of *Faith and* COURAGE

to Your Friends and Colleagues

CHECK YOUR LEADING BOOKSTORE OR ORDER HERE

❏ YES, I want _____ copies of *A Test of Faith and Courage* at $29.95 each, plus $4 shipping per book. (Mississippi residents please add $2.09 sales tax per book.) Canadian orders must be accompanied by a postal money order in U.S. funds. Allow 15 days for delivery.

❏ YES, I am interested in having Oscar B. Ladner speak or give a seminar to my company, association, school, or organization. Please send information.

My check or money order for $_____ is enclosed.

Please charge my: ❏ Visa ❏ MastersCard
❏ Discover ❏ American Express

Name_____

Organization _____

Address _____

City/State/Zip _____

Phone_____ E-mail _____

Card # _____

Exp. Date_____ Signature _____

Please make your check payable and return to:

Liberty & Freedom Productions
176 Allan Drive • Gulfport, MS 39507-1503

Call your credit card order toll free to: 866-610-2988
Fax: 228-604-1666

Austria

100 km

100 miles

Germany

Bavarian

Braunau
am Inn

B

Munich

Vöckla

Swiss

Salzburg

Bodensee

Ha

Bregenz

Reutte

Solbad
Hall

Kufstein

stenau

Dornbirn

Alps

Saalfelden

Feldkirch

Inn

Innsbruck

ohe

Taue

Bludenz

A

Landeck

l

ech.

Lienz

Drava

Switzerland

p

Rhaetian

Alps

Carnic

A

Italy